History from the Bottom Up
and the Inside Out

JAMES R. BARRETT

History from the Bottom Up and the Inside Out

Ethnicity, Race, and Identity in Working-Class History

Duke University Press · Durham and London · 2017

© 2017 Duke University Press
All rights reserved

Designed by Courtney Leigh Baker
Typeset in Trade Gothic and Arno Pro by Westchester Publishing Services

Library of Congress Cataloging-in-Publication Data
Names: Barrett, James R., [date] author.
Title: History from the bottom up and the inside out : ethnicity, race, and identity in working-class history / James R. Barrett.
Description: Durham : Duke University Press, 2017. |
Includes bibliographical references and index.
Identifiers:
LCCN 2017002151 (print)
LCCN 2017006258 (ebook)
ISBN 9780822369677 (hardcover)
ISBN 9780822369790 (pbk.)
ISBN 9780822372851 (ebook)
Subjects: LCSH: Working class—United States—History. | Minorities—United States—History. | Identity (Psychology)—United States—History.
Classification: LCC HD8066.B37 2017 (print) | LCC HD8066 (ebook) | DDC 305.5/620973—dc23
LC record available at https://lccn.loc.gov/2017002151

COVER ART: Lewis W. Hine, *Tenement Child with a Blank Wall to Stare At*, ca. 1910. Gelatin silver print, 11.4 × 16.6 cm. Courtesy George Eastman Museum.

In memory of
Thomas E. Barrett Jr.,
Mark Leff,
and David Montgomery

CONTENTS

Foreword · David R. Roediger · ix

Acknowledgments · xvii

INTRODUCTION
The Subjective Side of Working-Class History · 1

CHAPTER ONE
The Blessed Virgin Made Me a Socialist Historian:
*An Experiment in Catholic Autobiography and the Historical
Understanding of Race and Class* · 7

CHAPTER TWO
Was the Personal Political?
Reading the Autobiography of American Communism · 33

CHAPTER THREE
Revolution and Personal Crisis:
*William Z. Foster, Personal Narrative, and the Subjective
in the History of American Communism* · 58

CHAPTER FOUR
Blue-Collar Cosmopolitans:
*Toward a History of Working-Class
Sophistication in Industrial America* · 77

CHAPTER FIVE

The Bohemian Writer and the Radical Woodworker:
A Study in Class Relations · 102

CHAPTER SIX

Americanization from the Bottom Up:
*Immigration and the Remaking of the Working Class
in the United States, 1880–1930* · 122

CHAPTER SEVEN

Inbetween Peoples:
Race, Nationality, and the "New Immigrant" Working Class
James R. Barrett and David R. Roediger · 145

CHAPTER EIGHT

Irish Americanization on Stage:
*How Irish Musicians, Playwrights, and Writers Created
a New Urban American Culture, 1880–1940* · 175

CHAPTER NINE

Making and Unmaking the Working Class:
*E. P. Thompson, The Making of the English Working Class,
and the "New Labor History" in the United States* · 192

Notes · 209
Selected Bibliography · 273
Index · 277

FOREWORD · DAVID R. ROEDIGER

My first vivid memories of Jim Barrett, and of his wife Jenny, go back to the early 1970s and to a sadly underpopulated picket line in the parking lot of a small liquor store in the farm and university town of DeKalb, Illinois. The United Farm Workers had called for a boycott of Gallo wines and we gave what support we could—in this case a picket line of four people. There was plenty of time for our small group to talk, and a lot for me to like about Jim and Jenny. They were graduate students in history at Northern Illinois University, a department whose excellence resulted largely from a record of being willing to hire left scholars when other colleges hewed to Cold War exclusion based on politics. I was an undergraduate trying to balance sports with making the New Left last a little longer. Jim and Jenny, just slightly older, seemed to have access to the combination of ideas and action I sought. We were all lapsed, or lapsing, Catholics and, coming from working-class communities, we all gravitated toward labor causes, especially if racial justice were also involved.

Not too long after that picket line, the Barretts moved on to Warwick University in Coventry, England, where E. P. Thompson was a professor, and to the University of Pittsburgh, where Jim studied with David Montgomery. His recollections of those formative experiences, leavened by research on Thompson's enduring impact in working-class history, help to close this book. My decision to go to graduate school surely owed much to knowing radicals like the Barretts, who seemed in some general way to be like me.

The idea of doing history from the bottom up, so brilliantly actualized in Al Young's seminars at Northern Illinois, continued to animate large parts of what we endeavored to study. I set out to write about "slavery from the slave's point of view" under Sterling Stuckey's mentorship at Northwestern. Jim shared Montgomery's emphasis on the daily realities of the shopfloor, and added textured analyses of immigrants' daily lives from his wonderful early studies (scarcely represented in this collection) of black and immigrant packinghouse workers.

However, as a Marxist, Barrett, like Montgomery, avoided any naïve supposition that history is ever made only from below. Class, according to Thompson, is above all "a relationship," inconceivable without a study of how both labor and capital interact. Thus immigrant workers in Chicago's Back of the Yards neighborhood and meatpacking plants Barrett studied resisted, but often within rhythms set by the relentless "disassembly line" whose demands he so well described. Similarly, "Americanization from the Bottom Up," reprinted here and arguably the most influential and salutary article produced by his generation of labor historians, begins by describing the most dramatic of capital's efforts to enforce Americanization from above. Barrett raises vital questions—"But what did it mean to be 'Americanized,' and who was fittest and best placed to do the Americanizing?"—and provides dialectical answers.

The rigor of his training at Pitt and Warwick committed Barrett to taking no shortcuts by presuming to know what working people must have thought or felt. Instead, history from below involved a diligent search for sources, including official sources read against the grain and illuminated not only by historical materialism but also through social science methods. His introductory call here for histories of the personal and the emotional characteristically begins with the problem of sources. Strikingly, even his highly personal recollections of his childhood neighborhood send him straight back to the historical record, producing a memoir with copious citations.

In teaching with Jim at the University of Illinois during the first fifteen years of this century, we sat on dozens of graduate and undergraduate thesis defenses together. I can remember just one where he did not urge the inclusion of more maps, underscoring a reminder that large class forces contend in concrete settings. By then I was so trained by his example that I did the urging. In his emphasis on particular settings, he was moving toward the accent on individual experiences and the inner lives of workers long before he began to advocate in print for emphasizing such matters.

I begin on the personal note of a forlorn picket line walked by young people nevertheless on fire about the movements they supported and the ideas they encountered for more than nostalgic reasons. It is worth recalling that the new labor history matured during a period of significant class conflict with hundreds of large strikes each year, and with smaller wildcat strikes underlining the combativeness of workers. Moreover—and Barrett's accounts of his own coming to be a radical and a radical historian are most instructive on this score—the African American freedom movement and other freedom struggles had shown that creative mass actions coming from below could transform social relations rapidly. The electric mobilizations against the U.S. war on Vietnam reflected and imparted a similar sensibility regarding the power of popular mobilizations. However, things changed greatly during our working lives. The percentage of organized workers in the labor force declined by more than half, and the number of large strikes sometimes now falls short of a dozen per year.

During the decades since the 1970s, the social weight of the labor movement has declined so starkly that the question of how creative and indefatigable scholars of the working-class past such as Barrett have sustained their commitments deserves attention. The first generation of the new labor historians—Montgomery, Herbert Gutman, Alexander Saxton, and George Rawick, for example—similarly came to maturity during periods of great promise, in the Age of the CIO and often specifically in the post–World War II strike waves. However, the decline of labor's power which they experienced was less absolute and was interrupted by the rise of new working-class social movements and periods of militancy.

The late sixties and early seventies graduate student generations of labor historians faced—or rather experienced, as the subject of how we have navigated so long and hard a period of defeat has seldom been broached—a more challenging task of squaring youthful optimisms with hard times for workers and unions. To some extent this has also been true for labor history as a field. For a time, the idea that history moved in cycles provided some solace. Montgomery's 1988 classic *The Fall of the House of Labor* ended in labor's defeats of the 1920s, but everyone knew that the organizational successes of the 1930s and 1940s lay just around the corner. Our own "1920s," however, have now lingered and worsened for more than four decades, with many proclamations of new beginnings but no way forward yet in sight.

For many of us, especially those already thinking along those lines since the activism of the 1960s, one response to the crisis of the U.S. labor movement and the significant white working-class vote for antilabor politicians was a search for the roots of labor's weakness in white supremacy. As Barrett recounts here, he was positioned to embrace some of this critique, and we worked together on a series of essays building on his "Americanization from the Bottom Up" in order to consider how immigrants learned the racial system, what they made of it, and what it too often made of them.

Barrett's particular processing of how to sustain the writing of radical history in a period of constrained possibilities took broader forms, however.

It bears emphasis that here too setting mattered. In central Illinois, Barrett was able to participate directly in perhaps the most significant, militant, and extended set of class battles of the recent past, the "War Zone" lockouts and strikes, centered in Decatur's Caterpillar, Firestone, and Staley factories in the early 1990s. The University of Illinois has also been the scene of impressive and protracted organizing campaigns and conflict, resulting in representation for graduate student workers and adjunct faculty and ongoing efforts by professional employees and tenured/tenure-track faculty. Jim and Jenny Barrett were and are at the center of each of these efforts. Most recently, their son Xian's prominent role in the grassroots organizing of the Chicago Teachers Union has brought the Barretts to another high spot of recent working-class mobilization.

The writings collected in *History from the Bottom Up and the Inside Out* suggest how one leading historian has not only kept the faith during a long period of labor's decline but also rethought the boundaries of working-class history. The very structure of the book reflects this process. Although only one of the selections is completely new, many are so fully revised that they appear new to those of us who read them as they were published, or even drafted. The revisions help develop themes that make the various sections of the collection cohere. But those themes are often ones that only emerged as Barrett wrestled with questions over time. For example, his early work with the immigrant communist Steve Nelson might fairly be regarded as a rather straightforward collaboration of the Old Left and the New. As such it was partly animated by a desire to find a useful past and, in anticommunism, a reason for the decline of working-class militancy.

At the same time, the personal mattered, not the least in Barrett's seeing something of his own desires for a better world in the lives and risks of communists like Nelson and unrepentant ex-communists like David Montgomery. Perhaps the most salutary aspect of the revisionist accounts of the history of U.S. communism that Barrett helped to forward was a break from the Cold War practices identified by Vivian Gornick. Historians of communism, Gornick wrote, had long enforced "an oppressive distance between themselves and their subjects," and that distance was emotional as well as political. In acknowledging a kinship in sensibilities, if not in political line, with their subjects, young left historians of communism opened exciting new terrain. It might even be argued—Jim and I have probably argued about this—that seeing the humanity and hopes of those attracted to communism actually deepens our appreciation of the toll that Stalinism exacted.

The recent and revised writings included here on the communists also take on larger questions. Confronting the radical sadness running through the life of William Z. Foster, the subject of a superb biography by Barrett, doubtless contributed to his emerging emphasis on accounting for private and emotional lives on the left. Characteristically attuned to sources, and especially to the silences in communists' autobiographies, Barrett nevertheless finds much, especially in memoirs of women militants, reflecting on some aspects of gender and personal matters. Being on the right side of large structural processes of history hardly guarantees victories in the struggle for personal happiness. This realization in turn has helped to generate Barrett's challenging call for new histories of what he terms, after Robert Orsi, the "inner history" of ordinary people—a history taking the individual as seriously as it does the global.

During the late 1970s and 1980s Jim and I met mostly in Chicago, where I studied and then taught, and where he visited for family and research reasons. One of the old-time characters we both knew was Fred Thompson, longtime historian of and organizer for the Industrial Workers of the World (IWW). Fred, who was fond of saying that he was "just as old as the century," came to a number of academic presentations on working-class history, especially those held at Chicago's Newberry Library. He often digressed, telling stories that he, and I, regarded as important and entertaining. Others were less convinced. I came to regard how university-based historians related to Fred as something of a litmus test for how much I was likely to get along with them. Jim never showed the impatience that sometimes greeted Fred's interventions.

Thompson provides useful points of entry to two themes that Barrett pursues here. When the old Chicago-based socialist publisher Charles H. Kerr Company, on whose board Fred and I both sat, considered bringing out the autobiography of the radical organizer, painter, and writer Arne Swabeck, Fred surprised and even disappointed me. Swabeck, a Danish immigrant ten years Fred's senior, had serially and sometimes simultaneously been part of the IWW, the Socialist Party, and U.S. Communist, Trotskyist, and Maoist parties. A delegate to the workers' council running Seattle during the 1919 general strike, he was in Moscow during early Soviet rule. His memoirs certainly did not break far from the overemphasis on political matters that Barrett identifies, but they had their moments of sharp, extended personal observations, including notes on the personalities of early Soviet leaders. Before the Internet, we at Kerr passed around the same printed copy of the manuscript. My look came after Fred's, and I found that he had carefully crossed out almost everything that I found interesting and adventuresome. His reasoning followed along the lines that Barrett identifies as running through communist autobiography—class forces mattered, and individual personalities not so much. Fred in person was endlessly interesting, deeply curious, and at times wildly funny. He was as far from a Stalinist as anyone on the left. And yet he too thought broad structural explanations precluded an interest in things that would have fascinated him in everyday life. Barrett is probably right that such dynamics affect history writing as a whole insofar as academics, Marxist or not, pursuing explanations of historical process are tempted to minimize "inner history."

Fred Thompson also affords an opportunity to give flesh to the "working-class cosmopolitan" at the center of the one selection written expressly for this volume. Like many old-timers whom Jim would know, Fred was as likely to quote, at length and from memory, Shelley or Burns as he was Marx. He likewise broke into song at the drop of a hat, drawing on a pretty extensive repertoire. With a high school education, he edited newspapers, wrote books, led publishing ventures, and taught at the IWW's Work People's College. One healthy aspect of my early university career was that I was steadily surrounded at the Kerr Company by self-taught working-class intellectuals who knew far more about labor history—not to mention art, literature, music, dance, and politics—than I did. I would not have thought to call them cosmopolitans, but that's just what they were. Fred was educated in Canada and the United States, in boxcars and at San Quentin, by participants in the Knights of Labor and the world's revolutions. For a time David Montgomery was such a figure, though with college in his background; so too was labor folklorist Archie Green before a return to school later in life. The leading student of race in early America, Ted Allen, dropped out of college in record time and made his breakthroughs as a working-class cosmopolitan and militant. The most insightful student of social relations on the shopfloor, Stan Weir, did likewise. Sometimes the world came to working-class cosmopolitans, as with Rosa Parks and Fannie Lou Hamer. Barrett shows well the resources on which such working-class cosmopolitans drew and the ways in which they themselves functioned as a resource.

On reading Jim's new classic article on working-class cosmopolitans, I had a brief feeling that his earlier classic on Americanization from the bottom up had also provoked—a "Why didn't I think of that?" moment. The topics seemed absolutely familiar to me, both from the documents many of us have studied and from people I've known since growing up. The autobiographical selections in *History from the Bottom Up and the Inside Out* suggest that Jim had a jump on most scholars, experiencing the working-class intellectual first in his own household in the person of an older brother. But as is so often the case in the wonderful collection you are reading, Barrett mixed experience with study and discipline to produce profound insights. He recognized the working-class cosmopolitan in his studies of the relationship of Hutchins Hapgood, the much-traveled, Harvard-educated anarchist with the radical woodworker and "blue-collar cosmopolitan" Anton Johannsen, whom Hapgood came to know and admire.

In a still larger sense, the exemplary work sampled here is the product of persistent commitment—when picket lines had four pickets or four hundred, and when archives yielded much about working people and when they did not—joined to impatient desires to find better ways to understand and to act.

LAWRENCE, KANSAS
SEPTEMBER 2015

ACKNOWLEDGMENTS

These essays have been presented in a variety of venues, discussed and criticized by colleagues across several continents and around the United States, and improved considerably in this process. For their help in conceptualizing these studies, I thank audiences and discussants at conferences in England, Japan, Poland, China, and Australia, as well as those in Detroit, Chicago, Pittsburgh, Boston, and Urbana. Spread out over most of a scholarly lifetime, they have also benefited from the personal and intellectual support of family, friends, and colleagues. My oldest intellectual debts are to teachers and mentors who encouraged me in my work over many years. These include the following people and many others: the late David Montgomery, Al Young, Gilbert Osofsky, E. P. Thompson, Royden Harrison, Steve Nelson, Tom Barrett, Joe Hobbs, and Steve Sapolsky.

I have far too many people to thank properly in such a small space, but a number of individuals have been particularly helpful and supportive: As usual, Jenny Barrett was the key influence and provided the most support of all kinds, including help on the index. She helped with many technical aspects in the preparation of the essays, and she also read and commented on most of them in their original and revised forms. More importantly, her consistent love and support helped me get through a difficult period while I was preparing the manuscript for this book. Xian (Sean) Franzinger Barrett inspired much of this work by the way that he has lived his life and by the community of teachers and activists with whom he surrounds himself in the Chicago public schools, neighborhoods, and labor movement. Erin Franzinger Barrett has become vital to Xian and to this group in the past few years, and I am grateful to have her in our family. Xiobhan (Siobhan), the most recent and loveable addition to the family, has brought great joy and even inspiration. May she inherit and help build a better world.

I asked David Roediger to provide a foreword not only because he probably understands the work better than anyone else, but also because he has been involved in my thinking on some of these issues. Thanks to him for his foreword and other forms of support. Thanks also to Elizabeth Higginbotham, Kotaro Nakano, Vernon Burton, Leon Fink, and Sue Levine for their friendship and support, and for their discussions with me about these topics over many years. Shel Stromquist was a constant source of ideas and a model of patience when completing this project delayed our joint work. Toby Higbie and Kathy Oberdeck provided numerous comments and careful readings and suggestions for "Blue-Collar Cosmopolitans." Thanks also to Toby for letting me read and cite some of his unpublished work..

The Newberry Library provided a pleasant workplace and a stimulating intellectual environment during the preparation of this volume. Starting in my undergraduate years, it has become a scholarly home in the heart of the world's greatest city. I never expected to spend my career at a place like the University of Illinois at Urbana-Champaign. In finally collecting these essays, I realized again how much my colleagues at Illinois have shaped my thinking and writing over more than three decades. Illinois has been a challenging intellectual environment, and at the same time a supportive and encouraging community. Among the many people who deserve special thanks, I would like to single out Antoinette Burton, who encouraged this project, Diane Koenker, Clare Crowston, Kathy Oberdeck, Mark Steinberg, and the late Mark Leff—all of whom have been generous in reading and commenting on my work. And thanks also to all of my other unnamed Illinois colleagues, especially those in the History Workshop sessions. In Champaign-Urbana, friends in the Campus Faculty Association and Jobs with Justice and others, especially Dan Schiller, Susan Davis, Chip and Jayne Burkhardt, Jo and Doug Kibbee, Belden Fields, Pat Simpson, and Carol Leff provided some real-life meaning for my work. The late Jane Hedges provided mentoring and strength of a different kind. These colleagues and friends and many others helped me through a long and difficult illness, and in that and other ways contributed directly to the completion of this volume.

I have been lucky to have many wonderful graduate students at Illinois. Several of them served as research assistants while I was working on the original essays, and all of them influenced my thinking on these and other matters. I especially thank those who recognize the relationship between interpreting the past and creating a better future. These folks include Youn Jin Kim, Adam Stephanides, Kathy Mapes, Randi Storch, Caroline Merithew, Toby Higbie, Tom Mackaman, Adam Hodges, Nicki Ranganath, Val Littlefield, Dave Hageman, Steve Hageman, Dennis McNulty, Ian Hartman, Will Cooley, Kwame Holmes, David Bates, Bryan Nicholson, Anthony Sigismondi, Jason Koslowski, Melissa Rohde-Cherullo, Emily Pope-Obeda, Courtney Cain, and Michael Staudenmaier.

At Duke University Press, my editors Miriam Angress and Danielle Houtz were extremely supportive and patient, facilitating the work in many ways. I thank them heartily for their faith in the project and for all their efforts in my behalf. David Heath did an excellent job copyediting.

In considering the history of working-class identity, human relationships, and emotions, I have come to better understand my own life. And as I come a bit closer to its end, I understand better the importance of my immediate and extended families in shaping my personality, values, and ideas. The most important influences on my life have been my late parents, Catherine M. and Thomas E. Barrett, my wife Jenny Barrett, and my son Xian (Sean). In addition, my brothers and sisters—the late Tom Barrett, Janine Goldstein, Pat Fabsits, Jack and Bonnie Barrett, and Mike and Teri Barrett—have not only loved and supported me over the years but have also contributed to my thinking on working-class history in many ways that they may not recognize. My "inner-city" background was not a burden but a great resource in trying to understand the historical actors who have meant the most to me. It is doubtful I would have done my research, writing, and teaching in the way I have done them without the influence and rich culture of my own family and community. It was a long road to Urbana, but the West Side was a good place to start out.

The book is dedicated to three remarkable men. One is my wonderful friend and colleague Mark Leff—dedicated and talented teacher, brilliant historian, and *mensch*—whom we lost in February 2015. My brother Tom, the inspiration for one of the essays, passed away in July 2015. Finally, I honor the memory of David Montgomery who represents the most important intellectual influence in my life. Mark read and commented on much of the work represented here. His feedback was honest and at once both critical and supportive. He was also a dedicated humanitarian and liberal in the best senses of those terms. I and many others miss him every day, and this book is one way to carry on his memory. Tom was my mentor and role model throughout his life. In many ways his influence helps to explain why I am a college professor and writer rather than a well-read truck driver—as important as that profession is to us all. David showed that it was possible to be both a rigorous scholar and a committed citizen. The world would be a much better place with more people like Mark, Tom, and David.

INTRODUCTION

The Subjective Side of Working-Class History

By definition, working-class historians have concerned themselves with the collective—the community, social movement, union, or crowd—and their field has evolved in the United States and elsewhere in a distinctly materialist context. Theirs has also been a view of history "from the bottom up," that is, a reinterpretation of U.S. history from the perspective of laboring and poor people. Deeply influenced by postwar British Marxist historians, France's *Annales* school, and social science methods and theory, it is a perspective that has revolutionized our understanding of U.S. history.[1] The "new social history" of the late twentieth century succeeded in reconstructing the everyday lives of common people, and, at its best, it documented the significance of these anonymous lives for the broader sweep of American history.

All of these influences bear on my own intellectual lineage, and I am happy to associate myself with this approach. But I have also become increasingly concerned over the course of my career with how we might make room for the individual person in this story. What does this history look like from the personal perspectives of the common people who represent its subjects? While recent work has stressed the vital global character of working-class history, our next challenge may well involve the individual.² We need to raise the subjective side of our subjects' historical experience, and to do so in the very heart of a materialist approach. By the "subjective," I refer especially to identity—personal as well as group—and to issues of personality, personal relationships, and emotions. The study of such issues is not new, but it has received little attention from historians of the working class. What Robert Orsi has called the "inner history" of common people remains largely unexplored in the United States.³

The theme of the personal emerges in the book's first essay in an effort to understand the relationship between the historian's identity and values and her or his scholarly interests and interpretations. This autobiographical essay, expanded now with more autobiographical information relevant to the experiences and influences that shaped these essays, connects my own background with my research and with the development of working-class history as a field of study. The book ends with an essay on E. P. Thompson, the radical historian who did as much as anyone to shape this field, and who also had a great impact on my own development as a historian.

Chapters 2 and 3 take up a theme largely ignored by working-class historians: the relationship between the social and political movements that capture much of our attention and the individual experiences and identities of the people who built these movements. This individual dimension illuminates the more familiar history of such movements. In dozens of autobiographies, and then in the life of an individual radical, the two essays interrogate the relationship between the personal and the political in what may seem to be an unlikely venue for such an investigation—the Communist Party of the USA, from its heyday in the 1930s through the period of severe political repression and its decline in the postwar years.

Chapters 4 and 5 analyze what might be thought of as working-class intellectual history. These essays are intended to provoke a rethinking of those workers who took a more cosmopolitan view of the world as a result of travel, reading, political engagement, and cultural activities. Chapter 4, "Blue-Collar Cosmopolitans," raises, if it does not entirely answer, questions about the "life of the mind" in working-class communities and among certain occupational and political groups, while chapter 5 focuses on a particularly cosmopolitan woodworker and his relationship with a quintessential bohemian intellectual and "modernist." I hope this view of the intellectual dimensions of working-class life suggests a different vantage point for both intellectual and labor historians, and perhaps also a different way of understanding the "modern."

Another broad theme, *social* identity—racial, ethnic, gender, and class—remains central to American working-class historiography, and many of the essays here deal with this problem. Some of the most provocative work on racism, for example, has stressed the emergence of a distinct "white" self that developed in close relationship to working-class consciousness in the United States.[4] Chapters 6 and 7, "Americanization from the Bottom Up" and "Inbetween Peoples," have had an impact on the fields of immigration/ethnic and labor/working-class history and remain largely unrevised in order to provide benchmarks for our thinking concerning social identity. Each analyzes the gradual and uneven emergence of broader racial and class identities among immigrant workers, a theme which has emerged as central to the study of immigration and ethnic communities, as well as our understanding of race relations and what might be seen as the "ethnically segmented" character of American working-class movements.

This process of "Americanization from the bottom up" is also vital to understanding the cosmopolitan interethnic culture that emerged in American cities by the period of the Great Depression and World War II. Most immigrant workers and their children discovered America not in government and corporate "Americanization" classes, but rather in the streets and theaters of American cities. Chapter 8 considers Vaudeville, films, and urban realist literature as venues for the creation of a new, multiethnic urban culture.[5]

The problem, of course, in working on the subjective dimension in this field is, in part, one of sources. It is one thing to probe the psyches, emotions, and intimate relationships of the elite, rich in personal narratives, correspondence, and other introspective texts, and quite another to raise issues of personal experience in the lives of those long (and wrongly) considered "inarticulate." But so far we have not been looking very hard. Case files—for criminal or civil legal actions, for social service agencies, for employers—may be read against the biases of the middle-class and professional people likely to be overseeing such groups, and they often contain a wealth of data on personalities and relationships. Continued analysis of popular culture—song lyrics, for example—can suggest values and feelings. Clues to the intellectual and spiritual lives of common people might be embedded in religious ritual or prescriptive texts, and in religious practice itself. The systematic study of death, for example, and the ways in which it was handled by working-class people from various ethnic and religious backgrounds, remains in its infancy.[6] Above all, personal narratives—the autobiographies, letters, and interviews of workers, which are too often seen simply as empirical sources, might be read with the working-class subjective in mind—personal identity, relationships, and emotional responses to life experiences. Working-class autobiography is a distinct genre with its own characteristics and potential.[7]

Why is this important? Long wedded to frameworks of political economy and broad historical forces, why should social historians concern themselves with the personal? First, there is the matter of motivation. We assume the significance of emotion and the importance of personal relationships in explaining our own behavior, yet we seldom consider these explanations for the people we study. The nature of emotions has its own distinctive history, of course, and we cannot assume that our subjects experienced all this in the same way we do today.[8] But when we consider the factors shaping social movements, is it too much to ask how the more personal dimensions of working people's lives shaped their political activism, the movements they created, and the changes they made in their societies?

A more important reason to pursue the history of the working-class subjective has to do with the implications of ignoring this inner world. The individual looms large in explaining the evolution of bourgeois society, but the individuality of working-class people is seldom acknowledged. To some degree, this is a natural tendency given the collective character of those phenomena of most interest to social historians, but the effect of this can be to objectify our subjects. Phrases like "the anonymous crowd" mask the identities of thousands of purposeful individual actors. We can never hope to recover the individual experiences and emotions of all these people, but in acknowledging the significance of the personal in this context, we invest common people with a humanity often denied them in their own societies and times.

Often associated with postmodern theories and methods, the subjective side of history has often been counterposed to the more traditional concerns of working-class historians—work, material inequality, and protest. Why? Might it not enrich our work on these and other subjects to consider our blue- or white-collar actors not simply as atoms or as cogs in a great social and political machine, but also as individuals with their own affective lives? Why is it not possible to consider the role of personal relationships in the motivations of working people? It seems likely that strikes, for example, were often motivated as much by love and concern for one's family and community as by a broader notion of class struggle. Emotions may seem a world away from most labor history frameworks, but it is safe to assume that they played an important role in the lives of these people.[9]

Class was and still is not only a material and social, but also an emotional experience. What we call "class consciousness" involved not only social and political aspirations, but also a world of hurt, resentment, envy, and anger. As Richard Sennett and Jonathan Cobb observed many years ago, the deepest injuries of class are not on the surface, but rather "hidden" in working people's personal lives.[10] Yet more positive emotions like love and pride also played a role—as the basis for community and group solidarity and as the motivation for organization and struggle.

History from the Bottom Up and the Inside Out offers a different angle of vision on familiar topics. The book combines new and revised essays to raise the subjective side of common people's historical experience in a manner that retains a materialist analysis and enriches our study of social history. I ended up in an intellectual and political location I shared with many in my generation, but my own background is quite different from most of my colleagues in academia. I hope that the juxtaposition of some more personal writing with the essays I have written over the years and the new material produced for this volume suggest a different perspective on the relationship between personal life, scholarship, and politics. Although most of the published essays are revised, I hope readers will be able to trace not only the development of my own interests and approach, but also some of the major themes in the field over the past three decades.

CHAPTER ONE

The Blessed Virgin Made Me a Socialist Historian

*An Experiment in Catholic Autobiography and the
Historical Understanding of Race and Class*

Protestants, it seems to me, tend to have dramatic conversions. They are "born again" and do not look back. Catholics—and though I have been an atheist for many years, I am culturally and psychologically a Catholic—are forever backsliding, de-converting, returning to their previously sinful life. —MICHAEL HARRINGTON, *The Long Distance Runner: An Autobiography*

As Renee Remond has observed, historians are taught "to be on their guard against subjectivity, their own as much as others'. They know from experience the precariousness of recollection, the unreliability of first-person testimony.... Everyone has an unconscious tendency to introduce a factitious coherence into the path of his [sic] life. They have no reason to think that they have any better chance to avoid the tricks of memory that they have learned to spy out in others."[1] Is there a reason we might be interested in the details of any given historian's life for their own sake?

I have been asked to discuss the relationship between a particular religious background and the historical scholarship I have made my life's work.

As Remond suggests, there is a danger here of reading more coherence and intellectual development into one's background than was actually there and, in the process, missing the broader dimensions. For many, it seems, the essence of Catholicism involved guilt, fear, and sexual repression. Many Catholic women locate the essence of their own experiences in the Church's everyday patriarchy. I recognize both the validity of these observations and the diversity of Catholic lives. Mine is a recollection of a particular place and time, shaped by all those influences that I emphasize in analyzing the lives of my historical subjects—class, race, gender, and ethnicity.[2]

Aside from funerals and family celebrations, I have not attended Mass for over three decades. Thus, in considering the Catholic roots of my own historical interests, I am a little surprised to find how positive my recollections are—whether because of or in spite of my distance from the Church. My identity is deeply imbued with Catholicism, which has fundamentally shaped my political perspective and my approach to history. It is the *place* I came from—my old neighborhood, with my parish at its center; the *community*, *family*, and other people who nurtured me; the *worldview* that shaped my values. At its best, it is a promise that invests human life with the dignity it deserves. Growing up Catholic, Michael Harrington recalled, "meant, above all, that I accepted the idea that life was a trust to be used for a good purpose and accounted for when it was over.... In this fundamental conception of the meaning of existence I am as Catholic as the day on which I made my first communion." Long after leaving, Harrington continued to find the Church, "in its highest expressions, profound and beautiful. My only problem," he concluded, "was that I did not believe in it."[3] I could not forget my Catholic background if I wished to; it is an important part of who I am. I choose not to forget it.

It has taken a long time for me to realize the degree to which Catholicism has shaped the questions I am interested in as a historian and led me to view them a bit differently from many of my colleagues. Given the secular character of scholarly life, indeed the materialist bias in my own field of working-class history, the delayed recognition is hardly surprising. I want to explore several questions here: How did growing up in an ethnic, blue-collar, inner-city parish and coming to social and political awareness *through* the Church provide me with many of the concerns and ideas that have remained with me, particularly my interests in race, ethnicity, and class? How have these influences shaped my scholarship on such historical issues? Why have my "Catholic sensibilities" about these issues remained submerged for so long?

Incense and Miracles

My early memories of the Church are mostly sensual. I remember not only the visual images—the flickering red altar lamp in a dark church, ornate religious paintings on the vaulted ceilings, gilded banners with inscriptions in Latin and Slovak, sun streaming through stained glass, and the bloody stations of the cross—but also the sounds and smells, the call and response of the litanies in Latin, the altar bells, the candle wax and incense. All of this I found very attractive. Part of the church's aesthetic attraction probably derived from its juxtaposition with the outside world. My neighborhood was by no means a slum, but it was surrounded by factories and rail yards and filled with two-flats and drab apartment buildings—quite a contrast with the crafted beauty of the sanctuary. When you opened the large doors of the church and stepped inside, you left the clamor, noise, and dirt of the city, and you entered a world of grace and beauty. One aspect of working-class life I understood, then, as a result of growing up Catholic, was simply that amid the squalor and struggle embraced by working-class historians, many of these people also found great joy and beauty in their religious lives.

There was also a strong emotional bond that is more difficult to describe. American Catholicism in its 1950s high tide was, as Charles Morris noted, "highly formal, even mechanistic ... enshrouded in bewitching mysteries and ritual, combining a remarkable degree of theological rigor and a high degree of abstraction with a practical religion that was intensely personal and emotional." I believed that the spiritual part of my life was much more important than its other dimensions, and I took more interest in it, I think, than most kids. Being a part of the Mass gave me a strong sense of security and belonging as well as a sense of beauty. "For a trembling moment every week," Morris wrote, "or every day if they chose, ordinary people reached out and touched the Divine."[4]

The Church's theological rigor provided what I think of as an active intellectual life—even if, until recently, intellectual historians would not have recognized it as such. Catholic thinking about God and her/his relationship to man was universal in many respects. It provided a unified worldview and explained why things worked as they did, or did not. I came eventually to question the pat answers we memorized from *Father McGuire's New Baltimore Catechism No. 2*, but at the time I was glad to have them.[5]

On one level, ours was a quintessential "parochial" life, bounded physically by railroad overpasses and factory doors and spiritually by the boundaries of our parish and the teachings of the Church. Most of what gave my early life meaning occurred within a few blocks of my house and my church. This issue of parochialism is important. It helps to explain the social intolerance I noted eventually in my surroundings, and the intellectual intolerance that sometimes characterized the Church as an institution. Yet by the standards of a small parish on the West Side of Chicago, we were also taught to think "globally," a perspective that derived from the Church's universal character and claims. Its "apostolic" history and continuing mission activities took my imagination well beyond my parish and city to other parts of the world. I knew that Catholics in Asia and Africa were quite different from us in many respects, but I also knew that we shared with them that which was most important. Discussions of mission work often sent me to the storeroom in our basement. Here I consulted an old edition of *Compton's Pictured Encyclopedia*, where I could find various maps and descriptions of nations and peoples. A vivid photo diagram lined up the "Races of Mankind" in order of the shapes of their skulls and included photos of a Watusi warrior, a Native American chief in full headdress, a small Chinese guy, and, inexplicably, Benjamin Franklin.[6] Whatever my sources lacked in the way of subtlety with regard to race, the Church's reach did spark my interest in other peoples and cultures. I do not project later scholarly interests back onto these early forays, but in this limited sense at least, the Church introduced me to the broader world.

My first taste for history and politics came through the peculiarly Catholic approach in our texts, which seemed not only to organize the whole narrative around the development of the Church in various parts of the world, but also explained most historical change in terms of famous Catholics. *Treasure Chest*, a Catholic children's magazine that arrived twice monthly in comic book format, included a series on the discovery of the New World, the Revolutionary War, and the opening of the West, with a special emphasis on Catholic heroes.[7]

My introduction to the Cold War came not from the usual popular culture sources cited now in historical works on the subject (though I did follow events in *Life* magazine), but from *Treasure Chest*. Here or in other Catholic children's publications I encountered China and communism through the tragic fates of our missionaries. I admired Tom Dooley long before I ever heard of his classmate Michael Harrington. For us, the problem with the Chinese Revolution was not that it suppressed capitalism—I don't think the term ever came up—but rather that it suppressed Catholicism. An elaborate series, "This Godless Communism," introduced by no less than J. Edgar Hoover, ran throughout the 1961–1962 academic year (in the midst of the Cuban missile crisis). *Treasure Chest* also graphically laid out what the communist invasion of the United States would look like if we ever let our guard down. I saw Russian tanks rolling down a city street that looked a lot like Michigan Avenue, and the statue of a boy who had denounced his Catholic parents because they persisted in their lives of prayer (as always, it seemed, the Catholics had it the roughest). The new communist regime made mothers go to work in factories and placed their children in communal child-care centers. (I recall confusion on this score. Even without "communist authorities," many of my friends' mothers already worked in factories. It was true, however, that we had no communal day care; immigrant grandparents cared for most of the kids.)[8]

Catholic anomalies surfaced in the midst of all these Cold War fears. Our nuns first welcomed Fidel Castro, and not simply because of his Jesuit education (they were School Sisters of St. Francis, and clearly irritated by what they probably saw as Jesuit chauvinism in many of our texts). They objected to the lurid casino life in Havana, and also to the poverty in which many Cubans lived. Any enthusiasm for Fidel faded, of course, as the stories of Catholic suffering began to filter from Catholics in Florida to Catholics in Chicago, but it was our fellow communicants we worried about, not U.S. investments.

My lifelong interest in ethnicity and race started early, beginning with what I might term an "urban curiosity." My father fueled this with his stories of the city, but so did my own experiences amid the striking diversity that characterized Chicago's neighborhoods. My father (1912–1994) joined the Chicago Police Department during the Great Depression because he needed a job. He was the kind of person social historians need to think more about if they hope to understand American workers—precisely because his life reflects elements of working-class experience often ignored by labor historians. Raised by a fireman and his strong-willed, second-generation Irish wife, he was a good Irish Catholic boy. It seems that my grandparents, whom I remember only dimly, were both class-conscious and devout. Like many union workers in early twentieth-century Chicago, my grandfather wore only union suits and shoes and smoked only union cigarettes. He helped to organize the fire department engineers and claimed that the "bosses" transferred him from one firehouse to another around the city. Intended as punishment, this actually facilitated the organizing. One of my father's earliest memories was sitting with his sister in a double stroller as my grandmother pushed them through city streets, distributing union literature. The union was strong enough to launch an effective strike against the city in the midst of the great 1919 labor upheavals. My grandfather's engineers' strike was one of dozens that erupted, along with a great race riot, in the summer of 1919.[9]

But if strikes and unions were very much a part of my grandparents' lives, the Church was its center. The family started out on the old West Side, just south of Hull House and west of the old Jewish ghetto in Holy Family parish (established in 1857), which historian James Sanders called "the single great Irish Workingman's parish." Father Damen, the original pastor, refused more attractive locations and instead built the city's most impressive Catholic church and its premier men's and women's schools in a "desolate and uninviting locality" amid the shanties of Irish squatters accused of frequent "riots and ructions." The largely poor immigrants responded with lavish support for the church, which became "the undisputed symbol of Catholic confidence and respectability." The neighborhood was close to the Hull House settlement and the old Jewish ghetto. My father attended St. Ignatius, still one of the top Jesuit high schools in the country. Although we had little awareness that these roots placed us near the center of ethnic working-class history in Chicago, what little sense we had of history was tied to Holy Family. Aside from school texts, the only history book I can recall seeing around our house in my childhood was a history of this parish.[10]

Just before World War I, my grandparents moved to an ethnically mixed neighborhood much farther out on the West Side, the neighborhood where my father and all of his children grew up. They joined another huge parish, Our Lady of the Angels (OLA), which was tucked between two more middle-class neighborhoods of second settlement, Humboldt Park and Garfield Park. Until the 1950s, both these neighborhoods contained significant Jewish populations transplanted from the old West Side ghetto. By the time I was growing up in the late 1950s and early 1960s, however, both were changing, the latter quickly emerging as one of the city's largest black ghettoes, the former as its most important Puerto Rican *barrio*. In North Lawndale, two miles south of our church, the white population dropped from 87,000 in 1950 to 11,000 by 1960 and *none* of the forty-eight synagogues active in the previous decade still remained in the latter. While Jewish and Protestant congregations "fled," however, my own neighbors assumed the beleaguered parochial mentality John McGreevy has described so well: they dug in to "defend" their parish neighborhoods against "invasion."[11] Ours had long been considered a rough neighborhood. As the ghetto moved closer during the 1960s, however, my neighbors took on an embattled mentality and, some of them, a more militant kind of racism than I had seen earlier in my life.

In the year I was born (1950), West Humboldt Park had a steadily declining population of 39,000, including only twenty-three blacks. Most residents were native-born from immigrant families, with Italians and Poles predominating. Most were wage earners, almost half working in plants scattered throughout the neighborhoods—candy and toy factories, small metalworking shops, electrical manufacturing plants—and others in the skilled trades or lower-level white-collar jobs. My own census tract, about one mile west of OLA, was entirely white but quite mixed ethnically, with large numbers of Poles and Slovaks in our immediate area and greater numbers of Italians to the east, closer to the parish church. Ten years later, small numbers of Puerto Rican families had moved into some parts of West Humboldt Park; otherwise, little had changed. Originally dominated by the Irish, OLA parish was about 60 percent Italian and 30 percent Irish in the late fifties, the remainder largely Polish. By 1965, however, the population of West Garfield Park, directly south of my own neighborhood, was between 65 and 85 percent African American. By 1970, shortly after my family left the neighborhood, West Humboldt Park was over 20 percent nonwhite; by 1980, it was over 85 percent nonwhite.[12] I did not need the census figures to tell me that the neighborhood was changing while I lived there as a teenager; my neighbors were obsessed with the changes.

This age of racial transition on the West Side coincided with the golden age of American Catholicism, though I did not realize it as I was growing up. The number of Catholics in the country doubled between 1940 and 1960, and much of this growth came during the fifties through intermarriage, conversion, or immigration, but above all through high birth rates. At the time of John Kennedy's election in 1960, a critical moment of ethnoreligious and political awakening for many in my generation, Catholics were growing at a rate twice that of the rest of the population. Between 1949 and 1959, parochial school enrollments more than doubled, from 2.6 to 5.6 million, while more than 24 million subscribers read (or failed to read) a dense network of 580 Catholic publications.[13] The huge numbers, especially in the nation's older industrial cities, and the resources loyally provided by a largely working-class constituency, produced an elaborate parallel institutional structure and culture that was distinct from the WASP mainstream, though deeply patriotic. Nowhere was this dramatic growth more apparent than in Chicago. It is remarkable enough that half the city's population was Catholic in 1956, but I was surprised to find the figure was so low. Growing up on the West Side, I thought of Chicago as a Catholic city where one could walk for miles without encountering a Protestant or a Republican.[14] I was aware of but seldom considered other faiths. My parish, one of the largest ethnically mixed "territorial" parishes in the city, contained 4,500 registered families, a mixture of nationalities, spread out over 150 city blocks. Every school morning found me standing on Iowa Street in front of Our Lady of the Angels along with some 1,400 other uniformed children, lined up along with our priests and nuns, to pray and salute the flag.[15] Not surprisingly, I always assumed the power and the pervasive presence of the Church.

Although OLA was a territorial parish, as late as 1950, nearly half (at least 128) of Chicago's 281 parishes were instead ethnically homogeneous "national" parishes. Having created their own fairly isolated ethnoreligious cultures based on their parishes, often at great sacrifice, these congregations were the most determined to remain. Here the defensive mentality settled in deeply. Laypeople were determined to "preserve" their neighborhoods (that is, to preserve their racially segregated character), and pastors often cooperated in the project, at least until the early 1960s. Even among the more tolerant people, one found the slide that John McGreevy has noted from the deeply embedded tradition of distinct national parishes to overt racial segregation: "We have our churches (and schools and stores) and they have theirs." Studying Catholicism and race relations in Chicago in the 1960s, William Osborne and his colleagues found that the line of defense between white and black neighborhoods was most often a national parish like the one we transferred to in the fall of 1958.[16]

For me, American Catholicism's golden age was one of miracles. In September 1958, after my sister was stricken with a mysterious paralysis that made it increasingly difficult for her to walk the mile to OLA, my parents transferred us to Saints Cyril and Methodius, a Slovak parish. This was a typically closed national parish, with its parishioners jealously guarding their own ethnic subculture, hardly the place for a bunch of Irish kids. The pastor reluctantly accepted us as a hard-luck case, perhaps with encouragement from the archdiocese. My interests in immigration and ethnicity probably derive in part from my grade school years at St. Cyril's, where I was steeped in an ethnic culture that was not my own. We learned our prayers and songs in Slovak, while the kids down the street learned theirs in Polish. Refugees from Czechoslovakia and Hungary occasionally joined my classmates, their first-generation parents and their immigrant grandparents reinforcing the Old World atmosphere of the place. More than it had been at the ethnically mixed OLA, ethnic culture was promoted and palpable throughout my new parish. One could attend Mass and receive the sacraments, buy groceries or a beer, and read the day's news or listen to it on the radio—all with no recourse whatsoever to English.

The first miracle came on December 1, 1958, "the day Chicago wept," when a fire swept through the main building at OLA, killing ninety-two schoolchildren and three nuns and devastating a once-vibrant neighborhood around the school.[17] Arriving on the scene at the end of our own school day, we could still see many of the bodies under blankets. My sister's large seventh-grade class on the second floor of the school had been virtually wiped out. The illness that seemed to be destroying her muscles had saved her life. Another miracle followed within a year. After a series of novenas and prayers to Blessed Julie Billart and Our Lady of Fatima, my sister's paralysis left as quickly as it had come. The prayers took place in my living room, often with a group of neighbors and sometimes with a large statue of Our Lady of Fatima, which toured homes throughout the 1950s and early 1960s.[18] Doctors had considered my sister a lost cause, but she recovered completely.

It is easy enough for me today to dismiss my mother's claim that the unexpected recovery was the product of Julie's and the Virgin's intercession; at the time, it only increased my faith, a gift from my family and community. It probably also intensified my feeling that I was supposed to give something back for all of these gifts. I was delighted by my sister's recovery and our survival, but I was not shocked. Miracles, it seemed, were well within the realm of the possible. Yet the experience might also have set the stage for an eventual decline in faith. My development beyond the coming decade left little room for miracles.

By the 1960s, the kind of ethnic segregation among white Catholics that had characterized the older national parishes like St. Cyril's was clearly breaking down. My own and other ethnic neighborhoods were actually quite diverse, with street gangs and other characteristic forms of social organization reflecting a range of nationalities and individuals two or three generations removed from the immigrant experience. In the context of the massive in-migration of blacks to the West Side in the 1950s and 1960s, race rather than ethnicity became the dominant source of identity. In the wake of the tragedy at OLA, "block-busting" real estate agents moved into the neighborhoods south and east of ours. Throughout these years, the arrival of these black families produced racial confrontations, and we learned a new word: "ghetto." We still recognized one another by our parents' and grandparents' nationalities, but there was no mistaking who "we" were, and "they" were either black or Puerto Rican.[19]

Confronting Race

My confrontation with race and my efforts to understand it suggest the kind of influence Catholicism had in this environment and its transformation from the highly ritualized, isolated parish life of the fifties to the more cosmopolitan and liberal atmosphere of the sixties. I saw black people often as they went to work in the numerous factories, dairies, and rail yards around the neighborhood, but they were clearly outsiders—automatically suspect, watched rather closely. To be fair, this was generally quite a closed neighborhood, laced with street gangs who occasionally pounced on strangers thought to represent some kind of a challenge. Most outsiders who met this fate, as we did occasionally when we wandered away from our own turf, were white, not black.[20] I noticed, however, that blacks who had reason to be going through the neighborhood on their way to work never entered "our" stores or playgrounds or lingered anywhere to talk. If they did, what my mother called "a scene" would soon develop.

When I encountered a black person—a construction worker in front of my house or a black cop sitting with my father in our living room—this was an unusual event. I took advantage of the situation to investigate. If I asked my father about these friendly episodes afterward, in light of the racism I heard and saw all about me, I received no satisfactory answer except, "He's okay." Were some other blacks also okay? I became not only aware but also interested in race quite early. Why?

My father knew the city extremely well, from tough police precincts up and down the riverfront and a variety of other worksites he frequented on his days off for extra pay. He was at once attracted to and repelled by the drama he saw every day as a cop. He kept a good deal of this out of our house, and I only realized how much his job had scarred him emotionally when he came to the end of his life. But he was a wonderful storyteller and he carried the less grisly stories home with him. These were marked by a cynicism and intolerance shaped by having often seen people at their worst, but also by a genuine fascination with the complicated cultures people created amid such diversity. His mental map of the city, like that of most Chicagoans, was organized around race and ethnicity. Class was something taken for granted—less significant, it seemed, for sorting out the stories. He described our own neighbors as "the Polack (or Dago, or Bohunk) down the street." His worldview is suggested by the fact that he also used a derogatory term to refer to the Irish, who were "Turkeys" in his urban lexicon. Yet these people were our friends and neighbors in a much deeper sense than the terms connote today.

My dad sometimes took me with him on errands to more distant neighborhoods. A Chinese hand laundry where he took his uniform shirts became familiar, but remained exotic by my standards. The proprietor's little daughter seemed different—and fascinating. I was particularly struck by the Garfield Park ghetto, physically close to my own parish, but socially distant and mysterious—precisely because it was out of bounds. Except in retail stores, many of them still maintained by Jewish merchants, there were few white people here. It seemed to me like a parallel world with all of its own institutions, comparable to but different from ours. At least some of the mystique of the ghetto also rubbed off on my friends. At a time when one's musical tastes said it all, our gang listened only to rhythm and blues on the black radio station WVON, never to the Beatles, and we shopped for clothes in stores on Madison and Pulaski that catered to young black men. There was something here, then, besides all the racism. Young black guys provided a male model of bravado and style, and they were known to be tough. They might not have been welcomed in our neighborhood, but they were cool. Certainly part of this had to do with gender roles and symbolism, but I do not pretend to understand this attitude any better now than I did then.

I think what intrigued me about race from an early age was this combination of the frequent appearance of people of color, especially African Americans, and the almost total lack of personal contact or understanding. Racial difference was clearly important, judging from the amount of time people spent worrying about it and the energy they employed to enforce the various boundaries between races. Yet no one around me really seemed to understand blacks. In part, then, I was just curious. The widespread racism deeply embedded in my surroundings made me fear black kids a bit when I did encounter them . . . but I was still interested. Were their lives like ours? Were they like me, did they wonder about the white kids? The curiosity evolved as I moved out of my neighborhood into the broader city, and out of the city into the broader world. It became more theorized and hopefully more directed, but it remains.

The fact that such encounters produced more interest than fear or hatred was due in part to the Church and in part to my mother. If the daily routine and occasional surprises of inner-city life sparked an urban curiosity about such difference, Catholicism provided a framework within which to make sense of it all. Part of the Church's universal quality was that Catholics came in all races and nationalities.[21] Such teachings were not irrelevant. Notwithstanding conventional liberal wisdom, survey data from the 1940s through the 1960s suggested that ethnic Catholics in northern cities were consistently more tolerant on issues of race and more supportive of civil rights than other white groups.[22] This did not mean that laypeople or religious were free from racism and other forms of intolerance that surrounded us daily. What it seems to suggest is that urban Catholics were deeply conflicted over these issues. For me, the obvious disjuncture between the Church's formal teachings and the daily reality of racism, sometimes within the Church itself, was the source of great interest and many questions. Our pastor might worry about the neighborhood "changing," but the Church taught us that all people were brothers and sisters. And, like my reading of the *Baltimore Catechism*, I was inclined to accept the Church at its word. About the time I might have begun to question it, a new kind of Catholicism began to emerge. As the Church itself changed in the course of the 1960s, there seemed to be more room and even some encouragement for my questions.

Perhaps because she was more sheltered than my father, my mother (1913–2005) was more open, social, and tolerant in various respects, including in terms of racial and ethnic difference. From early on in her life, she had slightly more exposure to blacks than my father had, and, while she shared many of the fears common to my neighborhood, she taught us to treat all people with respect. She conveyed to her children the joy she found in meeting different sorts of people. If my father's stories displayed an urban panorama of people from diverse backgrounds, my mother's example taught us to value such diversity. She also taught us charity and the Church's "preference for the poor" at our own front door. She could be uncharacteristically rude with Jehovah's Witnesses, but she never turned away the people my father called "bums." If I asked her why she gave the guy a quarter or a can of soup, she simply said, "Because he was hungry." This was another face of Catholicism, a face I knew well and loved. I have no way to measure her influence on me; I have no doubt that it has been enormous.

Vatican II Arrives on the West Side

I would like to say that I gave up my original intention of joining the priesthood as I entered my teens for complex or idealistic reasons. In fact, the decision can be explained in one word: girls. I listened to visiting priests' descriptions of their seminaries with great interest, but I realized eventually that something was missing in the slides of bowling alleys and swimming pools. Once the recognition set in, I decided I could contribute to the Church in other ways, and I remained deeply involved in parish activities.

It is autobiographically convenient when a vital development in world history resonates with one's personal story. The source for a lot of my own social and intellectual development, even if I did not always recognize it, was the Second Vatican Council (1962–1965), which displayed what Philip Gleason has called "the Church in eruption."[23] I welcomed the council's more relaxed, understandable liturgy and its socially oriented practice. Naturally, my experience of this big transformation came locally and, like most other important changes in twentieth-century Chicago, this one involved race.

The eruption arrived in my own parish in the person of a new assistant pastor, Father John Spitscovsky—Slovak to be sure, but young, energetic, and full of passion for Vatican II. Our little parish had never had an assistant pastor before. I now realize that Vatican II's social implications were emerging at the same time that the Chicago archdiocese was implementing its own mission of creating peaceful integration. Father John was probably there not only to carry the message of the former, but also to begin advancing the latter. He arrived shortly after the council got going and quickly set about organizing a teen club and aiming to "drag religion into everyday life."[24]

A major turning point came in the summer of 1963 when Father John hatched a plan with the assistant at Our Lady of Sorrows basilica, in the heart of the West Side ghetto. The idea was deceptively simple—a joint religious retreat with the teen clubs of the two parishes. It is difficult to appreciate the revolutionary quality of this plan without understanding the breadth of the racial divide between these two neighborhoods on Chicago's West Side at this moment in their histories. The ghetto around Our Lady of Sorrows exploded soon after in the first of several major riots that claimed lives and wrecked large parts of the black neighborhoods. Newspapers were filled with lurid stories of black street gangs, and crime in the area was, in fact, rising.[25] These events greatly increased the fear in my own neighborhood, and this fear bred racism. Our retreat, which occurred amid all these racial tensions, was my first sustained encounter with young black people. I was uncomfortable at first, but my contacts with black kids at the retreat began to undermine whatever stereotypes I had embraced up to that point. The parish groups slept in different rooms of the same dormitory. A small group of the black guys came to our room in the middle of the night with a plan for a raid on the girls' dormitory. The fact that it was gender harassment that provided the basis for this tentative interracial overture was probably significant, but lost on me at the time. I thought this was a great idea. Most of the tough guys from my neighborhood demurred, though I am not sure whether they were more afraid of a bunch of black guys in their room in the middle of the night or what the priests would do to us. I was one of only two from our parish who joined the raid. We ran screaming through the girls' dorm, and retreated to a secluded spot on the grounds. I remember talking there for a long time in the dark. Miraculously, the priests made no issue of it the next morning.

In the following year, I paid more attention to the civil rights movement, in the city and nationally. In the years since my birth, Chicago had become the focal point for both Catholic civil rights activism—through the Catholic Interracial Council (CIC) and the archdiocesan Office of Urban Affairs under Father John Egan (a renowned liberal on civil rights and other matters who lived at OLA during my early school years)—and also some of the era's most violent racial confrontations. These occurred in parishes very much like my own. Each summer brought considerable racial tension, as in Visitation Parish just south of the stockyards where white teenagers attacked blacks moving into the neighborhood, or simply passing through. I considered such attacks on blacks wrong; *why* I considered them wrong had more to do with Catholicism than with 1960s liberalism. "Time after time," William Osborne wrote in the mid-sixties, "Negroes, in their efforts to break out of the ghetto, have encountered the resolute opposition of the city's white Catholics." At the same time, "In the interval between 1951 and 1965, the leadership of the Catholic interracial movement shifted from New York to Chicago."[26]

My own role in all of this was extremely modest, but it suggests the distance I traveled with regard to race and the route I took to get where I was going. As president of the parish teen club, I helped my assistant pastor plan a workshop with volunteers from the Catholic Interracial Council. I remember singing a lot of folk songs and planning the liturgy for the first "guitar Mass" I had ever seen, but the weekend also involved a hair-raising trip through the neighborhood to interview "typical teens" about their racial attitudes. We ran into a gang from the next playground with whom we had fought recently. I was saved only by my partner, a beautiful (and fearless) young woman from the Catholic Worker movement who attracted the attention of the various guys we encountered and actually got some of them to answer the questions (their answers were not very encouraging). Through this work, I became involved in the Young Christian Students (YCS) movement and had some contact with the CIC and the Catholic Worker. I remember few of the details. It is revealing, perhaps, that I clearly recall that the gatherings were racially mixed, including black kids from the West Side. These meetings were at once strange and gratifying.

My adherence to civil rights, and later to the antiwar movement, brought me into frequent conflict with my father during the sixties, but now a new kind of Catholicism provided me with some authority. I always reminded him of the Catholic support for these movements (though I clearly exaggerated in both cases) and used this, rather unfairly, to justify my own ideas and actions. My father was extremely proud of his education with the BVMs (Sisters of Charity of the Blessed Virgin Mary, an old Irish immigrant order) and the Jesuits. When I asked the old cop when he would join the movement, he always said he would be there as soon as he could see a Jesuit priest on one side of him and a BVM nun on the other. The inevitable moment came with a July 1963 *Chicago Daily News* photo that I displayed proudly on the kitchen table. Staring at the photo of nuns and priests in a July 1, 1963, civil rights demonstration to desegregate a Catholic facility, my father looked confused and hurt. He never showed up at any demonstrations. By the late 1960s, dinner conversations often revolved around race relations and peace demonstrations, with me talking about my involvement and him talking about locking people up.[27]

What was happening in our home was happening in households throughout the United States. Generational divisions within the Church over civil rights come alive in the letters to Father Daniel Mallette during the early to mid-sixties. Mallette served a black parish on the West Side and was one of the clergy frequently involved in civil disobedience in Chicago, Selma, and elsewhere. I cannot recall how aware I was of his particular activities, but he was the sort of priest who provided a role model for young Catholics becoming active in the movement. High school student Maria Romano tutored in an inner-city school, contributed her allowance to a civil rights organization, and explained to her classmates that the Church did not, in fact, condemn interracial marriage. Mallette's actions encouraged her to persist in her own commitment. "As long as there are Catholics like you in the world," she wrote, "I shall do my best to be a good Christian. Thanks a million." She enclosed five dollars. Mallette's correspondence is full of such letters, most of them from young people, sometimes from middle-aged Catholics, enclosing money, offering prayers, or proposing to join him working on the West Side. But there was another sort of letter, almost as frequent, usually from older Catholics. A person who signed only as "Irish Catholic" wrote in the wake of Mallette's Selma march, "When I think when I was a kid the respect we had for a priest or nun.... Take off the collar." The deep divide that McGreevy has noted in the Church from the mid-sixties between liberals and parish traditionalists, exacerbated by the escalation of the war in Vietnam, continued to be fought every night over our dinner table.[28]

My brush with the Catholic interracial movement underscores the conflicted Catholic attitudes about race that John McGreevy develops in *Parish Boundaries*. He describes the emerging chasm in the sixties between Catholic liberals and ethnic blue-collar parishioners, but my own experience suggests that the two categories sometimes overlapped. One might identify the CIC leadership, for example, as middle class, distinct from blue-collar ethnics, particularly if one classifies clergy as middle class and educated. It is difficult to assess the Catholic interracial movement's rank and file, however, without a good deal more research. What is compelling to me in the story of the Catholic Interracial Council, however, is not that most inner-city parishioners opposed its efforts, but rather that some defended them. There were civil rights supporters out in the parishes where it must have been difficult to take such a stand, and at least some of the movement's leaders came from backgrounds similar to my own.[29] It would be easy and wrong to romanticize the Church's mixed record on race. My point is not that working-class ethnic Catholics supported civil rights and integration, though some clearly did, but rather that the tension McGreevy finds between the liberal leadership and the conservative flock could run through local parish congregations as well.

Us and Them

Given my later preoccupation with class, it is ironic that it had little role in my early consciousness. I certainly saw differences in wealth, even within my own neighborhood, but none of these were very striking. I lived my life in a sea of blue collars and never thought much about it. Industrial unions and periodic strikes were taken for granted. We always sided with labor, but reflexively, not because of any well-developed ideology. Any ideas and values involved more likely came from the Church than from unions or any political organization. Catholics were expected to have what came to be called a "preference for the poor," and if we saw poor neighbors all about us, then that made the preference a little easier to come by. If class was reproduced in my neighborhood (and clearly it was), this happened at some more subtle level than most labor historians seem to have in mind. St. Patrick, my large boys' Catholic high school, provided little basis for class distinctions. With no girls present, the delicate situation of courting across class lines never came up. The girls with whom we socialized after school hours were either from Notre Dame, the girls' Catholic high school down the street, or, more often, from our own parishes. Uniforms meant few if any distinctions in appearance. Even most upper classmen arrived together on the same city buses. We did everything together, and any distinctions were based on issues other than wealth and family status. I remember the few black kids; I remember only one rich kid, and he was clearly an outcast.

All of this changed when I turned sixteen, shortly after my family fled the West Side for a blue-collar suburb on the edge of Hillary Clinton's excellent school district. For the first time in my life, I encountered considerable wealth and active class discrimination. The small minority of black and Latino kids at my old school was totally absent; this was the whitest place I had ever seen. The resulting alienation was stark and deep. Overnight, I went from being a leader in both my high school and my parish, with a large group of friends in both places, to being a social outcast. The occasional breaks, like making a friend or being invited to a formal dance, always seemed to end with my feeling marginalized. When a friend dropped me off, he thought my father, who was out trimming a hedge, must be our gardener. Labor historians are trained to think of class in terms of material deprivation and the political and organizational results of such deprivation in situations of class consciousness. We think of class in strictly social terms. But at the personal level, class is also experienced emotionally. My own feelings were mostly of resentment and insecurity. I lived my life as an outsider, a feeling that has stuck with me in many academic settings. But such marginalization was not all negative; it forced me to reflect on and value my family and parish background. I gave up on any effort to blend in at the new place, and retreated instead to the neighborhood my parents had just fled. I came to think of blue-collar Catholics, my people, as both victimized and superior in many ways to the teenage snobs I endured in my classes. Long before encountering social stratification theory or Marxism, I resented these people deeply. I identified closely with my old neighborhood, which soon took on mythic proportions in my imagination. Looking for a way to reconnect with all this—and to avoid the draft—I entered college in September 1968, just after the Democratic Convention in Chicago.

I realize now that the University of Illinois Chicago campus is a rather drab place by the standards of many university settings, but I thought it was beautiful. For me, it represented a vital liberation from my stifling suburban existence and a return to the city. The university had swallowed up a vibrant ethnic neighborhood around Hull House. Mexican and Greek enclaves were virtually wiped out, but part of the old Italian community remained. I traveled to campus every day on the El, and discovered parts of the city I had never known. I had a state scholarship, but like the overwhelming majority of first-generation college students on campus, I worked to pay for books and expenses. This was hardly an "ivory tower" existence. Once again, the Church gave me my bearings. A friend from the old neighborhood brought me to the Newman House, and I organized much of my life around the place. Like others of my generation, I became active in the antiwar movement, and went from a "peace now" position to a more elaborate critique of U.S. imperialism. Like some, this led me to an interest in Marxism and socialist politics. At Newman, we joined the United Farm Workers' (UFWA) movement, connected students with the Chicago Area Draft Resistance (CADRE), planned panels against the university's new Police Training Institute, and helped to organize antiwar demonstrations. I was never a leader in any of these movements, and my own evolution took place within a Catholic context, facilitated by the presence of an active Catholic Left in and beyond the city. I criticized particular aspects of the Church, but I lived within a progressive, interracial Catholic environment.

At the time, Newman was a politically active, diverse community with personal relationships crossing various racial and ethnic lines. The most important of these for me was my lifelong relationship with Jenny Wong Barrett. Born at St. Frances Cabrini Hospital on the old West Side just two weeks after her parents arrived in Chicago from China, she was raised in an inner-city parish and was making her own sense of race, politics, and history at the time we met. We went through our changes together, creating an emotional bond that has thrived for almost fifty years. Through this relationship, I came to better understand the city and its people, the implications of racial identity and race prejudice, and the pursuit of democratic aspirations well beyond the ballot box.

I never consciously left the Church, but rather drifted away. And the drifting had much less to do with specific disagreements (though I certainly had some) than with losing the "gift of faith." Such a drift, which started in college and accelerated in graduate school, was hardly peculiar to me. Marxism taught me to analyze problems in materialist terms, but I never developed the kind of faith in it as a universal theory that I once had for Catholicism. Socialism did not displace but rather grew out of religious values and sensibilities. My involvement in labor and socialist politics was always dictated far more by heart than by brain, and its ethical foundations remained what I still think of as "Catholic." Some of our political activities, first in the 1970s with support work for the UFWA and later, in the 1980s, organizing against U.S. intervention in Central America, provided links between Catholic social action and socialist politics, especially in the form of liberation theology. Both movements were based in part on Church groups, and included many other Catholics and former Catholics. I still cannot explain it, but my movement from Catholicism to socialism seemed very natural. I stopped attending Mass, but I retained contact with the culture through my family. My affinity for Catholicism continues to appear in many little ways.

Religion and Working-Class History

I encountered both working-class history and radical politics at the University of Illinois at Chicago in 1969, and the two were fused in my mind from the beginning. I sought out courses on race and ethnicity, which always had a mixed clientele, mostly blue-collar whites, but also Asians, Latina/os, and African Americans. I had no access to labor history courses, though a couple of my instructors encouraged this interest. My earliest research papers reflect the interests I have retained throughout my education and my professional life—rank and file organization and strikes among Jewish immigrant garment workers; Langston Hughes and the Harlem Renaissance; the Abraham Lincoln Brigade volunteers; immigration and ethnicity; racial identity and race relations; work, protest, and political radicalism. I hope my approach to each of these subjects has evolved over the past thirty years, but my general scholarly concerns were clearly set by the end of my college years. Why? And what, if anything, did this have to do with Catholicism?

I have never featured religion prominently in my work, much of which looks like the rest of the "new labor history." This has a great deal to do with the theory and politics of working-class history as a research field, characteristics that I embraced. Yet I believe that my blue-collar, ethnic Catholic background, a different one than most of my colleagues', has made a difference in my approach. The subjects of my work were never abstractions. Particularly when I wrote of immigrant factory workers and their families in city neighborhoods, I thought of these people as an earlier generation in communities very much like my own. More important, perhaps, the values that shaped my life and ideas up to the time I became a professional historian were still there, beneath the language of class analysis and systematic social history. The former translated into a set of sensibilities that informed the latter.

These sensibilities can be best viewed in my doctoral dissertation on the work, family, and community lives of Chicago packinghouse workers and in related projects. At nineteen, I read *The Jungle*, Upton Sinclair's classic novel of the destruction of immigrant workers at the hands of the great "meat trust." I was moved by the novel and identified with the characters, but I was also troubled by it in ways that I could not explain at the time. This neighborhood, though poorer, was not substantially different from my own, yet I did not recognize mine in the squalor of "Packingtown," or my friends and neighbors in Sinclair's degraded and defeated characters. In real life the neighborhood was dominated by vital parishes that formed the nuclei of the various ethnic communities "Back of the Yards," yet Sinclair ignored religion. I sensed that these people, like my neighbors, had not only poverty and hard work in their lives, but also love and beauty. I just did not know what to do about this. When I re-encountered the book in the midst of my doctoral research, I had developed an approach to labor history that helped me to place these misgivings into a broader framework and to write a history of Packingtown and its people that was at once more sympathetic and more realistic.[30] Yet I too missed much of the life in this neighborhood.

What drew me more than anything else in the "new labor history" was the notion of human agency—the idea that workers themselves made this history through the creation of their own institutions and movements, their own cultures and ideas. I wanted to do for "new immigrants," early mass-production industry, and big city life what Edward Thompson and his American followers were already doing for artisans and others in early industrialization—to re-create the worlds that Chicago's immigrant workers made for themselves and to put them at the center of my analysis.[31] All of this came from Thompson, Herbert Gutman, David Montgomery, and other historians, but I also had those vague misgivings about Sinclair's depiction of people I was having trouble recognizing. And those feelings derived far more from my own background than from reading the new labor history. The two influences came together for me in Pittsburgh in the late 1970s.

My central concern was certainly not religion, but rather work and its effects on people's lives. Four books were particularly important to my formulation of the project. *Outcast London*, Gareth Stedman Jones's brilliant history of poverty and social class relations, interested me in the problem of casual labor with which families in Chicago's stockyards district struggled on a daily basis. Carter Goodrich's *The Frontier of Control*, a study of the politics of work in the British metalworking industry, led me to think about the packinghouse work process, the nation's first assembly-line operation, in terms of "work rationalization." I concluded that such "rationalization" in the slaughterhouses and packing plants was a relative, class-based concept. Changes that appeared rational in terms of the profit motive often disrupted workers' lives and left their families destitute. David Brody's *Steelworkers in*

America provided a model by focusing on two distinct generations of steelworkers in the mill towns that I still saw about me in the Steel Valley around my new home of Pittsburgh, and on the psychologies (what we called the "mentalities") of both workers and management. David Montgomery's essays, which eventually appeared in *Workers' Control in America*, and his courses projected the pervasiveness of class in workers' lives at work and in their communities, and were by far the biggest influence.[32]

Yet none of these works successfully followed workers beyond the factory walls, into their homes and neighborhoods, and none of these scholars paid much attention to religion. I was convinced from the beginning that the real drama of this story lay in showing the impact of what Montgomery sometimes called "the long arm of the job."[33] Here I was particularly drawn by John Bodnar's argument that it was a commitment to family that motivated immigrant workers, and not Montgomery's notion of workers' control. Rather than juxtapose such traditional family values and the pursuit of workplace control, however, I insisted that these workers pursued work control issues, and working-class organization more generally, precisely because they saw these as vital to the protection of their families and communities. In this way, I linked Bodnar's "working class realism" to Montgomery's world of shopfloor politics and class conflict.[34]

The residents of Packingtown created vibrant and deeply religious lives organized around ethnic parishes—eleven in the space of less than a square mile, each of them with an elaborate array of voluntary organizations. Yet I tended to analyze religion in organizational terms and as a general influence in the community, never as the center of these people's lives and as the basis of their worldviews. Another study of this same community, Robert Slayton's more ethnographic *Back of the Yards*, picked up on this part of the story. Slayton was too nostalgic and optimistic in his readings of these religious communities. Like the Church generally, they were conservative in many respects, particularly with regard to issues of gender, and subject to all of their own conflicts along generational and other lines. But, as Leslie Woodcock Tentler notes, Slayton captured the centrality and even something of the meaning of religion "as a source of comfort and personal integrity, of social order and communal vitality" in the rather dismal setting of the stockyards and slaughterhouses. Slayton's more ethnographic and cultural approach, in contrast to my own emphasis on work and the quality of life, accounts to some degree for the centrality of religion in his evocation of the community and its one-dimensional treatment in my own. I certainly understood, however, that the mighty meat trust did not dominate the minds in Packingtown. These workers and their families found alternative sources for their values and ideals in their various ethnic and religious enclaves. As Tentler has observed for immigrant workers more generally, creating these cultures in the face of WASP cultural condescension and the acquisitive logic of the giant corporation represented an "act of resistance." "Religion provided them with perhaps their richest resources for shaping the world of everyday living, and with a potent counterweight to the dominant American ideology of competitive individualism."[35]

Their religion also invested their lives with a dignity that helps to explain their desperate struggles to maintain these precious cultures in the face of very real corporate threats. The same Lithuanian laborer who swept blood and offal amid commercialized death on a vast scale on the killing floor, or the Irish or Polish girl who spent her days stuffing chipped beef into cans, each also had music and beauty in her or his life, and a brush with the divine each Sunday. Like Mike Dobrejak, the central character in Thomas Bell's epic proletarian novel *Out of This Furnace*, their religious perspective was vital to their continuing struggles to protect their communities and build a better world.[36] Theirs were class struggles, but they were fundamentally shaped by their religious beliefs.

What I found most compelling in the human drama at the stockyards was *not* what riveted Sinclair—the destruction of these people by the meat trust—but rather their creation of vital family lives and rich cultures. I was attracted by this confirmation of the human spirit under such conditions, but this was not simply a good story. It is impossible to understand the emergence of strong social movements like the United Packinghouse Workers-CIO and the Back of the Yards Council at work and in the community without documenting the basis for this human spirit and the culture it spawned. The people "back of the yards" built these movements to protect their communities and their families, and Catholic conceptions of the sacred were at the basis of both of these concerns. Celebrated community activist Saul Alinsky concluded, "It is the Catholic Church that serves as the medium through which these people express their hopes, desires and aspirations."[37]

I never raised the obvious connections between a religious worldview and these kinds of traditional "family values," but I saw such values not as opposed to or even distinct from, but rather integral to class experience. As Leslie Woodcock Tentler suggests, "by preaching so conservative a version of marriage and family life, the clergy endorsed, albeit indirectly, a radical critique of existing economic arrangements." The vitality of religious values as a basis for what we analyze as class behavior is only one aspect of working-class religion that badly needs to be explored. The Back of the Yards was both a deeply religious community and the site of chronic class conflict in and outside the slaughterhouses, independent labor politics, and effective community organizing. Labor historians have largely ignored the nature of the relationship between such religious devotion and such class behavior—here and in comparable communities.[38]

The material manifestations of working-class religious devotion alone—the huge edifices built on laborers' and factory operatives' wages; the elaborate networks of schools carefully designed to shape the values and, thus, the characters and personalities of the communities' children; the voluntary groups and social service agencies erected to provide support for the poorest among the poor, in part because many of them would turn only to their own in times of need—all of this suggests religion's centrality in working-class life. Yet these creations represented only the more obvious dimensions of cultures that operated as potent intellectual and moral influences vital to the worldviews we seek to understand. A careful study of religion could at least begin to give us the basis for a new kind of plebian intellectual history and, at best, suggest the cosmology of poor and anonymous people in industrial communities throughout the country. Yet we have largely ignored the vast landscape of workers' religious lives.

And this failure to investigate such a vital aspect of working-class life was my failure as well. Catholicism, so embedded in my own life and in the lives of many of my subjects, has been largely absent from my research and writing down to the present. Why? First, I had changed. The loss of religious faith paralleled the development of a materialist conception of historical change, even if many of my earlier sensibilities remained. It is impossible to separate this personal shift from my immersion in a dynamic subculture of radical labor historians. In a profession where I might otherwise have felt even more marginalized than I did, I found in Pittsburgh a group of friends and colleagues, some of them from working-class backgrounds similar to my own, who shared my interests and values. Together, throughout the late seventies, we engaged in labor organizing, strike support, demonstrations against apartheid in South Africa, and other activity. This engagement provided the context for an enormously exciting intellectual journey that promised the opportunity to rewrite the history of the United States with common people at its very center, but it left little room for religion as a proper subject of historical inquiry.

Why have we learned so little about an influence that was clearly so important in workers' lives? Judging from Leslie Woodcock Tentler's surveys of the more general bias in U.S. social history, labor historians are in good company in ignoring the centrality of religion in general and Catholicism in particular. "Complaints about exclusion often strike a petulant tone," John McGreevy notes in a recent review of new religious history, "but it is noteworthy that historians of the most religious nation in the industrialized world understand their country's immediate past with little reference to religion."[39] Given their interest in anonymous common people, working-class historians face major sources and methods problems, especially if we wish to investigate personal thoughts and beliefs as well as buildings, organizations, and activities. But social historians have long faced similar research problems. Labor historians' resistance to the analysis of religious thought and behavior derives, in part at least, from the strong materialist bias in much of working-class history and the political perspectives of those of us who do this research. For all our discussion of consciousness and culture, we often embrace what William Sewell calls a "materialist common sense"—an assumption that the material precedes, shapes, and produces the cultural.[40] In a rare early foray into the significance of religion for labor history, Herbert Gutman discovered labor reformers' use of religious symbolism and language. But Gutman still tended to analyze religion in instrumental terms, as a resource rather than an elaborate worldview, and he continued to see politics as distinct from and more fundamental than religion. Some labor historians clearly believe not only that material conditions and the social relations surrounding them are causally more important than religious ideas, but also that religion is, after all, not a good thing. We often analyze it as an obstruction, a conservative influence and the source of conflict among workers from diverse backgrounds, something to be cleared away to allow for the construction of a progressive labor movement—but never as part of the very basis for class as well as ethnic identity or as an element in the motivation of workers engaged in class conflict.[41]

Much has happened in the past two decades to confront me once again with the significance of religion and with the subjective dimensions of historical experience more broadly. My shift to these concerns has less to do with the "death of communism," or the displacement of Marxism by postmodern theory and method, than with personal events. My parents' and other deaths among family and friends, the departure of my son for a life of his own, and my own natural process of aging and illness have forced me to think more about those vast realms of life that the "new social history," for all its accomplishments, has never approached. Such personal experiences have drawn me to the deceptively simple observation that our historical subjects clearly had their own emotional and spiritual lives that we have ignored at the risk of fundamentally misunderstanding them.

One result of this shift has been a tendency to simply consider the personal side of fairly traditional subjects like working-class radicalism. I began to think of radical movements like American communism not only as social movements but also in terms of the personal lives of individual activists.[42] Another result has been a renewed interest in race as a form of personal as well as social identity. Although race occupied a central place in my analysis of the rise and fall of the packinghouse workers' movement, like most labor historians of the time, I analyzed it largely as an obstacle to effective organization and struggle. I noticed, however, that most violence in the 1919 Chicago race riot had been perpetrated by second- and third-generation Irish American youth, and that the more recent Slavic immigrants played little part.[43] Yet homeowners from Slavic immigrant backgrounds became central in the racist violence following World War II. This reminded me of the observation a priest had made about recent Italian immigrants in Our Lady of the Angels parish in the sixties. It was remarkable, he said, how little they understood the racial conventions of the neighborhood, how little they embraced white racism when they first moved in—and remarkable too how quickly they absorbed the dominant attitudes of the resident white population. My own background among Slavic American Catholics made it difficult for me to abstract them as "typical working-class racists." Instead, I determined to understand racism as one part of a process of immigrant acculturation within distinctly working-class environments and situations—what I termed "Americanization from the bottom up." Several of my most recent articles, including some with my colleague Dave Roediger, concern this problem, and I continue to be interested in exploring working-class racism as part of a broader learning process rather than the "natural" product of a multiracial working-class population.[44]

The Irish Way (2012), which is often thought about as a study of Irish Americans per se, was always intended to be a book about the relationships between Irish American Catholics and other racial and ethnic groups in the twentieth-century American city. The book does argue for the central role of Irish Catholics in the creation of a new interethnic urban culture that was the product of their interactions with these other groups. It was a way of facing the agency of people from my own background in the creation of racial and ethnic discrimination and violence, but it was also an effort to reconstruct more progressive labor, political, and civil rights traditions among urban

Irish Americans. It is difficult to miss the personal motivations involved in writing the book.[45]

My continuing interest in the racial identity and attitudes of recent immigrants is just one dimension, however, of a broader concern with the personal lives of working-class people. This too certainly derives both from my own background, and also from more recent personal experience. Through a combination of method and perspective, social historians simply miss much of the personal, emotional, and spiritual side of life. There is little reason to think that such events were any less important in our subjects' lives than they are in our own, though surely attitudes about death and other life transitions differ from one culture to another and have changed over time. Indeed, it is clear that religion was far more important among most working-class people in the early twentieth century, for example, than it is among middle-class, secular humanist intellectuals today. Is it possible to fuse labor history's broad categories of structural and material analysis with a serious investigation of the subjective and the personal—the emotional content of life, strong personal relationships, particularly within families, and various forms of personal identity and sources of motivation? Though I am still not a practicing Catholic, for me, religion generally and my Catholic background in particular are critical to such concerns. Bringing a serious consideration of religion into the study of poor and wage-earning people's history not only rings true with my own experience; it also offers even those without this background an opening into a particularly important dimension of working people's lives.

CHAPTER TWO

Was the Personal Political?

Reading the Autobiography of American Communism

Amid calls for global approaches to the study of history, some labor historians have turned to the more personal dimensions of working-class life through the study of biography and autobiography. While an emphasis on social process, collective experience, and material conditions has largely defined social history for a generation, recent theory, the decline of the labor movement, and political transformations have encouraged some to consider the more subjective aspects of working people's lives. At the same time, the history of American communism has enjoyed a renaissance, with a new generation of anticommunist scholars contending with aging New Left interpreters over the meaning of communism in the broader sweep of U.S. history. One contention concerns the very nature of the Communist Party USA (CPUSA). The new anticommunists have documented at length the espionage activities of party members, and have returned us to a view of the party as essentially a tool of the Soviet state, while leftist interpreters argue that it represented a genuine social movement shaped by domestic situations. Rather than the influence of Stalinism, New Left historians have tended to emphasize the agency of party members.[1]

Historians of the left and the movement itself have long compiled biographical data on leading communists. An important international biographical turn in the history of communism is represented by Kevin Morgan and the group of scholars working at the University of Manchester, where they have constructed a very large database of biographical information on individuals associated with the Communist Party of Great Britain. Some of their published work has included biographical essays on figures from various national parties.[2] For the most part, however, even this work has employed biographical materials as data on which to generalize about the characteristics of party militants, largely steering clear of the personal and emotional issues addressed in this article. Likewise, biographies of several of the most important leaders in the American party over the past decade have dealt with their subjects' personal lives. The object of these studies, however, has been to assess their subjects' impact on the political movements they helped to build.[3] Most historians in the United States and elsewhere continue to think about communism with what Vivian Gornick, writing forty years ago, called "an oppressive distance between themselves and their subjects," which "conveys only an emotional and intellectual atmosphere of 'otherness'—as though something not quite recognizable, something vaguely nonhuman was being described."[4] What might be called the subjective history of communism tells us a good deal about the costs and also the attractions of the movement. The ideological and organizational character of communist parties might remain paramount in the writing of their histories, but the history of the subjective lends a personal dimension to the phenomenon that a strictly political reading of communism cannot grasp.

This essay draws on about forty communist and former communist memoirs, in addition to interviews and other forms of personal narrative. What can these texts tell us about the personal identity and intimate relationships within the party, and about the gendered quality of the communist experience? In the process of answering this question, I hope to encourage the notion among social historians that our worker-subjects were individuals as well as members of a social class, and that they traveled through their historical experiences with emotional and personal baggage that bear a relationship to the sensibilities and feelings that govern a good part of our own lives. Taking the communist memoir as a subgenre of working-class autobiography, I first analyze the characteristics of the communist autobiography, the conditions under which such works were produced, and their intended functions. In the second portion of the paper I ask: Was there a personal dimension to the history of American communism, and if so, of what does this history consist and how does it relate to the more familiar political narrative of the movement?

Working-Class Autobiography and Communist Autobiography

An autobiography represents not the unmediated story of a person's actual experience, but rather a constructed narrative full of conscious and unconscious choices on the part of its author. The notion that autobiographies are based on available models and shaped by the conditions under which they were produced and the goals they were intended to achieve represents a well-established understanding of what we mean by the term.[5] Autobiography, Phillipe LeJeune concludes, "is necessarily in its deepest sense a special kind of fiction, its truth as much created as discovered realities." Indeed, Joan Scott has gone so far as to argue that the "experience" of our historical subjects is itself a notion constructed by historians to provide a universalized understanding of the past, that "experiences" are themselves socially and culturally constructed.[6]

Autobiography appears by definition to be the province of the "sovereign self," "the genre par excellence of the emergent bourgeoisie," as Mary Jo Maynes has noted. Often traced back to Rousseau and Goethe, "It was the literary expression of individualism, and the faith in an integrated and coherent personality so central to the bourgeois economic and political philosophy that was groping its way to prominence ... part of the broader historical creation of the bourgeois personality."[7] The rare worker-autobiographer was, in this sense, "atypical" by virtue of having become a more or less self-reflective writer. They were what Maynes calls "boundary crossers," living their lives in working-class communities and often expending their energies and talents in creating and shaping working-class social and political movements, but also observing their own lives and those of their class-mates from a reflective perspective that owed something to bourgeois autobiographical traditions.[8]

Yet we must analyze proletarian autobiographers differently than we might their bourgeois counterparts. Scholars of working-class autobiography have long stressed its tendency to diminish or dissolve the self, to ignore the personal dimension of experience in favor of the collective, to stress the "ordinary" quality of its subjects. The convention of the individual as "social atom," as Reginia Gagnier notes, serves to distinguish working-class autobiography from the more introspective bourgeois genre.[9] This tendency has been particularly marked in the case of labor and socialist activists, for whom the central narrative seems always to be focused first on one's "conversion" to the movement and then on the development of the party or movement itself, rather than on the individual.[10]

Within the broader field of working-class autobiography, communist personal narratives would seem particularly problematic. Any sort of biographical approach might even seem superfluous because the movement's "proverbial conformism, intrusiveness and monolithicity were backed up by the strictest codes of party discipline."[11] Add to this the strong political interests of most historians of communism, regardless of political affiliation, and common assumptions about the character of communist parties and their negative effects on individual agency and autonomy, and there is little if any room left for the person or the personal in the history of communism.[12]

In describing the assumptions of most historians of communism, Kevin Morgan, a biographer of British communists, argues, "The historiography of communism is predicated on a group identity so intense and pervasive as to leave little room for distinctive life histories." All experience and thought is assumed to be "subordinate to the totalitarian logic of party discipline."[13]

Thus, few historians of any political description have been inclined to think about the autobiographical dimension of communist history. Communist autobiographers have included many middle-class authors, but their commitment to a working-class political organization and the collective quality of that commitment have discouraged the discussion of subjective experience in most of their personal narratives as well. Communist writers have focused instead on the party; the personal story was only significant insofar as it shed light on the evolution of the organization, its successes and failures, or broader lessons for communists and other radicals. Anticommunist writers have been particularly disinclined to dwell on the personal because they have viewed the party largely as an extension of the Soviet state—a monolithic, totalitarian instrument of a foreign power in which personal experience tells us little if anything about the history.[14] New Left historians of American communism have shown greater interest in the personal dimension of the story, perhaps because of their own roots in a political tradition claiming that "the personal is political."[15] But even many of the New Left scholars of communist biography have tended to be more concerned with the political dimension than with their subjects' personal lives.[16]

Yet the study of individual communist lives offers us what Morgan sees as "a way to move beyond traditional party historiographies . . . to an altogether more complex, nuanced and unsettling account. . . . If relating such stories constitutes revisionism, it is simply in the sense of a populated history, fragmented enough to embrace the extraordinary diversity of experiences it encompassed over the three-quarters of a century."[17]

In part, then, we pursue communist autobiography to "populate" our histories with flesh-and-blood subjects, not the cardboard characters that filled the scenery in older political histories of the movement. Given the strength of Cold War caricatures reemerging in the American historiography, this in itself is a contribution. It is more difficult to ignore the basis for communist loyalties in the everyday experiences of working-class people and others—to objectify individual identity in the name of a vast faceless international conspiracy—when we confront the diversity in human experience contained in personal narratives. In the context of the American historiographical debates, an approach based on autobiographies makes it more difficult to sustain the image of American communists as a collection of Soviet automatons. In this sense too, the personal side of communist history is political. Indeed, a great deal in the history of American communism is lost in deciding that the personal experiences of these activists are not a significant part of that story.

Autobiographies of American Communism

In fact, communist activists could speak in a different, more personal voice, given the right setting. Personal diaries might be one example, intimate correspondence with family or close friends another. Published autobiographies, however, are quite public by their nature, and we can employ them only very carefully, considering their purposes, the conditions under which they were produced, and their broader social and political contexts.[18]

In the case of the United States, a substantial set of autobiographies constitutes a base for such an analysis. We have several distinct genres, in fact, of communist personal narratives. The first of these was fundamentally shaped by the party itself. As in the case of most national parties, the CPUSA published numerous party autobiographies. Even more than most workers' personal narratives, these tend to be narrowly didactic texts geared to the party's own interests, useful primarily for clues as to how the party viewed such individuals, as well as for the details of organizational life they might convey.[19] The party's own autobiographies represent particularly striking examples of the constructed nature of personal narratives. Indeed, the narrative decisions were not simply made by the individual authors, but were deeply influenced by the party. Given the constructed nature of autobiographies, scholars of the genre stress the significance of the models autobiographers might have taken, consciously or subconsciously, in shaping their own stories. Here Soviet autobiography likely played a vital role. As in so many other aspects of party life, American communists seemed to shape their own personal narratives with Soviet models in mind.[20] But the intervention of other voices in the narrative could also be far more direct. Written under party direction and editing, and sometimes even subject to committee assessment, such autobiographies fulfilled several vital functions.

First, they conveyed lessons for revolutionaries. Particular episodes were developed to demonstrate such lessons. The party's most popular autobiographies, by Elizabeth Gurley Flynn and William Z. Foster, for example, were less narratives than collections of brief sketches, each intended to make a particular point about the experience of being a revolutionary worker.[21]

Party autobiographies also provided models of revolutionary commitment and genius. The Nicaraguan revolutionary Manuel Calderon captured their importance as vivid symbols of the revolutionary party. A scientific theory such as Marxism-Leninism provided a useful guide, he noted, but "in real life, it is the concrete, personal example that motivates people."[22] None of this means that such model narratives were identical in content. Even in party autobiographies, women tended much more than men to include personal details about family and children, love and friendship relations, and even emotions. The contrast in the autobiographies of Foster and Flynn is striking in this regard. Both were Irish American radicals who came out of the IWW with strong attachments to the labor movement, and both joined the Communist Party in middle age. Flynn includes extensive details about her first unsuccessful marriage, a miscarriage, the death of her infant child, and her long-term love relationship with the Italian anarchist Carlo Tresca. (Interestingly, Flynn includes no details at all about her ten-year lesbian relationship with the radical physician and birth control advocate Marie Equi, suggesting, apparently, the limits of party tolerance for the personal.) Flynn's sister Kathy, her parents, her son Fred, and her lover Tresca glide in and out of the story. In contrast, Foster's first autobiographical volume includes no mention at all of his first marriage, little on his family background, and only brief mention of his wife, and in his second volume there is no mention of her at all.[23]

Why women militants' narratives tended more toward the personal is an interesting question. Scholars of autobiography tells us that writers construct their personal stories on the basis of models and values close at hand and are deeply influenced by the conditions under which they produce their texts. It seems likely, then, that women activists, however radical they might appear by the standards of their time, were nevertheless influenced by some of the same values that shaped other women's autobiographies—a greater value on personal relationships and greater attention to the family, for example.[24]

These autobiographies, organized around a strong central narrative of party-building and class conflict, provided more than lessons. In the process of telling an individual's life story, they told the party's own. These were, in a real sense, histories of the working-class movement writ small, on a human scale, so that they conveyed a narrative of heroic struggle and a steady march toward the party as the ultimate instrument of working-class liberation. Indeed, William Z. Foster observed that his autobiography was less a personal narrative than "[a] contribution to the history of left trade unionism in the United States during the past forty years," and an "outline of the development of the Communist Party."[25] But because of their human scale, such narratives also provided model lives for individual militants.

What scholars of autobiography have come to call "conversion narratives" play a critical part in many of these autobiographies. The early narrative is often filled with details of poverty and disorganization that underline the misery of working-class life under capitalism, providing the material basis for class consciousness and the search for a political way out. The narrative builds to a moment of conversion to socialism and then marches through a process of movement-building in which the author is important only insofar as her/his story helps to explain the development of the party and its fate. Writing of similar conversions in French and German socialist autobiographies, Mary Jo Maynes notes that "these moments signify the point when the plots of their life stories were revealed to their heroes or heroines. . . . Through the reconstruction of these transformative moments, authors reconstructed the process by which they came to imagine and pursue possibilities for themselves other than ones to which had seemingly been born."[26]

As Nell Painter wrote of her experience working with the black communist Hosea Hudson on his personal narrative, "Hudson spoke as if his life were divided into forty six years in the Communist Party and thirty-five years groping toward it."[27] William Z. Foster's account is more or less typical of male autobiographers. He was walking the streets of his native Philadelphia slum in the summer of 1900 when he encountered a street-corner socialist speaker: "His arguments and analysis seemed to give real meaning to all my experience in the class struggle. . . . I began to count myself, from that time on, a Socialist. That street meeting marked a turning point in my life." Though the Communist Party was not born until nearly two decades later, and Foster did not join until 1921, the remainder of his story is organized around his ideological journey from socialism through syndicalism to Marxism-Leninism.²⁸

Though they might experience their own dramatic conversions, women militants were more often what American communists came to call "red-diaper babies," encountering the movement within their own families.²⁹ Peggy Dennis, Dorothy Healey, and Elizabeth Gurley Flynn were all born into socialist families and raised within the movement. An alternative route came through the rebellion of upper-class children, as in the case of Jessica Mitford, who first joined the Communist Party of Great Britain and ran off to Spain in the late 1930s, even as her parents and sisters cultivated their relations with high-ranking Nazis and developed alliances with homegrown British fascists. Mitford later became a local party activist and organizer for the Civil Rights Congress in the San Francisco Bay area and eventually, after leaving the party, a best-selling author.³⁰

A second genre of anticommunist narratives, what might be called "confessional antimemoirs," were particularly significant in the context of the Cold War, when the government sought to discredit domestic radicalism and much of the public was eager for lurid accounts of communist treachery and subversion.³¹ These texts have a central plot every bit as pronounced as the party autobiographies—the subversion of American democracy and its displacement by a mindless commitment to Soviet totalitarianism. Several involve a conversion or reconversion to Christianity. Such texts can be useful for conveying the seamier dimensions of communist experience that one is unlikely to find in authorized party biographies, but their intended political functions and the antagonistic frame of mind with which the authors took up their pens underscore the limits within which any autobiography, and certainly these, can be read as objective accounts of "experience." Virtually all of these memoirs focus particularly on their authors' and other communists' roles in Soviet espionage activities, an experience of particular concern in much of the older and more recent anticommunist historical writing, but one that was quite foreign to the lives of most rank-and-file American communists.³²

Finally, an interesting group of "oral biographies" produced between the late 1970s and the early 1990s were often the products of collaboration between communist veterans and younger scholars, dialogues of sorts between the Old and New Lefts. Several of these autobiographies constitute among our best cases of the integration of politics with personal experience. Most of these veterans had left the party or been expelled, either during the 1956–1957 crisis at the time of Khrushchev's revelations and the invasion of Hungary or during the next major party crisis with the Soviet invasion of Czechoslovakia in 1968.[33] Although some of these veterans undertook their writing independently, much of this work took the form of an oral history shaped by the political backgrounds of both the New Left historians and their respondents. The human dimension of American communism looms larger in many of these projects, and some of them involve what Camilla Stivers has called a "subject-to-subject" approach in which the interviewer/author is aware of his/her own perspective and interests in producing the book.[34]

One of the most important documentary films dealing with the party's history, based on extensive interviews, was produced with the explicit aim of putting a human face on the American communist movement.[35] Many of the New Left historians were shaped by a movement that held that the personal was indeed political, and they consciously investigated their subjects' personal lives in the course of researching, interviewing, writing, and editing the narratives. Raised during the Cold War and committed to fundamental social change, such historians sought in part to humanize a movement they had been taught to hate. Even in these cases, however, the narrative is often driven by the veterans' tendencies to discount personal experience and identity as secondary to the main plot of political organization and conflict, and by New Left scholars' own political agendas, which often involved the search for a "usable" historical past. The pursuit of the relationship between the personal and the political was particularly strong among feminist historians, whose approach was formed in the context of the new women's movement of the late 1960s and early 1970s.[36]

Given the strong bias for politics, what can these autobiographies tell us about the personal side of communist history? Acknowledging the bewildering array of human experience that confronts us in opening the subjective side of communist history, I have identified several realms that seem to exemplify the character of communist militants' personal lives: marriage and sexuality, child-rearing and family life, and personal identity and crisis.

Love and Marriage

Though perhaps in somewhat different ways and with different feelings, many male and female radicals opposed marriage on political grounds. The discourse in the early Communist Party (1919–1929), especially among those men who came up through the Industrial Workers of the World (IWW), was one of virile, romantic revolutionary roughnecks, living in a rough-and-tumble and dangerous capitalist world with little room for women.[37] For

Harvey O'Connor, who was not a member but remained close to the Communist Party for much of his adult life, marriage was "a bourgeois trap to hang a family on you, to enslave you to a steady job for the rest of your life, and to hell with it." As in patriarchal discourse more generally, women were seen as a burden on male revolutionaries. Recalling his attitude during his early years as a Wobbly, O'Connor recalled, "Women restricted your movement without adding a great deal to your life."[38]

Living together, however, was common, the writer Myra Page (Dorothy Markey) recalled, as were Russian liaisons for American communists. Indeed, the confessional antimemoirs of autobiographers who left the party, the popular press, and postwar Hollywood anticommunist films all stressed communists' rampant sexuality as part of their threat to the American way of life. But, contrary to sensational representations concerning casual sex, particularly in the 1920s, many party members disapproved. Earl Browder was living unmarried with one woman, Kitty, in the United States, but fell in love with Raissa in the USSR and lived with her there. Browder's rather turbulent love life was "shocking" to Page. Raissa had first fallen in love with party leader William Z. Foster and asked him to father the children she wanted, but Foster, a strict revolutionary ascetic, refused. "Foster had principles, especially about personal matters, and he refused because he had a wife," Page recalled. Browder, Raissa's second choice, accepted the offer. Page overstated her case, however, as Foster had at least one and possibly two lovers during his long marriage to Esther Abramovitz Foster. Again, communist attitudes and behavior were often vestiges of earlier movements. Both Foster and, especially, Esther had extended experiences with open relationships in the anarchist and syndicalist movements before ever joining the party, yet they established a lifelong and, by most accounts, loving marriage.[39]

Theoretically, many communists believed in open relationships, what American anarchists had called "varietism."[40] In real life this seldom turned out well. Working on a radical paper in Mexico with his wife Eleanor and another American radical, Charles Shipman soon came face to face with the contradictions between theory and practice. Early in their work, his wife Eleanor began an affair with the other comrade while the three of them were working together in a small office. "Theoretically libertarian in such matters, I was supposed to not care. But I did. Fiercely. When I insisted that it had to be him or me, she went to live with Clint. I thought I would never get over the loss of Eleanor."[41] While Dorothy Healey's second husband had been involved with other women "almost from the beginning" of their marriage, and always reported these affairs to her, she told herself and others it did not bother her. Clearly it did. When her third husband admitted that he was having an affair with another comrade's wife while Dorothy and the rest of the California leadership were on trial in the mid-1950s, Healey left him immediately.[42]

A lover hoping for romance, however, might be easily disappointed by a mate who was, above all, a professional revolutionary. Vera Buch Weisbord met and fell in love with her future husband Albert in the heat of the 1925 Passaic textile strike, but it was hardly candlelight and soft music. "[D]uring a brief, quiet interval in the office, Albert drew me over to the window and as we stood close said in a businesslike way, 'Smith, I want to live with you on a permanent basis, I believe you have the qualities I want in a partner. You have courage, intelligence, and the desire to be a Bolshevik.'" Vera, herself a dedicated organizer, embraced these terms. "The word LOVE, so essential to me, had never once been uttered by him," she later wrote. "Now, however, he had put into words what must have been to him the highest praise. I realized that I had just received a proposal. Now I could really love my man without reservation; now I experienced not merely the joy and elation of being in love, but with it a deeply felt satisfaction never known before."[43]

Liaisons could be even more instrumental. Charles Shipman, working for the Comintern in Moscow, took up with a young Russian woman, Natalia Alexandrovna Mikhailova, though she seemed to be using him as much as he was her. "Natalie" was one of a "bevy of highborn young Russian women" working as auxiliary personnel at the Second Comintern Congress. "[She] spoke perfect English and had good handwriting. Moreover, she was a thing of beauty with stormy eyes set deep in her ivory face.... She was surprisingly ignorant... liked being around foreigners.... As might have been predicted, we began to sleep together. Jokingly, I asked her if she would like to go to Mexico with me. She said yes so fast that I gasped." In order to be able to travel, he married her, making him a bigamist, as he still had a wife in the United States. "Though I never had any deep feeling for Natalie, nor she for me, we enjoyed each other, she wanted to get out of Russia, and I trusted her." She was a "staunch, undemanding companion" for several years.[44]

The obvious chauvinism suggested by such an account is important to gauging the character of some personal relationships within the party.[45] Such relationships often occurred between relatively younger, less experienced women and older male organizers, often their superiors. The adventurous quality of such affairs is undoubtedly important to understanding the women's motivation, but there is little doubt that difference in ages, experience, and status introduced an element of unequal power into the relationships.[46]

Shipman's story also conveys the cosmopolitan character of party activists who roamed the country and the globe, working in a wide range of environments with activists from diverse backgrounds in a worldwide political movement aimed at massive social, economic, and political transformation. The fact that most such activists came from working-class backgrounds suggests a particularly striking case of cosmopolitan experience that remains largely unexplored. To the extent that long-term sexual relationships were more open than typical marriages of the same era, this might have owed as much to this mobile lifestyle as to any particular ideological position regarding marriage or monogamy.

The instrumental approach to personal relationships suggested by Shipman's affair with Natalia could and did occasionally extend to the use of sex in the interests of party goals. "My 'liberation' from conventional standards of female behavior did not consist so much of getting what I wanted in my private life," Dorothy Healey recalled, "as in not attaching a great deal of importance to what I was missing." As a young woman, after the end of her first marriage, Healey became involved with a succession of men and lived with a communist seaman for about two years, "because I felt it was my Party duty to do it . . . he was lonely and he was one of our best members and if that's what he wanted, and it's what he did want, then it was my Party duty. . . . Later, I started thinking of this as my 'Salvation Army' approach to love and marriage. You're bestowing yourself because that's what somebody wants. . . . It shouldn't matter one way or the other."[47]

Communists clearly had models of love and marriage, often drawn from the history of the Russian Revolution, before them. As Russian personal and domestic lives were remade in the wake of the revolution, bourgeois observers often tended to exaggerate the more lurid aspects of these changes—notably, the notion that Soviet women's sexuality had been "collectivized." But change was real, nonetheless, in the areas of marriage, divorce, abortion, and other personal matters.[48] The new Soviet rulers were taken as models in their personal as well as their political lives. "You'll be my Krupskaya," Albert Weisbord promised in his proposal to his wife Vera. "You will go with me from one strike to another. . . . When we have the textile industry organized, we'll move on to steel, and so on, building the Party. You can never have children, not even a home. But you'll always be by my side, fighting with me, helping me."[49] When young communist labor organizers Joe and Sheba Rapoport decided to move in together before marriage, they were influenced by the Soviet example as well as by hormones. "The new freedoms and new forms in the Soviet Union strengthened the idealism of radical young people here," Joe later recalled. "I didn't see the need for anybody, the government included, to give us permission to come together."[50]

A stable marriage, whether formal or common law, was more typical among U.S. communists than an open one, it seems, especially after the 1930s. Earl Browder himself settled into a lifelong marriage and fatherhood of three children with Raissa. A love affair that started casually in the heat of political struggles could persist for a lifetime. The strength of such a union, as well as the domestic tensions it might produce, is suggested by the relationship between James Cannon and Rose Karsner, who began an affair while he was still married and both were raising children. Subject to the pressures of a revolutionary's life and trying to care for their children at a distance, Karsner and Cannon personify the problems of maintaining a family life in the party (and later in the Trotskyist movement). Yet they remained devoted to one another for life.[51] Myra Page's life might have been more typical than Browder's. She remained married to her "first love," John Markey, for sixty-six years, until his death. "We talked about it, but it never occurred to us to do anything but stay within traditional bounds ... throughout the sixty-six years of our marriage, John and I have been a team.... The partnership has been crucial. I don't believe I would ever have done it alone.... He's always been there—a strong person all the way through."[52]

While they owed a great deal to political affinities, such pairings often crossed other boundaries, some of which seemed insurmountable in mainstream society. Interracial marriage, still extremely rare in the United States and actually outlawed in some states as late as the 1960s, suggests how the subculture of American communism diverged from the mainstream at this most intimate level as well as in more explicitly political ways. Indeed, as in other cases, the decision to marry across racial lines was a political choice made in the context of white supremacist ideology and practice. With no hard data, autobiographical information provides our only guide, but it appears that interracial marriage was certainly much more common within the CP than in the broader society. Important African American leaders such as William Patterson, Claudia Jones, Lovett Fort Whiteman, Abner Berry, and Harry Haywood all had white partners, while the Japanese American activist Karl Yoneda married Elaine Black, a white communist organizer. Communist Party members figured prominently in the 188 interracial marriages sociologists studied in Chicago during the Depression. The pressure that such couples undoubtedly felt was mitigated, it seems, within the communist subculture, where such marriages were not only tolerated but nurtured, though even many party members remained sensitive about the issue. The black writer and poet Claude McKay recalled that as early as 1938 a group of black women communists in Harlem met to discuss the fact that most of the party's black male leaders had married white women (a practice that appears to have been more common than black women marrying white men). According to McKay, they drew up a resolution to Stalin and the Executive of the Communist International protesting the practice.[53]

Intermarriage between gentiles and Jews, a relatively common occurrence today, remained a taboo on both sides of the religious divide through the mid-twentieth century, yet such marriages were fairly common among American communists in the 1930s. While religious practice might have been rare among the radicals, important cultural differences were bridged in such marriages. Catholics from Eastern European backgrounds, for example, where anti-Semitism was fairly common, might learn some Yiddish, come to appreciate Jewish cooking, and, perhaps most importantly, agree to their children being raised as Jews. A young Jewish wife learned a bit of Polish and took great pleasure in Polish music and dance. In deference to a new son-in-law, a Jewish family excised a portion of the Passover ritual that called down plagues upon the heads of the gentiles. A young Jewish communist wife sang the old songs her Scottish Catholic husband had taught her and pined for him while he was fighting with the Loyalists in Spain. They had met in a Chicago branch of the Young Communist League.[54]

Political commitment was vital in breaching what might seem an insurmountable social barrier. The party not only provided rare common ground for two individuals who would otherwise not meet, but through its ideology it provided a strong sanction for such unions. A young Jewish communist woman continued to have misgivings about her decision to marry across religious lines. Although she was certainly not religious, she did identify as a Jew and regretted any estrangement the marriage caused with her family. When she traveled to the Soviet Union, however, and saw that such marriages were common and officially sanctioned in the society that she considered an ideal model, the lingering concerns she harbored dissipated.[55]

A Hungarian immigrant explained the process: "We were Roman Catholics and we got the whole religious works. . . . I was raised an anti-Semite," but Depression conditions pressed him to seek political answers to the problems he saw about him. And when he looked, he found the Communist Party, and with it, good Jews. "I was in closer contact. . . . It was a gradual change. I came to the conclusion, and especially through reading some of the Marxist literature, that anti-Semitism . . . was one of the tricks put over on us. . . . Now I don't consider whether people are Jews or not—I am not interested in that."

He married a Jewish woman in a civil ceremony, and their child was raised outside the religious traditions of both families.[56]

There were limits. A gentile husband felt the application of a *mezuzeh* to the couple's door was "superstitious stuff." A young radical Jewish woman was proud of her decision to step beyond established boundaries, disregard class prejudices, and marry a laborer of Polish Catholic descent. But when her husband refused to associate with her Jewish friends and continued to fraternize with anti-Semitic Poles, the marriage disintegrated. A University of Chicago researcher enumerated the controls on women particularly in such marriages: the family's resistance, gossip in the broader community, and the woman's own conscience and identity.[57]

Correspondence during the McCarthy era between imprisoned communists and their families offers a rare glimpse of the personal relations between party spouses in the postwar era. Many letters concern mundane details of daily life in and out of prison, and the Smith Act prisoners clearly sought to maintain their roles as spouses and parents through such communication. Because the letters were censored coming into and going out of the prisons, it is perhaps not surprising that they contain little of a political nature, and they do occasionally convey details about defense work and other party matters. But they also suggest the strain that long jail sentences must have placed on the families of political prisoners, and they convey above all the love between the correspondents. "I have been living from hour to hour every day," Aurelia Johnson wrote to her husband Arnold soon after he entered prison, "expecting you to come walking in.... It's good to read your letters sometimes as often as seven or eight times and I go back for a refresher every now and then.... Until tomorrow then—I shall close with love and thoughts of you always with me." "This morning I picked up your letter and my joy knew no bounds when I found the visit was being permitted," she wrote in March 1956, closing with "I love you and miss you so. I think of you and add the days. Lovingly always, Aurelia."[58] Arnold carefully counted each card and letter from his wife (118 letters and 187 cards in 1955 alone, 333 messages of all sorts in 1956). He read them over and over again. He himself wrote the maximum number of letters allowable under prison regulations, always conveying his deep love for his wife and reminiscing often about past vacations and celebrations, often trying to place her in his mind's eye.[59] Gil Green's children reported in detail on their school work, love lives, and neighborhood activities, and he often advised them on these and other matters.[60] In many respects, he was simply trying to maintain his role as husband and father, though at a great distance.

Some aspects of private life were best kept separate from the political. While the CPUSA leadership was wary of recruiting gay members, and gay communists often felt obliged to carefully separate their political and sexual lives, homosexual experiences were not uncommon, and some evidence suggests that local party groups were more tolerant in this regard. Attitudes on the left hardened, however, between the 1920s and the postwar era, according to Kathleen Brown and Elizabeth Faue. The early twentieth-century left and 1920s-era party were more open and tolerant of gay subcultures, while a less tolerant party culture was more common by the Popular Front era. The CPUSA leadership was particularly sensitive about homosexuality during the McCarthy-era repression of the early 1950s, when considerable numbers of gay and lesbian members were purged, ostensibly on security grounds. Even then, however, some local party leaders refused to expel trusted activists on the basis of sexual preference. Some activists in the emerging gay rights movements of the 1960s, such as Mattachine Society founder Harry Hay, relied on their communist organizing experience in establishing the basis for an early gay rights movement.[61]

Children and Abortion

In the context of a revolutionary party, particularly in periods of repression or revolutionary crisis, the decision to have children was even more complex than it would normally be, and, again, the stakes were rather different for male and female activists. In the 1920s and early Depression years, many party leaders actively discouraged the idea of raising children in the midst of trying to make a revolution. While such thinking was undoubtedly nurtured in the shadow of Soviet mythology, it was not born with the Communist Party. William Z. Foster clearly carried over from syndicalist days the principle that children inhibited militants and "provided a new supply of slaves" for capitalists. Harvey O'Connor, another Wobbly veteran, also refused to have children. He married a young socialist woman reluctantly and for largely practical reasons, but he "emphasized that I wanted no children and would not be tied down for the rest of my life. Love being what it is, Blanche agreed even to the point, eventually, of having a hysterectomy." When O'Connor succumbed to the idea of children in his second marriage, to Jessie Lloyd, it was less an enthusiastic conversion than a negotiated concession: "Well, that is the way women are and you have to humor them."[62] But such feelings were widespread, especially during the 1920s and early 1930s. "Among the Left, women as active as I was were not expected to have children," Myra Page recalled. "[W]omen were scarce, and those willing to work as leaders needed to put in their time... you made a choice." Again, the Soviet experience was invoked as a model, though more than one lesson could be drawn. Seeing activist mothers in the USSR emboldened Myra Page to have children of her own.[63]

Elizabeth Gurley Flynn's mother and sister cared for her only son, Fred, during her extended speaking and organizing tours, first for the IWW and later for the Communist Party. One of the few regrets she recalled in her copious autobiographical writings concerned her long absences from her son. "I recall a Christmas Eve, 1919, walking through Union Square, white with snow, with... the attorney who represented many of the Russian deportees, and realizing suddenly that I should be home, filling my child's stocking instead of attending a meeting."[64]

The extent to which the international communist movement might intrude on family life and the rearing of children—and the lengths to which party parents might go in following party directions—is suggested by the experience of Eugene and Peggy Dennis in the early 1930s. While he was sent on Comintern work in South Africa, the Philippines, and China, she was sent to various points in Europe, and their four-year-old son, Tim, was placed in the Comintern Children's Home for almost two years. Here he lived with the children of revolutionaries sent on Comintern missions around the world. By the time they returned, Tim spoke only Russian, and Comintern leaders feared that he would represent a security risk—for the international movement and the CPUSA—on the trip back and during his early months in the United States. They ordered the parents to return home without their son, who would be sent back at some other time, "under different circumstances." Peggy Dennis recalls the anguish she felt in this situation, but the parents made the decision to leave their firstborn son in the USSR, where Tim would be "safe, protected, given the best socialism had to offer." Tim remained in the Soviet Union for the rest of his life and saw his parents only a couple of times over the next two decades.[65] As difficult as this decision may be to understand, it does help to explain the resolve of some communists to avoid the responsibility of raising children—even when that meant abortion.

Diaphragms and other forms of birth control were likely even more common in the communist movement than in other areas of American life by the 1920s, but so were accidents and, as a result, abortions.[66] Dorothy Healey sustained a series of three abortions and at least one miscarriage during her early years in the party. "It was just taken for granted that we would have abortions. Who could think of a revolutionary having a child?"[67] When Vera Buch became pregnant in the midst of her organizing of the 1929 Gastonia strike, her lover and future husband, Albert Weisbord, insisted that she get an abortion because "the inconvenience would be great if we wanted to be active revolutionaries." He refused to accompany her, however, insisting that paying for the procedure was his only responsibility. Following a botched abortion by an amateur, Buch suffered as much emotionally as physically: "Something very strong and primitive in me had been violated.... Behind it all was resentment at what seemed to be Albert's callousness. Why had he refused to go there with me? Is it possible to love and feel no concern for the loved one?"[68]

Ironically, given this attitude toward children, party cadres often employed a family metaphor to explain the strength of personal bonds within the movement. "In some ways the Party was like a family," Myra Page recalled. "We formed very close relationships, but then we fought like families when we thought something was important enough.... We lost friends when we left. It was sad and painful."[69]

Party attitudes toward children seem to have loosened up during and immediately after the World War II era, in the midst of the baby boom. It might also make a difference, it seems, whether one was dealing with male or female leaders. In 1943, when Dorothy Healey decided she wanted a child, she asked her California state party secretary, and Oletta O'Connor Yates, county organizer in San Francisco, what they thought. Both agreed readily, though Healey admitted that if they had not done so, "I would have heeded party discipline and forgone the pregnancy."[70]

Peggy Dennis observed a close relationship between the domestic burdens of women activists and their small representation among the leadership cadres. Many who reached such heights had neither children nor a permanent personal relationship. "To comply with the methods governing party work, a woman had to be willing to relegate the children to an around-the-clock surrogate parent."[71] Dorothy Healey was determined that her son would not become such a "party orphan." Her mother assumed day-care duties when Healey had to be out of town. She insisted on leaving the party office at 3:30 every day to pick Richard up from child care, often held meetings at her home to avoid leaving him in the evening, and left meetings to answer his call and talk to him as he fell asleep.[72] But many activists became part-time parents because they remained full-time revolutionaries. Harvey and Jessie O'Connor left their children with caregivers daily and for extended periods of time.[73]

Some of the slack might be taken up by the various youth activities sponsored by communist parties throughout the world—sports programs and summer camps, the Young Pioneers, and relationships with other children in the party. As Deborah Gerson recalls in an autobiographical article, "In summer camp we lived out the Left's values... camp became the locus of our emotional relationships." The camp was a "respite" from the burden of living as part of a small political minority in an overwhelmingly hostile environment.[74] The demanding character of party membership and a very conscious effort to instruct members on "how to bring up communist children" undoubtedly shaped child-rearing. A striking array of children's publications, summer camps, and youth groups sustained a communist culture among the party's youth.[75]

Given all this, children's experiences varied enormously from one family to another, judging from the personal narratives of red-diaper babies. Some remembered their communist childhoods fondly; others recalled being neglected in the interests of political activity. Stephanie Allan's communist parents were careful to bring the family together for dinner every evening before the regular round of meetings, to save weekend time for the family from their busy political lives, and to bring children whenever they could to demonstrations and rallies so that the family would be together. She recalls hers as a "warm, loving family life."[76] But other red-diaper babies remember great distance from their parents.

Maxine DeFelice was verbally attacked almost daily and was later raped by a gang of boys, but her parents seemed always to be in meetings, and she felt unable to confide in them. "No one knew, no one noticed," she recalled. "Important things were happening." Living in North Carolina, where her parents were CIO union organizers, she found solace as the only white member of a black church.[77] Other children felt abandoned when their parents were imprisoned or sent underground during the McCarthy era. The most striking of the "red-diaper" autobiographies may well be Bettina Aptheker's.[78] While most commentators have focused on the author's charges of sexual abuse at the hands of her father, however, the story's main theme seems to be the daughter's efforts to frame her own identity and politics in the shadow of her father, Herbert Aptheker, a pioneer scholar of African American history and one of the party's main intellectual figures.

Living within the party could put enormous pressure on children, particularly in periods of political repression. On the night the Rosenbergs were executed, ten-year-old Gene Dennis awoke screaming with a fear shared by other children in communist families: "I don't want to die! They will kill him too. Bring my Daddy home; they will kill him too." His mother too had nightmares she shared with no one. "At night," she wrote at the time, "we each weep and surrender to the fears that grip our lives."[79] Particularly today, when revisionists are rehabilitating the image of McCarthyism, such accounts help us to grasp the damage wrought at the neglected personal level in this era of severe political repression.[80]

Political Crisis as Personal Crisis

The notion that communists were selfless conveys something of the quality of the political commitment and its implications for one's personal life, but it also reinforces the perception of communists as the other, people strangely different from us. The striking silence on personal issues in most Communist Party autobiographies was not only the product of design or conscious choice. It was also shaped by a very different understanding of the personal. In fact, many communists explained their commitments in terms of a particular kind of self-realization which was intense and fulfilling, but which also tended to subsume the personal in the political. This latter characteristic hobbled individual members and the party as an organization in trying to deal with serious personal problems. The pressure of daily communist political activity, let alone the sort of extreme stress to which communist men, women, and children were subject during the McCarthy era, produced numerous such personal crises, which remain largely unexplored.

Diane, an accomplished Broadway actress who left the party after fifteen years of strong commitment, recalled the personal fulfillment she experienced during her time as a communist: "They were good years, very good years. Richly alive with the sense of everything coming together, a fusion of world and being that made you drunk with life ... my life has been a long journey into myself. My years as a communist taught me things about human identity I would never have realized otherwise." Yet she regretted "the tragedy of identifying your entire self with anything outside of yourself."[81] When she faced an emotional crisis in the postwar period, her comrades were ill prepared to lend support, or even to understand what was happening.

> [S]omething began to happen inside of me ... imperceptibly, without my knowing it consciously, things began to come apart for me in the Party.... I struggled desperately to let them know what was happening to me.... They didn't know what I was talking about ... this was all personal and, therefore, trivial.... I should be more serious ... it was wrong to be so concerned with something as frivolous as my feelings.... I saw more and more that these people, my comrades, did not know themselves what they actually thought and felt.... Their iden-

tification with the Party had become so complete, so absolute, they no longer knew the difference between their own finite selves and what I could now only call Party dogma. I felt terribly lost. Who was I? What was I? Why was I here? What did it all mean? . . . The very fact that in the Party everything personal was suppressed and despised began to make it impossible for me to ignore the personal . . . if they had been clever enough to give me even a bit of understanding, I might have remained a communist for God knows how long.[82]

This emotional poverty appears most often in autobiographies in the context of political and personal crisis, for the two often went together. For Peggy Dennis, who spent more than forty years in the party, the moment came during the Smith Act trials when the entire party leadership, including her husband Eugene Dennis, was indicted and eventually imprisoned. Of the eleven defendants, one, Elizabeth Gurley Flynn, was an unmarried woman whose adult son had died earlier. Most of the rest left wives and families behind as they entered either prison or underground lives on the run. The party itself was completely preoccupied with defense work and in preparing the organization for what the leading faction saw as the imminent rise of fascism in the United States. "With husbands gone and the Party organization we had always relied on absent," Dennis recalled, "living with insurmountable family problems and fears and apprehensions, we were thrown upon our own resources and upon each other."[83]

These communist wives and mothers created the Families Committee of Smith Act Victims to support the prisoners and their children and to educate the public on the threat to civil liberties represented by the sweeping legislation under which the party was suppressed. In an era of hyperdomesticity and extreme nationalism, red-diaper baby Deborah Gerson notes, they adopted the language of family values to make their case. Women activists were doubtless influenced by a new postwar cult of domesticity, but it was also a political strategy. More than the constitutional issues involved in their cases, the committee's propaganda featured photos of the defendants with their families and emphasized their domestic roles as parents and spouses.[84]

Writing on behalf of the Smith Act defendants in the spring of 1956, the great African American intellectual W. E. B. Du Bois conceded that some Americans "believe that these victims have endangered this nation by what they have thought and said." "But I think that all of us can agree on one thing," he concluded, "and that is that the families and children of these persons should not be made to suffer."[85]

Many of these women were skilled and hardened political organizers. Their movement achieved some of its limited aims and provided extensive material and political support for the families, but few of them credited the committee with providing the day-to-day emotional support required to get through the crisis. Peggy Dennis recalls:

> As to the personal problems each of us had, none of us was equipped by our Party experience to respond to each other on a simple human level ... we had no experience in the Party to respond to each other as individuals, only in impersonal political concepts.... Like the other wives, officially and outwardly I was too calm, too impersonal, too political. Within myself, I cried silently.[86]

"In the CP there was no space for feelings as such," writes Deborah Gerson, who lived through the ordeal as a child. The party "placed no special value on the expression of one's own feelings; focusing on personal upsets bore the stigma of 'subjectivity' and was disdained."[87]

Whatever practical support the party provided its members, some of them felt this emotional deficit keenly. Diane, the actress quoted above, experienced her personal crisis in the context of McCarthy-era political repression, divorce, unemployment, and a call to testify before the House Un-American Activities Committee (HUAC). "My husband, the Party, my work—everything went up in smoke in one hideous moment."[88] She called the talented professional revolutionaries with whom she worked "politically astute, emotionally ignorant."[89] Another Communist Party veteran, a well-known editor, also noted what he called the "emotional distance" that "grew up between me and the world beyond the Party."[90]

While the McCarthy era was a particularly striking period of stress produced by political isolation and repression, one might well identify other situations in which such considerations are relevant to communist history—the extreme factionalism of the late 1920s and 1940s, when hundreds of people were driven out of the movement; the bitter class warfare of the early Depression "Third Period"; the declaration of the Hitler–Stalin Pact, which derailed the party's vibrant antifascist movement at a stroke; Khrushchev's excruciating 1956 litany of Stalin's crimes, which shattered the lifelong political commitments of thousands of individuals. In this sense, the personal side of the communist experience has a history every bit as much as its more public dimensions.

Life within the movement was often intense, and personal relationships might be quite intimate, but emotions were experienced and relationships developed through the political life of the party. A university physicist who had started a new life after twenty years in the movement came to realize that his "deepest emotions are engaged only in a political context.... Our political life is so deeply intertwined with our personal life.... It is our personal life. I mean, I'm not sure what else there is... apart from politics."[91] "For sixteen years," another veteran recalled, "I was suffused with the dogma of Communism.... My studies, my marriage, my friendships were all strained through the liquid flow of Marxist thought before they entered my brain and my feelings." Vivian Gornick emphasizes the passion of American communists, what she calls "this hook upon the soul," that invested the lives of militants with far more drama than those of most working people.[92]

What was most striking to Gornick in more than forty interviews with veteran communists, however, was the high development of what she termed "the gift for political emotion," while "the gift for individual sympathy" was "neglected, atrophied ... the experience of all things human lives primarily through the political act." Thus, as Gornick notes, a deep irony resides at the heart of communist history, for the same passion that plunged individual communists into this intense emotional experience also produced what she calls "a dogmatic purging of the self."[93] When an interviewer pursued details about William Z. Foster's private life, his subject resisted. "The movement," Foster concluded, "is the decisive matter."[94]

Conclusion

The conventions and exigencies of life in the movement discouraged American communists from expressing their personal feelings and shaped the character of their personal relationships. The more revealing autobiographies and interviews suggest a connection between this particularly (some might say peculiarly) strong political commitment and the subjective dimensions of one's life. Yet the distance most historians have placed between themselves and these historical subjects has warped our view of this history.

Communist autobiography, even more than most working-class autobiography, reflected a view of the world and a particular kind of political commitment that militated against the kind of introspection and subjectivity we might expect to find in this most intimate form of writing. Given the sort of organization to which they belonged and the very different political contexts within which they operated, this is not surprising. But this does not mean that party members lacked personal lives, or that these lives are superfluous to our understanding their movement. Even the self-realization that is the stuff of autobiography is present in some of these texts, particularly in the narratives of women activists, though perhaps in a form that appears strange to us.

While male autobiographers might concentrate entirely on the political, writing as if they had no personal lives, women's memoirs are far more apt to include personal details. Subject to the chauvinism that penetrated their movement, as it did other realms of American society, communist women faced a double standard in their personal as well as their political lives. Nor, despite their political activism, did they escape the gender norms of their times. As a result, their narratives provide rare glimpses and often insightful reflections on family life, personal relationships, and self-realization through political activism.

The lesson here is not that the personal was more important than or even equal to the political, but that the former can help us to understand the latter. Communist autobiographies suggest, for example, that self-realization came through collective experience and party activity, an extreme version perhaps of the collective quality scholars have found in working-class narratives more generally. We find not only a politically charged context, but also a fusion of the personal and the political in these life stories that is distant from our own conservative political climate and our radically depoliticized lives. But perhaps this distance from our own experience represents another characteristic that makes the study of such lives important—for political as well as historical reasons.

Serious consideration of the personal dimensions of communist activism provides a very different perspective on two important recent trends in the history of the United States. The first is an increasing tendency in revisionist literature to see the CPUSA simply as an arm of the Soviet Union and to diminish its role as a social movement, particularly at the local level in cities and towns throughout the United States. Some American communists clearly did operate as espionage agents, and the American party's subservient relationship to the Soviet party distorted its programs and political judgment. The second tendency in the historiography follows from this characterization. By focusing particularly on Soviet espionage work in the United States, some historians have justified the enormous damage done in the McCarthy era. Since it is clear now that some individual American communists were involved in such work, the tendency is to excuse the political repression of those years as a necessity for guarding national security.

An autobiographical approach not only underscores the emotional strain brought to bear on individual radicals and their families during such periods of repression. It also begins to suggest the fit, or lack of one, between personality, personal relationships, and emotions on the one hand and particular types of political organizations and policy on the other. Specifically, the patriarchal character of Stalinist parties like the CPUSA left little role for personal expression and identity—even less for women members than it did for men.

At its broadest level, the autobiographical approach to American communism suggests a level of experience that has remained largely submerged in labor history—for the United States and for other societies. It encourages us to consider radicals and other working people, not simply as members of a particular social class or participants in social movements, but also as individuals with personalities and private lives, each with his or her own strengths and frailties, which may have shaped their motivations and behavior beyond the political and social forces we find to be more familiar in our work. In this sense, autobiography affords a different angle not just on the history of the international communist movement but also on the historical experience of working-class people more generally.

CHAPTER THREE

Revolution and Personal Crisis

William Z. Foster, Personal Narrative, and the Subjective in the History of American Communism

In early 1919, the progressive novelist Mary Heaton Vorse found William Z. Foster sitting in the tiny Pittsburgh office where he directed the Great Steel Strike, the largest industrial conflict in the history of the United States up to that time. Foster remained calm and collected, selfless in the midst of this great social movement:

> He is composed, confident, unemphatic and impenetrably unruffled. Never for a moment does Foster hasten his tempo.... He seems completely without ego.... He lives completely outside the circle of self, absorbed ceaselessly in the ceaseless stream of detail which confronts him.... Once in a while he gets angry over the stupidity of man; then you see his quiet is the quiet of a high tension machine moving so swiftly it barely hums. He is swallowed up in the strike's immensity. What happens to Foster does not concern him. I do not believe that he spends five minutes in the whole year thinking of Foster or Foster's affairs.[1]

This was the image Foster projected throughout his early life and the reputation by which he was known: a brilliant strategist and organizational mind, an engineer and architect of working-class movements, a dedicated militant with no apparent personal life. Certainly for any historian looking for the links between the personal and the political, Foster does not appear to be a very promising subject.

But fourteen years later, in an October 1933 letter to his old friend and mentor Solomon Lozovsky, the Comintern's director of trade union work, Foster showed a very different side of his personality. Recovering at a Soviet sanatorium from a serious and complex illness with both physical and psychological dimensions, he was clearly depressed, subject to nervousness and anxiety attacks, bewildered by his current situation, and profoundly concerned about his future. "I am still very sick," he told Lozovsky. "Three months have passed since my arrival in the USSR, and the doctors say that my disease is nervous in nature, as if I am recovering, but the progress is so slow that I doubt any progress.... I feel that I cannot go on this way. Lying here, I am of no value to the movement, and the isolation is eating me up."[2] This crisis forced Foster to turn from his usual whirlwind of public speaking and organizing to a life of writing. He left a series of memoirs, letters, and other personal texts that suggest some aspects of the relationship between the subjective—personal identity and representation, emotional experience—and the political—ideology, organization, and action. As Kathleen Brown and Elizabeth Faue note, historians of both the "Lyrical Left," which preceded the Communist Party's heyday, and the New Left, which followed it, have been particularly concerned with the relationship between the "personal" and the "political." In contrast, most historians of U.S. communism have dwelt either on the machinations of the international movement and factional politics or on local studies of the Communist Party in action, seldom on the personal dimension of such political experience, a dimension that, as Brown and Faue argue, is critical to understanding this experience.[3] What can an analysis of Foster's crisis tell us about his career as a revolutionary, and perhaps also about the relationship between the personal and the political in the experiences of American communists more generally? How might this neglected personal dimension, the subjective problems of identity and emotion, relate to research in labor history, which has tended to emphasize the material and the objective?

I will describe some of the influences that shaped Foster's personality up to the time he joined the communist movement and the severe physical, psychological, and political crisis he faced in the mid-1930s just at the moment the Communist Party USA (CPUSA) was becoming a mass movement. Next, I focus on Foster's efforts in the late 1930s to reinvent himself as a communist writer and as a symbol of the party's proletarian roots, particularly through two autobiographical works. Finally, I distinguish my own approach from earlier Cold War efforts to interpret American communism from a psychological perspective, and I raise the broader problem of integrating the subjective elements of human experience into the materialist framework of most working-class historians.

As the Communist Party liked to remind people, Foster was a product of the Philadelphia slums. Bitter poverty, the deaths of most of his siblings, crime and violence in the streets of his own Philadelphia neighborhood, his father's alcoholism and erratic work life, and the failure of his mother's hopes and dreams marked his early life. His work life could only have underscored the insecurities that encumbered his youth: enforced transiency, constant uncertainty about his livelihood, dangers embedded in many of his work situations.[4]

Such experiences shaped a rather grim outlook on life, best conveyed perhaps in the language of Foster's early syndicalist tracts and in the zeal with which he embraced the hyperbolic revolutionary language of the Comintern's Third Period (1928–1935).[5] The syndicalist, Foster wrote in 1912, has "placed his relations with the capitalists on a basis of naked power.... He knows he is engaged in a life and death struggle with an absolutely lawless and unscrupulous enemy, and considers his tactics only from the standpoint of their effectiveness. With him the end justifies the means."[6] "The only possible guard for the future security of the working class," Foster told congressional investigators in December 1930, "is the dictatorship of the proletariat and a Soviet government."[7] Writing in 1932, he concluded: "The working class cannot come into power without a civil war."[8] Such language reflected not only the international line, but also the very real class violence of Foster's early life and the early Depression years. It also characterized his personality and political perspective throughout his life. Indeed, it seemed to Foster that his own experiences constituted a living indictment of capitalism. As an old man, he could not remember "the time when I was not imbued with that class hatred against employers which is almost instinctive to workers."[9]

In his youth, Foster fashioned a sense of his rather bleak surroundings from the ideas and values at hand, notably his mother's devout Catholicism and the Fenianism for which his father had been exiled from Ireland. He also embraced the comradery, loyalty, and inchoate class pride that he found in his street gang and in early strikes. In his memoirs. Foster describes these early influences as primitive thinking he left behind on his steady ideological progress toward communism. In fact, unlike Elizabeth Gurley Flynn and some other Irish American communists, he did eschew all identification with his ethnic and religious background, and was openly hostile to organized religion in some of his writings.[10] Yet Foster's revolutionary asceticism, his formulaic approach to matters of history, theory, and ideology, and his extreme discipline all suggest the lingering effects of Catholicism. There are rumors, originating apparently with members of his family, that he requested and received the services of a priest when he was near death in Moscow.[11]

When he turned from the daily struggle for survival to the world of ideas, Foster acquired what he described as an "insatiable spirit of observation." His mother encouraged his long hours in the Philadelphia Free Library, though it was here that he abandoned his religious faith for Darwin, Gibbon, and Spencer, and here that he began a slow journey to the political left. Leaving school after the third grade to contribute to the family economy, Foster remained an avid reader throughout his life, eventually learning to read in French and German, also picking up some Russian, and producing dozens of books and thousands of articles and pamphlets. Despite his formulaic approach in his writing and his reliance on the rather dogmatic language of orthodox Marxism-Leninism, this was a remarkable personal achievement, given his background.[12]

After the deaths of both parents and the disintegration of his family around the turn of the century, Foster drifted for many years around the country and throughout the world, working at a wide range of jobs: railroad laborer, camp cook, deep-water sailor. Such experiences also shaped his worldview and provided him with an extensive anecdotal repertoire concerning working-class life, an encyclopedic knowledge of the labor movement and the world of work, and an almost instinctive sense about organization and strategy. Even his enemies acknowledged him as a master builder of workers' movements. Between 1917 and 1919, he provided the organizational genius behind two massive organizing campaigns that swept hundreds of thousands of immigrant and African American meatpacking and steel workers into the burgeoning wartime labor movement.

The instability in his own life produced a strong attraction for system, organization, science: first Darwin, Spencer, and the pioneer American sociologist Lester Frank Ward, later Marx and Lenin. In his early writings, he spent considerable time and effort in describing precisely what the new syndicalist society might look like, and he located the solution to social and economic problems not in democratic representation and practice, but rather in technical expertise and systematic organization.[13] Historians have argued for the attraction of system and organization for intellectuals and the new professionals of the early twentieth century, Foster's formative years. But the significance of strong, centralized organization, discipline, and planning likely meant something else to workers like Foster who had grown up with and endured for so long poverty, disorder, instability, and insecurity.[14] In the unstable and chaotic environment in which he matured, he was strongly attracted to Ward's vision of a society rationally organized on the basis of human needs. Ward provided Foster with his first notion that the rampaging market and the social carnage in its wake might somehow be brought under control.[15] Searching for a systematic political way forward, Foster first found Marxist socialism, then the syndicalist model, and finally Soviet communism. When he embraced communism and during his later Russian travels, he was most impressed with the details of Russian industrial and union organization, not Soviet ideology. The fact that the Russians seemed to have created an effective, exportable workers' system was what attracted Foster, not Marxist-Leninist theory.

When he secretly joined the Communist Party at the age of forty in 1921, Foster was already middle-aged and at a political dead end.[16] The impressive organizations he had built in the open shop bastions of meatpacking and steel, which had won him a reputation as his generation's most talented labor organizer, were largely destroyed. Blacklisted from the railroads where he had made his living, having passed through the left wing of the Socialist Party, the IWW, and a series of his own syndicalist groups, he was waiting impatiently for a new opening in the political scene.

Foster had, by this time, developed his argument that the "militant minority" of dedicated radicals must "bore from within" the conservative mainstream unions to transform them into effective class weapons. He had created a new organization, the Trade Union Educational League (TUEL), to achieve this end. As it happened, Lenin also urged boring from within, at least at the moment when Foster visited Soviet Russia for the first time in the summer of 1921. As the wartime revolutionary upheavals subsided and political reaction set in in capitalist societies throughout the world, Lenin urged revolutionaries to create "united fronts" with socialists, labor party supporters, and trade union activists. "It appeared that our ten year fight for work within the conservative unions was at last going to be successful," Foster later recalled. Searching for a way to galvanize his new TUEL, and swept up in the enthusiasm of the Russian Revolution, Foster joined the new party that fall, and the TUEL became the American section of the new Red International of Labor Unions.[17]

Throughout the 1920s and beyond, Foster was by far America's most important communist—the party's perennial presidential candidate, the architect of its trade union work, a link to American radical traditions and to indigenous labor militants, and the person whom the public identified most closely with American communism. Deeply embedded in the world of industrial work, union organizing, and strikes, his Chicago-based party faction and subculture constantly battled the group they called the "City College Boys," a more urbane and cerebral group of professional revolutionaries in the New York headquarters. The latter held the party franchise through much of the 1920s, but Foster remained the great symbol of American radicalism, and his group represented the only hope for a base in the labor movement. The result was almost constant factional warfare throughout the 1920s.[18]

The particular role he carved out for himself within the communist movement put a tremendous strain on Foster. In March 1930, he was arrested while leading a giant, violent, unemployed demonstration in New York City, one of several such mobilizations throughout the nation, which put the party's unemployed work on the map. Imprisoned at the age of fifty for six months in a small cell on Riker's Island, Foster was subject to all sorts of deprivation. He emerged at the end of 1930 and, instead of resting, quickly immersed himself in the party's unemployed organizing.[19] The following spring, he assumed direction of the largest party-led strike to date, the 1931 bituminous coal strike. Touring the southwestern Pennsylvania, eastern Ohio, and West Virginia fields for several months, organizing picketing and relief work in the midst of extreme deprivation and considerable violence, Foster later admitted that he was "almost finished" by the end of the strike. In the midst of the strife, he clashed repeatedly with Earl Browder, who publicly accused him before the Comintern of neglecting party work in the interests of a hopeless industrial struggle. When the strike finally collapsed in the fall of 1931, Foster took the blame.[20]

Foster's physical and emotional exhaustion were likely aggravated by his frustrations with party factionalism and the danger it posed to the industrial organizing he valued above all other political work, and by his disappointment with the elevation of Browder to party leadership in the early 1930s. All of this reached a climax in the fall of 1932, contributing to a severe crisis that took him out of the movement entirely for several years and left an indelible mark on his personality.

As the nation's most visible communist, Foster was the party's natural standard bearer in the 1932 election, but his nomination at once removed him from his industrial organizing and saddled him with a crushing itinerary. Beginning the campaign "already in rundown condition," he traveled more than 17,000 miles coast to coast, giving dozens of speeches.[21] Crowds were often jubilant, local authorities less enthusiastic. He was driven out of an Illinois coal town by armed deputies, arrested in Lawrence, Massachusetts, beaten and jailed in Los Angeles. Foster never made it to a huge September 12 rally on Chicago's South Side. He suffered a severe heart attack and stroke and collapsed while addressing a crowd in Moline, Illinois. The party always referred to this illness as a heart attack, but the crisis clearly had emotional and psychological dimensions. Foster himself later described it as a "smash-up: angina pectoris, followed by a complete nervous collapse."[22]

In his 1933 letter to Lozovsky, Foster revealed an uncharacteristic despair. Such a long recovery would have been difficult for any person, but Foster's self-image as a vigorous, selfless revolutionary made it "real hell." He could not research, write, or even play cards or chess, his favorite pastimes. If he tried to do anything, all of his symptoms returned. "The result of this endless isolation and frustration is that I am constantly agitated and nervous," he wrote:

> You might say that I should ignore my loneliness, but I have struggled now for thirteen and half months, including five months flat on my back in bed, and it is very difficult to live with such involuntary rest.... I cannot imagine staying here week-by-week, waiting.... In the past, my strength had no limits. I could, and many years did, work sixteen-hour days without a rest, even on Sunday, not to mention a vacation. But now even unimportant things get me down.[23]

Six months later, recuperating in San Francisco during the 1934 strike wave, Foster told Browder he felt "just like one in chains." "[It] just about breaks my heart to be laid up in the midst of this developing struggle." A friend described him at this late point in his recovery: "He was in shocking physical condition," he recalled. "His head shook constantly, his hands trembled, and he walked with great difficulty."[24]

Without being clear which condition precipitates the other, medical researchers now identify a close relationship between heart disease and clinical depression. Foster was clearly plagued by both. Like many stroke victims, perhaps particularly those who had possessed great strength and endurance before the illness, he lost confidence in his abilities. He was often anxious, a condition that stood in stark contrast to the coolness he had displayed in even the worst situations before the early 1930s. For several years after his recovery, he required assistance crossing the busy streets near the party's Union Square headquarters. When he did speak publicly, he cut his usually long speeches to a minimum and always had a small glass of gin, indistinguishable from water, on the rostrum, apparently to steady his nerves. Oddly, Foster, who abstained from alcohol most of his life, never took a drink, but he clearly derived some security from the glass being there. Some of these insecurities diminished over time, but he always seemed to be measuring out his strength so as not to risk another collapse. Foster estimated that he never regained more than half of his former stamina. This frustrated him enormously, but he "learned to live with himself." Foster's highly disciplined workdays at his small, crowded apartment near Yankee Stadium in the South Bronx involved a kind of ritual "to prevent the leakage of time": "So many hours for sleep, up early in the morning (6:00 A.M.) to scan the morning newspaper, then to write a thousand words."[25]

In the wake of this severe crisis, Foster reinvented himself, turning to two types of writing. First, he drew on his vast experience and reputation as a "practical" militant for a series of pamphlets aimed at industrial union organizers. His *Organizing Methods in the Steel Industry* (New York: Workers' Library, 1935) became what Lizabeth Cohen calls a "blueprint for CIO policy." Loaded with detailed advice, this and similar pamphlets often included remarkable insights.[26] They represented a sort of substitute for the field organizing and speaking tours Foster was no longer capable of sustaining, allowing him to connect with the industrial work that he always stressed. Given the importance of communists in industrial union organizing, these pamphlets and his continuing contacts with organizers gave Foster an important, if less direct, role in the 1930s upsurge.[27]

In the late 1930s, he turned to a far more ambitious project—his own life story. Why did he make this choice, and why at this moment in his life? One possible motivation was simply his age and the recent brush with death. It would not have been unusual for a person with Foster's experience to be thinking about the meaning of her/his life. The idea that the autobiographical impulse also was prompted by political considerations, however, is suggested not only by Foster's declaration of his aims, but also by the whole trajectory of his career. Judging from the didactic quality of his memoirs, he did his writing "for the party" with regard to both his intended audience and the work's function. He aimed for an audience composed primarily of party activists, in the United States certainly, but perhaps also abroad—Soviet and Comintern leaders. In fact, the books were translated and read in socialist countries throughout the world. In this sense, Foster, like other socialist autobiographers, saw himself placing his practical experience and insights at the service of the party, hoping activists and the movement would benefit from his story. Displacing his typical industrial organizing efforts to his writings, he may also have aimed to retain a place for himself in the party at a time when he was politically marginalized. At the very moment of the mass upsurge of the 1930s, precisely those activities he most prized had been placed well beyond the limits of his physical strength and endurance. As Browder centralized party authority in his own hands, he pushed Foster to the margins. Yet through his writing, Foster remained a powerful symbol of the party, particularly among industrial organizers. "Although Browder supervised the behind-the-doors contacts with top CIO brokers," veteran activist Dorothy Healey recalled, "most of us in the unions assumed that the Party's chairman, William Z. Foster, was an equal spokesman when it came to trade union affairs.... In our eyes he remained the authoritative public spokesman on issues confronting the labor movement."[28]

Foster's autobiographical writing can no more be taken as a direct and unmediated reflection of his personality than any other personal narrative. Autobiography, Phillipe LeJeune writes, "is necessarily in its deepest sense a special kind of fiction, its self and its truth as much created as discovered realities." Reginia Gagnier suggests that workers' biographies are best used "not as historians have, as data of varying degrees of reliability reflecting external conditions, but as texts revealing subjective identities embedded in diverse social and material circumstances." Most important are the narrative choices an author makes and the plot he or she develops in telling the story. What we learn from Foster's autobiographies comes partly through silences—his calculated inattention to his own personal identity and relationships—and partly through the structure of the narratives in his two autobiographical works.[29]

In 1937, Foster published *From Bryan to Stalin*, which he accurately described as not so much an autobiography as "a contribution to the history of left wing trade unionism in the United States during the past forty years" and an "outline of the development of the Communist Party."[30] Organizational in form, formulaic in tone, *From Bryan to Stalin* stood in for an official party history until Foster produced *History of the Communist Party of the United States* (New York: International Publishers, 1952). Reflecting Foster's explicit goals in writing it, *From Bryan to Stalin* is peculiarly impersonal. He divides his narrative into pre–Communist Party and post–Communist Party sections. In the first, Foster himself enters the story only through his organizational efforts. Even then, the real genius he displayed in some of these early efforts has no independent role, but is subordinated to the narrative of movement-building, with all roads leading toward communism. In the section of the book dealing with the Communist Party and its various organizational efforts, Foster hardly appears at all. When he does, he refers to himself in the third rather than the first person, as if not to distract readers from the narrative of party development. The book is full of individuals but not personalities. People enter the story in so far as they affect the success or failure of the movement.

Two years later Foster published *Pages from a Worker's Life*, a series of fascinating, often humorous, sometimes touching pieces drawn from his experiences at work and on the road. *Pages* offered a more personal, anecdotal perspective: "the hopes and illusions, the comedy and tragedy, the exploitation and struggles of an American worker's life." Right around the same time Foster was writing *Pages*, he criticized communists and other radicals for a "hyper-objective tendency" and being "too cold and impersonal" in their mass agitation, a flaw that created "a barrier to establishing the broadest mass contacts." Communists and other progressives must bring a "human element" into their work. Perhaps, as Ed Johanningsmeier has suggested, this new memoir was an effort in that direction. Certainly it was more engaging than his previous effort. But it is still difficult to chart any sort of personal development, something that clearly held little interest for Foster. Indeed, here there is no explicit plot at all, just "sketches, recollections and snapshots." He understood even this more personal book in explicit, rather narrow political terms, emphasizing "the forces that led me to arrive at my present opinions."[31]

Both books served important functions for the party, though judged by the standards of bourgeois autobiography, as personal investigations, both were failures. Yet Foster's neglect of the personal was not an oversight, but a conscious narrative choice, and to some degree also a reflection of his personality. As his friend and fellow Wobbly Elizabeth Gurley Flynn observed in her review of Foster's autobiographical works, *From Bryan to Stalin* "was a veritable guide book to the American labor movement in the past half century." If you wanted to know something about the "actual experiences of Bill Foster," however, they had to be "glimpsed between the lines." Even when Foster did recount personal experience, as in *Pages from a Worker's Life*, "there is no ego here; no cultivated 'complex'; no soul searching to find himself; no personal glory, amorous conquests nor 'success' recipes. . . . This is the key to Foster," Flynn concluded. "He lives and moves and has his being as a worker; conscious of his class and its struggles, its needs and what its final aims must be. He has no personal life nor ambition outside of theirs."[32]

Peculiarly impersonal from the perspective of bourgeois autobiography, with its emphases on the individual, the personal, and self-realization, Foster's personal narrative is characteristic of radical and, to some degree, most working-class memoir literature. This notion of the individual as "social atom" is, as Reginia Gagnier notes, characteristic of working-class autobiography more generally, and helps to distinguish it from the more introspective bourgeois genre. Foster's tendency to stress the insignificance of the personal and to subordinate the individual to the collective is predictably strong, not only in American communist personal narratives, but also in the memoirs of socialist revolutionaries worldwide, though his autobiographies provide a particularly striking case.[33]

To the extent that *Pages* can be taken in some sense as a reflection of Foster's life, what is perhaps most remarkable about its episodes is the almost total absence of women. The most striking case is Esther Abramovitz Foster, the remarkable woman whom he met in 1912 and married soon after, and with whom he lived until his death in 1961. A Russian Jewish immigrant garment worker, Esther was an anarchist militant, a free love advocate, and the mother of three children (none of them with Foster, who from his early syndicalist days counseled revolutionaries against raising families). Friends might describe their relationship as warm and loving, but Foster's few references to her are all very impersonal. He dedicated *From Bryan to Stalin* to her, but described her in characteristic political terms: "An intelligent and devoted comrade . . . my constant companion and a tower of strength to me in all my activities for these many years." Esther maintained a very low profile throughout their married life—and certainly in Foster's memoirs. Foster mentions her once in the 345-page *From Bryan to Stalin*, in a brief paragraph concerning her role in his Syndicalist League of North America; once in *Pages*, in relation to his recovery from his illness; and almost never in any of his other writings.[34]

Foster's silence about Esther and heterosexual relationships more generally is explained in part at least by the homosocial worlds he inhabited for much of his life. His early work environments—isolated lumber and metal mining camps and sawmills, sailing ships, and railroad freight yards and boxcars—were exclusively male settings. His life as a hobo was also an experience that accentuated both male bonding and the alienation typical of transient workers' lives. In *From Bryan to Stalin*, individuals are mentioned only in relation to particular organizations or political activities, never in terms of their relationships with Foster. *Pages from a Worker's Life* contains a few references to personal friends and companions from these early years, but these are virtually all to other men. To the extent that Foster developed the kind of close personal relationships that Brown and Faue argue were crucial to sustaining the left, and it is difficult to judge this from his narratives, such relationships were most likely with men who shared not only his political orientation but also his personal experiences as itinerant worker and organizer. Likewise, although he mentioned and sometimes worked with women comrades, Foster's political spaces, populated largely by men, resonated with an ostentatiously proletarian and "muscular" form of trade union–based politics. This was true of his TUEL circle and his Chicago Communist Party faction in the 1920s ("a rough-and-ready group" with "few niceties in mutual relations"), and his earlier engagements with the left wing of the Socialist Party, the IWW, and his own succession of syndicalist groups. The Communist Party was far more open to women's participation and even leadership than most heterosocial organizations of the time, but very few women served in the top leadership during Foster's first decade in the party. The proportion of women on the central committee rose throughout the 1930s, but Foster's illness largely removed him from these circles in the years preceding his autobiographical writing in the late 1930s. Throughout his life, he had a close friendship with Elizabeth Gurley Flynn, another "old Wobbly," and he apparently had at least two extramarital affairs. Yet Foster's worlds of work and politics were largely male worlds.[35]

Fortunately, in trying to understand Foster, we can draw not only on his own writings, but also on the observations of those who knew him. During his early party career, Foster's insecurity found expression particularly in the realm of theory, where he clearly felt inadequate. These tendencies became more pronounced in the Popular Front years, when the Communist International encouraged activists to work in broad political formations with reformist organizations, and to focus less on revolutionary transformation and more on the struggle against fascism.[36] Foster visualized himself as a class warrior and was simply far less comfortable than Browder with the more expansive theoretical renderings and the social democratic drift of the Popular Front era. Less theoretically inclined than that of other party leaders, his own thinking remained what political scientist and communist veteran Joseph Starobin called "an amalgam of his trade union origins and his 'fundamentalist' understanding of Marxism."[37] Having matured politically in the rough-and-tumble world of hobos and industrial workers, strikes, and Wobbly free speech fights, Foster based much of his approach to revolutionary change on his experiences in the labor movement. Not surprisingly, perhaps, he preferred the company of radical workers, and not only because their ideas and strategies seemed to square better with his own, but also because he felt more comfortable around them than with intellectuals and professionals. Yet Foster's apparent anti-intellectualism was more complex than it appeared. Though clearly not a profound thinker, he had an active intellect and read widely—history, biography, and science, as well as politics—and enjoyed classical and folk music. He had a great love of learning from an early age. The disregard Browder and other leaders showed for his ideas clearly bothered him.

Foster's career as a party leader was one of repeated frustrations, notably with the party's persistent, humiliating factionalism, which often derailed his projects to radicalize the American labor movement. He clashed repeatedly with Jay Lovestone, the party's consummate factionalist, and bitterly opposed the 1928 international turn from "boring from within" to dual revolutionary unions, a tendency he had fought throughout his adult life. After a long conflict, Foster lost control of his own faction and came close to expulsion before finally capitulating. Stalin was particularly irritated with Foster's factionalism and the enduring effects of his struggle against Lovestone. Up to this point, Foster's politics had been shaped by his strong syndicalist tendencies and an eclectic application of his own ideas and experiences to party policy, an approach some party activists called "Fosterism." His final capitulation on the issue of dual unionism marked a decisive turn in his career. His role in the factionalism of the late 1920s and his stubborn resistance to the dual union line—all carefully noted in his Comintern file—cost him leadership of the party. It went instead to Foster's "clerk" and "man Friday," Earl Browder, who reigned throughout the party's heyday in the 1930s and World War II. James P. Cannon, who knew both men well, recalled, "The appointment of Browder to the first position in the Party with Foster subordinated to the role of honorary public figure without authority, really rubbed Foster's nose in the dirt." In this sense, Foster's crisis had practical political effects. Conversely, these political effects shaped his psychological state in the Depression and war years. When he regained the upper hand with the reassertion of orthodox Marxism-Leninism at the end of the war, it was on the eve of severe political repression and decline. He spent his final years in the mid-1950s locked in another factional battle, defending orthodoxy against those who sought to reform the party along more democratic lines.[38]

Oddly perhaps for one who steeped himself in American work environments and consciously identified with American radical traditions, Foster sustained himself throughout his career with international connections and recognition. His early travels in Europe before World War I provided him a purer form of syndicalism that linked him with revolutionaries throughout Europe and influenced his approach long after joining the party. On the heels of the steel strike defeat, he found exhilaration and vindication of his strategies on his first trip to Soviet Russia, where he was pleased to learn that Lenin had read his book on the strike. Elected to the executive committees of both the Communist International and the Red International of Labor Unions, Foster visited the Soviet Union frequently and maintained relationships with communist leaders throughout the world. Often viewed as a "practical" trade union communist in his own party, he eventually found recognition abroad as a great Marxist thinker. The historical works he produced during the 1950s might meet with contempt in his own country, but their translations into Russian, Polish, German, French, Italian, Japanese, and other languages brought adulation in the international communist press. They introduced the United States to a generation of youth and party activists in the Soviet bloc. In March 1956, on his seventy-fifth birthday, in the midst of severe government repression and a dramatic decline in party membership, on the eve of the organization's greatest crisis, Foster set his eyes on the Soviet world and remained optimistic. "In this period of capitalist decay and socialist advance," he told the crowd of well-wishers, "it gives me the boundless satisfaction of knowing that my life's efforts have been spent on the side of progress, and that the great socialist cause is marching on rapidly to triumph throughout the world." Foster was particularly thrilled when, at the very end of his life, he received an honorary professorship at Moscow State University in recognition for his writing. In his view, this "splendid and exclusive honor" was the highest form of recognition for a Marxist intellectual.[39]

What can all this personal stuff tell us? The easiest piece of the story for us to grasp is the political significance of the personal crisis. Foster's breakdown, his long and painful recovery, his loss of confidence were all *products* in some sense of his political work over the previous decade or longer. At the same time, they had political *effects*, removing him from the field at a critical turning point in the party's history; clearing away the personality most clearly identified with its proletarian elements and the Third Period's class war rhetoric; making room for Browder, the person most clearly identified with the Americanist reform language of the Popular Front.

We are all still on familiar ground here—putting the personal experience in the broader (and presumably more important) political context. But what happens when we turn to less familiar terrain and try to place the political in the context of human experience and personal development? At the very least, Foster's physical and psychological illnesses, and particularly his crisis of confidence throughout the 1930s, suggest the enormous personal toll revolutionary politics could exact from even (or perhaps particularly from) as tough and highly disciplined an individual as Foster.[40] More broadly, Foster's story begins to suggest some fit between personal experience and political expression. His early insecurities, for example, rooted in material conditions, and his later ones, rooted in party factionalism, each contributed to particular ideological inclinations, the first to his quest for system and method, the latter to his tendency toward Marxist-Leninist orthodoxy.

Foster's and other communist memoirs, as well as the large spate of personal narratives produced over the past two decades through the collaboration of New Left with Old, all suggest a tendency to submerge the personal in the political. While most communist autobiographers made this decision to eschew the details of personal life, however, gender seems to make a difference. Men's memoirs—of those who remained in the party as well as those who left long before writing—are very short on personal information and largely devoid of emotional content. Any personal narrative is subordinated to the story of movement-building. Women party activists, representing well over one-third of party membership during the Popular Front era, were also supremely political people. "As to the personal problems each of us had," Peggy Dennis wrote, "none of us was equipped by our Party experience to respond to each other on a simple human level. . . . I was too calm, too impersonal, too political." In fact, Dorothy Healey recalled, for the party "there was no such thing as a division between your personal and your political life. You were supposed to be totally selfless and dedicated to the revolution."[41] But the balance between the personal and the political in women's memoirs, including those by Dennis and Healey, is different from that in the male narratives. They were more likely to deal with relationships and emotions, to structure their stories around crises that were personal as well as political. Anyone interested in grasping the personal dimensions of the communist experience is much more likely to find them in the autobiographies and interviews of women veterans than in the best of the male narratives.[42] Still, the political overwhelms the personal in both groups of memoirs. Why?

The proletarian writer Joseph Freeman developed a close relationship with Foster in the late 1920s, and made an observation in the midst of his friend's personal crisis that seems to apply to other veteran communists. "Foster talked chiefly about the class war," Freeman noted, and only mentioned personal experiences to make some broader political point. "Actually, Foster was a man of wide cultural interests; his library was as full of literary classics as of socialist classics. . . . But when he questioned me about Europe, he wanted to know about the trade unions, the growth of the communist movement, international politics. Anything he said about himself was a parenthetical illustration of a general law of revolutionary strategy or a trade-union principle."

Foster tended to see personal conduct and values strictly in relation to the political struggle, Freeman wrote. "The problems of personal conduct which agitated us in the [Greenwich] Village, did not seem to matter to him. He was ascetic by a standard which determined all his actions. The class struggle was the most important thing in the world, and for that struggle he wanted to keep physically, mentally, and morally fit." Most significantly, Freeman found that Foster identified so closely and personally with the working class that his own identity tended to fuse with that of his class. His recollections echo Flynn's observations about Foster's tendency to describe his own experiences as part of the class struggle. "Within the Party, Foster had an engaging modesty," Freeman wrote, "but in contact with the class enemy there emerged a powerful pride in which his person and his class were identical."[43]

This fusion of personal identity with political struggle, which is apparent in so many communist memoirs, undoubtedly made Foster a brilliant organizer, but it limited his ability and language in analyzing and understanding his own personal situation. His asceticism facilitated while it rationalized the extreme sacrifices and deprivation he endured throughout much of his life, but it also made it difficult for him to deal with personal crisis, and particularly with the crisis of confidence he faced in the 1930s. The strikingly impersonal quality of his life narratives undoubtedly reflected the conscious conviction of a devoted revolutionary that the personal simply did not count, but the submergence of the self in the struggle was also a reflection of Foster's personality.

It may be, however, that the whole notion of a "private life" needs redefining in the case of revolutionaries. Wendy Goldman writes: "dedication to an ideal of revolution in a revolutionary situation is synonymous with a fully 'public' life." The human and individual costs can be enormous, and should be a part of the story we tell. "But the gains were great as well. The powerful sense of comradeship as something going deeper than friendship or love, the sense of mission and purpose, the feeling of possibility, the new avenues for talents, potentials never before known, the excitement . . . the power to create a new future."[44] It is difficult, perhaps impossible, to reduce this experience to an emotional balance sheet, but the personal dimension of the experience is relevant and worth exploring. Even if it is only political motivation that we seek to understand, it seems likely that the more personal aspects of life are relevant.

To avoid misunderstanding, let me conclude by explaining what I am not suggesting. The last time issues of personal psychology were raised in relation to American communism was during the 1950s, when the movement was analyzed not as the product of social and economic conflicts, but rather as a form of psychological deviance. This idea of communism as neurosis permeates much of the Cold War–era analysis of the CPUSA, though its roots are older.[45] Some scholars explained communist activism as the product of "social disorganization" leading to feelings of isolation and vulnerability, others as a form of secular religion fulfilling deeply rooted human needs. Most employed some kind of psychological approach to explain what they viewed as a political aberration. After interviewing nearly three hundred former communists and considering a range of answers to the question "Why did they join?" Morris Ernst and David Loth concluded: "The party would appear to be heavily populated with the handicapped—some of them physically, but more of them psychologically, to a point that might be called emotionally crippling.... In the Communist party they find a certain amount of relief, often temporary, but always welcome."[46]

In *The Appeals of Communism*, perhaps the most sophisticated of these studies, Gabriel Almond and his colleagues analyzed the question of motivation comparatively, using a sample of 221 former communists in France, Italy, England, and the United States. It was misleading, they concluded, to speak of an appeal; "rather we must talk of types of appeals, to various types of persons, in different kinds of situations." Still, "types of neurotic susceptibility" loomed large in their analysis. Noting that the incidence of neurotic isolation was higher among American and British subjects, they attributed much of their motivation to hostility, self-rejection, or isolation. "The image of the Communist militant is that of a dignified, special person, dedicated, strong, confident of the future.... These aspects of Communism have an obvious attraction for persons who carry within themselves feelings of being weak and unworthy."[47]

Psychohistorians embraced Freudian theories in the 1960s and 1970s. While somewhat different in their interpretations of particular individuals, many believed it was possible to identify an ideal "revolutionary personality." Bruce Mazlish combined Weber's notions of ascetics and charisma with Freud's of displaced libido, uneven psychological development, and the crisis of adulthood to produce a new personality type—the "revolutionary ascetic." He traced this revolutionary type all the way back to the Puritan revolutionary and then transformed him into a Bolshevik in the early twentieth century. Both Wolfenstein and Mazlish were confident in employing rather abstract personality theories to generalize over hundreds of years of political agitation and conflict in strikingly diverse political and cultural settings.[48]

Today, most psychologists have abandoned the quest for ideal personality types. Their Cold War political and intellectual context helps to explain these psychological theories, just as our own situation in the postcommunist era undoubtedly shapes our interpretations of communist militants in various settings. In their case, a particularly optimistic reading of postwar American politics and living standards produced the search for a psychological explanation for the "aberration" of American communism. With the fall of communism and the rise of more conservative interpretations of the party's history, perhaps such theories will reemerge as some scholars return to a view of American communism as an irrational malignancy.

Yet for decades, communist movements throughout the world won and held the loyalty of millions of people from a wide variety of class and cultural backgrounds. To employ psychology as the ultimate explanation for the development of such social and political movements is to oversimplify a complex political phenomenon and understate the significance of both individual and group reason and agency. The rise and fall of major social movements cannot hinge on the psychological states of even their more important participants. They are best understood in terms of the broad social, economic, and political contexts within which they operated, rather than as collections of more or less neurotic individuals.

It seems reasonable to consider psychological, as well as social and political, factors that influenced a person to join the party, sustained them through decades of thankless work and extreme hardship, and perhaps eventually shaped their decision, in the midst of the party's ultimate crisis, to leave or to stay—but only if one concedes that such factors are at work in all political commitments, and indeed in other types of individual dedication to impersonal goals. As historian Leo Ribuffo puts it, "Earl Browder entered public life to satisfy drives and dreams, but so did Herbert Hoover, Alfred E. Smith, and Abraham Lincoln."[49]

Much of the recent, more sympathetic scholarship on the Communist Party has tended to ignore this subjective dimension of the experience.[50] Psychological factors and personal relationships are apt to show up more frequently in personal narratives and correspondence, particularly in accounts of the extreme pressure brought to bear on cadres during the political repression, underground activity, and subsequent factional struggles of the 1950s. To consider psychological along with other factors at the level of individual motivation and rationalization can be an important interpretive strategy, one that historians of social movements as well as biographers might use to better understand the experiences and motivation of activists.

It is probably not a coincidence that labor historians have turned increasingly to biography over the past decade. A biographical approach to American communism and other aspects of working-class life allows us to consider elements of individual development and personality in relation to broader social and political contexts. Foster's own politics were molded in part by the subjective—his individual personality—which in turn was shaped by experiences in his childhood and early adult life, by the crises he faced at various points in his life, and by the quality of the relationships he forged. But they were also shaped by his experiences in a variety of industrial and political situations, by his own efforts to understand these, and, finally, by the exigencies of life in an international Marxist-Leninist party.

Foster's trouble grasping the personal dimension of his crisis tells us something not only about him and other working-class revolutionaries, but perhaps also about ourselves as labor historians. We have been experiencing our own crisis in the past few years, one that involves the place of the subjective in our understanding of historical change: problems of personal identity, emotion, and experience, and the relationship of these to what we term "politics."[51] Foster's story suggests both the importance of considering this relationship and the fact that it was sometimes as difficult for our historical subjects to grasp its meaning as it seems to be for us.

CHAPTER FOUR

Blue-Collar Cosmopolitans

Toward a History of Working-Class Sophistication in Industrial America

Up in Tom's Room

Until I was about ten years old, we lived in a two-bedroom flat in an old brick house on the West Side of Chicago. When my policeman father was promoted and the young couple upstairs moved to the suburbs, the five kids flowed into the upstairs apartment, where we finally had a little more room. My favorite spot was a bedroom surrounded with windows, the preserve of my oldest brother, Tom. After high school he went directly to a job at the telephone company, and by his early twenties he had a skilled position which he prized for its solitude, especially in off-hours, and for the frequent, well-paid overtime work. The job, troubleshooting connections on huge electrical frames, allowed him to read for evening courses when he finally returned to school at the Chicago City Colleges—psychology, sociology, humanities. The relatively good wages allowed him to travel throughout the West, and he came back with amazing photos and stories of locations and events beyond the imagination of a kid on the West Side.

Many things drew me to Tom's room. It was the place in the house with the most books, so it was the place where I began to read—classic novels, but also books on "social problems." Tom also had fairly sophisticated tastes in music, so this was where I came to appreciate jazz—Oscar Peterson, Ella Fitzgerald, Dave Brubeck; adult comedy, especially Lenny Bruce; and even a bit of classical music. It was a quiet place where I could think, and I preferred sitting on the bed, reading and listening to music, to playing softball in the neighborhood's alleys and open lots.

My father was a good person, but we had little in common, and the distance only grew as I came into my own ideas about politics, civil rights, and other issues. Tom filled up the space between my father and me. He gave me books he was studying in his night school courses, took me to the Art Institute, and talked with me about ideas. Only many years later did I understand that he was nurturing something he could see inside me, something that was also a part of him—a love of learning, a sensitivity to things of beauty, a curiosity about distant places and different kinds of people. Tom returned to school years later, eventually earning a PhD in psychology in middle age and providing me with an example that such things were possible for people like us.

In many ways, Tom was a fairly typical young worker; in other ways he was different. Perhaps as a result, working-class historians have little room for him in their narratives. He was a white guy who supported civil rights, a straight guy who accepted gay people, a man who showed respect for women's intelligence and skills. He was a union member and a liberal, but he was not particularly political. He took part in strikes, and he was certainly class conscious, but as a matter of course, not as a conscious political commitment. He assumed rich people were out for themselves and we had better stick together. He was an intellectual in his own right, but not the sort of "organic intellectual" Antonio Gramsci had in mind. In a word, he was "cosmopolitan"—a blue-collar cosmopolitan, and he was not alone.

Blue-Collar Cosmopolitanism

For a term used so often in academic parlance—the social science literature in particular is saturated with the word—"cosmopolitanism" is rather difficult to define. For political scientists and others concerned with international politics, it connotes a relatively more sophisticated international or transnational perspective, usually on the part of policymakers.[1] For anthropologists, cosmopolitanism connotes a familiarity with or at least an interest in "others," and perhaps also some greater knowledge of the world outside one's local community, often as the result of travel.[2] For sociologist Robert K. Merton, "localists" were more firmly rooted in their communities, saw voluntary associations in functional terms, and concerned themselves with the impact of change on their own communities. "Cosmopolitans" lived in and exerted influence in their own communities, but they saw themselves as integral parts of a broader outside world. They were more apt to be influenced by ideas from outside the community and more apt to migrate.[3]

What all of these theories of cosmopolitanism have in common is that they focus largely on elites.[4] Indeed, the term cosmopolitan seems almost by definition to apply to better educated, better connected, more sophisticated upper- and upper-middle-class people, especially intellectuals. But what happens when we consider the concept in the context of working-class communities and its value for understanding working-class intellectuals?

Most early twentieth-century working-class people were Merton's "localists." Their workplaces were often close to their homes. Their cultural lives were circumscribed by their religious institutions down the street. Their aspirations were usually wrapped up in their own families, not in those of a global working class. Historians and sociologists have likened their communities in the midst of large industrial cities to the rural villages from which many of them sprang.[5] After decades of work, we still don't know enough about the personal lives and everyday dramas of such people. And so we tend to abstract them, to assume that, though they might differ by race, ethnicity, and religion, they were somewhat interchangeable. We speak of them in the plural; we blend them together with one another; we notice them only when they become part of some mighty whole—a riotous crowd, a socialist movement, a strike.

But there were others: Today we might think of travel and technology as being particularly important in the creation of a "global" culture, and it is true that the scale of experience for common people and the frequency with which they move across national boundaries is unprecedented. Yet immigrants who traversed different societies in the late nineteenth and early twentieth centuries, employing several languages and interacting with diverse peoples were in some sense quite cosmopolitan. And so were many dockers and sailors who spent their work lives at the intersections of transnational trade networks and political movements, developing in the process broader perspectives on the world. Radicals' worldviews were global by definition, and their aspirations were indeed linked to those of other workers spread across the face of the globe. And then there were working women and men like Tom who broadened their own horizons in their spare time through reading, travel, and wondering about the world beyond their workplaces and neighborhoods. If cosmopolitanism is thought of as a spectrum of experience rather than as some sort of threshold, then perhaps there was a sizable portion of the working-class population who were cosmopolitan in these ways.

Formal political and social ideas—ideologies that were self-consciously transethnic or transnational—are vital to my study; many of the more radical cosmopolitans embraced such ideologies. They were perhaps closest to Gramsci's notion of the organic intellectual—sprung from local working class cultures and connected to transnational political movements and ideas. But I am also alluding to a more quotidian understanding of the term—a kind of working-class intellectualism: the effect of daily reading, travel to diverse locations, the experience of diverse cultures and peoples. The cosmopolitans' relationship to place varied. The hobo and the sailor were often rootless by definition, but many immigrant radicals created and sank deep roots in their respective communities even as they maintained a relationship with family and friends in the Old World.

Some of these cosmopolitans have caught our attention by virtue of their sheer brilliance—proletarian writers like Jack Conroy, for example, and Richard Wright. Conroy worked at various factory jobs and wandered about the country, but he also produced brilliant novels and short stories, edited a series of radical literary journals, mentored younger working-class writers, and worked closely with African American writers on black migration and folklore.[6] Born to sharecropper parents in 1908 on a Mississippi plantation, Wright attended school only sporadically and worked at a series of menial jobs before migrating to Chicago. There he worked as a postal clerk and joined the Communist Party and its literary group, the John Reed Club. In 1937, Wright moved to Harlem, where he wrote the novel *Native Son* (1940) and an autobiography, *Black Boy* (1945), both of which became staples in the American canon, before breaking with the party in the late forties and moving to Paris.[7] But most blue-collar cosmopolitans remained obscure, unacknowledged thinkers in a world that largely ignored their thoughts.

Timing and gender are both important to our story. The period under consideration is roughly from the 1880s through the Great Depression. There were working-class readers and thinkers in the eighteenth and earlier nineteenth centuries, of course, but the opportunities to indulge one's reading and travel interests expanded significantly after the end of the nineteenth century. While the expansion and refinement of the railroad system and the merchant fleet made movement faster and cheaper, creating millions of jobs demanding travel, child labor and compulsory education laws meant that opportunities for at least a basic literacy came within reach of many more working-class people. With new printing and distribution technologies, a flood of cheap printed texts—radical and religious tracts; cheap stories; corporate, labor, foreign language, and daily newspapers—opened to working-class readers new worlds reflecting a remarkable range of subjects and perspectives.[8] As in earlier eras, such texts might circulate among many readers, while cigar makers, garment workers, and others often employed one of their number to read to the whole group—radical publications, novels, even poetry.

Many of the venues probed here, like much of the early twentieth-century public sphere, were homosocial, the preserves of male manual workers. There were spaces populated by female worker-cosmopolitans, however—educational programs developed by the largely female garment workers unions and the Women's Trade Union League, for example, and adult education classes offered by New York's People's University and comparable institutions in other parts of the country.[9] The female constituencies for such efforts were disproportionately young and single, and the prospects for travel, reading, and serious discussions were likely diminished for working-class housewives and mothers. Yet women's clubs, study groups, and intercultural music and art programs at settlement houses in the slums of New York, Chicago, and other large cities; union women's auxiliaries; and informal occasions offered venues for working-class housewives and mothers for discussion and learning.[10]

This essay is intended to be provocative and prescriptive rather than definitive, suggesting a different angle of vision on the experiences of some common people we thought we knew well, but whose intellectual lives remain largely unacknowledged. Their story suggests a working-class world that was more vibrant and diverse than we have recognized. It asks not only, "Who were the blue-collar cosmopolitans?" but also, "What does their existence suggest about our understanding of working-class life and presence in the industrial era?" In placing such experiences in relation to our understandings of the cosmopolitan, we not only illuminate the former but also broaden our notions of the latter.

Although the essay is organized around archetypes in an effort to display the content of the experience and contributions more concretely, the reality was more likely a kind of continuum—with an obvious degree of overlap between types and a range of cosmopolitan experience and thought among workers from diverse backgrounds. Thus, many immigrants experienced not only extensive travel and diverse languages and cultures, but also exposure to a range of social and political ideas. Sailors often became hoboes between voyages, traveling from one coast to the other to connect with their ship. With a good deal of down time aboard ship or, in the case of railroad workers, between runs, they were often among the most avid working-class readers, and in the process they were often exposed to radical political ideas. If the term "cosmopolitan" is defined broadly in order to capture an array of experience with reading, travel, or experiences with diverse cultures and peoples, then the range of characters here is perhaps much broader than we might expect.

The Radical Hobo and the Working-Class Reader

A hobo by the name of Doyle exemplified the unlikely connection between rough, unskilled labor and migration on the one hand, and a truly unique perspective and robust life of the mind on the other. Doyle had been born in Cork, but, as economist Don Lescohier found, "He has been all around the earth several times, visited every important port and interior city of South America, every important city in Europe and on this continent." Doyle's "occupation" depended upon the season. He followed the wheat and sugar beet harvests, then turned to lumbering work or picked oranges in California. "This hobo, this bum, who had never been inside of a school . . . knew the classical economists well and quoted from Ricardo and Adam Smith . . . Hobson, [John R.] Commons, Seager, Scott Nearing, Marshall. . . . He is an adherent of Carl [sic] Marx from the ground up . . . [and he] quoted from Carlyle and Ruskin." When Lescohier met him, Doyle was gathering a stake so that he could spend six months in New York taking a course with the radical economist Scott Nearing at the Rand School. A member of the Industrial Workers of the World (IWW), Doyle took for granted that the proletariat would eventually triumph, and he seemed to be preparing himself for that crucial moment.[11]

Perhaps few hobo intellectuals could match Doyle's reading or travels, but his type was not unusual. The journalist-lumberjack Stewart Holbrook came across a toolshed which the workers in a lumber camp seemed to use as a lending library, filled with the works of Dumas, Dickens, Brontë, Carlyle, Darwin, the *Encyclopaedia Britannica*, and the ever-present Darwin and Tom Paine.[12] It is a rather compelling image: manual workers sitting around an isolated camp in the woods, reading literature and Darwin. Often the first step in radicalism was not an engagement with socialism but disenchantment with religion, an attraction to science, and an affinity for atheism. Anton

Johannsen, who embraced the new lifestyle with great enthusiasm, began to read in a boxcar when a friendly fellow sojourner gave him some radical pamphlets. Later, a follower of the atheist speaker Robert Ingersoll introduced Johannsen to Tom Paine's *The Rights of Man*, and be became a convinced freethinker. The reading, together with the conversations surrounding it, changed his life. For some, a radical hobo experience might well have been a stage in the working-class life course. For others like Johannsen, it was the beginning of a life of radicalism, organizing—and continuous learning.[13]

The notion that late nineteenth- and early twentieth-century radical and even union publications were narrowly instrumental in content is misleading. English and foreign-language Socialist Party publications, freethought magazines, and union journals and newspapers frequently included not only political analysis and trade news, but also book and theater reviews, fiction, popular science essays, cartoons, and in some cases, readers' letters.[14] The apparent audience for such fare suggests the scope of working-class reading interests as well as cultural activities outside of reading.

Even when self-educated workers were not reading radical tracts, their interests tended to be serious and wide-ranging. A 1931 American Library Association study reported that workers, farmers, housewives, and teachers were most interested in self-improvement articles and in subjects like "the next war" and "laws and legislation."[15] The Haldeman-Julius "Little Blue Books" cost only a nickel and were designed to fit into the pocket of a worker's overalls. The radical publisher Charles H. Kerr's Pocket Library played a similar role. The range of subjects was particularly broad. Among the earliest authors in the "Little Blue Book" series were Voltaire, Wilde, Emerson, and Poe. In addition to books on Christianity and popular science, the list included introductions to Buddhism, Confucianism, Islam, and yoga, and self-improvement treatises on marriage, sexuality and birth control, gardening, baseball, homeownership, psychoanalysis, hypnosis, and other topics.[16]

Historian Toby Higbie points out that even westerns and other escapist novels could broaden a worker's horizons. Reading the novels of Zane Grey in the depths of Mississippi, the future African American writer Richard Wright was transported. They "enlarged my knowledge of the world more than anything I had encountered so far," he recalled. "To me, with my roundhouse, saloon-door, and river-levee background, they were revolutionary, my gateway to the world."[17] Pulp fiction westerns and detective novels might represent an escape from the problems of work, family, and community, transporting the working-class reader to new places and situations, though such readers could also recognize aspects of their own lives in such texts.[18]

The personal library of a rank-and-file, semiskilled worker in the Pullman Company's Chicago shops provides a fascinating glimpse into a worker's intellectual life. John Edwin Peterson collected more than three hundred books in his lifetime (1884–1949). His purchases, usually at IWW headquarters or radical bookstores in Chicago, corresponded rather closely with his political activities. Peterson seemed to purchase more books and read more during periods of intense organizing and struggle, fewer during periods of repression and defeat. His purchasing also reflected economic conditions. He acquired the most books under full employment and relatively high wages during World War II, far fewer during a period of unemployment in the mid-twenties. About one-third of his books dealt with Marxism, socialism, and the IWW, but the collection was remarkable for its range of topics. It included classics cited by worker radicals throughout the early twentieth century—Tom Paine's *Common Sense* and Bunyan's *Pilgrim's Progress*, for example, but also a great deal of contemporary fiction, especially authors reflecting a critical view of American society—Dos Passos, Steinbeck, Sinclair Lewis. The yearning for self-education was reflected in the purchase of multivolume encyclopedias and atlases, as well as in books on the natural sciences, philosophy, history, law, and economics. He acquired a number of books on feminism, birth control, and sexuality, and he showed a marked interest in Darwin. Peterson was an internationalist, not only in political perspective, but also in his reading. He read on the Soviet Union but also on China, Mexico, and a range of European societies.[19]

To some extent, such ubiquitous reading should not be surprising, though it has certainly remained obscure in the eyes of most historians. On the one hand, most working-class people in the early twentieth century left school early. On the other, most had at least some elementary schooling and might well have been interested enough to seek out sources for continued learning. They were also highly literate; even most immigrant workers could read in their own languages, if not in English.[20] Books were important, it seems, to the working-class reader; they occupy an important place in many workers' autobiographies, with authors remembering precisely which books they read and when they read them.

It would be ironic if, in calling attention to elements of sophistication in the hobo's life, we managed to romanticize a lifestyle that was often degraded and dangerous. The mobility for which the hobo was known was often simply flight from unemployment and a search for work. Most hobos were essentially labor migrants moving with the change of seasons between railroad and other construction work in the spring and summer; following the wheat harvest in the late summer and fall; cutting ice, lumbering, working briefly in a factory, or simply laying by in a "flophouse" in Chicago or another casual labor center for the winter. In the process, a hobo often risked his or her life on moving freight cars. Between 1901 and 1905 alone, nearly 25,000 railroad "trespassers" died on the nation's trains. They were pursued by police and railroad detectives, hungry and sick, sometimes victimized by sexual predators and "yeggs," the small core of criminal itinerants often shunned by the settled population.[21] Yet such travel brought engagement with a broad range of characters, regional and ethnic cultures, and a kind of practical traveler's knowledge—a knowledge not only of the various railroads, but also the nation's big cities and smaller towns, and more importantly, a broader range of people than if the hobo had instead remained in one place.

The phenomenon of the well-read hobo was not a coincidence. Many of the characters they encountered were people who had consciously rejected the values of the mainstream culture, and some were radicals. The IWW in particular built a whole organizational culture around the itinerant worker, his daily routine and habits, his grievances and dreams, his values and prejudices. We know that the IWW thrived amid these itinerant workers, but we have usually thought about the movement in organizational terms. In fact, with cheap printing, a hobo would have found both the city and the road awash in texts. The literature and music of the IWW has long been considered part of a radical culture of the "dispossessed," but it is only more recently, with the work of Toby Higbie, that we have begun to think about this world as a kind of working-class intellectualism. Such learning came not only in boxcars, but through a striking array of blue-collar venues. Higbie writes, "American working people ... pieced together their education through personal experience, reading, political organizing, public lectures, and discussions with others." He invokes the spaces in which such learning might take place—"workplaces, union libraries, street speaking venues, even boxcars, bunkhouses, and park benches."[22]

Wanderlust was also as much a part of the hobo's life as the hardships, and it was often what motivated him or her to continue the lifestyle into old age. Extensive travel and exposure to new places and cultures often produced a more expansive view of life. For most hoboes, life on the road was part of the pursuit of work, punctuated by labor that also involved travel—on the railroad, long voyages at sea, or a turn on the docks. In each of these cases, travel brought exposure to diverse working-class cultures throughout the United States and in ports well beyond.

The hobo's was an overwhelmingly homosocial world, though there were, in fact, women hobos who represented a small proportion of the population. Restricted in their options by family life and the expectations of a patriarchal world, women cosmopolitans sought—and found—their intellectual lives in other spaces. Some of these lay in the ethnic cultures that immigrant workers created in the industrial city.[23]

The Immigrant

Few experiences convey the transnational quality of historical change more dramatically than global migration. The movement of millions of immigrants to the United States in the late nineteenth and early twentieth centuries, for example, was clearly molded by economic and social changes that crossed national boundaries, transforming the Old World as well as the New. We understand better now than we once did that the migration process itself was transnational not simply in the sense that people moved between nations, but that they often did so repeatedly and in various directions over the course of a lifetime. It is easier to point to the economic and technological changes that stimulated and facilitated such migration, however—the expansion of international markets, the transformation of skilled trades into unskilled mass production work, the refinement of railroad and steamship travel—than it is to approximate what such transnational migration meant on a human scale.

This experience shaped people who were themselves transnational in a profound sense, embracing cultures and consciousness that were the products of not one but often several different societies that the immigrant encountered in the course of migration and settling into multiethnic societies in the New World. Indeed U.S. immigration historians have probably spent too much time lovingly reconstructing the histories of particular immigrant communities and not enough on what might be termed an "interethnic" approach to their subject that would stress contacts between diverse ethnic groups and the creation of transnational cultures in the very heart of the American industrial city early in the last century.

The labor migrant was in many respects the quintessential American worker of the early twentieth century. She/he lived in two distinct cultures simultaneously, and often displayed cosmopolitan characteristics—multilingualism; an immersion in music, art, literature, and performance; religious belief and everyday cosmologies; transnational experience and perspectives. Often taken for granted in studies of immigrant workers, the juxtaposition of heavy or tedious manual work and active cultural and intellectual lives was often quite remarkable.

Nineteenth-century German working-class culture provides a striking example. This was a more cerebral world than we might envision for a nineteenth-century laboring community, a world of workers who might quote Goethe or Shakespeare as readily as Marx. Theirs was a largely male world of gymnastic and shooting groups, singing and theatrical societies, reading and discussion circles. Several of the Haymarket martyrs were such people, but there were many others who will never make it onto the pages of most history books. These were self-taught freethinkers who were, like the anarchist Adolph Fischer, "exceedingly well read in philosophy, history, literature, and political economy." They spent their days at manual labor and their evenings, often in saloons and Turner halls, reading and debating the issues of the day. Such radicalism—in its various incarnations from the Knights of Labor's capacious labor reformism through the Marxist socialists' electoral campaigning to the anarchists' violent rhetoric of class war—was a way of life for thousands of working people in Milwaukee, Detroit, Chicago, New York, and other cities marked by industrialization: the transformation of work through extreme division of labor and the creation of distinct ethnic communities through massive immigration.[24]

Perhaps the most famous of these radical immigrant cultures sprang from the crucible of New York's Lower East Side in the late nineteenth and early twentieth centuries. The community produced countless writers, poets, artists, actors, and playwrights—creators of all kinds—and it did so amid considerable squalor and deprivation. Middle-class observers like Hutchins Hapgood were often amazed at the cultural and intellectual life they found on the streets there. On the Lower East Side, thousands of people toiled under brutal conditions in the city's sweatshops, then engaged an active life of the mind in its streets. A *New York Times* reporter described what he termed "peripatetic philosophers" who sprouted on the streets of Lower Manhattan along "with the flowers that bloom in the Spring," bringing with them a wide range of issues—Zionism, socialism, anarchism, women's suffrage, drama, literature.[25]

The activity of the Women's Trade Union League and the garment unions meant that many of the soapboxes were mounted by young women eager to share their ideas and engage with others. This culture produced writers like Anzia Yezierska and worker-activists like Fannia Cohen, who devoted her life to workers' education, but also a generation of nameless women workers who wrote poetry and journalism at night after working at their machines in sweatshops during the day.²⁶ Young women of the Lower East Side, Chicago's West Side ghetto, and other Jewish working-class communities quenched their thirst for knowledge at the People's University or in cultural activities at settlement houses, but radical and all kinds of other ideas were easily accessible on city streets. "For who cares, after a hard day's work," the *Times* reporter concluded, "to sit in a close room and listen to a discourse ... and what is more charming than to stroll about in the open air and think high thoughts in good company.... The rich man has his clubs ... the clubless poor man has the streets."²⁷ Both the radicalism and the learning carried over into the International Ladies' Garment Workers' Union and the Amalgamated Clothing Workers of America, where vibrant Yiddish cultures thrived and a host of reading groups and workers' education initiatives maintained these traditions through the 1930s. As the industry's demographics changed, Jewish women activists brought this intellectual work to a new generation of black and Puerto Rican women.²⁸

Like their Jewish counterparts, Italian American socialists and anarchists were well connected to transnational movements, but they also created vibrant radical subcultures in American cities and smaller industrial and mining towns throughout the United States. As in the larger cities, women in coal mining towns carried a good deal of the organizational burden as well as the responsibility for the reproduction of radical ideas across the generations. They literally came to terms with life and work in industrial America through their radical movements, and in the process they helped to create oppositional and alternative urban cultures. In New York, Chicago, and San Francisco, but also in Paterson, New Jersey; Ybor City, Florida, where *lectores* read to the Cuban and Spanish cigar workers as they rolled; and in little Spring Valley, Illinois, a regular stop on Emma Goldman's speaking tours, highly literate radical working-class thought and culture blossomed.²⁹

Such communities were early sites of what the anthropologist Arjun Appadurai calls the "global production of locality." They developed very distinct, even combative neighborhood identities and cultures, and were not only populated by, but often deeply shaped by the vast migrations of diverse peoples that transformed American cities between the late nineteenth century and the early 1920s. The Lower East Side might be remembered as a monolithic Jewish neighborhood, but Jews themselves, drawn from numerous societies throughout Russia and Eastern Europe, were diverse in many respects, often speaking several different languages as well as a common Yiddish in order to cope. They also shared their streets and public transportation and recreational spaces with Italians, Irish, Germans, and many others. Ybor

City's Cuban cigar makers shared their workplaces and engaging neighborhoods with Spanish, Italian, and other radical workers, forming a hybrid Latin working-class culture.[30] Likewise, Harlem and Chicago's Bronzeville, perhaps the two most important locations for black working-class politics and cultural production, drew together "northern blacks" with recent southern migrants and a range of Caribbean and some second-generation European immigrants. These were cosmopolitan urban worlds in the fullest sense of the term.

The Well-Read Sailor

Herman Melville was neither the first nor the last sailor to spend a great deal of his seagoing time with a book before him. The phenomenon of sailors as readers and the significance of ships' libraries were both apparent in the eighteenth century, and they remained a constant on both merchant and navy vessels throughout the nineteenth century and well into the twentieth. Most naval and many commercial ships maintained small libraries, and sailors exchanged the few books they had carried on board. Even when they sailed without organized libraries, they read. William Z. Foster discovered few worthwhile books and no real libraries aboard the four deep-water sailing ships he served on between 1901 and 1904, but he found his shipmates generally well read. Although he had never progressed beyond third grade, Foster himself picked up the habit early in life and spent much of his free time below deck reading, finishing Hugo's *Les Misérables* while rounding the Cape of Good Hope. Charles Rubin ran into quite a good ship's library on a voyage to Australia. Many of the sailors read magazines or westerns, but Rubin and others read Dickens, Hugo, and Dostoevsky. He claimed never to have read a book before this voyage, but once back in New York, he eagerly scooped them up by the dozen.[31]

Bill Bailey, who grew up in Manhattan's Hell's Kitchen and shipped out on merchant vessels at the age of fourteen, found that "the American seaman is an avid reader. Most of his off-duty time was spent reading." In addition to a small ship's library, books were often tucked into sailors' bunks. Very different sorts of literature might compete for the sailor's attention. In the early thirties, when Bailey tried to interest his mates in the radical literature of the Marine Workers' Industrial Union, he found there was simply too much competition romances, adventure stories, religious tracts. He and a friend solved the problem by collecting all the books they could find and heaving them out a large porthole. With little to distract them, the seamen soon took up the radical newspapers and pamphlets.[32]

As important as reading was aboard ship, it was not the only way to absorb ideas. Sailors might read aloud to one another so that the illiterate among them might still engage new values and ideas. Likewise, the frequent telling of what Rediker calls the "sailor's yarn," stories that conveyed a wide range of experiences, represented a vital dimension of a shared oral tradition.

Diversity itself, and an appreciation for it, are often taken as markers of cosmopolitanism. In the case of sailors, and perhaps more generally among immigrants living in diverse neighborhoods, a "competence"—"a personal ability to make one's way into other cultures, through listening, looking, intuiting, and reflecting"—was an essential.[33] As trade routes became more expansive and complicated by the late nineteenth century, the "motley crew" that Peter Linebaugh and Marcus Rediker found on eighteenth-century ships became even more diverse.[34] A late nineteenth- or early twentieth-century sailor was apt to encounter peers from a bewildering array of nations. Older Irish, Scandinavian, and British predominated, but African American, black West Indians, and even Puerto Rican sailors were common. Depending on the size of the ship, this could mean considerable ethnic and racial mixture in rather confined quarters or, on larger ships, a series of on-board ethnic niches. Though there were few hard and fast divisions even on larger ships, Scandinavian, British, and native-born white American sailors tended to be on deck, black and Asian workers in the mess and other serving positions, and the Irish in the "black crew" of the engine room, stoking and maintaining the machinery that drove the ship. Conflict across ethnic lines was not unusual, but unlike a large factory, it was difficult to maintain strict ethnic segregation on board even a larger ship, and impossible on many of the smaller ships where sailors made their livelihoods.

The sailor's radicalism derived from his daily experience as well as his reading, and this raises the old question of the sources for political and other ideas. It was not always a matter of reading, as complex ideas might be absorbed more easily through concrete experiences. Perhaps even more than among industrial workers in a factory, some experiences drove sailors together across ethnic and racial lines—particularly bad work conditions up to and even after the period of World War II—long hours, rotten food, unsanitary conditions, unusually tight and sometimes brutal forms of labor discipline and control, and a stark division between officers and crew reinforced by separate eating, rest, and even toilet facilities. Summing up the reasons for the poor living and working conditions aboard early twentieth-century commercial vessels, a Royal Navy fleet surgeon concluded, "The truth was that ship owners took no interest in their men."[35] With a considerable number of Wobbly and other radical sailors always prepared to argue for a shared class identity and action across ethnic lines, the motley crew was often more cohesive than a comparable group of workers might have been in a different setting.

For all of its problems, the sailor's life also held strong attractions. "Spending many months at a time on its broad bosom," William Z. Foster recalled of his shipmates, "they grew insensibly to love the sea, which profoundly shaped their psychology and their whole outlook on life." Most sailors took pride in their skills and respected those of their shipmates. The lengthy time in close quarters on board ship meant that sailors talked constantly, often developing "the warmest relationships." When they were not reading, they spent their leisure time in collective pursuits—singing, cards or cribbage, swimming, and boxing.[36] One can only imagine the reactions of a young person transplanted from the slums and factories of New York or Philadelphia to exotic ports of call around the globe.

As Foster's and other sailors' stories suggest, and as Leon Fink has noted in his work, "sea labor functioned through the decades (and indeed centuries) not only as a forum for interethnic and interracial contact but also as a conveyor belt for political radicalism." In the United States, socialists, IWWs, and eventually communist militants all thrived aboard ship. And, as Fink notes, although racial and ethnic mixture on board could lead to conflict, the diversity of the sailors who manned these ships often reinforced whatever international class solidarity might have derived from the transnational travel. Just as historians Peter Linebaugh and Marcus Rediker tracked the "hidden history of the Revolutionary Atlantic" for an earlier era, one could certainly extend their narrative (though that is not the task here) of oceanic rebellion through the early twentieth century. "In and of themselves," Fink concludes, "seafaring occupations offered some degree of political and personal openings whatever the formal policies of employer, nation, or even trade union dictated."[37] Indeed, what is striking in many of the sailors' narratives is that adherence to radicalism often came less through reading per se and more through personal relationships and interaction with politically experienced sailors.

Having grown up in the early twentieth century in a Brooklyn immigrant neighborhood, Charles Rubin's world began to expand when he joined the U.S. Navy just after World War I. Though Rubin eventually read Marxism and became active in the Communist Party USA, his earliest understanding of global politics came through direct observation and conversations with those from other nations in the course of broad travel. Before encountering the concept of imperialism from reading Lenin, Rubin observed the system at work in the ports of China during the 1920s. A boxer of some talent, he came across the sport in ports as diverse as Manila and Baltimore. His political education came through conversations with an older Irish American seaman who pointed out the parallels between the social structure of the ship and that of capitalist societies, the fighting between seamen from various ethnic backgrounds and the ethnic divisions among American workers generally, the need for working-class solidarity aboard ship and in capitalist societies around the world. When Rubin was temporarily stranded in an Italian port in 1923, local longshoremen explained the rise of fascism there and what it was likely to mean for the world's workers. In the Crimea he encountered Russian communist sailors, and in Buenos Aires, demonstrations against the executions of Sacco and Vanzetti, whose names he had never heard in the United States. A voyage to Africa exemplified the racial dimensions of imperialism.[38]

A sailor, hobo, or radical woman worker might also transgress the "normal" in the realm of sexuality. On the one hand, engagement with anarchist or communist subcultures often brought an opportunity for free love, or what the bohemians called "varietism." At a time when monogamy was the norm, radicals might take a number of lovers. Certainly, Hutchins Hapgood's evocation of Chicago's bohemian working-class anarchist culture and the memoirs of numerous radicals are littered with recollections of diverse sexual experiences. Likewise, life on a ship, in prison, or simply engagement with bohemian lifestyles introduced the possibility for homosexual experience. While such experimentation was likely rare in Catholic and Orthodox Jewish cultures, the existence of both free love and homosexual activity suggests that the line between the bohemian intellectual and radical working-class cultures might have been more permeable than we often assume.[39]

The Pullman Porter

While railroaders as a group were unusually well traveled, the Pullman Porter occupied a unique position within the railroad trades, and certainly in the African American community. His mobility and status might have been envied by many black workers, yet his daily experience and very identity were shaped by the constant reality of racism on board the train, in ports of call, and in the society at large. As the black academics Spero and Harris noted, "To the general public, the Pullman Porter is above all a Negro. He is in fact the only contact which thousands of white persons will have with the race."[40]

He was an important cosmopolitan within the black community, yet his social situation remained ambiguous.

Journalist Murray Kempton cautioned us against viewing the porters as a kind of elite. In fact, they were hemmed in at every turn by white supremacy, confined most of their working day to a subservient position in relation to the whites who rode their cars.

> They were grown men without formal education, with no obvious talent, and with no access upward.... The Pullman porter in those days [1920s] had a certain stature among Negroes as a cosmopolite, because he lived so much of his life among white persons of substance, a fortunate auxiliary to a great world so far from the lives of most Negroes. The Pullman porter's presumed superiority was one compensation for the $27.50 a month wage at which Thomas Patterson (a Brotherhood organizer) began in the system. But it was the smallest of compensations. To respond automatically to the generic call for "George" was after all a confession that you had no identity as an individual.[41]

Kempton is not entirely correct. Some of the porters, facing employment discrimination, were actually well educated, and there is no doubt that they represented a kind of sophisticated stratum within the black community. "[P]orters enjoyed an envied lifestyle," historian William Harris notes. "Many people looked upon them as cosmopolites and believed that their constant travels made them somehow important figures. Porters went daily to places that most blacks merely heard of, and their conversations about these 'exotic' spots stirred the imaginations of those not fortunate enough to be on the road. In a sense, porters were folk heroes in the black community, as well as pillars of black society."[42] Something of the porters' status and the upper reaches of the African American social structure they represented are suggested by the death of Theodore Seldon. Killed when his train left the tracks at high speed, Seldon's body was so mangled that he had to be identified on the basis of his ring—Phi Beta Kappa from Dartmouth College. If the porters were "servants on wheels," they were unusual servants.[43]

Required to appear at all times in their spotless uniforms and impeccably shined shoes, Pullman porters stood out in a crowd. While such standards undoubtedly placed a burden on the porter and his family, they could also be sources of distinction and pride. Pullman porters contrasted in appearance, and perhaps also in deportment within their communities, which were populated largely by domestics and laborers. More importantly, they connected black neighbors, who were often confined to local spaces by poverty and the demands of their own work, with the outside world. This was true not only symbolically but sometimes quite literally. "On the road," Beth Bates writes, "Pullman porters connected rural African Americans with news from urban areas. Black youth, in particular, looked up to them as agents of exotic ideas from faraway places, like New York, Chicago, and Los Angeles."[44] Edgar Daniel Nixon, a retired porter and civil rights activist, recalled that "Everybody listened because they knowed [sic] the porter been everywhere and they never been anywhere themselves."[45] The young Malcom X saw a dining car job as an opportunity to get to Harlem, where he would find the jazz and nightlife he had heard so much about back in Lansing, Michigan, and Roxbury, Massachusetts.[46]

Moving back and forth between northern cities and between the South and the urban North, the porters became urban cultural emissaries in the wake of the First Great Migration. While acoustic forms of Delta blues moved north along with the migrants on the Illinois Central and other lines, the porters often brought urban blues—Bessie Smith and Ma Rainey—back in the opposite direction to rural southern communities. "The market [for blues records] was definitely there, waiting to be tapped," the great W. C. Handy recalled. "In Clarence Williams' place and in Thomas' Music Store in Chicago I had seen cooks and Pullman porters buying a dozen or two dozen records at one time... [the] blues—always blues."[47] "Pullman porters bought them by the dozens at a dollar per copy," blues artist Perry Bradford observed, "and sold them in rural districts for two dollars."[48] Thus, the porters played a vital role in the spread of a distinctive American musical form embraced not only by African Americans, but eventually by millions of urban whites.

But the porters carried with them more than blues records and gossip. Before the advent of mass communications in the poorest rural communities, the porter literally brought the news: "In cafes where they ate or hotels where they stayed, they'd bring in the papers they picked up, white papers, Negro papers," Edgar Nixon recalled. "He'd put 'em in his locker and distribute 'em to black communities all over the country. Along the road, where a whole lot of people couldn't get to town, we used to roll up the papers and tie a string around 'em. We'd throw these papers off to these people. We were able to let people know what was happening."[49] In other ways as well, porters who had migrated to northern cities conveyed vital information back to southern communities and encouraged continuing migration and the formation of large communities up north.

At the least, the porter dealt constantly with individuals from a wide range of locations and backgrounds, and his tips depended upon his knowledge and his ability to negotiate conversations with this diverse white clientele. In this sense, they operated in two quite distinct worlds and developed a talent for moving between the two. "The Pullman porter had to be a trickster to survive," Santino writes, "the better the tricks, the stronger the survival. . . . Ernest Ford says he would prepare for certain trips by researching the areas. He went so far as to learn some French for his trips to Montreal, so he might tell a Canadian passenger that he was a French-speaking Creole from Louisiana, thus fascinating the passenger to no end and ensuring a healthy gratuity." The intimacy of the Pullman car also meant that the porter witnessed at close range the habits and foibles of the white elite, even fine distinctions on the basis of social class, an opportunity afforded regularly to black women as domestics, but seldom to black males.[50]

Like sailors and other groups of workers on the move, the porters spent considerable time together on layovers, often in shared hotel rooms and flats or in dormitory-style accommodations provided by the company, playing cards and trading stories. The bonding that took place on and off the trains can only be guessed, but there is no doubt that the occupation and its peculiarities strengthened it. Between trips, they found themselves drawn from large cities and smaller black communities throughout the nation. In the course of card games, baseball games, singing, and other frivolity, they absorbed information about these diverse black cultures. Based on his extensive interviews with retired porters, Jack Santino concludes: "Porters faced dualities every day. It was a good job and a bad job; they were hosts and they were servants; they had the highest status in their communities and the lowest on the train."[51] It is this bifurcated existence that might help to explain the porters' turn toward labor organization.

This social solidarity in ports of call and the long conversations during down times on-train served the porters well as their conditions began to decline and they turned toward unionization in the 1920s—the Brotherhood of Sleeping Car Porters, which became the nation's most important black labor organization. The Brotherhoood's literate publication, *The Messenger*, edited by socialist A. Philip Randolph, contained fiction, poetry, and theater reviews, as well as news of the labor movement and the situation of the porters and black workers generally. The Brotherhood's story has been well told, but the porters' role in winning the black community to a strategy of mass organization and protest is less understood. As Beth Bates has shown, the Brotherhood produced many of the most important black protest leaders in a new generation and helped to convert early civil rights organizations like the NAACP from supplicants appealing to white liberals and philanthropists to more militant protest organizations.[52]

The Radical

Overlapping many of these occupational categories was the "militant minority"—those activists who not only did the organizing but also created rich radical cultures in the heart of the working-class community. International socialism, anarchism, and communism were, of course, transnational in their organizational forms as well as their visions for the future. Mobilizing in the interests of international proletarian solidarity, such movements at their best challenged not only imperialism and colonialism but also the racial, ethnic, religious, and gender barriers dividing people from one another. They sought to speak in the name of a universal humanity and brought a message of international revolution to the local community and factory. In all this, they might be seen as the ultimate form of working-class cosmopolitanism.[53]

The international socialist ideal was always in tension, of course, with both ethnic nationalism and often with one's ethnic identity in the context of diverse American working-class communities. One result was the formation of fairly distinct ethnic working-class cultures based in the various immigrant communities. Yet there were many situations in which workers from diverse ethnic backgrounds came together in ethnically mixed, hybrid socialist and syndicalist movements. This was particularly true during the first two decades of the twentieth century, when immigration and its effects were at a high point. Mass strikes rocked cities and industrial towns throughout the country during the second and third decades of the twentieth century, and these movements suggest a kind of cosmopolitanism, with workers finding a language and symbolism that might provide the basis for broader identities. One center of such activity was Lawrence, Massachusetts, where an earlier generation of British and Irish workers had largely given way to Poles, Lithuanians, Italians, and Russian and Eastern European Jews. The jumble of ethnic, national, and international solidarities displayed in such strikes, which suggest the complexity of immigrant workers' mentalities, is conveyed in David Montgomery's observation that immigrant strikers could often be seen arranged by ethnic group, marching behind the American flag and singing the *Internationale*.[54]

It is a scene relived over and over in dozens of working-class autobiographies: A workmate, usually an older person, often from the subject's own ethnic community introduces the immigrant novice to radical literature and ideas and, in the process, to a radically different perspective on their new society. For the Croatian immigrant Stjepan Mesaros (later Steve Nelson), it was a Serbian vegetarian and atheist member of the Serbo-Croatian branch of the Socialist Labor Party who explained the functioning of the factory and the economic system, the varieties of workers' organizations, and the pervasive racism Nelson saw about him.[55] For John Wiite, a Finnish railroad laborer and lumber worker, the mentor was another, more experienced Finn, Victor Staudinger, who shared his subscription to *Tyomies*, the Finnish socialist paper. "This was the beginning of the transformation of my life," Wiite recalled. "No longer was I to spend my free time in saloons. Instead I was beginning to think about social, political, and economic matters, and self-education of myself on the problems of the working people."[56]

The radical cultures that produced such acculturation represented a remarkable range in terms of both ideology and ethnicity—Finnish freethinkers, Wobblies, and communists on the Minnesota iron range; Italian- and Yiddish-speaking anarchists in big-city enclaves in New York and Chicago; Spanish-speaking radicals in smaller manufacturing centers like Ybor City in Tampa; and immigrant coal and metal miners in isolated company towns throughout the West and Midwest. What did working-class radicalism mean at the level of individual experience?

Vivian Gornick, who grew up in a Jewish communist family in the forties in the Bronx, describes the cosmopolitan character of her family's outlook: Her father worked for thirty years in a garment factory pressing dresses, but he and her mother lived for the intellectual world they built around the Communist Party. "Before I knew I was Jewish or a girl I knew that I was a member of the working class." Her father was "Labor," her uncles who owned the factory, "Capital." "We" were the working-class socialists she met around her parents' kitchen table, and everyone else was "them." "Oh, the talk! That passionate, transforming talk! Something important was happening here, I always felt, something that had to do with understanding things. And 'to understand things,' I already knew, was the most important, most exciting thing in life." "Ideas, dolly, ideas," her Yiddish teacher Rouben told Vivian, "Without them life is nothing. With them, life is *everything*."[57]

She asked her mother who these people were: "My mother would reply in Yiddish: 'He is a writer. She is a poet. He is a thinker.' ... He, of course, drove a bakery truck. She was a sewing machine operator. That other one over there was a plumber, and the one next to him stood pressing dresses all day next to my father. So powerful was the life inside their minds ... these people ceased to be what they objectively were—immigrant Jews, disfranchised workers—and, indeed they became thinkers, writers, poets."[58]

> Every one of them read the *Daily Worker*, the *Freiheit*, and the *New York Times* religiously every morning. Every one of them had an opinion on what he or she read.... That river of words was continually flowing.... They were voyagers on that river, these plumbers, pressers and sewing machine operators.... They took with them on this voyage not only their own narrow, impoverished experience but a set of abstractions as well, abstractions with the power to transform.... They were not simply the disinherited of the earth, they were proletarians. They were not people without a history, they had the Russian Revolution. They were not without a civilizing world view, they had Marxism.[59]

Living in a Bronx cooperative apartment building, working in a garment factory every day, Gornick's friends and family nevertheless felt themselves connected to other workers throughout the world. "The people in that kitchen had remade the family in the image of workers all over the world.... They sat at that kitchen table and they felt themselves linked up to America, Russia, Europe and the world."[60] She evokes the life of the mind that unfolded each day around her family's kitchen table, fueled by the Yiddish and English-language party press, political meetings and demonstrations, debates among family and friends.

In a very different sort of neighborhood halfway across the continent, Richard Wright witnessed a similar connection in the midst of a very different culture, between the intimate world of everyday exploitation, in this case of black workers, and the worldwide revolution. The meeting was a trial of a black party leader accused of various infractions, but it did not start with these accusations. Rather, a series of speakers evoked the political world at its various levels: The party's central committee described the worldwide crisis and the threat of fascism. The next speaker described the historic role of the Soviet Union.

> Finally, a speaker came forward and spoke of Chicago's South Side, its Negro population, their suffering and handicaps, linking all that also to the world struggle. Then still another speaker followed and described the tasks of the Communist Party on the South Side. At last

the world, the national, and the local pictures had been fused into one overwhelming drama of moral struggle in which everyone in the hall was participating.... With the exception of the Church with its myths and legends, there was no agency in the world so capable of making men feel the earth and the people upon it as the Communist Party.[61]

For understandable reasons, communist history is normally considered in organizational terms, and its formulaic view of the world seems to tell us all we need to know, but the personal experiences of individual militants testify to the transformation in perspective that occurred in their lives. Through the Communist Party and other radical groups, workers with very limited educations learned public speaking and began to read more broadly. A coal miner or a sharecropper might leave the Anthracite Region or rural Alabama for training or other assignment in the Soviet Union, parts of Europe, or Asia. For many, party publications, schools, and reading groups opened entirely new vantage points that were global by definition. Working-class radicals considered their own problems in relation to workers around the world, and saw their own efforts as part of a global movement. Often isolated from mainstream middle-class culture, especially in periods of political repression, militants constructed an alternative culture. Children were socialized in such radical cosmopolitan cultures, attending summer camps and reading stories and books designed to reproduce those cultures and worldviews.[62]

The sources and situations of black working-class thinkers were different. Robin Kelley offers a particularly compelling case in his study of black tenant farmers and a communist sharecroppers' union they built amid the everyday racial violence of rural Alabama during the Great Depression. Black farmers, isolated, semi-literate, and under constant threat, came to identify their own struggles with those of the Soviet Union and other workers' movements around the world, though they often expressed these feelings of solidarity through the language and symbolism of Pentecostal Christianity.[63]

For black workers, migration to the big city often brought an enormous expansion of one's perspective, range of contacts, and ideas. The civil rights militant Ella Baker grew up poor in Jim Crow Norfolk, Virginia, and rural North Carolina. Though her parents owned their own farm and Ella excelled in high school and at Shaw University, her grandparents had been slaves. Her father's work as a waiter on a steamer involved extensive travel. Both he and his wife, a pillar in the community's Baptist church, graduated from high school and nurtured a love of education in their children. From an educated, upwardly mobile family, Ella turned her face toward the black working class and spent her life as a grassroots organizer, first for the NAACP and later for the Student Non-Violent Coordinating Committee and the Mississippi Freedom Democratic Party. She located the roots of her activism in her mother's religion and aspirations for racial uplift, but the turning point in her life came through library reading, lectures, and informal discussion in that seat of black urban cosmopolitan life, Harlem of the 1920s and 1930s, which she termed a "hotbed of radical thinking."[64]

Is this idea of a blue-collar cosmopolitanism a recognizable phenomenon? If so, how do we go about investigating the problem? How common were such cosmopolitan experiences, and what were their implications for what we call working-class consciousness and political radicalism? Other venues seem relevant. Military service often brought young working-class men into contact with peers from throughout the United States, took them to distant lands, and exposed them to new cultures and ideas. Despite the fact that it often served as the focus of local urban cultures, religion might also suggest one's place in the broader world or a connection with co-religionists in other societies. Although working-class reading habits deserve more research, it seems likely that working people were more literate—in English, their home language, or both—than we have supposed. Universal free public education certainly contributed to this, and as child labor and compulsory school attendance laws took hold in the course of the early twentieth century, more workers realized such educations. The frequent discussions of books and reading in autobiographies and the extensive publications produced by and aimed at working-class people are clues that such a readership was quite broad. Reading during the high tide of industrialization and mass immigration built on earlier nineteenth-century working-class reading traditions, but the working-class print culture grew enormously in the late nineteenth and early twentieth centuries. Immigrants without a command of English had ready access to foreign-language newspapers, pamphlets, and books reflecting a wide range of ideological perspectives.[65]

The most serious readers may have been motivated by a strong ethic of self-improvement derived not only from particular ethnic cultures, but also from free thought, labor, and socialist milieus. For the radicals, perhaps, it was a matter of improving and strengthening oneself for the struggle against the class enemy, but even for more typical workers, there was always the notion that education, often self-education, was something "they" could never take away from you. The turn of the century brought a dramatic expansion of the black press amid Jim Crow repression, and many black workers brought a special perspective of racial uplift to their reading in Marcus

Garvey's and other movements stressing the elevation of the race.[66] Not all workers were avid readers, of course, but for those who were, reading opened new ideas and new possibilities—for broader experience through travel and, of course, more reading. Some signed up for what we would term "adult education" courses offered through public school evening programs, settlement houses, trade unions, or political groups. Others simply continued to read on their own. And we likely underestimate the degree of engagement with ideas out in the streets and at work.

Work could reinforce cosmopolitan perspectives. Consider, for example, longshore workers and sailors who labored at the interstices of vast imperial systems in ethnically diverse ports connected to other cities throughout the world; or the sense of power that railroad workers derived from piloting huge trains over vast expanses of the continent. Jobs that involved extensive travel brought the lowly sailor or Pullman porter into contact with more diverse cultures than the typical middle-class person might have experienced.

Migration itself, so common to working-class life, not only brought workers into new labor markets and cultures but also into contact with new ideas. The broad abstractions they might have encountered in politics, economics, and human relations came alive through their encounters with such new places and people. In their travels, worker-migrants saw these ideas emerge in the experience of those around them. As we reconstruct the lives of common people, it is essential to our understanding of them to recognize that many of them were quite cosmopolitan in their own ways.

CHAPTER FIVE

The Bohemian Writer and the Radical Woodworker
A Study in Class Relations

I don't know that people who are professional thinkers or philosophers or students do all the thinking; perhaps other people who are at work have an opportunity to think that the others have not got. —ANTON JOHANNSEN, WORKING-CLASS ANARCHIST, 1905

On a late spring day in 1905, Hutchins Hapgood walked into the saloon in the Briggs House Hotel, a hangout for Chicago labor activists. He was looking for someone he had never met, only imagined. "Before I went to Chicago, I had in mind what I wanted to find," he later recalled. "I felt certain that, somewhere in that turbulent world of labor, there must be a man who stood at the center of all the converging elements and who was at least dimly conscious of the development of a labor philosophy. I felt certain I would recognize him if I came into contact with him."[1] He found that person in Anton Johannsen.

This unlikely pair produced a most remarkable book, *The Spirit of Labor* (1907), a mixture of a worker's personal narrative with a study of the radical labor movement at its most developed and volatile, in early twentieth-century Chicago, though the book's voice is most often that of Hapgood.

Here I consider this rare personal relationship between two very different men from two very different backgrounds, their motivations in the project, and the broader context of class conflict which shaped their collaboration, along with some of the elements of working-class life in early twentieth century Chicago that Hapgood missed in his evocation of radical labor, and what might be viewed as a kind of "working-class modernism."

Hutchins and Anton

The two men inhabited very different worlds at the beginning of the twentieth century. Born in Chicago in 1867 and raised in the Mississippi River town of Alton, Illinois, Hapgood traced his family back two centuries to the Massachusetts Puritans. His father, a progressive businessman educated at Brown, was the first in the family to have left Petersham, Massachusetts, in many generations. With ancestors on both sides in the American Revolution, one a Tory and the other a revolutionary who served in the Continental and U.S. Congresses, Hutchins Hapgood could hardly have been more deeply rooted in American myths and traditions. He graduated Phi Beta Kappa near the top of his class at Harvard. At a time when a small minority of Americans went to high school, Hapgood went on for a master's degree and then taught English at Harvard and the University of Chicago. His subsequent life, one of literature and leisure, was spent in travel around the world or settled in Greenwich Village, Dobbs Ferry, New York, Tuscany, Provincetown, or Key West.[2]

His brothers were equally remarkable. William Powers Hapgood (1872–1960) launched the Columbia Conserve Company, a cooperative factory and experiment in industrial democracy that featured a workers' council and profit-sharing, and dedicated his life to a range of reform causes. Norman Hapgood (1868–1937) built a successful career as a progressive journalist and served as ambassador to Denmark.[3] A nephew, Powers Hapgood (1899–1949), worked for many years as a miner and joined the Socialist Party after graduating from Harvard. He went on to be an important organizer for the United Mine Workers of America and the Amalgamated Clothing Workers of America, and a leader of the Congress of Industrial Organizations (CIO) in the late 1930s and 1940s.[4]

Raised in this environment, Hutchins Hapgood became that rare bird—a well-educated WASP elite who questioned not only his own privilege but the system on which it rested. "I am helped by a whole set or system of circumstances which have nothing to do with my individual value," he wrote his friend Mabel Dodge Luhan. "It is unjust that I should have so many privileges."

In his writing and in his personal life, Hapgood looked toward a new kind of society based more on human worth than personal privilege. For a generation he remained at the center of radical intellectual life in the United States. A key figure in both Mabel Dodge's Greenwich Village salon and in the Provincetown Players, a radical group at the very cutting edge of modern theater, he was a close friend and collaborator of playwrights Eugene O'Neill and Susan Glaspell; writers Floyd Dell, Theodore Dreiser, Sinclair Lewis, Upton Sinclair, and Sherwood Anderson; artists Alfred Stieglitz and Georgia O'Keefe; and journalists John Reed, Louise Bryant, Lincoln Steffens, Anna Strunsky Walling, and Walter Lippmann.[5]

Like so many turn-of-the-century workers, Anton Johannsen was an immigrant. His father, a roofer with little education, fled the rural poverty of Germany for the small-town poverty of Clinton, Iowa, where he first worked as a brewery teamster and then prospered briefly as a saloon keeper. With little formal education, Anton left school early and went to work in a brick and, later, a window sash and door factory. He left town on a boxcar at the age of eighteen and educated himself while tramping around the country and working at a variety of jobs. It was this travel and the people he met while traveling that provided him with what might be called a "blue-collar cosmopolitanism"—a new world of ideas and a tolerance of, even an interest in, that which was different, new. A literate hobo "intellectual," Anton's "first real friend," introduced him to socialism as well as the social structure and culture of the open road. He met Greenhill, a follower of freethinker Robert Ingersoll, in an Iowa furniture factory. The old man lent him copies the *The Truth Seeker* and Tom Paine's *The Rights of Man*, which Anton read many times over and aloud to his wife, at the time a devout Lutheran. Both became skeptics, atheists, and freethinkers.[6]

In this at least, his cosmopolitan attitudes actually paralleled Hapgood's, though the men developed their values and ideas in very different settings. "Life on the road," Anton concluded, "with all its chance meetings with many men and ways of living makes one tolerant of everything except tyranny."[7] At the end of the nineteenth century, he settled down with his wife and children in Chicago, where he earned his living by day in a woodworking shop, led his local union, and became active in the city's labor federation and anarchist circles. Like Hapgood, Anton was driven by his own "spirit of protest," which pressed him to consider some broader context for his own life and those of the working people around him.[8]

While their collaboration on *The Spirit of Labor* might seem strange, by the time they met in Chicago, both men had already made a habit of crossing the kind of social boundaries that separated them. Even in his shop or union meetings, Anton was the cosmopolitan worker, the one likely to bring in an anarchist book or a free thought newspaper, to strike up a conversation about the meaning of life or the need for women's suffrage. His intellectual curiosity, his thirst for ideas drove him beyond his workplace and his union. His days might be spent making window or door frames, but his evenings were likely to include conversations with artists, poets, and influential reformers. Nor were such exchanges simply a matter of the humble worker soaking up ideas from his social betters. What struck Hutchins Hapgood about Chicago, on the contrary, was the degree to which the opposite seemed to be the case, that middle-class and elite people were stimulated by and absorbing ideas from the labor movement. In the university, the settlements, even in business and professional life, Hapgood noted, the details of daily life "show in a hundred implicit ways the degree to which the radical ideas of the common people have affected all grades of society. . . . Most radicals are either working people or else persons who have come in contact with the feelings and ideas evolved by the laboring class, and have come to express them."[9] Surging forward in Chicago and elsewhere at the turn of the century, "the spirit of labor" seemed to pull all else in its wake. For a bright worker like Anton, this situation meant, among other things, considerable contact with middle-class and elite "radicals."

Working-Class Life from Two Vantage Points

Hutchins Hapgood was one of the intellectuals drawn by this spirit. Like some other young writers and artists of his generation, he took his interest in the immigrant worker, the street merchant, and petty criminal "past genteel amusement to a conviction that meetings with social 'others' might not simply entertain but foster more fully realized selves."[10] For Hapgood, this quest for self-realization through contact across the class divide began in 1897 when he took a job as reporter with the *New York Commercial Advertiser*, edited by the soon-to-be-famous muckraker Lincoln Steffens. Journalism was the closest Hapgood ever came to a vocation, and he worked on and off at it for the next two decades. Aiming for a newspaper that was a cut above the common fare, Steffens assembled a group of talented young writers who recognized the human drama at work in the city and rendered it with a literary flair unusual in the mainstream press. The *Advertiser* was lyrical by the newspaper standards of the day. The writers around Hapgood and his brother Norman were drawn by the excitement and beauty they found in city life. They saw "murder as a tragedy rather than a crime," historian Moses Rischin writes, "a fire as a drama rather than police news, pushcart traffic as a vibrant pageant rather than as a nuisance."[11] "Their observations appealed to an inquisitive public who wanted to peek across the 'Social Gulf,'" historian Christine Stansell concludes, "without actually straying into the territory themselves."[12] Over the next two decades Hapgood produced literally hundreds of columns embracing a striking panorama of urban life for various papers in New York and Chicago.

Hapgood was particularly drawn to the Lower East Side, and he produced wonderful columns evoking the community created there by the burgeoning population of poor Russian and Eastern European Jews. His wife Neith Boyce, also a reporter at the *Advertiser*, convinced him to combine these pieces into *The Spirit of the Ghetto* (1902). Never a great success in its day, *Spirit of the Ghetto* now stands as a minor classic of immigrant life. In a pattern he often repeated in his early career, Hapgood was able to penetrate the life of the Lower East Side only with the aid of native collaborators, in this case the socialist editor Abraham Cahan of the Yiddish *Jewish Daily Forward* and the brilliant artist Jacob Epstein, who produced dozens of drawings for the book.[13] After publishing *The Autobiography of a Thief* (1903), Hapgood shared the proceeds from the book with Jim Caulfield, the petty thief whose life provided its substance. He did the same with his next two books involving collaborations across class lines.[14]

The conditions under which Hapgood and Anton produced *The Spirit of Labor* tell us a great deal about both the authors and the book. Hapgood had intended to use Anton's life story to capture the energy and pervasive influence of Chicago's organized working-class movement, to offer someone like Anton as an archetype of the new working-class radical. He had used this autobiographical strategy successfully in *The Autobiography of a Thief*. But quickly he came up against the clear-cut differences between the genres of bourgeois and working-class autobiography. Hapgood had trouble getting Anton to focus on his own story and even getting him slowed down long enough to talk at all. When he did talk, Anton wanted to discuss the union movement, politics, and strikes. Such tendencies were typical of worker autobiographers in many countries, and they suggest the influence of social class on notions of self and identity.

Whereas Hapgood himself and other middle-class intellectuals might place the emphasis on the individual and his or her search for the self, workers' narratives tended to be told very differently. They often subordinated the personal to the social and political, and described themselves as what one scholar has termed "social atoms"—more or less representative pieces of a much larger whole. Particularly with labor radicals, the movement and not the self was the focus of the narrative.[15] There was an individualist anarchism abroad in the early twentieth century, but Anton, an ideological eclectic in any case, was clearly drawn by the ideas of anarcho-communism, which emphasized the social and collective over the self, and social movements over individual acts of terror.

At a more practical level, Anton was far more concerned with his life in the movement and was reluctant to take time away from that for what he tended to view as the bourgeois enterprise of autobiography. "He felt I belonged to another class," Hapgood recalled, "and that my motives were probably profoundly suspect."[16] He absorbed a certain amount from simply visiting with Anton and his family and observing him at large in the city, and he was sometimes able to question Anton at length in meetings at Hapgood's own room. Such meetings were productive, Hapgood wrote his wife from Chicago, but "he is nervous about having to give up many of his trade union meetings. I have many problems connected with him—how to hold him and his interest as well as how to get and use the material." "I can get a good thing from Johannsen," Hapgood concluded in another letter, "if I can keep him up to the work. He is restless, wants to go to his meetings, etc."[17]

For these and other reasons, Hapgood chose a more biographical approach, hoping to place Anton in his element and, in the process, bring some notion of the labor movement to middle-class readers. Although Hapgood's book is essentially a biography, extensive quotations from Johannsen convey something of the thinking of a radical worker. It would be a mistake, however, to assume that these quotations convey Anton's unalloyed worldview. Not only did the interviews, the questions Hapgood asked, and the way he chose to ask them all reflect his own interests and biases, but the words themselves come from Hapgood's notes. These have not survived, but it seems unlikely that they represented a verbatim rendering of Anton's words. None of this reduces the value of *The Spirit of Labor*, but it is worth considering when we ask ourselves what the text represents. The two men worked together on the book, but clearly it was conceived and conceptualized by Hapgood. Thus, what he brought to the book was at least as important as what Johannsen brought to it. Hapgood's choices in constructing the narrative can tell us as much about the world of a radical intellectual as they can about the world of a radical woodworker.

Love and the Working Class

Inspired as much by the personal as the political lives of the workers he encountered in Chicago, Hapgood produced a second book, *An Anarchist Woman* (1909), which told the stories of his friends Terry and Marie Carlin, working-class anarchists who appear at several points in *The Spirit of Labor*.[18] Hapgood's telling of Terry and Marie's love story represented his special interest in the love lives of such proletarian radicals. As Christine Stansell notes, "*The Spirit of Labor* eroticized the subject of labor and the figure of the radical workingman, striking a connection between working-class life and sexual license. Hapgood set out to describe the 'expressiveness' of the American workers and that expressiveness turned out to be, in good measure, a superabundance of sex. The democracy that beckoned across the class line was erotic as well as industrial, a liberalized regime of heterosexual love." Hapgood's account does little to dispel a common confusion about the notion of what has come to be called "free love." A principled position against any legal restraints on individuals' sexual habits, the position had roots in American reform movements of the mid-nineteenth century, though it was more common at the turn of the century among immigrant working-class anarchists. Contrary to popular conceptions about sexual promiscuity, it neither prescribed this nor precluded monogamy. The emphasis was on individual freedom in this and other realms of one's personal life. Free love in this sense became a strong principle among bohemian intellectuals as part of a more general revolt against bourgeois morality. By his own account, Hutchins Hapgood learned the free love ethic from Chicago anarchists; it was a habit he continued to embrace for much of his life.

Working women play a frustratingly minor role in Anton's personal narrative; his was in many ways a man's world. Yet we do get some intriguing glimpses of their lives. How and why were the lives of women radicals different from those of the male workers around them? Radical women like Marie Carlin and Emma Goldman struggled to build not only a new world, but also a new way of life for themselves. In their relations with the men in their lives, as much as in their relations with urban elites, they fought for a place in the world, and they did so outside the mainstream women's rights movement. Trade union activists like Margaret Haley of the Chicago Federation of Teachers demanded their place in the burgeoning labor movement, but their criticisms were not confined to their male labor colleagues. They also demanded that their sisters join this class movement and support male unionists.[19]

The most intriguing female figure in Anton's narrative is his wife, Maggie. A "typical working-class housewife" to middle-class observers, perhaps, Maggie turned out to have her own ideas. Hapgood left little room for her in either *The Spirit of Labor* or *An Anarchist Woman*, perhaps because in her personal life she was what he considered a rather typical wife and mother, perhaps because he was largely blind to her personality. The writer dwelled instead on a number of single female anarchists and their active love lives. Maggie Johannsen, like her husband, was a freethinker and a labor radical. She supported the work of the Women's Trade Union League as time allowed, but caring for a household and children, she lacked the opportunity to engage the outside world as Anton did. In midlife, Maggie realized her lifelong dream of being an artist. She took a course at Chicago's Art Institute and created a series of portraits of women who had contributed to labor and the welfare of working-class families—Jane Addams, Mary McDowell, Mary Dreier Robbins, and others. Any older woman "has the right to develop her talents and interests," she told an interviewer. Her story reminds us of the hidden aspects of the spirit of labor.[20]

The Class War

One problem with *Spirit* is that Hapgood was so absorbed with Anton's and others' personalities that he often failed to establish the broader context required to understand the labor movement, and the particular context was crucial in this case.[21] If, as Christine Stansell suggests, New York was the soul of the intellectual bohemian phenomenon of the early twentieth century, the crucible for literary and intellectual modernism, then Chicago was, as Hapgood recalled in his memoir, "the heart of the radical labor movement in America."[22]

Both social reformers like Jane Addams and writers like Jacob Riis and Hapgood himself were moved by the enormous social distance at the turn of the century between the nation's native middle-class population and the ocean of immigrant poor. Riis addressed this problem in his book *How the Other Half Lives* (1890), Addams founded Hull House (1889) as a kind of beachhead for middle-class culture and values in the heart of Chicago's West Side slums, and Hapgood sought to explain the radical labor movement to middle-class reformers and intellectuals through *The Spirit of Labor*. Nowhere was the social gulf characterizing U.S. cities in this era greater than in Chicago; nowhere were workers more fully organized or more class conscious. Throughout the late nineteenth century, the city's diverse working-class communities had created the strongest and most progressive labor movement in the United States. A series of epic political and industrial conflicts, including both the Haymarket tragedy (1886) and the great Pullman strike (1894), accentuated the social chasm between the immigrant working class and the city's elites. Yet the greatest drama might well have resided not in such dramatic episodes, but rather in the quotidian class war played out in the streets of Chicago and other industrial cities and towns.

We are also introduced to the underground world of the proletarian intellectuals, worker-radicals who sought to transform the world through an anarchism that remained embedded in the lives of Chicago's workers. In the late nineteenth century, the city had produced one of the strongest anarchist labor movements in the world. The background for the Haymarket tragedy of 1886 was a rich subculture of labor radicalism rooted in the city's ethnic communities and ranging from trade unionism and the reformist Knights of Labor to Marxist socialism and the anarchist International Working Peoples Association, a potent force on Chicago's proletarian scene. In the midst of a demonstration during the great May 1886 strike for the eight-hour day, an unknown bomber killed several policemen and workers and touched off a "red scare" aimed at suppressing the city's radical movement. The political repression following this tragedy undoubtedly weakened that movement, but *The Spirit of Labor* shows that it never really died. Much smaller, it was vibrant at the moment of Hapgood's visit. And more than its predecessor, which was strictly a working-class and largely male affair, this turn-of-the-century anarchist movement crossed the boundaries of sex, class, and nationality.

Hapgood missed dimensions of the even more radical wing of the labor movement in *The Spirit of Labor*. The Industrial Workers of the World (IWW), that quintessentially American radical labor organization, was founded in Chicago the very summer he visited. One might have expected him to encounter the IWW, a new revolutionary industrial union organization with considerable anarchist influence in its early years, as he made his way in Chicago's labor circles in the fall of 1905. One founder of the new labor organization, Lucy Parsons, was at the center of anarchist activity in the city. Yet Lucy, the wife of Albert Parsons, the central figure in the Haymarket story, is not even mentioned. She personified whatever link remained between the Haymarket movement and the one Hapgood found in Chicago two decades later. One possible explanation for this gap in the story is the existence of two rather distinct anarchist subcultures, one focused more on the world of unions and strikes, the other focused more on cultural phenomena. In fact, at the moment of his visit, a major controversy split the Chicago movement between a more culturally inclined group that soon left for the Home Colony in Washington State and a more industrially inclined group around Lucy Parsons that continued to work on the city's West Side and to focus on unions, strikes, and working-class politics.

The Best-Organized City in the World

While the 1890s are often considered the pinnacle of class conflict in the United States, the level of union organization and strike activity actually increased in the following decade. In 1903 alone, Chicago unions doubled their membership and launched 251 strikes. By September of that year, the Chicago Federation of Labor boasted more than 243,000 members, over half of the city's labor force, and the breadth of the movement was even more impressive than its size. It embraced not only building tradesmen, railroad workers, and a broad range of unskilled male operatives in heavy industry, but also 35,000 female factory workers, scrub women, waitresses, and four thousand of the city's elementary schoolteachers. The reproduction of class sentiments in the city is suggested by the fact that schoolchildren, prominent in many strike photos of the era, organized their own "skilled pupils unions" and strikes in support of their unionized parents and teachers. Union organization and strikes spread throughout Chicago at the turn of the century as the movement passed from an older generation of German, Irish, and native-born skilled workers to the thousands of unskilled "new immigrants" pouring into the city's mills, foundries, and factories. The *Arbeiterzeitung*, the city's main German-language working-class newspaper, declared the city the "trade union capital of the world."[23]

Chicago's movement reflected a broader growth in the size and ambitions of American labor at the turn of the century. From 1897 to 1904, union membership soared from 447,000 to more than two million. The American Federation of Labor tripled in size between 1900 and 1904, and unions also became far more aggressive. From their typical numbers of 1,000 to 1,300 in the mid-1890s, strikes rose to almost 3,000 in 1901 and nearly 4,000 in 1903, with an increasingly large proportion of these conflicts won by unions.[24]

Chicago was engulfed in severe class conflict at the moment Hapgood set out to capture the essence of American labor radicalism in the spring of 1903. The Chicago Employers' Association had launched an all-out campaign against the unions in a bid to rid the city of this "tyranny" and to run the place "open shop." The key target in this offensive was the powerful teamsters' union, which represented the linchpin in the city's movement for several reasons.

Made up of 35,000 blacks, native-born and immigrant Irish, and workers from a variety of other ethnic backgrounds, they had managed to build an unusually powerful movement, employing their wagons to stop traffic in what came to be termed "street strikes." As historian David Witwer notes, "The nature of the teamsters' trade and the geography of the early-twentieth-century city made non-union vehicles vulnerable." Strikebreakers attempting to navigate congested city streets were attacked by large crowds drawn from the city's densely populated working-class neighborhoods. In return, the teamsters seemed ever-willing to support other groups of workers in sympathy strikes that became endemic in the city around the turn of the century.[25] Doctors at the County Hospital labeled the teamster "the roughest, toughest scrapper of the working classes."[26] The teamsters' power was particularly obnoxious to the city's large merchants. One them predicted in the spring of 1904 a confrontation between Chicago's militant unions and its increasingly class-conscious employers. "Some day," he declared, "the unions and the business community will have to fight it out to see who owns Chicago."[27]

As the economy dipped and unemployment rose in the summer and fall of 1904, the Chicago Employers' Association launched an ambitious (and quite successful) open shop drive. By July of that year, the city was convulsed by ninety-two strikes and lockouts involving 77,000 workers. The net effects were disastrous, particularly in the city's largest factories. Strong organizations of largely unskilled immigrant workers at Illinois Steel, International Harvester, and in the slaughtering plants at the giant Union Stock Yards were completely destroyed. As with the great upsurge at the turn of the century, the decline of the Chicago unions mirrored a national trend. From 1904 on, in the face of a massive and well-coordinated open shop drive, union growth stalled, AFL membership actually dropped briefly, and the numbers of workers involved in strikes declined precipitously, with workers tending to lose an ever-larger proportion of those strikes. While employers had launched an open shop campaign in the city's building industry as early as 1900, the cataclysmic struggle for the Chicago unions came in April 1905 during a massive and violent teamsters' strike. Hapgood did his first round of research in the midst of this dramatic conflict, which highlighted for him and other observers the high degree of class feeling in the city's immigrant working-class communities.[28]

Graham Taylor, a liberal minister and settlement house reformer, was struck by the pervasive and violent class consciousness which he saw all about him.

> It was the disclosure of the intensity and intolerance of class-conscious feeling prevailing not only among those on both sides who were im-

mediately involved in controversy, but as pronouncedly throughout one whole class as the other... our non-union neighbors... became as class-conscious, almost overnight, as were the striking teamsters.... [M]en from the sidewalks, women from the tenement-house windows, and even the little children from the playground, cried with one voice, "Down with the scabs," some of them hurling any missile at hand at the frightened drivers.... [T]he "solidarity of labor" extends beyond the membership of unions.... [O]n occasion the class-conscious spirit emerges from the whole working class, expressing the personal claim to the job as inviolate.[29]

In such situations, Jane Addams observed, "the entire population of the city becomes divided into two cheering sides.... Any one who tries to keep the attitude of non-partisanship... is quickly under suspicion by both sides."[30] Like Jane Addams before him, Taylor was saddened by what he saw as a form of intolerance. Settlement house reformers like Taylor and Addams dedicated their lives to building social and cultural bridges between immigrant workers and the more "respectable" elements in the city's population. Strikes enlarged the chasm between social classes in a particularly dramatic fashion. To his credit, Hapgood saw the pervasive class consciousness of early twentieth-century Chicago in very different terms. "I was impressed over and over again, when living among the mechanics," he wrote, "with a certain kind of altruism, of a fairly wide-spread emotion of solidarity, akin to the religious; for when men band together in an effort to attain things they deem necessary to their deepest material and spiritual welfare, they are not far from conceiving of the movement, at least in moments of self-consciousness, as being from one point of view religious."[31] Even Addams agreed that the "most valuable result" of the mass strikes involving immigrant workers was "the expanding consciousness of the solidarity of the workers."[32] The highest principle in working-class subcultures, Hapgood concluded, was that of "organized solidarity." Upon this, all else depended.

Hapgood told a story that illustrated the extent of such sentiment in the city at the time. Friends introduced him to a hardcore criminal who calmly recited a long litany of his violent and rather degraded activities. Raised in a working-class neighborhood, he retained friends in the labor movement, though he lived most of his life in the city's underworld. "Here," Hapgood thought, "was a man whom it was not possible to insult. He probably had no sensibility." Yet when the author asked if he had ever acted as a scab or worked on the side of corporations during strikes, the man's feelings were genuinely hurt. "Oh, no," he said. "I may be bad, but I'm not as bad as that. That is against my principles."[33]

A Working-Class Modernism?

If Chicago was the heart of industrial radicalism, it was also the vital center of a vibrant working-class intellectual and cultural life that shaped not only the lives of the city's workers but also the social, cultural, and political life of the city as a whole. It was the convergence of this labor and cultural radicalism, a kind of proletarian modernism that Hapgood sought to capture in his study of Johannsen and his world. The essence of the "modern," Hapgood believed, lay not in his own group of *déclassé* radical intellectuals, as many writers at the time and since have assumed, but rather in people like Anton and his friends. "I feel he is really nearer the truth of the immediate future than I or any of my leisure class friends," Hapgood wrote his wife Neith.[34]

Chicago's strong free speech traditions went back to Haymarket and well before, but there were also more recent traditions. Hapgood found that Jane Addams ran "a kind of salon" at Hull House, "an exchange of ideas where all the surging social conceptions find expression."[35] At dinners and public forums in the old house on Halsted Street, one might indeed find some of the leading writers and artists of the day, but they would be rubbing elbows with Women's Trade Union League activists, immigrant anarchists and socialists, labor organizers.[36] Christine Stansell notes that New York drew off many of the most talented Midwestern writers and artists who might otherwise have raised literary and artistic standards in Chicago, but the bohemian scene that remained, and it was an extremely dynamic scene, was much closer to working-class radical politics and culture than its New York counterpart. The city's "Bughouse Square," Radical Bookshop, Ben Reitman's "Hobo College," and later the Dill Pickle Club seemed to meld bohemian intellectuals and working-class activists, politics, and art, more easily than comparable New York venues.[37] These Chicago institutions and others like them were far more open than Mabel Dodge's Greenwich Village salon, attracting many of the era's leading literary lights and artists to spaces they shared with anarchists and socialists and more typical migratory workers.

Drawing on his relationships with Robert Morss Lovett and the novelist Robert Herrick, both friends from Harvard now teaching English at the University of Chicago, Hutchins made extensive contacts among Chicago's intellectual circles and immersed himself in the city's remarkable cultural life. He developed a close relationship with the radical lawyer Clarence Darrow and met with the economist Thorstein Veblen to discuss *The Theory of the Leisure Class* (New York, 1899). He also spoke often with settlement house reformers Jane Addams and Graham Taylor, University of Chicago sociologist W. I. Thomas, and other intellectuals. A regular "Lunch Group" included Algie Simmons, editor of the *Chicago Socialist*, Lovett, and writers I. K. Friedman, Raymond Robins, and William English Walling. "In fact," Hapgood wrote to Robert Herrick, "Chicago is full of good humans." While in Chicago, Hapgood read Kropotkin's *Memoirs of a Revolutionist* (Boston, 1899), Oscar Wilde's *The Soul of Man under Socialism* (Boston, 1910), and other books "along an anarchist line." But he also had no trouble meeting a range of labor activists including Con O'Shea, president of the teamsters, a number of other teamsters, the garment workers' leader Abraham Bisno, and several of the leading figures in the Chicago Federation of Labor, as well as anarchists Ben Reitman, "the Hobo Doctor," Hippolyte Havel, and Emma Goldman.[38] The radicalism he evoked derived less from the texts than from experiences and the culture surrounding them.

The Mainstream

The radical modernism of Chicago's intellectual elite and professional reformers, the bohemian radicalism of the city's "proletarian intellectuals," the tough idealism of its labor activists, and the almost "religious" class solidarity of much of its working-class population—Hapgood illuminated each of these worlds for his readers, but there was another world that he never penetrated during his time in Chicago, perhaps because he never looked for it.

Anton Johannsen was certainly not a "typical" early twentieth-century urban worker, if such a person had ever existed. He was an anarchist radical at a time when most Chicago workers continued to support one of the two main parties; a free love advocate at a time when most working families held to traditional family values; a sophisticated cosmopolitan in an era when most working-class people organized their lives around their local communities; an atheist freethinker at a time when the city's churches and synagogues were full. Anton's story does convey a radical dynamic that was a vital part of working-class life in these years, but it does not capture the everyday experience of millions of immigrant workers and their families.

The rather bewildering ethnic diversity of the city and others like it eluded Hapgood and other middle-class writers of the time. Chicago's broader working-class community was fragmented into dozens of ethnic subcultures.

Between 1880 and 1930, as the city's labor force grew by 600 percent, a massive migration drew more than 600,000 people from around the world into the city's shops and factories. By the time of the Great Depression, Chicago had the largest Polish, Scandinavian, Czech, Lithuanian, and Slovak, and the third largest Italian populations of any city in the United States. Even at the turn of the century, Chicago had a substantial African American population, some of them integrated into the labor movement Hapgood observed, others marginalized by it. In the World War I years and the twenties, this original black community and the "new immigrants" who arrived in Hapgood's Chicago years were joined by tens of thousands of black migrants who fled the Deep South to escape the worst aspects of Jim Crow segregation and organized racial violence, and to take advantage of the opportunities for industrial employment that cities like Chicago provided.[39]

What was true in Chicago in these years was also true for many other industrial cities in the Northeast and the Midwest: Millions of unskilled immigrant workers met black (and, later, Mexican migrant) laborers on the streets and in the workplaces of American cities. What difference would this have made in Hapgood's telling of Anton's story? As early as the time of Hapgood's research and writing, this momentous meeting of immigrant and African American was already breeding cooperation and solidarity in some places and massive conflict in others. In the course of 1904 and 1905, for example, large strikes at the stockyards, among the teamsters, in the city's restaurants, and elsewhere all involved the fundamental issue of the integration of black workers along with recent immigrants. In a real sense, the future of the labor movement in countless industrial communities throughout the country depended upon the resolution of what the great black intellectual W. E. B. Du Bois called the central problem of the new twentieth century—the race issue.[40]

One part of the story Hapgood missed, then, in concentrating solely on the world of labor radicalism and ignoring the ethnic and racial diversity of Chicago, is the rather compelling story of the ways in which the city's workers strove to cross ethnic and racial lines to create a strong working-class movement—their failures as well as their successes. For him, it seems, the central question was one of class and not race. Yet for workers on both sides of the color line, race could not be ignored. Little more than a decade later (1919), the city exploded in violence, wrecking much of its interracial labor organizing and distorting its race relations for decades.

Distinct ethnic cultures shaped the lives of many of Chicago's workers. Each community sustained a wide array of religious, cultural, social, and economic institutions, and many immigrant and black workers in Chicago and elsewhere lived rich lives within the contours of such networks. The cultural and intellectual lives of the city's myriad ethnic communities remained opaque to most writers of the era. Each sustained a wide array of institutions—reading circles, play groups, choruses, bands and orchestras, a cultural panorama beyond the purview, or perhaps the interest, of the educated middle class. Indeed, the music that left its deepest mark on the city, for example, was arguably not that of the Chicago Symphony Orchestra, but rather the jazz and blues that percolated from black bars and cafés over the first half of the twentieth century.

Religion was particularly important in many of these communities, yet we find no recognition of such ethnic subcultures in *The Spirit of Labor*. They were not on Hapgood's radar, and Johannsen himself was actively hostile to them. In a sense, the emphasis on community that made Hapgood's earlier book *The Spirit of the Ghetto* such a captivating work is largely missing here. It is as if he was so taken with the spectacle of widespread class solidarity that he missed the conspicuous ethnic, religious, and racial divisions among Chicago's workers. How might a consideration of these parallel worlds change our image of working-class life? Such communities offered alternative values and perspectives to both those of elite and corporate cultures and also those espoused by radicals like Anton Johannsen.

Life Itself

For all the social distance between these men, Anton and his world had a profound effect on Hapgood. "The last two months have meant a great deal to me," he wrote to Neith Boyce in late 1905.

> They have made me see the real sadness of things more deeply than I did before and they have removed the last vestige of snobbishness and "class" feeling that I had. My relations in the past years with thieves, vaudevillians, etc. etc. seem now to me quite unimportant, socially. But these working people and the radical atmosphere in which the thought of the working class results—this seems significant to me in a tremendous, almost terrible way.... [They] fascinate, please, sadden, and excite me.[41]

Neith Boyce, writing to their friend Robert Morss Lovett, reported in early 1906, "Hutch has been here five weeks now and has talked steadily for about four weeks. He did have some fearful and wonderful experiences in radical Chicago. When he got here he seemed to feel that he had been rudely torn from the one spot on earth where he really desired to root himself."[42]

As his biographer concludes, "Hutchins Hapgood discovered labor in Chicago."[43] He had already shown a marked sympathy with common people and outsiders of all kinds, and a radical disposition. Raised by an antibusiness businessman father, he was steeped in an alternative intellectual culture. But until his visit to Chicago, he had little sense of either the labor movement or radical labor politics. The Lower East Side evoked in Hapgood's *Spirit of the Ghetto* was certainly saturated with a vibrant Yiddish radicalism, but this culture remained largely divorced from New York's unions and English-speaking radical world at the end of the nineteenth century. Anton's world sensitized Hapgood to a working-class critique of modern capitalism and won him over to a support for labor that persisted throughout his life. Writing of the labor ethic he discovered in Chicago, he recalled in the late 1930s, "my own consciousness and therefore my life was [sic] affected by it. I had always sympathized with the underdog. But now I began to give more serious endorsement to the philosophy of those who have not." "As I look back upon my long life," he wrote in 1939 in the midst of a new era of labor insurgency, "I find there is only one faith that burns in me as brightly or more brightly than ever. That is what may be called roughly the faith in the labor movement."[44]

Their lives after their collaboration on *The Spirit of Labor* suggest the remaining distance between Hutchins Hapgood and Anton Johannsen, the ways in which these two radicals shared deep human experiences, and how their respective class positions determined their futures. Having gathered all of this "human material" in the heart of Chicago's labor and radical communities, Hapgood finished *The Spirit* in New York in 1906, and then read the proofs for the book at a villa in Florence, leaving the slums of Chicago far behind.

For several years after, Hapgood was very productive. He continued to write newspaper columns on a vast array of subjects and collected some of these in another book on the "lower classes," *Types from City Streets* (New York, 1910). *The Story of a Lover*, a book on his relationship with Neith Boyce, was not published until 1919, but, in fact, he wrote it in 1914. An early commercial success, *The Story of a Lover* was confiscated by the New York City Police Department's Vice Squad. Although the book was ruled nonpornographic, Hapgood attributed its slumping sales thereafter to the scandal. He finished his only play, *Enemies*, which he coauthored with Neith, in 1915.[45]

From about 1914 until at least the early 1930s, Hutchins Hapgood struggled with depression. He produced little journalism and no major works. It seems likely that whatever tendencies he might have had toward depression and alcoholism were severely aggravated by the death of his eldest son, Boyce

Hapgood, in the 1918 influenza epidemic. "For years," Hapgood wrote, "Neith and I were unable in any full measure to live either in work or with our children." While Neith Boyce wrote her way out of her own depression to some degree with *Harry* (1923), a book based on her dead son's personality and life, Hutchins seems never to have recovered from the tragedy.[46] Hutchins Hapgood died on November 26, 1944, and was buried in Petersham, Massachusetts, his family's home for almost three centuries.

Anton Johannsen suffered his own tragedies, but remained deeply enmeshed in the labor movement. He served as state organizer from 1909 to 1914 for the California Building Trades Council and was indicted along with J. B. and J. J. McNamara of the Structural Iron Workers for a dynamite campaign aimed at antiunion employers in the Los Angeles area. Although Johannsen was never tried for these offenses, the indictment hung over him for two years. The McNamara brothers were placed on trial in late 1911, while labor anarchists David Kaplan and Johannsen's close friend Matt Schmidt fled. Eighty thousand unionists and socialists met in Chicago to protest the indictments. Johannsen traveled throughout the United States raising funds for the legal case, and Clarence Darrow came to California to defend the brothers in court. Johannsen and workers throughout the country were outraged when the McNamaras confessed to dynamiting the *Los Angeles Times* building. Convinced, apparently, that his plea would avoid further repression, James McNamara later insisted on his innocence. Kaplan and Schmidt were tracked down and sentenced to long prison terms. The trial's outcome ended the prospects for a Socialist Party victory in the Los Angeles municipal elections, and also led to a precipitous decline in the state's union movement. In the midst of this tragedy, Johannsen's young daughter died; he and his wife buried her in the family's yard.[47] Although he certainly had what Hapgood once called a "dynamiting mind" in terms of his intellectual radicalism, it seems unlikely that Johannsen was directly involved in the violence. The government apparently concurred, as the charges were eventually dropped.[48]

Still an anarchist, Anton spent much of the rest of his time bringing organizations to life. He served as a general organizer for the carpenters in California from 1914 to 1917, and as an organizer for the Labor Defense Council the following year. In 1918, he returned to Chicago, where he worked for seven years as business agent for the carpenters' district council. During the Red Scare period, 1919 to 1922, he was elected chair of the Chicago Federation of Labor's Organizing Committee. The federation's progressive president, John Fitzpatrick, trusted and worked closely with Johannsen without regard to politics, as he did with Chicago communists and a host of other radicals in the early twenties. When he last wrote Hapgood in 1933, the liberal Democratic Governor Henry Horner had appointed Anton to the state's Industrial Commission. "[I]f by chance you ever come to Chicago," Anton concluded, "I could probably give you plenty of material for a new edition of the '*Spirit of Labor*.'"[49] Toward the end of his life, between 1935 and 1946, Johannsen achieved his highest office in the labor movement, serving as vice president of the Chicago Federation of Labor.[50] Anton Johannsen died in Chicago on February 9, 1951, and was buried in Waldheim Cemetery near the monument honoring the Haymarket martyrs and alongside numerous other activists associated with the city's rich history of labor radicalism.[51]

Considering Anton Johannsen's reading habits, listening to his insights about social and personal relations, the state of the world, and various matters of ethics and aesthetics, it becomes more difficult to think of him any longer as simply a pair of strong arms or even a "class-conscious worker"—though this label certainly applies. He forces us to ask if there is an "intellectual history" far beyond what we normally associate with that term, a world of ideas and values created and exchanged in the working-class neighborhoods, factories, saloons, and other common spaces throughout cities like Chicago. And if such a world of ideas and values did exist, how does that change our understanding of working-class people in the industrial era?

Again, the particular context for a study of class relations, and especially of working-class intellectual and cultural life, makes a difference. Hutchins Hapgood and Anton Johannsen both stressed Chicago's deep and expansive class consciousness. Yet, while the city might have been unusual in the extent to which such consciousness pervaded every aspect of its life, certainly class divisions and working-class organization had become characteristic of American cities by the end of the nineteenth century. In terms of a vibrant working class full of literature, music, and theater, New York's Lower East Side during the era of massive Russian and Eastern European Jewish immigration may well be a better example than Chicago. But both the level of class conflict and the resonance of radical labor ideas and culture were much more widespread in early twentieth-century Chicago.

Like our own, Anton's world intersected with many others, and such intersections provide us a fascinating window onto relations between the social classes. There are, of course, the worlds of the trade union activist, racketeer, and reformer. One boundary crossed—in the collaboration that produced this book as well as in saloons and meeting halls around working-class Chicago—was the one that separated "proletarian intellectuals" from people like Hapgood. Hutchins Hapgood and other bohemian radical intellectuals were caught between classes that were at war with one another in the early years of the twentieth-century city. And they were "in-between," not only in the sense of their divided sympathies and sensibilities, not only in terms of lifestyle, but also in the sense that these "modern radicals" were trying to forge a new way of living and a new way of looking at the world around them.

The story of Hutchins Hapgood and Anton Johannsen and their relationship suggests other features of social class in the early twentieth century. Perhaps most importantly, it illuminates a vibrant world of radical cosmopolitan worker-intellectuals as interested in ideas and culture as they were in creating an effective working-class movement. Indeed, their practical goals were linked to their interest in these ideas. It also suggests a juncture between this world and that of the radical middle class, the world of the bohemian intellectual. The persistence of such hybrid class cultures in New York, Chicago, and other cities around the country suggests that the roots for American bohemianism lie as much in the working class as among young writers and artists.

For all their affinities, however, Johannsen and Hapgood were very different people, and the gulf between them was never quite bridged. The distance was not simply a matter of social and economic inequality, though it is difficult to overstate the impact of such forces in shaping individual lives. It was also a matter of how one viewed culture. Many radical intellectuals embraced a modern culture and values for their own sake, and because these outlets offered a way to break with a bourgeois world they despised. For working-class cosmopolitans like Anton, the significance of ideas and values lay in their promise to liberate people and to provide the basis for a new society without class distinctions.

CHAPTER SIX

Americanization from the Bottom Up

Immigration and the Remaking of the Working Class in the United States, 1880–1930

The scene is the athletic field at the Ford Motor Company's famous Model T assembly plant at Highland Park, Michigan, on the Fourth of July in the midst of World War I. The occasion is a graduation ceremony for the Ford English School, a language and civics program for the company's immigrant workers, part of Ford's ambitious Five Dollar Day corporate welfare program. The pageant incorporates a symbol that has acquired peculiar importance in Americans' self-image. While the ritual is heavy-handed and perhaps in rather bad taste, its importance lies in the meaning it holds for both the immigrant workers and their corporate sponsors. Ford's director of Americanization describes the scene.

> All the men descend from a boat scene representing the vessel on which they came over; down the gangway representing the distance from the port at which they landed to the school, into a pot 15 feet in diameter and 7½ feet high, which represents the Ford English School. Six teachers, three on either side, stir the pot with ten foot ladles representing nine months of teaching in the school. Into the pot 52 nationalities

with their foreign clothes and baggage go and out of the pot after vigorous stirring by the teachers comes one nationality, viz, American.

Lest anyone miss the point, each of the workers emerges from the pot dressed in an identical suit and carrying a miniature American flag.[1]

Scenes like this one, perhaps without its contrived drama, were occurring in factories, public school rooms, and settlement houses throughout the United States in the early twentieth century. Between 1880 and 1924, the year immigration was severely restricted, more than twenty-five million immigrants poured into the country; they transformed the face of America's laboring population. From the late nineteenth century on, in a movement that gathered momentum after the turn of the century, teachers, settlement house workers, and professional patriots aimed to "Americanize" these immigrants, to guide and hasten the process of acculturation by which they might embrace the values and behavior of mainstream America. During and immediately after World War I, the movement became a kind of crusade as employers, nationalist groups, and various state and federal agencies sought to remold the values and behavior of immigrant workers and their families.[2]

But what did it mean to be Americanized, and who was fittest and best placed to do the Americanizing? Typically, the term Americanization has had conservative connotations. It conveyed a unified notion of what it meant to be American and more than a hint of nativism. It was something the native middle class did to immigrants, a coercive process by which elites pressed WASP values on immigrant workers, a form of social control. That side of Americanization was very real, particularly during the era of World War I and the Red Scare. But it is a rather narrow understanding of Americanization. I employ the term critically, to suggest the broader acculturation of immigrants, the day-to-day process by which they came to understand their new situation and to find or invent ways of coping with it. Americanism was, in fact, a contested ideal. There were numerous understandings of what it meant to be an American, divergent values associated with the concept, and so, many ways that an immigrant might "discover" America.

Ethnic culture certainly persisted in the New World, and immigrants employed older cultural values and behavior in facing the problems of urban industrial society. Immigration historians have emphasized the striking diversity and complexity of American society, demonstrating that there is not one American story, but many of them that must be told in relation to one another. But if we wish to understand how working-class formation took place in the midst of great ethnic, cultural, and racial diversity and change, then we must study the widespread contacts and interaction between workers from diverse ethnic and racial backgrounds, the gradual acculturation of new immigrants, and the transformation of immigrant worker consciousness.

We need an analytical framework that acknowledges the very uneven and continual quality of American working-class formation, shaped by constant migration, and that allows us to do more than simply describe instances of interethnic class cooperation—one that also enables us to explain how and why they occurred. Such an analysis would incorporate the sequential character of the process and the element of cultural continuity noted by immigration historians, but would also assess the impact on the newcomers of existing working-class culture and organizations. The arrival of these immigrants and the prospect of integrating them into existing communities and institutions represented as much of a challenge to the maturing working class as it did to employers and the state. Through formal and informal efforts, working-class people, themselves from quite diverse backgrounds, introduced and explained American society to the immigrants.

This process undoubtedly occurred in many ways and in many settings for various age, gender, and occupational groups in immigrant communities—at the dancehall or on the street corner, at a club meeting, in a city park, in a movie theater, or in a saloon.[3] Labor organizations were not necessarily involved. For my purposes here, however, the "bottom" refers to wage-earning people, and by "Americanization from the bottom up," I mean the gradual acculturation of immigrants and their socialization in working-class environments and contexts—the shopfloor, the union, the radical political party. These settings provided immigrants with alternatives to the worldview and the values advocated in programs sponsored by employers and the government. They absorbed alternative views from their own ethnic communities, from cosmopolitans of various sorts, and from an earlier generation of older immigrant and native-born workers. Immigrant workers constructed their own identities, embracing those perspectives and ideas that made sense to them, rejecting those that seemed to be at odds with what they recognized as reality. Conceptualizing the "remaking" of the working class in the early twentieth century as the interaction between two historical generations, and class formation itself as an Americanization from the bottom up, provides a new perspective on both working-class and immigration history.

The notion of historical generations illuminates this relationship between workers either native-born or long resident in the United States and recent immigrants who were still constructing new identities and coming to terms with life in the United States. Used in this way, the term "generation" refers to a cohort with comparable historical experiences, rather than the biological generations in any particular immigrant community.⁴

Two fairly distinct generations of workers lived in many American industrial communities between the end of the nineteenth century and the 1920s. The first consisted of native-born and "old" immigrant workers and their children—British, Germans, and Irish, with smaller numbers of Scandinavians, English-speaking Canadians, and others. By the late nineteenth century, these workers had not only had years of industrial and urban experience; they had also created institutions and developed and popularized ideas that they used to cope with the rigors of wage labor. They had organized and now led trade unions, Knights of Labor assemblies, co-ops, and labor parties. To use E. J. Hobsbawm's famous phrase, they had learned "the rules of the game."⁵ They might be steeped in their own ethnic cultures, as were the Irish and Germans as late as the early twentieth century. But they also had experience in dealing with other ethnic groups, and though some retained a measure of prejudice, they often recognized the value of interethnic cooperation.

By the turn of the century, a new generation of workers, drawn to the United States largely from Eastern and Southeastern Europe, shared the cities and industrial towns with these older, more experienced groups and their American-born children. By the end of World War I, these "new immigrants" were joined by black and Mexican migrants to create a new working-class population. Few of these newcomers were ignorant peasants recently uprooted from the land and casting about in the city, disoriented and demoralized, but all of them faced major adjustments if they were to cope with life in large factories and in city neighborhoods.⁶ To some degree, they relied on the material and cultural resources of their own ethnic communities, but for good or ill, they had also to contend with the structures already in place, those created by the earlier generation of industrial workers, who played major roles in acculturating and socializing the newcomers.

Various forms of old-country radicalism and social mobilization shaped the development of labor radicalism in the United States. The precise content of such cultural and ideological continuity varied in important ways from one ethnic group to another, but we might think about such continuity as part of what might be termed either ethnocultural or segmented class formation. I use the phrase ethnocultural class formation to underscore the fact that some immigrant workers did indeed create viable working-class cultures with distinct institutions, political ideas, forms of socialization, organizations, and strategies. But they tended to do this within their own ethnic communities, often developing such cultures partly on the basis of Old World experiences and then adapting them to the conditions of the New.

The phrase segmented class formation suggests a different vantage point on the same process. Class formation in the United States was segmented in the sense that it took place simultaneously in various ethnic communities. But describing workers' cultures within each ethnic community is not enough, especially since ethnic socialization often had exclusivist strains that inhibited broader working-class solidarity. Especially by the early twentieth century, American working-class formation was of necessity interethnic, emerging from the mixture of people from diverse backgrounds and depending on contact across ethnic boundaries. We should be looking rather carefully at the relations between the generations of immigrant workers and the various ethnic working-class communities, not simply telling the story of each group of ethnic workers.

In industrial communities throughout the country during the late nineteenth century, skilled German, British, Irish, and native-born male workers built strong craft unions and settled into comfortable communities. The cultures they built, based on associational life and homeownership, were imbued with notions of class, but they were largely defensive in nature. New immigrants might be viewed with as much suspicion as bosses. Where they were organized, these skilled workers used their leverage to protect their standards and prerogatives, but even with no union organization at all, they might achieve some of the same security by employing ethnic and kinship connections to secure work and to retain their hold on the better jobs. Through their craft unions, churches, fraternal organizations, and other institutions, they created their own cultural worlds, ones that often left little room for newcomers.[7]

These older native-born and immigrant workers often embraced a "social republicanism" that fused notions of economic and social reform with democratic nationalist ideals. Indeed, the concept of a distinctive working-class republicanism has even been advanced as a kind of synthesis for labor history. But there are several problems with employing republicanism to reintegrate the story of American workers in the wake of the massive immigration at the turn of the century. It is questionable whether even the earlier generation of immigrants all understood republicanism in the same sense as native-born workers. The traditions with which many of the earlier immigrants identified were those of 1848, not those of 1776; both those traditions had more to do with nationalism than with internationalism and class solidarity. Finally, whatever the republican consensus that may have obtained among earlier immigrants, it had clearly fragmented by the turn of the century.[8]

Nor was such ideology always progressive in content. The same defensive mind-set that might impart great cohesion and solidarity for resistance against employers and state authorities could also manifest itself in exclusionary impulses that shaped responses to new immigrant workers. A common reaction to labor's decline in status during the late nineteenth and early twentieth centuries, for example, was the demand for immigration restriction, which enjoyed great popularity among not only the native-born but also many Irish and British and some German labor activists. Even as an instrumental approach to problems of unemployment or low wages, the demand for restriction revealed an exclusionary quality to workers' thinking, and it sometimes betrayed a narrow, nativist conception of "labor" shared not only by American Federation of Labor (AFL) craft unionists but also by Knights of Labor activists and even socialist militants.[9]

In its extreme form, that perspective infused the anti-Chinese movement that swept the West and other parts of the country in the late nineteenth century. Here the element of race added an enduring and explosive quality to the mixture of defensive sentiments characterizing conservative and even some radical workers. Some Socialist Party leaders, for example, held profoundly racist attitudes toward Asian, black, and many immigrant workers, and strongly supported immigration restrictions.[10]

Immigrant socialization in working-class settings could perpetuate this negative strain of thought and feeling: Older immigrants and natives passed their own prejudices on to the newcomers. Irish immigrants, who had been in job competition with Asians and blacks for more than a generation before Eastern European immigrants arrived, and who had themselves suffered discrimination and violence at the hands of nativists, often developed racist attitudes and repertoires of behavior. Inside the labor movement, the Catholic Church, and the political organizations of many working-class communities, the Irish occupied vital positions as Americanizers of later groups.[11] Racism was a learned value, deeply ingrained in the worldviews of many workers by the end of the nineteenth century; it was passed on to immigrants along with values enhancing class solidarity.

The AFL's craft unionism was, of course, exclusionary by definition; keeping nonmembers out of the labor market through control of hiring was its raison d'être. In the context of mass immigration, craft organization reinforced any nativist tendencies derived from other sources. The contempt some craft unionists had for new immigrants and women was often based more on their cultural, gender, ethnic, or racial "otherness" than on any threat they posed to the livelihood and living conditions of skilled workers and their families. But these two aspects of the newcomers' image—otherness and lack of skill—fused. When they did, exclusion from a trade might be based not simply on the question of skill, but either implicitly or explicitly on race, ethnicity, or gender. To overdraw the point, it was possible to be a "good union man" and at the same time a racist, a nativist, and a chauvinist.

The earlier generation, then, sometimes reacted to new immigrants defensively, seeking to exclude them from the labor market and from the broader working-class community. Yet the older, entrenched generation often could not afford to shut out the newcomers. Relations between the two generations occurred in a context of massive technical and economic upheaval, something like a second industrial revolution. The American working-class population was transformed in the course of the early twentieth century precisely because the economy and the nature of work itself were also being transformed. In some sectors of the economy, for instance, the building trades, where skills were still required and complex work rules hung on, craft unions might retain control over the labor market. In many industries, however, such unions faced a sustained crisis throughout the late nineteenth and early twentieth centuries. The desperation of their struggle to retain some control over the work process and jobs varied considerably from one trade to another, but most skilled workers felt the pressure. Most of the literature about this problem has focused on the control struggles of the skilled, yet many old-line AFL unions did reach out to unskilled immigrants in these years, if only because the transformation of the labor process and the labor market left them little choice.[12]

The ongoing social transformation and the related technological revolution in industry presented the labor movement with an enormous challenge, one with both social and organizational dimensions. The integration of the newcomers into the labor movement called not only for new forms of organization, new organizing strategies, and new strike tactics, but also for a new means of socializing and acculturating the new people, a "remaking" of the working class between the turn of the century and the Great Depression. That involved the organized efforts of unions and other labor organizations, myriad informal contacts between workers in various settings, and a long struggle with management for the loyalty of the immigrant worker.

We know most about the impulse for immigrant acculturation that came from the native middle class in public school classrooms, settlement houses, and factories. Because most of the new immigrant's waking hours were spent at the workplace, much of his or her learning about what it meant to be an American occurred there. Certainly employers had their own lessons to teach. They experimented with English instruction and citizenship classes during the early years of this century, and they took a special interest in the movement during the labor shortage and unionization of the World War I era.[13]

Henry Ford launched the most ambitious of these plans at his Highland Park Model T plant as part of the Five Dollar Day plan, which, beginning in 1914, combined assembly-line technology with a shorter work day, incentive pay, and an elaborate personnel management system. Accepting prevailing Progressive notions that environment shaped one's behavior and attitudes, Ford engineers established a Sociology Department to remake the lives of their immigrant workers and win them over to thrift, efficiency, and company loyalty. Case workers fanned out into Detroit's working-class neighborhoods, ready to fight for the hearts and minds of the immigrant auto workers. They investigated each worker's home life as well as his work record, and one could qualify for the Five Dollar Day incentive pay only after demonstrating the proper home environment and related middle-class values. Thus the company sought to show workers not only the "right way to work" but also the "right way to live." In describing the work of his Sociology Department, Ford argued that "these men of many nations must be taught American ways, the English language, and the right way to live." (And he meant business. When about nine hundred workers of Greek or Russian extraction missed work to celebrate Orthodox Christmas—on the Julian calendar, hence thirteen days after Christmas on the Gregorian calendar—he summarily fired them all. "If these men are to make their home in America," he argued, "they should observe American holidays.") Meatpackers, steel mills, farm implement manufacturers, textile plants, and companies in other industries established similar plans. By the spring of 1919, there were at least eight hundred industrial plants sponsoring their own classes or working in conjunction with the YMCA and other agencies to put on evening or plant classes.[14]

Of course, learning also went on at work outside the structured programs. The workplace was by its nature an authoritarian environment, and foremen and other supervisors were always "teaching" immigrants—to do what they were told, to act promptly, to keep working. There was one phrase "every foreman had to learn in English, Polish, and Italian," recalled William Klann, a Ford Motor assembly foreman: " 'Hurry up.' " The verbal abuse of immigrant workers for which steel mills and some other factories were notorious derived in part from the heartfelt prejudices of lower-level management, but it was also a crude effort to teach the immigrant "who was boss." Blast furnaces, rolling mills, slaughterhouses, and freight yards were brutal places where the foreman or straw boss undoubtedly felt obliged to assert his authority with whatever force seemed justified. He too had a lesson to teach the immigrant, in this case a lesson about power in the workplace.[15]

But there were other teachers—older, more experienced, sometimes politicized workers, who conveyed different notions of what was right or wrong in the workshop and in the United States as a society. Immigrants learned restriction of output and other aspects of a new work culture from their workmates, and, according to David Montgomery, "exchanged portions of their traditional culture, not for the values and habits welfare plans sought to inculcate, but for working-class mores."[16] Immigrant strikers' frequent demands for humane treatment and for the discharge of abusive foremen suggest the importance of such socialization. Clearly, immigrants themselves were constructing identities and embracing values that reflected situations they faced in the workplace.

Not all workplace conversations were concerned with work itself. Nor did all one's lessons come from earlier immigrants. Some had broader implications that might be conveyed by more experienced and sophisticated workers from within one's own community. Something like the ethnocultural class formation that characterized the "old immigrant" communities in the late nineteenth century was occurring in "new immigrant" communities in the early twentieth. Here too workers developed the ideas, organization, institutions, and movements commonly associated with the phrase "working-class culture." Once again, such cultures were built in part on Old World experiences and values, but they were soon tailored to American industrial settings. Sicilian peasants and artisans who created Italy's "red towns" and then carried a radical oral tradition to Tampa, Chicago, and New York are examples of this phenomenon, as are the Jewish socialists of the ghettos of Eastern Europe and America, or the Finnish leftists of the Mesabi Range. Comparable radical minorities flourished throughout America's Eastern European ethnic communities and in workplaces around the country.[17]

John Wasko of United States Steel's Homestead Works might have been one of these people. By 1919 he had been in the country only seven years, but he was already married with two children and a home. He had taken out his first papers and spoke English fluently. He learned the language and a number of other things down in the anthracite mines. There he had seen the United Mine Workers of America handle all the common complaints he encountered in the mill—arbitrary and abusive foremen, unpaid overtime, and phony pay scales—and it was a lesson learned well. Wasko read several

Slavic-language papers and New York City's socialist *Call* every day. When the organizing started in the mill, he knew what to do, and he "spread the principles of trade unionism among his fellow countrymen."[18]

Stjepan Mesaros, a twenty-year-old Croatian immigrant, met a man like Wasko when he arrived for his first day on the job at Berk's slaughterhouse in Philadelphia. He was overwhelmed by what he found there and in the streets of his neighborhood. Among the many mysteries was the verbal abuse meted out to a young black man with whom Stjepan shared his duties. Noticing a Serbian laborer who seemed to spend every free moment reading Serbo-Croatian pamphlets and newspapers, Stjepan took a chance and asked him about it. Almost sixty years later, he recalled the conversation which took place amid the blood of the slaughterhouse and changed the course of his life. "The Serb sat down next to me and explained that both bosses and workers were prejudiced against black people. 'You'll soon learn something about this country,' he said. 'Negroes never get a fair chance.'" The next day the Serb brought a newspaper clipping in to work.

> The picture showed the Berk family on its way to vacation in Florida for the winter. The picture showed the young men in white pants and shoes and the young ladies in white summer dresses. The whole family was boarding a Pullman parlor car. The explanation proceeded in Serbo-Croatian. "'What's Florida?' I asked. "'That's a place that's warm in the winter. . . .'" "'Who goes there?'" "'You can see who goes, only bosses.'" "'But the boss [the foreman, as I understood the setup] is still here.'" "'The Berks just hire him to run the factory. They get all the money.'"[19]

The Serb described the sort of life that came with the requisite amount of money, and the young Croatian was astounded by the wealth he heard described. Did Stjepan wish to know how all this was possible? The Serb handed him some Socialist Labor Party pamphlets and soon after gave him other reading matter of the sort favored by self-educated worker radicals around the world—not just on politics but on popular science, temperance, health foods, atheism. Such literature conveyed more than a formal political ideology—socialism—it also incorporated a new worldview. This too was Americanization, but not the sort that employers or most adult educators had in mind when they used the term. Stjepan had discovered America.

Stjepan Mesaros's slaughterhouse conversation raises the important question of how other immigrant workers discovered the significance of race in American life. The black migrants arriving from the Deep South in the war years and the 1920s were part of the same generation as the new immigrants, and the two groups had a great deal in common. Yet we know very little about the relations between them, or for that matter about the more general problem of the evolution of racism among white workers. It seems likely, however, that racial attitudes were part of the legacy that older, more Americanized workers passed on to newcomers. In some cases, these might have included the sort of enlightened perspective displayed by Stjepan's Serbian friend. The anarchist Luigi Galleani often wrote in the Italian-language press about the problem of white racism, and concluded that in America the proletariat's motto should be "Not race struggle but class struggle." Surely there were others like these men. More often, however, recent immigrants encountered the hostile attitudes toward blacks that had developed among the Irish and other older groups in the late nineteenth century, exacerbated by the competition for jobs and resources in the early twentieth. The fact that newer immigrants played little part in the race riots of the World War I era suggests that it took some time for them and their children to make these prejudices their own, but their prominent presence in post–World War II racial conflicts demonstrates that many learned their lessons only too well.[20]

The results of Stjepan's friendship with the Serb and his later career also suggest another context for Americanization—radical working-class politics. Stjepan joined a South Slav branch of the Socialist Labor Party and later the Communist Party. He changed his name to Steve Nelson, learned to read the party press in English with the help of a young German American radical, and studied public speaking, organizing methods, economics, Marxist philosophy, and labor history at party schools in New York and Moscow. He became a union organizer and later an organizer of the unemployed. He worked in Detroit, Chicago, and the anthracite coal fields of eastern Pennsylvania. During the Spanish Civil War he served as commissar of the American Abraham Lincoln Battalion, fighting for his own notion of democracy. Jailed for his political activities during the McCarthy era, he left the Communist Party in 1957 but remained a committed socialist.

The Communist Party gave Nelson more than language and speaking skills. It brought him into contact with educated and politically committed young people from a wide range of ethnic backgrounds, provided him with a key to understanding the world around him, and gave him a vision of a new and better world. Ironically, Steve Nelson's Americanization came in the context of a revolutionary party, a path he trod with a small but important group of immigrant radicals.

The early Socialist Party was ethnically segmented through a system of foreign-language federations, and socialist culture was often ethnic culture, but immigrant socialists were not isolated either from one another or from their native-born counterparts. Many recognized that the party's long-term viability rested on links between foreign and native-born radicals, on creating an American mass movement. In each ethnic community, whether it was preponderantly new immigrants or old, small groups of radicals assumed a disproportionate significance in the acculturation of immigrant workers. Already sympathetic to the goals of the movement, perhaps a bit more articulate or cosmopolitan than their workmates, they provided labor activists with invaluable links to the immigrant communities. As newspaper editors, street-corner speakers, and organizers, they carried the socialist message into their communities in a language workers could understand, and in the process they provided a framework within which the individual immigrant could comprehend the American political and economic system and her or his place in it.[21]

The Communist Party in the 1920s was a bit different from earlier socialist organizations. In the mid-twenties, the communists made a conscious decision to "Americanize" the party (their term). They dissolved language federations, shifted immigrant activists into neighborhood branches, shop nuclei, and other ethnically mixed mass organizations, and even asked foreign-born comrades to change their names. During the Popular Front of the late 1930s, Americanization was even more elaborate. Proclaiming that "Communism Is Twentieth Century Americanism," Earl Browder and other party leaders consciously cultivated an American image, using patriotic symbols and language to convey their message. The new line came easily to second-generation immigrants who eagerly identified themselves as American radicals. A veteran of this movement later recalled beginning to feel "like we were really part of the American Scene. We were looking for some kind of legitimation of our feeling about becoming even more American. Browder came along and sort of articulated this!"[22]

Labor organizations striving to organize in the era of mass immigration also became contexts for acculturation. Indeed, when organizers reached out to the newcomers—and this happened rather more often than we have realized during the early twentieth century—they had little choice but to engage the immigrants in a dialogue about unionization. Too often union drives are thought of in purely institutional terms—as attempts to build up organizations. Surely, this was the goal and sometimes the end result. But each of these efforts was a process of socialization as well, an effort to convey to the immigrants basic values as well as the structure and function of unions and other working-class organizations. To some degree, this was simply a matter of "selling the union," and this effort itself was important. In coal mining, steel production, clothing manufacturing, slaughtering and meatpacking, and other industries, organizers, business agents, and shop stewards had to convey to the immigrants the specific goals, strategies, and structures of the labor movement. But they also conveyed the values and ideas that gave the movement its rationale, its soul. What in the union's appeal attracted immigrants more than official programs? Why were they willing to make the sorts of sacrifices that were clearly necessary to sustain organization in the face of staggering odds? Such questions might help us begin to sketch out some of the characteristics of immigrant workers' mentalities in the early twentieth century.

There were several elements to labor's version of Americanism. Not surprisingly, activists frequently emphasized basic civil liberties, particularly free speech, and encouraged immigrants to speak up and defend their rights. Nor were these ideals abstract. In coal company and steel mill towns and in many other industrial communities, labor's ability to organize depended on the maintenance of such rights, and immigrants frequently learned the values of these freedoms in the midst of organizing activities, strikes, and demonstrations. Workers' notions of these rights, moreover, were often much broader than the law itself. They tended to reflect rights that were more idealized than real. "It is time that some people learned," wrote a West Virginia miner in the midst of the 1921 coal strike, "that working men have some rights under the Constitution, among them the right to organize for mutual protection, the right of collective bargaining and the right to quit work when conditions surrounding their employment become unbearable. And these rights we are going to maintain at any cost." Another miner wrote to President Warren Harding the same year to complain that "the coal operators are depriving the coal miners of the right to belong to the labor organization which is their inherent right given to all citizens of the United States." A steelworker who termed his forty-one years in the mill "slavery and persecution" claimed that the long work day and poor conditions were "against the Constitution."[23]

Organizers frequently invested their material demands with the power of democratic rhetoric and patriotism by speaking of an American standard of living, by which they meant higher wages, shorter working hours, and decent working conditions. Reference to the "American" standard could be and sometimes was used to exclude newcomers, as in the case of the working-class agitation against Chinese immigrants. But it could also be the basis for integrating newcomers and imparting the basic values of the movement, while establishing legitimacy in the eyes of the public at large. During World War I, the "American standard of living" provided the unions with a patriotic image and immigrant workers with the prospect of an ideal American life for themselves and their children. "We cannot bring up our children as Americans on 15 and a half cents an hour," a Polish stockyards worker argued. "We cannot live decently. Our wives, our children, our homes demand better wages."[24]

Finally, many labor activists embraced the concept of cultural pluralism, if only in the interests of labor solidarity, and tried to impart this value to immigrants. What this might have looked like at the level of the local union is suggested by the scene at a meeting of Local 183, which included all women working in the Chicago stockyards, regardless of race, nationality, or trade. When the young Irish chairwoman called for a discussion of grievances, a young black woman complained that a Polish member had insulted her. The chairwoman asked both to come forward.

> "Now what did yez call each other?" "She called me a Nigger." "She called me a Pollock first." "Both of yez oughta be ashamed of yourselves. You're both to blame. But don't you know that this question in our ritual don't mean that kind of griev-e-ances, but griev-e-ances of the whole bunch of us?"[25]

Ethelbert Stewart, the U.S. commissioner of labor, observed labor's version of Americanization as it unfolded in Chicago's slaughterhouses and meatpacking plants during the early years of this century. Here ethnic hostilities had been rife, and ethnic communities tended to be dominated by charismatic "clan leaders" who fought the unions for influence over the immigrants. Since the workers' worlds were organized largely on the basis of nationality, the union "represented the first, and for a time the only, point at which [the immigrant] touches any influence outside of his clan.... The Slav mixes with the Lithuanian, the German, and the Irishman—and this is the only place they do mix until, by virtue of this intercourse and this mixing, clannishness is to a degree destroyed, and a social mixing along other lines comes into play." In the anthracite coal fields, labor economist John R. Commons noted, "foreigners were given over to the most bitter and often murderous feuds among the ten or fifteen nationalities and the two or three factions within each nationality.... When the union was organized all antagonisms of race, religion and faction were eliminated. The immigrants came down to an economic basis and turned their forces against the bosses." "The only effective Americanizing force for the southeastern European," Commons concluded, "is the labor union."[26] Later conflicts suggest that Commons was too optimistic, but there was no question that the union's focus on common grievances helped to break down ethnic barriers. Why? Immigrants themselves were the critical element in this process. They responded better to unions than to official programs because the unions stressed issues that were vital to the welfare of ethnic communities but simply could not be resolved without looking beyond their boundaries to class-based organization.

Besides teaching immigrants interethnic solidarity, unions did more than any civics lesson to impart the principles and methods of democratic government by relating them to practical matters: wages, hours, and working conditions. For most immigrants, introduction to the American political and economic system came not through night-school classes but through discussion and debate at union meetings (with interpreters), informal conversations with fellow workers, and labor movement publications (often printed in various languages). And the union's version of Americanism was likely to be different from the one conveyed in employers' programs, emphasizing the free expression of one's opinions and the importance of standing up with fellow workers to demand one's rights.[27]

This kind of socialization took great effort, but could yield impressive results. After they had hired Polish, Slovak, and Hungarian organizers and made contacts in the various ethnic communities around the turn of the century, the United Mine Workers of America quickly gained a loyal following among recent immigrants. During World War I, one laborers' local of the Stockyards Labor Council recruited more than ten thousand Polish and Lithuanian butcher workmen inside a month's time. Council organizers found that once the immigrants understood the union's goals, they were easier to organize than the native-born and the more skilled, and generally made better union members. William Z. Foster drew similar conclusions from his experiences in steel. At the end of World War I, the National Committee for Organizing Iron and Steel Workers swept through the thoroughly open-shop steel mill towns, penetrating deep into the immigrant communities and conveying the union message to workers in their own languages.[28] The huge numbers can easily overshadow the vital element here—the human agency of the immigrants themselves. They fashioned their identities out of their own experiences, the language and ideas they brought with them, and those they confronted in such union campaigns.

Americanization, whether official or labor, was also fundamentally shaped by issues of gender. Concentrated in precisely those professions—teaching, settlement house work, public health—that brought them into close contact with immigrant families, women assumed major roles at the highest reaches of the corporate and government bureaucracies that provided the Americanization movement with its structure, ideas, and legitimacy. Thousands of them taught English and civics in evening school, settlement house, Young Women's Christian Association (YWCA), and factory programs, conveying the Americanization message. But the message itself encoded notions of domestic orthodoxy and other gender values in English primers, loyalty parades, and citizenship plays. In its early stages, when it chiefly emphasized naturalization and the right to vote, the movement focused almost entirely on men. When Americanizers did begin to address women, it was because of their key role in child-rearing and for fear of the dangers posed by the "un-Americanized mother." Long after woman suffrage, Americanizers placed far more emphasis on the immigrant mother's role in the home than on her duties as a citizen. She was urged to maintain the new American standard of living in diet, hygiene, and infant and child care, and to be mindful of her crucial role in producing a second generation of "true Americans."[29]

Working-class Americanizers made their own approaches to immigrant women. Organizing them presented special problems, some created by the changing occupational structure of women's work in the early twentieth century, others by the patriarchal values of the immigrant household and the labor movement itself. Yet the proportion of the female labor force in unions doubled during the first two decades of the twentieth century, and the Women's Trade Union League (WTUL), a coalition of working women and middle-class reformers, played a particularly important role in socializing immigrant women. In organizing garment workers, the league employed activists from the communities involved and printed leaflets in various languages. During and after the garment strikes of 1909 and 1910, Jewish and Italian organizers visited women in their homes to explain the issues involved in the strikes and the importance of unions. The Chicago WTUL set up neighborhood committees to organize social and educational events, a tactic that was later used in immigrant neighborhoods in New York. Chicago teachers' union volunteers assumed a function comparable to that of "home teachers" in the official Americanization movement, bringing English to immigrant women in their own homes. The New York league produced a labor-oriented English primer, *New World Lessons for Old World Peoples*, in Lithuanian, Italian, Yiddish, Bohemian, and English. It contained illustrated stories "designed to provoke lively discussion and to stimulate students to think out their own answers to the various questions surrounding unionization."

Most of the characters were women living in immigrant neighborhoods and facing situations that the students themselves might encounter. The texts emphasized women activists and their accomplishments, and in this way provided realistic role models. These immigrant women learned English in a way that developed important values of class solidarity and personal relationships that they relied on in later organizing and strikes. "For the WTUL," Colette Hyman concludes, "teaching English was a point of entry into these women's lives through which lessons of unionism could be taught. It was the first step in female institution-building among immigrant women."[30]

World War I and the years immediately following represented a watershed in the Americanization process. Labor's own notions about Americanism stood out in bold relief against the war's backdrop. The massive immigration of the preceding decade had produced a remarkably diverse population that might come to see their chances for a decent life in America embodied in labor's efforts. In this context, interethnic and often interracial organizing was vital to union efforts. The economic effects of the war—increased demand, labor shortages, and steep inflation—sharply raised the issue of living standards and mutual sacrifice for the good of the war effort. In the process, the war greatly strengthened unions' bargaining position and ability to organize, and raised questions of democratic ideology, providing union organizers and immigrant workers with a vocabulary with which to express their grievances and aspirations.

Because of large war orders and labor shortages, both employers and the government sought to co-opt the labor movement into the war effort and avoid strikes, while inflation provided workers with incentive to organize. An ideological dimension was less tangible but probably just as important. In the interests of stimulating sacrifice and hard work on the part of immigrant workers, employers and government agencies couched their propaganda in a democratic idiom. For their part, labor activists sought to appropriate such democratic rhetoric and symbols in the name of labor. More than ever before, the plight of the immigrants, their status as workers, and their vision of the labor movement became part of a discourse on Americanism. The concept was hotly contested, and the immigrants were very much at the center of this symbolic struggle.[31]

For their part, the unions, seizing on the war situation to launch ambitious organizing drives in nonunion basic industry, where most of the immigrants were employed, framed their appeals in patriotic terms. The March 17, 1918 issue of the *United Mine Workers Journal* put the issue forcefully: "If this war is waged for the destruction of political autocracy, we demand ... the elimination of industrial autocracy in this country. The workers demand a voice in the conditions of their service, in all sections of the country; thus shall they be assured that this is indeed their war."

The National Committee for Organizing Iron and Steel Workers geared its campaign around this theme and drove it home repeatedly at mass meetings and in publications produced in various languages. Ironically, it was the recent immigrant rather than the native-born worker who was most receptive to the democratic rhetoric. The committee's large red, white, and blue campaign badges were favorites in the immigrant neighborhoods. Far from being abstract, David Brody concludes, "The democratic theme made unionism comprehensible." A Polish steelworker made the connection between trade unionism and democratic war aims in rather more eloquent terms: "just like a horse and wagon, work all day.... For why this war? For why we buy Liberty Bonds? For the mills? No, for freedom and America—for everybody. No more horse and wagon. For eight-hour day."[32]

Similar scenarios unfolded in many industries throughout the country. During a 1919 conflict at Scovill Manufacturing in Waterbury, Connecticut, a strike leaflet framed the issue in patriotic terms: "Where is the democracy our boys gave their lives for? Wake up American workers; can't you see that we have another Kaiser, another von Hindenburg, another czar who is conspirating to destroy humanity?" The workers, most of them of Italian or Eastern European parentage, demanded a decent "American wage," and frequently used democratic and patriotic language in expressing their grievances.[33]

In steel, coal, and metal mining, in meatpacking, in textile and garment manufacturing—across the whole spectrum of American industry—unions or loose federations of unions launched large organizing drives designed to integrate the new, unskilled immigrants. In the short run, the efforts were remarkably successful, and union membership doubled between 1917 and 1920. In steel, the strongest bastion of the open shop, earlier organizational efforts had failed repeatedly, though the new immigrants were certainly active in several of those efforts. During World War I, the National Committee for Organizing Iron and Steel Workers launched an ambitious organizing drive, and had garnered more than 100,000 workers, most of them recent immigrants, by the spring of 1919. In textiles and clothing and in many other industries, the emergence of the so-called "new unions" represented efforts on the part of an earlier generation of activists, or of radicals within the various "new immigrant" communities, to integrate the second generation of immigrant workers into the movement by creating new sorts of unions with new organizing and strike strategies. A massive strike wave, the largest in

American history to that point, involving more than a million strikers per year for several years, accompanied this organizing, and many of the activists who led the strikes emerged from radical subcultures in the various ethnic communities.[34]

Union locals, national unions, and city labor federations across the country launched educational programs for new immigrant members. These incorporated not only English and civics instruction but also courses in economics, political economy, history, and literature taught by lawyers and college professors as well as labor activists and socialist elected officials. Sam Levin, business agent of the Amalgamated Clothing Workers' Chicago Council, explained why it was essential to teach such classes from labor's perspective: "It is not sufficient to tell the workers that they are entitled to all profit since they create all wealth. They know this, but it is important to tell them how each individual institution of our political and economic system is composed, how it works, and how it is possible to improve upon it, and whether it is possible or necessary to abolish it."[35]

The successful wartime organizing among very recent immigrants and the related strike wave raise two crucial questions that deserve a great deal more research. The first has to do with the immigrants themselves: What do these phenomena suggest about their thinking? The second is equally vital: What happened to this impressive movement?

One might begin to think of the consciousness characterizing many of the new immigrants of the early twentieth century as a sort of transitional mentality, an amalgam of Old World traditions, values, and behaviors with new working-class ideas, forms of organization, and strategies. Whatever the content of the transition, it was neither linear nor inevitable. Perhaps it was a sort of conversation in the immigrants' own minds and between older voices and newer ones, which were still not quite clear. There was undoubtedly an infinite variation to such thinking, beginning with differences between various ethnic groups and ranging down to the personality of each individual immigrant. Each person embraced multiple identities shaped by her or his experiences as a woman or man, an Italian or Pole living in a particular type of community in the United States, working in a particular industry. But conceptualizing consciousness as transitional lends the analysis a dynamic and fluid dimension and suggests that such identities were not entirely idiosyncratic, that they were created within a specific historical context that is vital to explaining them. It also directs our attention away from particular ethnic communities and toward the relationship between ethnicity and class identity. The transitional quality of the unskilled immigrants' worldviews is suggested in part by the words and the symbols they chose. Employers were described as "czars" or "Kaisers," unjust rulers without the support of their subjects—and the police as "Cossacks," a particularly apt word for the mounted officers mobilized in steel mill towns and ethnic working-class city neighborhoods in the World War I era. The strong support for the Polish army in immigrant neighborhoods and the centrality of nationalism in the political discourse of Eastern European immigrants both suggest continuing ideological links with the Old World. Many immigrants lacked what might be termed an "industrial lexicon," and found it difficult to even describe their work to folks back home without resorting to Old World metaphors and analogies. Yet these same immigrant workers often led their parades and picket lines with the American flag, marched in their own American military uniforms, and employed patriotic rhetoric to attack their employers and express their grievances, especially during World War I. Increasingly integrated into the working-class movement, they were becoming proletarians by the war years.[36]

But if there was a gradual transformation in the consciousness of unskilled recent immigrants, reflected in the changing strategies and social composition of the labor movement, then what happened to the new movement that was emerging in these years? Labor history, like other fields of social history over the past two decades, has tended to steer away from the analysis of particular events and toward the delineation of processes and trends. Yet specific events are often crucial to explaining historical change. Working-class fragmentation, for example, is too often thought of as an eventuality rather than a problem to be explained with reference to a particular historical situation that shaped the process. In this case, the war, which had first brought dramatic breakthroughs in the integration of recent immigrants into the labor movement, also set the stage for the political reaction to follow. Several short-term factors in the postwar years devastated the immigrant-based movement that had provided a context for Americanization from the bottom up, fragmenting the impressive wartime movement along ethnic, racial, and political lines.[37]

In the midst of a serious depression, which had a particularly disastrous effect on the new unions of unskilled immigrants, employers attacked in one industry after another between late 1919 and early 1922. Among the strikebreakers in many of these conflicts were the most recent migrants to join the labor force, southern blacks and Mexicans. Race emerged as the decisive division within many working-class communities, and employers clearly manipulated this development to deepen racial tensions. Race riots broke out in two dozen American cities and towns in 1919, leaving any dream of an interracial labor movement in tatters.

In the wake of war, the Americanization campaign took on a distinctly nativist cast and a patriotic frenzy. Ritual and symbolism had a peculiar importance to both government and corporate Americanizers. As nationalism and the fear of subversion grew, the government and employers put more effort and resources into the crusade to turn foreign-born workers into citizen patriots: On July 4, 1918, in cities across the country, federal agencies and voluntary organizations staged giant patriotic celebrations featuring dozens of ethnic groups demonstrating the gifts they had brought with them to the New World and affirming their loyalty to the government. The Flag Day program at Wilson and Company's Chicago meatpacking plant was typical of the events staged in industrial establishments. The drive for one-hundred-percent Americanism began with a brass band, a parade, and patriotic songs; thousands of loyalty leaflets were distributed. But the corporate programs were not notably successful. At Wilson's plant, disappointed organizers noted that few of the immigrants joined in the songs, presumably because they did not know the words, and the leaflets, all of them in English, went unread. By 1919, Ford had traded its melting pot and elaborate welfare program for an extensive network of spies and a practice of firing workers for disloyalty to the nation or the corporation. Employers saw these programs as part of a broad effort to inoculate immigrant workers against the dangers of bolshevism and other forms of radicalism. They called their new offensive, which mixed lockouts, industrial espionage, and private armies and police forces with welfare plans and company unions, the "American Plan."[38]

State and local governments' own version of one-hundred-percent Americanism involved the widespread use of injunctions and mounted police to quell strikes. Workers usually lost these struggles, and the new organizations that had provided the context for integrating the new immigrants were demolished. During the Red Scare, federal and local authorities raided meeting places, closed down presses, seized organizational records, and jailed or simply deported immigrant activists, decimating the ranks of radical labor in immigrant communities. Never more than a tiny minority in any immigrant community, the radicals had played key roles in organizing and leading the mass strikes of recent unskilled workers, and they linked immigrant communities to trade unions, the Industrial Workers of the World (IWW), the Socialist and Communist Parties, and other organizations that provided alternative forms of socialization for people who were still trying to understand the society in which they found themselves.[39] The Red Scare amounted to a kind of enforced Americanization.

Again labor radicals contested the term's meaning. The Farmer-Labor Party's 1920 platform demanded democratic control of industry, abolition of imperialism, public ownership and operation of railroads and mines, the legal right to collective bargaining, the eight-hour day, unemployment compensation, and government old-age pensions. The document also called for its version of one-hundred-percent Americanism:

> Restoration of civil liberties ... including free speech, free assemblage, right of asylum, equal opportunity, and trial by jury ... amnesty for all persons imprisoned because of their patriotic insistence upon their constitutional guarantees, industrial activities or religious beliefs.... As Americanism means democracy, suffrage should be universal. We demand full, unrestricted political rights for all citizens regardless of sex, race, color, or creed.[40]

But the Red Scare undeniably enhanced the more general development of nativism and other forms of intolerance that split the working class and the labor movement in the early 1920s. Already on the defensive, unions made fewer efforts to reach new immigrant and black migrant workers as nationality, race, and patriotism once again became sources of identification for many native-born and old immigrant workers. Indeed, the resulting fragmentation represented the social basis for labor's organizational decline in the course of the 1920s.

It might be tempting to think of the 1920s as a period of triumph for more conservative notions of Americanism, as a time when ethnic workers were culturally and institutionally integrated through the rise of a mass consumer culture and corporate welfare programs, but the reality was much more complex. Certainly elements of the new mass culture penetrated blue-collar ethnic communities and the burgeoning ghettos of northern cities, but often what emerged was a fusion of new and old. Likewise, corporate programs and the daily routine of work in giant mass-production factories spawned a new workplace culture and collective identity, especially among second-generation immigrants, but the values actually created were seldom those promoted by the companies involved. When the corporate welfare system collapsed and jobs disappeared in the Great Depression, traditional sources of support in immigrant communities were overwhelmed, and workers turned increasingly toward government programs, self-organization, and protest, first through unemployed councils and later through the industrial union movement that ultimately produced the Congress of Industrial Organizations (CIO).

This rhetorical and symbolic Americanization was also very real for workers who experienced the bloody union struggles and the fight to maintain democracy from the late thirties through World War II. The second generation in immigrant communities came of age during those struggles, and there was never any question that they thought of themselves as American workers. Political discourse was once again dominated by a democratic idiom, a working-class Americanism.[41]

CHAPTER SEVEN

Inbetween Peoples

Race, Nationality, and the "New Immigrant" Working Class

JAMES R. BARRETT
AND DAVID R. ROEDIGER

By the eastern European immigration the labor force has been cleft horizontally into two great divisions. The upper stratum includes what is known in mill parlance as the "English-speaking" men; the lower contains the "Hunkies" or "Ginnies." Or, if you prefer, the former are the "white men," the latter the "foreigners." —JOHN FITCH, *The Steel Workers*

In 1980, Joseph Loguidice, an elderly Italian American from Chicago, sat down to give his life story to an interviewer. His first and most vivid childhood recollection was of a race riot that had occurred on the city's near North Side. Wagons full of policemen with "peculiar hats" streamed into his neighborhood. But the "one thing that stood out in my mind," Loguidice remembered after six decades, was "a man running down the middle of the street hollering... 'I'm White, I'm White!'" After first taking him for an African American, Loguidice soon realized that the man was a white coal handler covered in dust. He was screaming for his life, fearing that "people would shoot him down." He had, Loguidice concluded, "got caught up in... this racial thing."¹

Joseph Loguidice's tale might be taken as a metaphor for the situation of millions of Eastern and Southern European immigrants who arrived in the United States between the end of the nineteenth century and the early 1920s. The fact that this episode made such a profound impression is in itself significant, suggesting both that this was a strange, new situation and that thinking about race became an important part of the consciousness of immigrants like Loguidice. We are concerned here in part with the development of racial awareness and attitudes, and an increasingly racialized worldview among new immigrant workers themselves. Most did not arrive with conventional U.S. attitudes regarding "racial" difference, let alone its significance and implications in the context of industrial America. Yet most, it seems, "got caught up in . . . this racial thing." How did this happen? If race was indeed socially constructed, then what was the raw material that went into the process?

We are also concerned with how these immigrant workers were viewed in racial terms by others—employers, the state, reformers, and other workers. Like the coal handler in Loguidice's story, their own ascribed racial identity was not always clear. A whole range of evidence—laws; court cases; formal racial ideology; social conventions; popular culture in the form of slang, songs, films, cartoons, ethnic jokes, and popular theater—suggests that the native-born and older immigrants often placed these newer immigrants not only *above* African and Asian Americans, for example, but also *below* "white" people. Indeed, many of the older immigrants, and particularly the Irish, had themselves been perceived as "nonwhite" just a generation earlier. As labor historians, we are interested in the ways in which Polish, Italian, and other European artisans and peasants became American workers, but we are equally concerned with the process by which they became "white." Indeed, in the United States the two identities intertwined, and this explains a great deal of the persistent divisions within the working-class population. How did immigrant workers wind up "inbetween"?

Such questions are not typical of immigration history, which has largely been the story of newcomers becoming American, of their holding out against becoming American, or, at best, of their changing America in the process of discovering new identities. To the extent—and it is a very considerable extent—that theories of American exceptionalism intersect with the history of immigration, the emphasis falls on the difficulty of enlisting heterogeneous workers into class mobilizations, or, alternatively, on the unique success of the United States as a multiethnic democracy.[2] But the immigration history Robert Orsi has recently called for, one which "puts the issues and contests of racial identity and difference at its center," has only begun to be written. Proponents of race as an explanation for American exceptionalism have not focused on European immigrants, at best regarding their racialization as a process completed by the 1890s.[3]

Even with the proliferation of scholarship on the social construction of race, we sometimes assume that such immigrants really were "white," in a way that they were not initially American. And, being white, largely poor, and self-consciously part of imagined communities with roots in Europe, they were therefore "ethnic." If social scientists referred to "national" groups as races (the "Italian race") and to Southern and Eastern European pan-nationalities as races (Slavonic and Mediterranean "races"), they did so because they used race promiscuously to mean other things. If the classic work on American exceptionalism, Werner Sombart's 1906 *Why Is There No Socialism in the United States?* has a whole section on "racial" division with scarcely a mention of any group modern Americans would recognize as a racial minority, this is a matter of semantic confusion. If Robert Park centered his pioneering early twentieth-century sociological theory of assimilation on the "race relations cycle," with the initial expectation that it would apply to African Americans as well as European immigrants, he must not have sorted out the difference between race and ethnicity yet.[4] Indeed, so certain are some modern scholars of the ability of "ethnicity" to explain immigrant experiences that contemporaries described largely in terms of race and nationality that a substantial literature seeks to describe even the African American and Native American experiences as "ethnic."[5]

Racial identity was also clearly gendered in important ways, and historians are just beginning to understand this gendered quality of racial language, conventions, and identity. It is apparent even in the sorts of public spheres privileged here—citizenship, the state, the union, the workplace. But we are *most* apt to find the conjunctions between gender and race in places that are not probed here—at those points where more intimate relations intersected with the rule of law. The taboo against interracial sex and marriage was one obvious boundary between low-status immigrant workers and people of color with whom they often came in contact. As Peggy Pascoe has noted, "although such marriages were infrequent throughout most of U.S. history, an enormous amount of time and energy was spent in trying to prevent them from taking place . . . the history of interracial marriage provides rich evidence of the formulation of race and gender and of the connections between the two." Yet we have little understanding of how this taboo was viewed by immigrant and African or Asian American workers. One obvious place to look is at laws governing interracial marriage and court cases aimed at enforcing such laws. Native-born women who became involved with immigrant men could lose their citizenship, and, if the immigrant were categorized as nonwhite, they could be prosecuted for "race-mixup." "Race mixing" occurred in spite of all this, of course. Chinese men, who lived under particularly oppressive conditions because of restrictions on the immigration of Chinese women, tended to develop relationships with either African Americans or Poles and other "new immigrant" women.[6] We have not attempted to unravel this fascinating and complex problem or the racial identity of immigrant women here. Except where clearly indicated, we are describing situations where racial identity was informed and shaped by, often even conflated with, notions of manhood.

Thus, we make no brief for the consistency with which "race" was used, by experts or popularly, to describe the "new immigrant" Southern and Eastern Europeans who dominated the ranks of those coming to the United States between 1895 and 1924 and who "remade" the American working class in that period. We regard such inconsistency as important evidence of the "inbetween" racial status of such immigrants.[7] The story of Americanization is vital and compelling, but it took place in a nation also obsessed by race. For immigrant workers, the processes of "becoming white" and "becoming American" were intertwined at every turn. The "American standard of living," which labor organizers alternately and simultaneously accused new immigrants of undermining and encouraged them to defend via class organization, rested on "white men's wages." Political debate turned on whether new immigrants were fit to join the American nation and on whether they were fit to join the "American race." Nor do we argue that Eastern and Southern European immigrants were in the same situation as nonwhites. Stark differences between the racialized status of African Americans and the racial inbetween-ness of these immigrants meant that the latter eventually "became ethnic" and that their trajectory was predictable. But their history was sloppier than their trajectory. From day to day they were, to borrow from E. P. Thompson, "proto-nothing," reacting and acting in a highly racialized nation.[8]

Overly ambitious, this essay is also deliberately disorderly. It aims to destabilize modern categories of race and ethnicity and to capture the confusion, inbetween-ness, and flux in the minds of native-born Americans and the immigrants themselves. Entangling the processes of Americanization and of whitening, it treats a two-sided experience: new immigrants underwent racial categorizing at the same time that they developed new identities, and the two sides of the process cannot be understood apart from one another. Similarly, the categories of state, class, and immigrant self-activity, used here to explain how race is made and to structure the paper, can be separated at best arbitrarily and inconsistently. Expect, therefore, a bumpy ride, which begins at its bumpiest, with the vocabulary of race.

Inbetween in the Popular Mind

America's racial vocabulary had no agency of its own, but rather reflected material conditions and power relations—the situations that workers faced on a daily basis in their workplaces and communities. Yet the words themselves were important. They were not only the means by which native-born and elite people marked new immigrants as inferiors, but also the means by which immigrant workers came to locate themselves and those about them in the nation's racial hierarchy. In beginning to analyze the vocabulary of race, it makes little sense for historians to invest the words themselves with an agency that could be exercised only by real historical actors, or meanings that derived only from the particular historical contexts in which the language was developed and employed. The word *guinea*, for example, had long referred to African slaves, particularly those from the continent's northwest coast, and to their descendants. But from the late 1890s, the term was increasingly applied to Southern European migrants, first and especially to Sicilians and southern Italians who often came as contract laborers. At various times and places in the United States, *guinea* has been applied to mark Greeks, Jews, Portuguese, Puerto Ricans, and perhaps any new immigrant.[9]

Likewise, *hunky*, which began life, probably in the early twentieth century, as a corruption of "Hungarian," eventually became a pan-Slavic slur connected with perceived immigrant racial characteristics. By World War I, the term was frequently used to describe any immigrant steelworker, as in *mill hunky*. Opponents of the Great 1919 Steel Strike, including some native-born skilled workers, derided the struggle as a "hunky strike." Yet Josef Barton's work suggests that for Poles, Croats, Slovenians, and other immigrants who often worked together in difficult, dangerous situations, the term embraced a remarkable, if fragile, sense of prideful identity across ethnic lines. In *Out of This Furnace*, Thomas Bell's 1941 epic novel based on the lives of Slavic steelworkers, he observed that the word hunky bespoke "unconcealed racial prejudice" and a "denial of social and racial equality." Yet as these workers built the industrial unions of the late 1930s and took greater control over their own lives, the meaning of the term began to change. The pride with which second- and third-generation Slavic American steelworkers, now including women as well as men, wore the label in the early 1970s seemed to have far more to do with class than with ethnic identity. At about the same time, the word *honky*, possibly a corruption of *hunky*, came into common use as black nationalism reemerged as a major ideological force in the African American community.¹⁰

Words and phrases employed by social scientists to capture the inbetween identity of the new immigrants are a bit more descriptive, if a bit more cumbersome. As late as 1937, John Dollard wrote repeatedly of the immigrant working class as "our temporary Negroes." More precise, if less dramatic, is the designation "not-yet-white ethnics" offered by Barry Goldberg. The term not only reflects the popular perceptions and everyday experiences of such workers, but also conveys the dynamic quality of the process of racial formation.¹¹

The examples of Greeks and Italians particularly underscore the new immigrants' ambiguous positions with regard to popular perceptions of race. When Greeks suffered as victims of an Omaha "race" riot in 1909, and when eleven Italians died at the hands of lynchers in Louisiana in 1891, their less-than-white racial status mattered alongside their nationalities. Indeed, as in the case of Loguidice's coal handler, their ambivalent racial status put their lives in jeopardy. As Gunther Peck shows in his fine study of copper miners in Bingham, Utah, the Greek and Italian immigrants were "nonwhite" before their tension-fraught cooperation with the Western Federation of Miners during a 1912 strike ensured that "the category of Caucasian worker changed and expanded." Indeed, the work of Dan Georgakas and Yvette Huginnie shows that Greeks and other Southern Europeans often "bivouacked" with other "nonwhite" workers in western mining towns. Pocatello, Idaho, Jim-Crowed Greeks in the early twentieth century, and in Arizona they were not welcomed by white workers in "white men's towns" or "white men's jobs." In Chicago during the Great Depression, a German American wife expressed regret over marrying her "half-nigger," Greek American husband. African American slang in the 1920s in South Carolina counted those of mixed American Indian, African American, and white heritage as Greeks. Greek Americans in the Midwest showed great anxieties about race, and were perceived not only as Puerto Rican, mulatto, Mexican, or Arab, but also as nonwhite because of being Greek.¹²

Italians, involved in a spectacular international diaspora in the early twentieth century, were racialized as the "Chinese of Europe" in many lands.¹³ But in the United States their racialization was pronounced and, as *guinea*'s evolution suggests, more likely to connect Italians with Africans. During the debate at the Louisiana state constitutional convention of 1898 over how to disfranchise blacks, and over which whites might lose the vote, some acknowledged that the Italian's skin "happens to be white" even as they argued for his disfranchisement. But others held that "according to the spirit of our meaning when we speak of 'white man's government,' [the Italians] are as black as the blackest negro in existence."[14] More than metaphor intruded on this judgment. At the turn of the century, a West Coast construction boss was asked, "You don't call the Italian a white man?" The negative reply assured the questioner that the Italian was "a dago." Recent studies of Italian and Greek Americans make a strong case that racial, not just ethnic, oppression long plagued "nonwhite" immigrants from Southern Europe.[15]

The racialization of Eastern Europeans was likewise striking. While racist jokes mocked the black servant who thought her child, fathered by a Chinese man, would be a Jew, racist folklore held that Jews, inside-out, were "niggers." In 1926, Serbo-Croatians ranked near the bottom of a list of forty "ethnic" groups whom "white American" respondents were asked to order according to the respondents' willingness to associate with members of each group. They placed just above Negroes, Filipinos, and Japanese. Just above them were Poles, who were near the middle of the list. One sociologist has recently written that "a good many groups on this color continuum [were] not considered white by a large number of Americans."[16] The literal inbetween-ness of new immigrants on such a list suggests what popular speech affirms: The state of whiteness was approached gradually and controversially. The authority of the state itself both smoothed and complicated that approach.

White Citizenship and Inbetween Americans: The State of Race

The power of the national state gave recent immigrants both their firmest claims to whiteness and their strongest leverage for enforcing those claims. The courts consistently allowed "new immigrants," whose racial status was ambiguous in the larger culture, to be naturalized as "white" citizens and almost as consistently turned down non-European applicants as "nonwhite." Political reformers therefore discussed the fitness for citizenship of recent European immigrants from two distinct angles. They produced, through the beginning of World War I, a largely benign and hopeful discourse on how to Americanize (and win the votes of) those already here. But this period also saw a debate on fertility rates and immigration restriction that conjured up threats of "race suicide" if this flow of migrants were not checked and the fertility of the native-born increased. A figure like Theodore Roosevelt could stand as both the Horatio warning of the imminent swamping of the "old stock" racial elements in the United States and as the optimistic Americanizer to whom the play which originated the assimilationist image of the "melting pot" was dedicated.[17]

Such anomalies rested not only on a political economy that at times needed and at times shunned immigrant labor, but also on peculiarities of U.S. naturalization law. If the state apparatus told new immigrants that they both were and were not white, it was clearly the judiciary that produced the most affirmative responses. Thus U.S. law made citizenship racial as well as civil. Even when much of the citizenry doubted the racial status of European migrants, the courts almost always granted their whiteness in naturalization cases. Thus, the often racially based campaigns against Irish naturalization in the 1840s and 1850s and against Italian naturalization in the early twentieth century aimed to delay, not deny, citizenship. The lone case that appears exceptional in this regard is one in which U.S. naturalization attorneys in Minnesota attempted unsuccessfully to bar radical Finns from naturalization on the ethnological grounds that they were not Caucasian and therefore not white.[18]

The legal equation of whiteness with fitness for citizenship significantly shaped the process by which race was made in the United States. If Southern and Eastern European immigrants remained "inbetween people" because of broad cultural perceptions, Asians were in case after case declared unambiguously nonwhite and therefore unfit for citizenship. This sustained pattern of denial of citizenship provides, as the sociologist Richard Williams argues, the best guide to who would be racialized in an ongoing way in the twentieth-century United States. It applies, of course, in the case of Native Americans. Migrants from Africa, though nominally an exception in that Congress in 1870 allowed their naturalization (with the full expectation that they would not be coming), of course experienced sweeping denials of civil status both in slavery and in Jim Crow. Nor were migrants from Mexico truly exceptional. Despite the naturalizability of such migrants by treaty and later court decisions, widespread denials of citizenship rights took place almost immediately—in one 1855 instance in California as a result of the "Greaser Bill," as the Vagrancy Act was termed.[19]

Likewise, the equation between legal whiteness and fitness for naturalizable citizenship helps to predict which groups would not be made nonwhite in an ongoing way. Not only did the Irish, whose whiteness was under question in the 1840s and 1850s, and later the "new immigrants" gain the powerful symbolic argument that the law declared them white and fit, but they also had the power of significant numbers of votes, although naturalization rates for new immigrants were not always high. During Louisiana's disfranchising constitutional convention of 1898, for example, the bitter debate over Italian whiteness ended with a provision passed extending to new immigrants protections comparable, even superior, to those which the "grandfather clause" gave to native white voters. New Orleans's powerful Choctaw Club machine, already the beneficiary of Italian votes, led the campaign for the plank.[20] When Thomas Hart Benton and Stephen Douglas argued against Anglo-Saxon superiority and for a pan-white "American race" in the 1850s, they did so before huge blocs of Irish voters. When Theodore Roosevelt extolled the "mixture of blood" making the American race, a "new ethnic type in this melting pot of the nations," he emphasized to new immigrant voters his conviction that each of their nationalities would enrich America by adding "its blood to the life of the nation." When Woodrow Wilson also tailored his thinking about the racial desirability of the new European immigrants, he did so in the context of an electoral campaign in which the "foreign" vote counted heavily.[21]

In such a situation, Roosevelt's almost laughable proliferation of uses of the word race served him well, according to his various needs as reformer, imperialist, debunker, romanticizer of the history of the West, and political candidate. He sincerely undertook seemingly contradictory embraces of Darwin and of Lamarck's insistence on the heritability of acquired characteristics, of melting pots and of race suicide, of an adoring belief in Anglo-Saxon and Teutonic superiority, and in the grandeur of a "mixed" American race. Roosevelt, like the Census Bureau, thought in terms of the nation's biological "stock"—the term by now called forth images of Wall Street as well as the farm. That stock was directly threatened by low birth rates among the nation's "English-speaking race." But races could also progress over time, and the very experience of mixing and of clashing with other races would bring out, and improve, the best of the "racestock." The "American race" could absorb and permanently improve the less desirable stock of "all white immigrants," perhaps in two generations, but only if its most desirable English-speaking racial elements were not swamped in an un-Americanized Slavic and Southern European culture and biology.[22] The neo-Lamarckianism that allowed Roosevelt to use such terms as "English-speaking race" ran through much of Progressive racial thinking, though it was sometimes underpinned by appeals to other authorities.[23]

We likely regard choosing between eating pasta or meat, between speaking English or Italian, between living in ill-ventilated or healthy housing, between taking off religious holidays or coming to work, between voting Republican or Socialist, as decisions based on environment, opportunity, and choice. But language loyalty, incidence of dying in epidemics, and radicalism often defined race for late nineteenth- and early twentieth-century thinkers, making distinctions between racial, religious, and antiradical varieties of nativism messy. For many, Americanization was not simply a cultural process but an index of racial change, which could fail if the concentration of "lower" races kept the "alchemy" of racial transformation from occurring.[24] From its very start, the campaign for immigration restriction directed against "new" Europeans carried a strong implication that even something as ineluctable as "moral tone" could be inherited. In deriding "ignorant, brutal Italians and Hungarian laborers" during the 1885 debate over the Contract Labor Law, its sponsor framed his environmentalist arguments in terms of color, holding that "the introduction into a community of any considerable number of persons of a lower moral tone will cause general moral deterioration as sure as night follows day." He added, "The intermarriage of a lower with a higher type certainly does not improve the latter any more than does the breeding of cattle by blooded and common stock improve the blooded stock generally." The restrictionist cause came to feature writings that saw mixing as always and everywhere disastrous. Madison Grant's *The Passing of the Great Race* (1916), a racist attack on recent immigrants that defended the purity of "Nordic" stock, the race of the "white man par excellence," against "Alpine," "Mediterranean," and Semitic invaders, is a classic example.[25]

Professional Americanizers and national politicians appealing to immigrant constituencies for a time seemed able to marginalize those who racialized new immigrants. Corporate America generally gave firm support to relatively open immigration. Settlement house reformers and others taught and witnessed Americanization. The best of them, Jane Addams, for example, learned from immigrants as well, and extolled not only assimilation but also the virtues of ongoing cultural differences among immigrant groups. Even progressive politicians showed potential to rein in their own most racially charged tendencies. As a southern academic, Woodrow Wilson wrote of the dire threat to "our Saxon habits of government" by "corruption of foreign blood," and characterized Italian and Polish immigrants as "sordid and hapless." But as a presidential candidate in 1912, he reassured immigrant leaders that "We are all Americans," offered to rewrite sections on Polish Americans in his *History of the American People*, and found Italian Americans "one of the most interesting and admirable elements in our American life."[26] Yet Progressive Era assimilationism, and even its flirtations with cultural pluralism, could not save new immigrants from racial attacks. If racial prejudice against new immigrants was far more provisional and nuanced than anti-Irish bias in the antebellum period, political leaders also defended "hunkies" and "guineas" far more provisionally. Meanwhile the Progressive project of imperialism and the Progressive nonproject of capitulation to Jim Crow ensured that race thinking would retain and increase its potency. If corporate leaders backed immigration and funded Americanization projects, the corporate model emphasized standardization, efficiency, and immediate results. This led many Progressives to support reforms that called immigrant political power and voting rights into question, at least in the short run.[27] In the longer term, big business proved by the early 1920s an unreliable supporter of the melting pot. Worried about unemployment and about the possibility that new immigrants were proving "revolutionary and communistic races," they equivocated on the openness of immigration, turned Americanizing agencies into labor spy networks, and stopped funding for the corporate-sponsored umbrella group of professional Americanizers and conservative new immigrant leaders, the Inter-Racial Council.[28]

Reformers, too, lost heart. Since mixing was never regarded as an unmitigated good, but as a matter of proportion with a number of possible outcomes, the new immigrants' record was constantly under scrutiny. The failure of Americanization to deliver total loyalty during World War I and during the postwar "immigrant rebellion" within U.S. labor made that record one of failure. The "virility," "manhood," and "vigor" that reformers predicted race mixture would inject into the American stock had long coexisted with the emphasis on obedience and docility in Americanization curricula.[29] At their most vigorous, in the 1919–1920 strike wave, new immigrants were most suspect. Nationalists, and many Progressive reformers among them, were, according to John Higham, sure that they had done "their best to bring the great mass of newcomers into the fold." The failure was not theirs, but a reflection of the "incorrigibly unassimilable nature of the material on which they had worked."[30]

The triumph of immigration restriction in the 1920s was in large measure a triumph of racism against new immigrants. Congress and the Ku Klux Klan, the media and popular opinion all reinforced the inbetween, and even the nonwhite, racial status of Eastern and Southern Europeans. Grant's *The Passing of the Great Race* suddenly enjoyed a vogue that had eluded it in 1916. The best-selling U.S. magazine *Saturday Evening Post* praised Grant and sponsored Kenneth Roberts's massively mounted fears that continued immigration would produce "a hybrid race of people as worthless and futile as the good-for-nothing mongrels of Central America and Southeastern Europe." When the National Industrial Conference Board met in 1923, its director allowed that restriction was "essentially a race question." Congress was deluged with letters of concern for preservation of a "distinct American type," and of support for stopping the "swamping" of the Nordic race. In basing itself on the first fear and setting quotas pegged squarely on the (alleged) origins of the current population, the 1924 restriction act also addressed the second fear, since the U.S. population as a whole came from the northern and western parts of Europe to a vastly greater extent than had the immigrant population for the last three decades. At virtually the same time that the courts carefully drew a color line between European new immigrants and nonwhite others, the Congress and reformers reaffirmed the racial inbetween-ness of Southern and Eastern Europeans.[31]

Americanization therefore was never just about nation, but always about race and nation. This truth stood out most clearly in the Americanizing influences of popular culture, in which mass-market films socialized new immigrants into a "gunfighter nation" of westerns and a vaudeville nation of blackface; in which popular music was both "incontestably mulatto" and freighted with the hierarchical racial heritage of minstrelsy; in which the most advertised lures of Americanized mass consumption turned on the opportunity to harness the energies of black servants like the Gold Dust twins, Aunt Jemima, and Rastus, the Cream of Wheat chef, to household labor. Drawing on a range of anti-immigrant stereotypes as well, popular entertainments and advertisements cast newcomers as nationally particular and racially inbetween, while teaching the all-important lesson that immigrants were never so white as when they wore blackface before audiences and cameras.[32]

Occasionally, professional Americanizers taught the same lesson. In a Polish and Bohemian neighborhood on Chicago's lower west side, for example, social workers at Gads Hill Center counted their 1915 minstrel show a "great success." Organized by the center's Young Men's Club, the event drew 350 people, many of whom at that point knew so little English that they could only "enjoy the music" and "appreciate the really attractive costumes." Young performers with names like Kraszewski, Pletcha, and Chimielewski sang "Clare De Kitchen" and "Gideon's Band." Settlement houses generally practiced Jim Crow, even in the North. Some of their leading theorists invoked a racial continuum that ended with African Americans "farthest in the rear," even as they goaded new immigrants toward giving up particular Old World cultures by branding the retention of such cultures as an atavistic clinging to "racial consciousness."[33]

"Inbetween" Jobs: Capital, Class, and the New Immigrant

Joseph Loguidice's reminiscence of the temporarily "colored" coal hauler compresses and dramatizes a process that went on in far more workaday settings as well. Often while themselves begrimed by the nation's dirtiest jobs, new immigrants and their children quickly learned that "the worst thing one could be in this Promised Land was 'colored.'"³⁴ But if the world of work taught the importance of being "not black," it also exposed new immigrants to frequent comparisons and close competition with African Americans. The results of such clashes in the labor market did not instantly propel new immigrants into either the category or the consciousness of whiteness. Instead, management created an economics of racial inbetween-ness, which taught new immigrants the importance of racial hierarchy while leaving open their place in that hierarchy. At the same time, the struggle for "inbetween jobs" further emphasized the importance of national and religious ties among immigrants by giving those ties an important economic dimension. The bitterness of job competition between new immigrants and African Americans has rightly received emphasis in accounting for racial hostility, but that bitterness must be historically investigated. Before 1915, new immigrants competed with relatively small numbers of African Americans for northern urban jobs. The new immigrants tended to be more recent arrivals than the black workers, and they came in such great numbers that, demographically speaking, they competed far more often with each other than with African Americans. Moreover, given the much greater "human capital" of black workers in terms of literacy, education, and English language skills, immigrants fared well in this competition.³⁵ After 1915, the decline of immigration resulting from World War I and restrictive legislation in the 1920s combined with the Great Migration of Afro-southerners to northern cities to create a situation in which a growing and newly arrived black working class provided massive competition for a more settled but struggling immigrant population. Again, the results were not of a sort that would necessarily have brought bitter disappointment to those whom the economic historians term SCES (Southern and Central Europeans).³⁶ The Sicilian immigrant, for example, certainly was at times locked in competition with African Americans. But was that competition more bitter and meaningful than competition with, for example, northern Italian immigrants, "hunkies," or white native-born workers, all of whom were at times said to be racially different from Sicilians?

The ways in which capital structured workplaces and labor markets contributed to the idea that competition should be both cutthroat and racialized. New immigrants suffered wage discrimination when compared to the white native-born. African Americans were paid less for the same jobs than the immigrants. In the early twentieth century, employers preferred a labor force divided by race and national origin. As the radical cartoonist Ernest Riebe understood at the time, and as the labor economists Richard Edwards,

Michael Reich, and David Gordon have recently reaffirmed, work gangs segregated by nationality as well as by race could be and were made to compete against each other in a strategy designed not only to undermine labor unity and depress wages in the long run, but also to spur competition and productivity every day.[37]

On the other hand, management made broader hiring and promotion distinctions which brought pan-national and sometimes racial categories into play. In some workplaces and areas, the blast furnace was a "Mexican job"; in others, it was a pan-Slavic "hunky" job. "Only hunkies," a steel industry investigator was told, worked blast furnace jobs, which were "too damn dirty and too damn hot for a white man." Management at the nation's best-studied early twentieth-century factory divided the employees into "white men" and "kikes." Such bizarre notions about the genetic "fit" between immigrants and certain types of work were buttressed by the "scientific" judgments of scholars like the sociologist E. A. Ross, who observed that Slavs were "immune to certain kinds of dirt . . . that would kill a white man." "Scientific" managers in steel and in other industries designed elaborate ethnic classification systems to guide their hiring. In 1915, the personnel manager at one Pittsburgh plant analyzed what he called the "racial adaptability" of thirty-six different ethnic groups to twenty-four different kinds of work and twelve sets of conditions, and plotted them all on a chart. Lumber companies in Louisiana built what they called "the Quarters" for black workers and (separately) for Italians, using language very recently associated with African American slavery. For white workers they built company housing and towns. The distinction between "white" native-born workers and "nonwhite" new immigrants, Mexicans, and African Americans in parts of the West rested in large part on the presence of "white man's camps" or "white man's towns" in company housing in lumbering and mining. Native-born residents interviewed in the wake of a bitter 1915 strike by Polish oil refinery workers recognized only two classes of people in Bayonne, New Jersey: "foreigners" and "white men." In generalizing about early twentieth-century nativism, John Higham concludes: "In all sections native-born and Northern European laborers called themselves 'white men' to distinguish themselves from Southern Europeans whom they worked beside." As late as World War II, new immigrants and their children, lumped together as "racials," suffered employment discrimination in the defense industry.[38]

There was also substantial management interest in the specific comparison of new immigrants with African Americans as workers. More concrete in the North and abstract in the South, these complex comparisons generally, but not always, favored the former group. African Americans' supposed undependability, "especially on Mondays," intolerance for cold, and incapacity for fast-paced work were all noted. But the comparisons were often nuanced. New immigrants, as Herbert Gutman long ago showed, were themselves counted as unreliable, "especially on Mondays." Some employers counted black workers as more apt and skillful "in certain occupations," and cleaner and happier than "the alien white races." An occasional blanket preference for African Americans over immigrants surfaced, as at Packard in Detroit in 1922. Moreover, comparisons carried a provisional quality, since ongoing competition was often desired. In 1905, the superintendent of Illinois Steel, threatening to fire all Slavic workers, reassured the immigrants that no "race hatred" [against Slavs!] motivated the proposed decision, which was instead driven by a factor that the workers could change: their tardiness in adopting the English language.[39]

The fact that recent immigrants were relatively inexperienced vis-à-vis African American workers in the North in 1900 and relatively experienced by 1930 makes it difficult for economic historians to measure the extent to which immigrant economic mobility in this period derived from employer discrimination. Clearly, timing and demographic change mattered alongside racism in a situation in which the immigrant SCEs came to occupy spaces on the job ladder between African Americans below and those who were fed into the economic historians' computers as NWNPs (native-born whites with native-born parents). Stanley Lieberson uses the image of a "queue" to help explain the role of discrimination against African Americans in leading to such results.[40] In the lineup of workers ordered by employer preference, as in so much else, new immigrants were inbetween. In a society in which workers did in fact shape up in lines to seek jobs, the image of a queue is wonderfully apt. However, the Polish worker next to an African American on one side and an Italian American on the other as an NWNP manager hired unskilled labor did not know the statistics of current job competition, let alone what the results would be by the time of the 1930 census. Even if the Polish worker had known them, the patterns of mobility for his group would likely have differed as much from those of the Italian Americans as from those of the African Americans (who in some cities actually outdistanced Polish immigrants in intra-working-class mobility to better jobs from 1900 to 1930).[41]

Racialized struggles over jobs were fed by the general experience of brutal, group-based competition, and by the knowledge that black workers were especially vulnerable competitors who fared far less well in the labor market than any other native-born American group. The young Croatian immigrant

Stjepan Mesaros was so struck by the abuse of a black coworker that he asked a Serbian laborer for an explanation. "You'll soon learn something about this country," came the reply. "Negroes never get a fair chance." The exchange initiated a series of conversations that contributed to Mesaros becoming Steve Nelson, an influential radical organizer and an antiracist. But for most immigrants, caught in a world of dog-eat-dog competition, the lesson would likely have been that African Americans were among the eaten.[42]

If immigrants did not know the precise contours of the job queue, nor their prospects in it, they did have their own ideas about how to get in line, their own strategies about how to get ahead in it, and their own dreams for getting out of it. These tended to reinforce a sense of the advantage of being "not nonwhite," but to also emphasize specific national and religious identifications rather than generalized white identity. Because of the presence of a small employing (or subcontracting) class in their communities, new immigrants were far more likely than African Americans to work for one of "their own" as an immediate boss. In New York City, in 1910, for example, almost half of the sample of Jewish workers studied by Suzanne Model had Jewish supervisors, as did about one Italian immigrant in seven. Meanwhile, "the study sample unearthed only one industrial match between laborers and supervisors among Blacks."[43] In shrugging at being called "hunky," Thomas Bell writes, Slovak immigrants took solace that they "had come to America to find work and save money, not to make friends with the Irish." But getting work and "making friends with" Irish American foremen, skilled workers, union leaders, and politicians were often very much connected, and the relationships were hardly smooth. Petty bosses could always rearrange the queue.[44] But over the long run, a common Catholicism (and sometimes common political machine affiliations) gave new immigrant groups access to the fragile favor of Irish Americans in positions to influence hiring, which African Americans could not achieve. Sometimes such favor was organized, as through the Knights of Columbus in Kansas City packinghouses. Over time, as second-generation marriages across national lines but within the Catholic religion became a pattern, kin joined religion in shaping hiring in ways largely excluding African Americans.[45] Many of the new immigrant groups also had distinctive plans to move out of the U.S. wage-labor queue altogether. From 1880 to 1930, fully one-third of all Italian immigrants were "birds of passage," who in many cases never intended to stay. This pattern likewise applied to 46 percent of Greeks entering between 1908 and 1923 and to 40 percent of Hungarians entering between 1899 and 1913.[46]

Strong national (and subnational) loyalties obviously persisted in such cases, with saving money to send or take home probably a far higher priority than sorting out the complexities of racial identity in the United States. Similarly, those many new immigrants (especially among the Greeks, Italians, and Jews) who hoped to (and did) leave the working class by opening small businesses set great store by saving, and often catered to a clientele composed mainly of their own group. But immigrant saving itself proved highly racialized, as did immigrant small businesses in many instances. Within U.S. culture, African Americans symbolized prodigal lack of savings, as the Chinese, Italians, and Jews did fanatical obsession with saving. Popular racist mythology held that if paid a dollar and a quarter, Italians would spend only the quarter, while African Americans would spend a dollar and a half. Characteristically, racial common sense cast both patterns as pathological.[47] Moreover, in many cases Jewish and Italian merchants sold to African American customers. Their "middleman minority" status revealingly identifies an inbetween position which, as aggrieved southern "white" merchants complained, rested on a more humane attitude toward black customers and on such cultural affinities as an eagerness to participate in bargaining over prices. Chinese merchants traditionally and Korean merchants more recently have occupied a similar position. Yet, as an 1897 New York City correspondent for *Harper's Weekly* captured in an article remarkable for its precise balancing of antiblack and anti-Semitic racism, the middleman's day-to-day position in the marketplace reinforced specific Jewish identity and distance from blacks. "For a student of race characteristics," the reporter wrote, "nothing could be more striking than to observe the stoic scorn of the Hebrew when he is made a disapproving witness of the happy-go-lucky joyousness of his dusky neighbor."[48]

Other immigrants, especially Slovaks and Poles, banked on hard labor, homeownership, and slow intergenerational mobility for success. They too navigated in very tricky racial cross-currents. Coming from areas in which the dignity of hard, physical labor was established, both in the countryside and in cities, they arrived in the United States eager to work, even if in jobs that did not take advantage of their skills. They often found, however, that in the Taylorizing industries of the United States, hard work was more driven and alienating.[49] It was, moreover, often typed and despised as "nigger work"—or as "dago work" or "hunky work" in settings in which such categories had been freighted with the prior meaning of "nigger work." The new immigrants' reputation for hard work and their unfamiliarity with English and with American culture generally tended to lead to their being hired as an almost abstract source of labor. "Hunky" was abbreviated to "hunk," and Slavic laborers in particular were treated as mere pieces of work. This had its advantages, especially in comparison to black workers; Slavs could more often get hired in groups, while skilled workers and petty bosses favored individual "good Negroes" with unskilled jobs, often requiring a familiarity and subservience from them not expected of new immigrants. But being seen as brute force also involved Eastern Europeans in particularly brutal social relations on the shopfloor.[50] Hard work, especially when closely bossed, was likewise not a badge of manliness in the United States in the way that it had been in Eastern Europe. Racialized, it was also demasculinized, especially since its extremely low pay and sporadic nature ensured that new immigrant males could not be breadwinners for a family. The idea of becoming a "white man," unsullied by racially typed labor and capable of earning a family wage, was therefore extremely attractive in many ways, and the imperative of not letting one's job become "nigger work" was swiftly learned.[51] Yet no clear route ran from inbetween-ness to white manhood. "White men's unions" often seemed the best path, but they also erected some of the most significant obstacles.

White Men's Unions and New Immigrant Trial Members

While organized labor exercised little control over hiring outside of a few organized crafts during most of the years from 1895 until 1924 and beyond, its racialized opposition to new immigrants did reinforce their inbetween-ness, both on the job and in politics. Yet the American Federation of Labor also provided an important venue in which "old immigrant" workers interacted with new immigrants, teaching important lessons in both whiteness and Americanization. As an organization devoted to closing skilled trades to any new competition, the craft union's reflex was to oppose outsiders. In this sense, most of the AFL unions were "exclusionary by definition" and marshaled economic, and to a lesser extent political, arguments to exclude women, Chinese, Japanese, African Americans, the illiterate, the noncitizen, and the new immigrants from organized workplaces, and, whenever possible, from the shores of the United States. So clear was the craft logic of AFL restrictionism that historians are apt to regard it as simply materialistic and to note its racism only when direct assaults were made on groups traditionally regarded as nonwhite. John Higham argues that only in the last moments of the major 1924 debates over whom to restrict did Gompers, in this view, reluctantly embrace "the idea that European immigration endangered America's racial foundations."[52]

Yet Gwendolyn Mink and Andrew Neather demonstrate that it is far more difficult than Higham implies to separate appeals based on craft or race in AFL campaigns to restrict European immigration. A great deal of trade unions' racist opposition to the Chinese stressed the connection between their "slave-like" subservience and their status as coolie laborers, schooled and trapped in the Chinese social system and willing to settle for being "cheap men."[53] Dietary practices (rice and rats rather than meat) symbolized Chinese failure to seek the "American standard of living." All of these are cultural, historical, and environmental matters. Yet none of them prevented the craft unions from declaring the Chinese "race" unassimilable, nor from supporting exclusionary legislation premised largely on racial grounds. The environmentalist possibility that over generations Asian "cheap men" might improve was simply irrelevant. By that time the Chinese race would have polluted America.[54]

Much of the anti-Chinese rhetoric was applied as well to Hungarians in the 1880s and was taken over in AFL anti–new immigration campaigns after 1890. Pasta, as Mink implies, joined rice as an "un-American" and racialized food. Far from abjuring arguments based on "stock," assimilability, and homogeneity, the AFL's leaders supported literacy tests designed specifically "to reduce the numbers of Slavic and Mediterranean immigrants." They supported the nativist racism of the antilabor Senator Henry Cabot Lodge, hoped anti-Japanese agitation could be made to contribute to anti–new immigrant restrictions, emphasized "the incompatibility of the new immigrants with the very nature of American civilization," and both praised and reprinted works on "race suicide."[55] They opposed entry of "the scum" from "the least civilized countries of Europe" and "the replacing of the independent and intelligent coal miners of Pennsylvania by the Huns and Slavs." They feared that an "American" miner in Pennsylvania could thrive only if he "Latinizes" his name. They explicitly asked, well before World War I: "How much more [new] immigration can this country absorb and retain its homogeneity?" (Those wanting to know the dire answer were advised to study the "racial history" of cities.)[56]

Robert Asher is undoubtedly correct in arguing both that labor movement reaction to new immigrants was "qualitatively different from the response to Orientals" and that AFL rhetoric was "redolent of a belief in racial inferiority" of Southern and Eastern Europeans. Neather is likewise on the mark in speaking of "semi-racial" union arguments for restriction directed against new immigrants.[57] Gompers's characterization of new immigrants as "beaten men of beaten races" perfectly captures the tension between fearing that Southern and Eastern Europe was dumping its "vomit" and "scum" in the United States and believing that Slavic and Mediterranean people were scummy. Labor sometimes cast its ideal as an "Anglo-Saxon race . . . true to itself." Gompers was more open, but equivocal. He found that the wonderful "peculiarities of temperament such as patriotism, sympathy, etc.," which made labor unionism possible, were themselves "peculiar to most of the Caucasian race." In backing literacy tests for immigrants in 1902, he was more explicit. They would leave British, German, Irish, French, and Scandinavian immigration intact but "shut out a considerable number of Slavs and other[s] equally or more undesirable and injurious."58

Such "semi-racial" nativism shaped the AFL's politics and led to the exclusion of new immigrants from many unions. When iron puddler poet Michael McGovern envisioned an ideal celebration for his union, he wrote, "There were no men invited such as Slavs and 'Tally Annes,' Hungarians and Chinamen with pigtail cues and fans." The situation in the building trades was complicated. Some craft unions excluded Italians, Jews, and other new immigrants. Among laborers, organization often began on an ethnic basis, though such immigrant locals were often eventually integrated into a national union. Even among craftsmen, separate organizations emerged among Jewish carpenters and painters and other recent immigrants. The hod carriers' union, according to Asher, "appears to have been created to protect the jobs of native construction workers against competing foreigners." The shoe workers, piano makers, barbers, hotel and restaurant workers, and United Textile Workers likewise kept out new immigrants, whose lack of literacy, citizenship, English-language skills, apprenticeship opportunities, and initiation fees also effectively barred them from many other craft locals. This "internal protectionism" apparently had lasting results. Lieberson's research through 1950 shows new immigrants and their children having far less access to craft jobs in unionized sectors than did whites of northwestern European origin.59

Yet Southern and Eastern European immigrants had more access to unionized work than African Americans, and unions never supported outright bans on their migration, as they did with Asians. Organized labor's opposition to the Italians as the "white Chinese," or to recent immigrants generally as "white coolies" usually acknowledged and questioned whiteness at the same time, associating whites with nonwhites while leaving open the possibility that contracted labor, and not race, was at issue. A strong emphasis on the "brotherhood" of labor also complicated matters. Paeans to the "International Fraternity of Labor" ran in the *American Federationist* within fifteen pages of anti-immigrant hysteria such as A. A. Graham's "The Un-Americanizing of America." Reports from Italian labor leaders and poems like "Brotherhood of Man" ran hard by fearful predictions of race suicide.⁶⁰

Moreover, the very things that the AFL warned about in its anti-immigrant campaigns encouraged the unions to make tactical decisions to enroll Southern and Eastern Europeans as members. Able to legally enter the country in large numbers, secure work, and become voters, "hunkies" and "guineas" had social power that could be used to attack the craft unionism of the AFL from the right or, as was often feared, from the left. To restrict immigration, however desirable from Gompers's point of view, did not answer what to do about the majority of the working class, which was by 1910 already of immigrant origins. Nor did it speak to what to do about the many new immigrants already joining unions in the AFL, in language and national federations, or under socialist auspices. If these new immigrants were not going to undermine the AFL's appeals to corporate leaders as an effective moderating force within the working class, the American Federation of Labor would have to consider becoming the Americanizing Federation of Labor.⁶¹

Most importantly, changes in machinery and Taylorizing relations of production made real the threat that crafts could be undermined by expedited training of unskilled and semiskilled immigrant labor. While this threat gave force to labor's nativist calls for immigration restriction, it also strengthened initiatives toward a "new unionism" that crossed skill lines to organize recent immigrants. Prodded by independent, dual-unionist initiatives like those by Italian socialists and the United Hebrew Trades, by the example of existing industrial unions in its own ranks, and by the left-wing multinational, multiracial unionism of the Industrial Workers of the World, the AFL increasingly got into the business of organizing and Americanizing new immigrant workers in the early twentieth century. The logic, caught perfectly by a Lithuanian American packinghouse worker in Chicago, was often quite utilitarian: "[B]ecause those sharp foremen are inventing new machines and the work is easier to learn, and so these slow Lithuanians and even green girls can learn to do it, and the Americans and Germans and Irish are put out and the employer saves money. . . . This was why the American labor unions began to organize us all." Even so, especially in those where new immigrant women were the potential union members and skill dilution threatened mainly immigrant men, the Gompers leadership at times refused either to incorporate dual unions or to initiate meaningful organizing efforts under AFL auspices.⁶²

However self-interested, wary, and incomplete the AFL's increasing opening to new immigrant workers remained, it initiated a process that much transformed "semi-racial" typing of recently arrived immigrants. Unions and their supporters at times treasured labor organization as the most meaningful agent of democratic "Americanization from the bottom up"—what John R. Commons called "the only effective Americanizing force for the southeastern European."[63] In struggles, native-born unionists came to observe not only the common humanity, but also the heroism of new immigrants. Never quite giving up on biological/cultural explanations, labor leaders wondered which "race" made the best strikers, with some comparisons favoring the recent arrivals over Anglo-Saxons. Industrial Workers of the World leader Covington Hall's reports from Louisiana remind us that we know little about how unionists, and workers generally, conceived of race. Hall took seriously the idea of a "Latin race," including Italians, other Southern Europeans, and Mexicans, all of whom put southern whites to shame with their militancy.[64] In the rural West, a "white man," labor investigator Peter Speek wrote, "is an extreme individualist, busy with himself," a "native or old-time immigrant" laborer, boarded by employers. "A foreigner," he added, "is more sociable and has a higher sense of comradeship" and of nationality. Embracing the very racial vocabulary to which he objected, one socialist plasterer criticized native-born unionists who described Italians as "guineas." He pointed out that Italians' ancestors "were the best and unsurpassable in manhood's glories; at a time when our dads were running about in paint and loincloth as ignorant savages." To bring the argument up to the present, he added that Italian Americans "are as manly for trade union conditions as the best of us; and that while handicapped by our prejudice."[65]

While such questioning of whiteness was rare, the "new unionism" provided an economic logic for progressive unionists wishing to unite workers across ethnic and racial lines. With their own race less open to question, new immigrants were at times brought into class-conscious coalitions, as whites and with African Americans. The great success of the packinghouse unions in forging such unity during World War I ended in a shining victory and vastly improved conditions. The diverse new immigrants and black workers at the victory celebration heard Chicago Federation of Labor leader John Fitzpatrick hail them as "black and white together under God's sunshine." If the Irish American unionists had often been bearers of "race hatred" against both new immigrants and blacks, they and other old immigrants could also convey the lesson that class unity transcended race and semi-race.[66]

But even at the height of openings toward new unionism and new immigrants, labor organizations taught very complex lessons regarding race. At times, overtures toward new immigrants coincided with renewed exclusion of nonwhite workers, underlining W. E. B. Du Bois's point that the former were mobbed to make them join unions and the latter to keep them out. Western Federation of Miners (WFM) activists, whose episodic radicalism coexisted with nativism and a consistent anti-Chinese and anti-Mexican racism, gradually developed a will and a strategy to organize Greek immigrants, but they reaffirmed exclusion of Japanese mine workers and undermined impressive existing solidarities between Greeks and Japanese, who often worked similar jobs.[67] The fear of immigrant "green hands," which the perceptive Lithuanian immigrant quoted above credited with first sparking the Butcher Workmen to organize recent immigrants in 1904, was also a fear of black hands, so that one historian has suggested that the desire to limit black employment generated the willingness to organize new immigrants.[68]

In 1905, Gompers promised that "Caucasians are not going to let their standard of living be destroyed by Negroes, Chinamen, Japs, or any others."[69] Hearing this, new immigrant unionists might have reflected on what they as Caucasians had to learn regarding their newfound superiority to nonwhites. Or they might have fretted that "guineas" and "hunkies" would be classified along with "any others" undermining white standards. Either way, learning about race was an important part of new immigrant's labor education.

Teaching Americanism, the labor movement also taught whiteness. The scattered racist jokes in the labor and socialist press could not, of course, rival blackface entertainments or the "coon songs" in the Sunday comics in teaching new immigrants the racial ropes of the United States. But the movement did provide a large literature of popularized racist ethnology, editorial attacks on "nigger equality," and in Jack London a major cultural figure who taught that it was possible and desirable to be "first of all a white man and only then a socialist."[70] But the influence of organized labor and the left on race thinking was far more focused on language than on literature, on picket lines than lines on a page. Unions that opened to new immigrants more readily than to "nonwhites" not only reinforced the "inbetween" position of Southern and Eastern Europeans but attempted to teach immigrants intricate and spurious associations of race, strikebreaking, and lack of manly pride. Even as AFL exclusionism ensured that there would be black strikebreakers and black suspicion of unions, the language of labor equated scabbing with "turning nigger." The unions organized much of their critique around a notion of "slavish" behavior, which could be employed against ex-slaves or against Slavs, but indicted the former more often than the latter.[71] Warning all union men against "slave-like" behavior, unions familiarized new workers with the ways race and slavery had gone together to define a standard of unmanned servility. In objectively confusing situations, with scabs coming from the African American, immigrant, and native-born working classes (and with craft unions routinely breaking each other's strikes), Booker T. Washington identified one firm rule of thumb: "Strikers seem to consider it a much greater crime for a Negro who had been denied the opportunity to work at his trade to take the place of a striking employee than for a white man to do the same thing."[72] In such situations, whiteness had its definite appeals.

But the left and labor movements could abruptly remind new immigrants that their whiteness was anything but secure. Jack London could turn from denunciations of the "yellow peril" or of African Americans to excoriations of "the dark-pigmented things" coming in from Europe. The 1912 Socialist Party campaign book connected European immigration with "race annihilation" and the "possible degeneration of even the succeeding American type." The prominence of black strikebreakers in several of the most important mass strikes after World War I strengthened the grip of racism, perhaps even among recent immigrants, but the same years also brought renewed racial attacks on the immigrants themselves. In the wake of these failed strikes, the *American Federationist* featured disquisitions on "Americanism and Immigration" by John Quinn, the national commander of the nativist and antilabor American Legion. New immigrants had unarguably proven the most loyal unionists in the most important of the strikes, yet the AFL now supported exclusion based on "racial" quotas. Quinn brought together biology, environment, and the racialized history of the United States, defending American stock against Italian "industrial slaves" particularly, and the "indigestion of immigration" generally.[73]

Inbetween and Indifferent: New Immigrant Racial Consciousness

One Italian American informant interviewed by a Louisiana scholar remembered the early twentieth century as a time when "he and his family had been badly mistreated by a French plantation owner near New Roads where he and his family were made to live among the Negroes and were treated in the same manner. At first he did not mind because he did not know any difference, but when he learned the position that the Negroes occupied in this country, he demanded that his family be moved to a different house and be given better treatment." In denouncing all theories of white supremacy, the Polish-language Chicago-based newspaper *Dziennik Chicagoski* editorialized, "if the words 'superior race' are replaced by the words 'Anglo-Saxon' and instead of 'inferior races' such terms as Polish, Italian, Russian and Slavs in general—not to mention the Negro, the Chinese, and the Japanese—are applied, then we shall see the political side of the racial problems in the United States in stark nakedness."[74] In the first instance, consciousness of an inbetween racial status leads to a desire for literal distance from nonwhites. In the second, inbetween-ness leads to a sense of grievances shared in common with nonwhites.

In moving from the racial categorization of new immigrants to their own racial consciousness, it is important to realize that "Europeans were hardly likely to have found racist ideologies an astounding new encounter when they arrived in the U.S.," though the salience of whiteness as a social category in the United States was exceptional. "Civilized" northern Italians derided those darker ones from Sicily and the *mezzogiorno* as "Turks" and "Africans" long before arriving in Brooklyn or Chicago. And once arrived, if they spoke of "little dark fellows," they were far more likely to be describing southern Italians than African Americans. The strength of anti-Semitism, firmly ingrained in Poland and other parts of Eastern Europe, meant that many immigrants from these regions were accustomed to looking at a whole "race" of people as devious, degraded, and dangerous. In the United States, both Jews and Poles spoke of riots involving attacks on African Americans as "pogroms." In an era of imperialist expansion and sometimes strident nationalism, a preoccupation with race was characteristic not only of the United States but also of many European regions experiencing heavy emigration to the United States.[75]

Both eager embraces of whiteness and, more rarely, flirtations with nonwhiteness characterized these immigrants' racial identity. But to assume that new immigrants as a mass clearly saw their identity with nonwhites, or clearly fastened on their differences, is to miss the confusion of inbetween-ness. The discussion of whiteness was an uncomfortable terrain for many reasons, and even in separating themselves from African Americans and Asian Americans, immigrants did not necessarily become white. Indeed, often they were curiously indifferent to whiteness. Models that fix on one extreme or the other of immigrant racial consciousness—the quick choice of whiteness amid brutal competition or the solidarity with nonwhite working people based on common oppression—capture parts of the new immigrant experience.[76] At times Southern and Eastern Europeans were exceedingly apt, and not very critical, students of American racism. Greeks admitted to the Western Federation of Miners saw the advantage of their membership and did not rock the boat by demanding admission for the Japanese American mine workers with whom they had previously allied. Greek Americans sometimes battled for racial status fully within the terms of white supremacy, arguing that classical civilization had established them as "the highest type of the Caucasian race." In the company town of Pullman and adjacent neighborhoods, immigrants who sharply divided on national and religious lines coalesced impressively as whites in 1928 to keep out African American residents.⁷⁷ Recently arrived Jewish immigrants on New York City's Lower East Side resented reformers who encouraged them to make a common cause with the "schwartzes." In New Bedford, "white Portuguese" angrily reacted to perceived racial slights and sharply drew the color line against "black Portuguese" Cape Verdeans, especially when preference in jobs and housing hung in the balance.⁷⁸ Polish workers may have developed their very self-image and honed their reputation in more or less conscious counterpoint to the stereotypical "niggerscab." Theodore Radzialowski reasons that "Poles who had so little going for them (except their white skin—certainly no mean advantage but more important later than earlier in their American experience) may have grasped this image of themselves as honest, honorable, non-scabbing workers and stressed the image of the black scab in order to distinguish themselves from . . . the blacks with whom they shared the bottom of American society."⁷⁹

Many new immigrants learned to deploy and manipulate white supremacist images from the vaudeville stage and the screens of Hollywood films, where they saw "their own kind" stepping out of conventional racial and gender roles through blackface and other forms of cross-dressing. "Facing nativist pressure that would assign them to the dark side of the racial divide," Michael Rogin argues provocatively, immigrant entertainers like Al Jolson, Sophie Tucker, and Rudolph Valentino "Americanized themselves by crossing and recrossing the racial line."⁸⁰

At the same time, immigrants sometimes hesitated to embrace a white identity. Houston's Greek Americans developed, and retained, a language setting themselves apart from *i mavri* (the blacks), from *i aspri* (the whites), and from Mexican Americans. In New England, Greeks worked in coalitions with Armenians, whom the courts were worriedly accepting as white, and with Syrians, whom the courts found nonwhite. The large Greek American sponge-fishing industry based in Tarpon Springs, Florida, fought the Ku Klux Klan and employed black workers on an equal, share-the-catch system. Nor did Tarpon Springs practice Jim Crow in public transportation. In Louisiana and Mississippi, southern Italians learned Jim Crow tardily, even when legally accepted as whites, so much so that native whites fretted and black southerners "made unabashed distinctions between Dagoes and white folks," treating the former with a "friendly, first name familiarity." In constructing an anti-Nordic supremacist history series based on the "gifts" of various peoples, the Knights of Columbus quickly and fully included African Americans. Italian and Italian American radicals "consistently expressed horror at the barbaric treatment of blacks," in part because "Italians were also regarded as an inferior race." Denouncing not only lynchings but "the republic of lynchings," and branding the rulers of the United States as "savages of the blue eyes," *Il Proletario* asked: "What do they think they are as a race, these arrogant whites?" and ruthlessly wondered, "and how many kisses have their women asked for from the strong and virile black servants?" Italian radicals knew exactly how to go for the jugular vein in U.S. race relations. The Jewish press at times identified with both the suffering and the aspirations of African Americans. In 1912, Chicago's *Daily Jewish Courier* concluded that "In this world . . . the Jew is treated as a Negro and Negro as a Jew," and that the "lynching of the Negroes in the South is similar to massacres on Jews in Russia."[81] Examples could, and should, be piled higher on both sides of the new immigrants' racial consciousness. But to see the matter largely in terms of which stack is higher misses the extent to which the exposed position of racial inbetween-ness could generate both positions at once, and sometimes a desire to avoid the issue of race entirely. The best frame of comparison for discussing new immigrant racial consciousness is that of Irish Americans in the mid-nineteenth century. Especially when not broadly accepted as such, Irish Americans insisted that politicians acknowledge them as part of the dominant race. Changing the political subject from Americanness and religion to race whenever possible, they challenged anti-Celtic Anglo-Saxonism by becoming leaders in the cause of white supremacy.[82]

New immigrant leaders never approximated that path. With a large segment of both parties willing to vouch for the possibility of speedy, orderly Americanization, and with neither party willing to vouch unequivocally for their racial character, Southern and Eastern Europeans generally tried to change the subject from whiteness to nationality and loyalty to American ideals. One factor in such a desire not to be drawn into debates about whiteness was a strong national/cultural identification as Jews, Italians, Poles, and so on. At times, the strongest tie might even be to a specific Sicilian or Slovakian village, but the first sustained contact between African Americans and "new immigrants" occurred during World War I, when many of these immigrants were mesmerized by the emergence of Poland and other new states throughout Eastern and Southeastern Europe. Perhaps this is why new immigrants in Chicago and other riot-torn cities seem to have abstained from early twentieth-century race riots to a far greater extent than theories connecting racial violence and job competition at "the bottom" of society would predict. Important Polish spokespersons and newspapers emphasized that the Chicago riots were between the "whites" and "Negroes." Polish immigrants had, and should have, no part in them. What might be termed an abstention from whiteness also characterized the practice of rank-and-file Eastern Europeans. Slavic immigrants played little role in the racial violence, which was spread by Irish American gangs.[83]

Throughout the Chicago riot, so vital to the future of Slavic packinghouse workers and their union, Polish American coverage was sparse, occurring only when editors "could tear their attention away from their fascination with the momentous events attending the birth of the new Polish state." And even then, comparisons with pogroms against Jews in Poland framed the discussion. That the defense of Poland was as important as analyzing the realities in Chicago emerges starkly in the convoluted expression of sympathy for riot victims in the organ of the progressive, prolabor Alliance of Polish Women, *Glos Polek*: "The American Press has written at length about the alleged pogroms of Jews in Poland for over two months. Now it is writing about pogroms against Blacks in America. It wrote about the Jews in words full of sorrow and sympathy, why does it not show the same today to Negroes being burnt and killed without mercy?"[84]

Both "becoming American" and "becoming white" could imply coercive threats to European national identities. The 1906 remarks of Luigi Villiari, an Italian government official investigating Sicilian sharecroppers in Louisiana, illustrate the gravity and interrelation of the two processes. Villiari found that "a majority of plantation owners cannot comprehend that ... Italians are white," and instead considered the Sicilian migrant "a white-skinned negro who is a better worker than the black-skinned Negro." He patiently explained the "commonly held distinction ... between 'negroes,' 'Italians' and 'whites' (that is, Americans)." In the South, he added, the "American will not engage in agricultural, manual labor, rather he leaves it to the Negroes. Seeing that the Italians will do this work, naturally he concludes that Italians lack dignity. The only way an Italian can emancipate himself from this inferior state is to abandon all sense of national pride and to identify completely with the Americans."[85]

One-hundred-percent whiteness and one-hundred-percent Americanism carried overlapping and confusing imperatives for new immigrants in and out of the South, but in several ways the former was even more uncomfortable terrain than the latter. The pursuit of white identity, so tied to competition for wage labor and to political citizenship, greatly privileged male perceptions. But identity formation, as Americanizers and immigrant leaders realized, rested in great part on the activities of immigrant mothers, who entered discussions of nationality and Americanization more easily than those of race.[86] More cast in determinism, the discourse of race produced fewer openings to inject class demands, freedom, and cultural pluralism than did the discourse of Americanism. The modest strength of *herrenvolk* democracy, weakened even in the South at a time when huge numbers of poor whites were disfranchised, paled in comparison to the opportunities to try to give a progressive spin to the idea of a particularly freedom-loving "American race." In a fascinating quantified sociological study of Poles in Buffalo in the mid-1920s, Niles Carpenter and Daniel Katz concluded that their interviewees had been "Americanized" without being "de-Polandized." Their data led to the conclusion that Polish immigrants displayed "an absence of strong feeling so far as the Negro is concerned," a pattern "certainly in contrast to the results which would be sure to follow the putting of similar questions to a typically American group." The authors therefore argued for "the inference that so-called race feeling in this country is much more a product of tensions and quasi-psychoses born of our own national experience than of any factors inherent in the relations of race to race." Their intriguing characterization of Buffalo's Polish community did not attempt to cast its racial views as "pro-Negro," but instead pointed out that "the bulk of its members express indifference towards him." Such indifference, noted also by other scholars, was the product not of unfamiliarity with, or distance from, the U.S. racial system, but of nationalism compounded by intense, harrowing, and contradictory experiences between whiteness and nonwhiteness.[87]

Only after the racial threat of new immigration was defused by the racial restriction of the Johnson-Reed Act would new immigrants haltingly find a place in the ethnic wing of the white race. This brief treatment of a particularly complicated issue necessarily leaves out a number of key episodes, especially in the latter stages of the story. One is a resolution of sorts in the ambiguous status of inbetween immigrant workers, which came in the late 1930s and the World War II era. In some settings, these years brought not only a greater emphasis on cultural pluralism and a new, broader language of Americanism that embraced working-class ethnics, but also a momentary lull in racial conflict. With the creation of strong, interracial industrial unions, African American local officials and shop stewards fought for civil rights at the same time they led white "ethnic" workers in important industrial struggles.[88] Yet in other settings, sometimes even in the same cities, the war years and the period immediately following brought riots and hate strikes over the racial integration of workplaces and, especially, neighborhoods. Most second-generation ethnics embraced their Americanness, but, as Gary Gerstle suggests, this "may well have intensified their prejudice against Blacks, for many conceived of Americanization in racial terms: becoming American meant becoming white."[89]

During the 1970s, a later generation of white ethnics rediscovered their ethnic identities in the midst of a severe backlash against civil rights legislation and new movements for African American liberation.[90] The relationship between this defensive mentality and more recent attacks on affirmative action programs and civil rights legislation underscores the contemporary importance of understanding how and why these once inbetween immigrant workers became white.

CHAPTER EIGHT

Irish Americanization on Stage

How Irish Musicians, Playwrights, and Writers Created a New Urban American Culture, 1880–1940

In January 1907, a wave of riots broke out in New York's theaters. Irish American audiences heckled actors, pelting them with rotten vegetables. Twenty-two men were arrested in one melee alone, though an Irish American judge dismissed all charges. Organized by the United Irish Societies, the protests were aimed at a vaudeville skit called "The Irish Servant Girl." Once one of vaudeville's most popular acts, the Russell Brothers had been performing it without incident for many years. Dressed in drag, the actors depicted dim-witted Irish maids, but now the protests forced the Russells out of New York and eventually out of vaudeville entirely.[1] "The Irish Servant Girl" reflected vaudeville's preoccupation with ethnic stereotypes, while the protests, part of a broader movement against ethnic caricature, were emblematic of evolving attitudes toward ethnic difference in the Irish American community and in urban society generally.

A new popular culture that reflected urban themes and a sense of realism reached maturity in the Great Depression era, but its roots lay earlier in the striking ethnic and racial diversity of the American city at the turn of the century. The curiosity and conflict this social difference engendered, and the realities of social class in American cities, emerged on stage and screen, in the narratives of late nineteenth-century musical comedies, in early twentieth-century vaudeville routines, in the pages of realist fiction, in the lyrics of Tin Pan Alley songs, and in newspaper columns and cartoon strips. Vaudeville—the variety shows embracing a series of music, comedy, and dance acts—became synonymous with this new urban culture. It was the product not of the Irish alone but of interactions between them and other city dwellers from diverse backgrounds. Irish efforts to interpret this urban diversity to themselves, to the immigrant peoples around them, and to the mainstream public reflected their biases toward and their conflicts with other ethnic groups, but they all reflected life in the streets of America's great cities, and they shaped popular understandings of the city. The cultural expressions they passed on to more recent arrivals ranged from low humor to what came to be recognized as part of the literary canon.

Blackface Irish

The roots of Irish American urban performance lay in blackface minstrelsy of the mid-nineteenth century. Irish immigrants did not invent blackface minstrelsy, the first truly popular American cultural form, but they dominated the form in hundreds of national touring companies and thousands of local performances. Their stage presence continued to reflect minstrelsy's norms long after the form had declined. Profoundly racist, minstrelsy represented the sort of ethnic composite that came to characterize Irish American performance throughout the early twentieth century. As the United States became more ethnically diverse in the late nineteenth century, minstrel shows featured not only Irish immigrants taking on the personae of absurd black characters in story, song, and dance, but also polka, Italian opera, German and Irish folk song, and other performances.[2]

The rather tenuous social footing of the Irish is evident in the fact that they had been the main focus of ethnic humor on the English stage for centuries by the time they reached the United States. Irish comic figures appeared in Shakespeare's plays and remained a central feature of British theater from the seventeenth century through the Victorian era. This "stage Irishman" stereotype transferred easily to the nineteenth-century American scene; traces of the tradition continued into the twentieth.[3]

Blackface minstrelsy was central to the formation of white supremacist values in the nineteenth-century United States generally, and among the despised Irish Catholic minority in particular.[4] Irish performers employed blackface to ridicule and distance themselves from African Americans in the course of establishing their own white identity, assuming a crucial role in the formation and reproduction of racist values. They took on other ethnic roles as well, and actors from a variety of ethnic backgrounds also took on comic Irish personae. In the process, stage performers interpreted an increasingly complex social world to audiences from a variety of backgrounds.

The stock ethnic characters in nineteenth-century ethnic music hall and theater—"Paddy," the drunken and stupid stage Irishman, and his partner "Biddy," the lovable but stupid Irish maid—were probably at the height of their popularity in the midst of the later Irish immigration of the 1880s. Like the black characters "Sambo" and "Mose" in minstrelsy, these were comic characters that fed on racism and discrimination. Even when they laughed at them, the Irish resented such stereotypes.[5]

The American Dickens

Astride the older musical variety shows of the 1860s and 1870s and the emerging vaudeville explosion at the end of the century stood the musician, performer, and playwright Edward Harrigan (1844–1911), the "American Dickens." Born on the Lower East Side, that classic crucible of immigrant culture, and steeped in Irish American culture, Harrigan witnessed the city's ethnic transformation firsthand. He created a series of enormously popular late nineteenth-century plays portraying ethnic life on the city's Lower East Side. Harrigan and his collaborators—his father-in-law David Braham, the son of an Orthodox Jew, and Tony Hart, a second-generation Irish American—all shared extensive minstrel experience. They graduated from songs, sketches, and dialogues to full-fledged musicals that captured the imagination of late nineteenth-century New Yorkers who saw their city changing about them. The fact that twenty-three of his plays each ran for more than one hundred performances, while hundreds of thousands of copies of his songs circulated on sheet music throughout the United States demonstrates Harrigan's popularity. His main theme was the relations between the Irish and a range of other ethnic groups.

Harrigan's own goal was clear enough. "Though I use types and never individuals," he wrote, "I try to be as realistic as possible." His characters, locations, and situations were exaggerated but easily recognizable. His lyrics employed familiar slang and dialect, and he purchased his costumes directly from individuals on the streets of New York. His setting, carefully designed with an eye to detail, was invariably Five Points, New York's most famous slum, his characters assorted immigrant politicians, petty merchants, washerwomen, laborers, and cops.[6] The middle-class nationalist John Finerty's complaint that Harrigan and Hart produced "drama from the slums" was not far off the mark. "Mr. Harrigan realizes in his scenes what he realizes in his persons," the critic William Dean Howells wrote at the time. "He cannot give it all . . . and he has preferred to give its Irish American phases in their rich and amusing variety, and some of its African and Teutonic phases."[7]

Harrigan brought his own well-developed sense of racial hierarchy to his creations and held the Irish up as a sort of model.[8] Yet along with this notion of hierarchy came a very real appreciation for the city's diversity. Harrigan's lyrics captured *both* the casual ethnic prejudice and the unmistakable fascination with urban diversity that characterized much of Irish American culture.

Relations between these groups were often antagonistic. The *Boston Herald* called Harrigan's plays a "war of the races in cosmopolitan New York," and this was particularly true in the case of the Chinese.[9] Yet Harrigan's plays also alluded to the presence of Chinese–Irish couples, a common theme in late nineteenth-century song lyrics and musical variety performance, but also a sensitive issue at the time.[10] This competition hit the New York stage before audiences consisting heavily of Irish Americans who resented the encroachment of the Chinese. The laundry became a frequent site of ethnic tension and a source for racism among Irish women, as in the popular song "Since the Chinese Ruined the Thrade":

> It makes me wild, whin I'm on the street,
> To see those haythen signs:
> Ah Sung, Ah Sing, Sam Lee, Ah Wing,
> An' the ilegant spread on ther lines.
> If iver I get me hands on Ah Sing,
> I'll make him Ah Sing indade—
> On me clothesline I'll pin the leather skin
> Of the haythen that ruint the thrade.[11]

Harrigan's lyrics resonated in the Irish American community because they reflected very real attitudes toward the Chinese and concrete changes in New York's labor market. When anti-Chinese agitation began to gather steam in New York in the late 1870s, the competition between Irish women and Chinese men for laundry work represented a specter haunting the Irish. "They have already two hundred laundries in New York," the *Irish World* reported. "Six months ago they had not twenty." "Their passage to San Francisco costs less than a steerage passage from Liverpool to New York. And crowded up in China there are some 400,000,000 of them, and they can live on ten cents a day."[12]

What separated Harrigan's plays from earlier minstrelsy and later musical theater, both of which included extensive ethnic performance, was the extended interaction between ethnic groups. In *The Mulligan Guards' Ball* (1879), interethnic marriage was a central theme. Dan Mulligan and wife Cordelia are at odds with their neighbors the Lochmullers, in part because they fear that their son Tommy will marry Katrina Lochmuller. (Ironically, Katrina's own mother is not German but Irish.) Blacks, Germans, and Irish are often in conflict with one another, but they also find common ground.

Another of Dan Mulligan's antagonists, Sim Primrose, leader of the competing African American Skidmore Guard, runs a barbershop that provides a common ground for the various ethnic groups. Sim complains loudly of the cost to launder his towels with the Irish washerwoman and threatens to turn to the neighborhood's Chinese laundryman. Class tensions and anxieties also abound. The main characters are not workers but small businesspeople looking for the means to rise—a reflection of Irish America's struggling lower middle class. The play's denouement comes when the competing black and Irish guard units schedule their fancy balls on the same day at the same building. The black couples dance with such enthusiasm in the hall above that the floor collapses and they literally fall to the level of the Irish in the hall below.[13]

These were certainly comic scenes, but they differed significantly from those in minstrelsy, where stereotypical characters like Mose or Pat appeared on stage only briefly to sing, dance, or deliver stock gag lines. They seldom interacted, and there was no story line. Harrigan invested his African American, Irish, and other characters with greater depth and agency, and brought them into sustained conversation with one another.

Vaudeville: Americanization on the Stage

With their urban tenement setting, their concern with ethnic difference and race relations, their often crude characterizations of various racial and ethnic groups, and their enormous popularity among immigrants and their children, the Harrigan musicals represented in some ways an overture to George M. Cohan's vaudeville.[14] Vaudeville theater stood at the very center of popular culture in the increasingly diverse turn-of-the-century American city. Through its songs, dances, and jokes, vaudeville integrated immigrant city life into a national theater industry and set the stage for modern American show business.[15]

Characterized by cheap variety acts that ran continuously through the day and evening, vaudeville was designed as family entertainment, with a little something for everyone. Like minstrelsy, it spoke to the displaced rural migrant coping with daily life in the big city and trying to make sense of the people around him/her. No group had been more deeply immersed in this experience and its expression on stage than the Irish. For them, blackface performance had been a ritual of Americanization, and they remained center stage with the emergence of vaudeville, which became the same sort of ritual for later immigrants.[16] But now the performers, their audiences, and the urban life they re-created were far more diverse.

Vaudeville theaters of various sizes and quality sprouted in big-city neighborhoods, and their performers also toured smaller towns throughout the country. This brought aspects of the urban life and culture that disparate ethnic groups held in common before a much larger national audience, and set the stage for the electronically based movie and radio mass culture of the interwar years.[17]

New York City audiences were drawn from a remarkably wide social spectrum. Nearly two-thirds came from the working class, while the comparable figure for the "legitimate theater" was only 2 percent. But the vaudeville audience also included vagrants and "gamins," and more than one-third came from clerical occupations. The overwhelming majority of the audience consisted of working adults, and more than a third was female.[18] Vaudeville attracted more settled immigrants and their children because of the language factor, but skits often employed a mixture of English, Yiddish, and other languages, and physical comedy ensured laughs even when audiences faced a language barrier. After small, cheap "nickelodeon" film arcades were added to neighborhood houses, even recent immigrants were drawn into the vaudeville orbit, as the new silent films required little command of English.[19] Increasingly, such mass leisure was an experience that older immigrants like the Irish shared with more recent arrivals.

Vaudeville offered a common ground among the city's social classes. The native-born middle class found their more refined culture of restraint challenged by brash immigrant comedians, singers, and dancers.[20]

Irish performers could appeal to these mixed audiences for many reasons. They regularly took on the personae of other ethnic groups and peppered their performances with a good dose of self-deprecation, a characteristic of Irish humor. Even when it focused on Irish American themes, vaudeville resonated across ethnic lines with the urban experience of immigrant people and their children who were trying to grasp the diversity of the city world, which furnished the main source for the material. The characters were stereotypes, but they were based on racial, class, sexual, and ethnic stereotypes drawn from city streets.[21] As they morphed from minstrels to vaudeville performers, the Irish developed a distinctive style and an urban sensibility. They played a variety of ethnic groups, and these groups likewise took on the persona of Irish characters.

As vaudeville blossomed, there were Dutch (German), Jewish, Irish, black, and Italian acts performed by artists from a bewildering array of backgrounds. In this tendency to ethnically cross-dress, vaudeville owed a great deal to minstrelsy. Like its forerunner, it was a distinctly American art form, with its preoccupation with ethnic and racial difference. This humor could be intentionally crude and often insulting to the targeted group, but its popularity with immigrants themselves demonstrates what the cultural historian Joyce Flynn calls a "cautious cosmopolitanism." Stereotypes served to categorize the multitude of others inhabiting the city. They might console the Irish and other older groups about their higher place in this evolving ethnic hierarchy, but there is no doubt of their popularity among later immigrants, and especially their children. Audiences were drawn to the very diversity that characterized their neighborhoods and their daily lives.[22]

While late nineteenth-century songs and musical plays often reflected tensions between the Irish and the Chinese, turn-of-the-century vaudeville songs and skits tended to focus on racist comparisons between the Chinese and African Americans. Kelly and Catlin's routine "The Coon and the Chink" featured the comedy team in blackface and yellow face, portraying a range of derogatory stereotypes of the two groups. Drawing on longstanding nineteenth-century tropes often employed by Irish American minstrels, such routines remained popular throughout the early twentieth century.[23] Irish American impersonators of the Chinese arrived on stage in yellow face at least as early as the 1870s, while Chinese impersonations of the Irish had arrived by the turn of the century. African American performers often displayed an uncanny ability to mimic the Irish brogue.[24] Again, it was the transgression of ethnic lines—the spectacle of a Chinese performer singing in Irish dialect, sometimes in Irish dress, which attracted audiences.

Such ethnic caricature signaled xenophobia and boundary-marking by native middle-class audiences, but there was far more going on in the skits than an attack on one or another immigrant group. In larger and even in many of the smaller houses, both the vaudeville audience itself and its performers were ethnically mixed by the turn of the century. The comedy and performance thrived on this diversity. "The show dramatized the spectrum of humanity in the city," urban historian Gunther Barth wrote, "and the diversity of urban life through its subject matter and variety."[25]

The ethnic characters were stereotypes, but they often bore a resemblance to people that immigrants and their children were apt to see walking the streets of the Lower East Side, Chicago's near West Side, and other immigrant neighborhoods. A critic noted "how quick patrons of vaudeville are to recognize an act that comes near to the truth."[26] Each ethnic group was reduced to a distinct set of characteristics, some favorable, some unfavorable, but just enough reality made the scenes familiar, if not entirely plausible. Performers often integrated issues of local interest—political scandals, strikes, or international events—as they traveled around the country and through the neighborhoods of large cities. And it was this perceived authenticity as much as any slapstick humor that gave the acts their enormous popularity with remarkably diverse audiences. The performers' evocation of urban situations and characters helped to make the immigrant audience's surroundings more intelligible and negotiable.[27]

It was in these darkened theaters that many immigrants learned about their new urban world. The great Jewish American writers of the mid-twentieth century, literary critic Alfred Kazin wrote, were shaped not in the universities, but in vaudeville theaters, music halls, and burlesque houses, "where the pent-up eagerness of the penniless immigrant youngsters met the raw urban scene on its own terms."[28] "Greenhorn" caricatures were particularly popular, perhaps because they allowed the more experienced immigrants and the Americanized second generation to distinguish themselves from these symbols of their Old World pasts and to take on the mantle of sophisticated American city dwellers.[29]

One of the most popular acts of the late nineteenth and early twentieth centuries was the Jewish comedy team of Weber and Fields, who appeared in blackface impersonating African Americans, Germans, and Irish. The speed with which such comics sailed through a variety of ethnic groups was itself characteristic of vaudeville's quick-change pace and variety. "Here we are, a colored pair," Weber and Fields announced in heavy Yiddish accents and minstrel outfits. Then they quickly changed their ethnic makeup and costumes to fit the next stereotype—green satin breeches, black velvet coats, green bow ties, and green derbies to signal the Irish—but they changed not a word in any of their jokes. The audience loved seeing the Jewish comics singing songs in the Gaelic language with their heavy Yiddish accents.³⁰ An Irish comic impersonating a Jewish or Chinese immigrant in heavy brogue likewise was considered hilarious.³¹

Down with the Stage Irishman

Negative Irish caricatures were rife in the late 1880s and early 1890s, overlapping with the surging anti-Catholicism of those years. But as the Irish rose gradually in the early twentieth century, the crudest of the ethnic stereotypes departed the legitimate theater and even became less acceptable in vaudeville.³² Some of the comic laborers were replaced by ward politicians and small businessmen, but characters like "Mike Haggerty," who wore *both* the laborer's hobnailed boots and a respectable frock coat, reflected the audience's continuing anxieties about the experience of social climbing and the tensions between the Irish American middle and working classes. This is a theme that recurs throughout not only Irish American music, theater, literature, and song, but the popular culture of Jews and other immigrant people as well.³³ One explanation for the fading of the caricatures, then, is a quest for respectability on the part of old Pat and Biddy or their offspring, who had generated considerable social capital and political influence by the early twentieth century.

The theater riots of which the Russell Brothers protests were a part require a related but more complex explanation. These protests highlighted a special concern with the status of Irish American women, which surfaced in many of the other protests. Increasingly, vaudeville audiences objected to negative stereotypes. Irish-dialect comedians were received with stony silence from Boston audiences. In other cases, viewers showered offensive actors with eggs and vegetables.³⁴

The Ancient Order of Hibernians launched boycotts against stage Irishmen in Chicago, Philadelphia, and elsewhere, and by 1904 they were also calling for an end to Irish comic stereotypes in cartoons and newspaper features. New York's United Irish Societies began collecting reports of performances "that brought the Celtic people into plain contempt."³⁵ Reporting on a comedian, a Boston manager wrote the home office in 1903, "Look out and have him cut his comedy Irishman if your town is strongly A.O.H. [Ancient Order of Hibernians]."³⁶ The protests had some effect. Comic Irish characters, which had been a staple in the 1890s, did not vanish, but they diminished considerably by the World War I era.

Irish Americans had roared at some of the cruder caricatures in Harrigan's plays and in musical variety shows; now many of them had stopped laughing. Why? Social class, social mobility, and audience composition certainly explain part of the change. More subdued Irish comic caricatures persisted in vaudeville, where audiences were more mixed in class and ethnic terms. The audience in legitimate theater and musicals plays, however, was relatively more respectable by the turn of the century, and the Irish Americans among them were often particularly sensitive. In this sense, the reaction was one example of what literary historian Charles Fanning has called "the seismic shocks to the Irish-American community brought on by the emergence of a middle class."[37]

Historian Kerby Miller found the late nineteenth-century Irish American bourgeoisie "morbidly sensitive to real or imagined threats to their tenuous grasp on respectability." The resurgence of anti-Catholicism in the 1890s, aimed largely at Irish Americans, undoubtedly heightened such anxieties.[38] This search for respectability helps to explain why some of the most brilliant Irish American writers, such as Eugene O'Neill, F. Scott Fitzgerald, and John O'Hara, pursued acceptance from upper-class WASPs while isolated from and despised by the Irish American middle class whom they satirized.[39]

Yet there was another source for such protests—a newly militant, more muscular Irish nationalism. The Russell Brothers protest and other theater riots were not spontaneous, but rather organized by the Gaelic League, Clan na Gael, and A.O.H. They were populated largely by working-class males and exhibited a belligerent masculinity that came to the fore in the emergent nationalist agitation.[40] This more militant nationalist culture was rising in precisely these years, reaching its zenith during World War I and the early twenties to become a mass movement embracing hundreds of thousands of working-class Irish Americans. In this context, such performances touched a nerve in the broader Irish American community, not just its middle class. Far enough to command some degree of respect, Irish Americans were close enough to their despised origins in Ireland and American cities to resent any slight.[41]

"Some day," a vaudeville manager wrote the home office in 1903, "the Hebrews are going to make as big a kick as the Irish did against this kind of burlesque of their nationality."[42] And indeed other ethnic communities soon voiced their own objections to such stereotypes. Negative African American stereotypes were particularly persistent, but agitation within the black community forced vaudeville management to limit the number and roughness of "coon" acts in the early twentieth century.[43] When Jews launched their own protests, they distinguished, as Irish protesters had, between ethnic humor per se and offensive caricatures in particular. They also modeled their boycotts and agitation on those of the Irish. Dr. Emil Hirsch, a founder of the Anti-Defamation League in Chicago in 1913, highlighted the difference in the depictions of Irish and Jews. "A stage Irishman is funny and not offensive because he is a good humored caricature," Hirsch reasoned. "We wouldn't mind being laughed at in that way." Many Jewish stage characters were more sinister.[44]

Irish comic caricatures, which had been a staple at the turn of the century, declined in the decade before World War I, while "Hebrew" and other caricatures persisted. By the early 1920s, at which point a second generation was maturing in even more recent immigrant communities, vaudeville performers themselves expressed reservations about ethnic acts and hesitated to employ ethnic dress and stock ethnic caricatures.[45]

The Irish and the Jews

Tin Pan Alley songs, which enjoyed huge popularity in the decade before the First World War and through the 1920s, were often based on traditional Irish melodies and themes, evoking nostalgia for an idealized Ireland that city dwellers pined for—even if it never existed. To the extent that the Irish *were* moving up, it was precisely this distance from their roots that produced such nostalgia in the second and third generations. The Irish remained as both creators and subjects of Tin Pan Alley lyrics in sheet music, recordings, and live performance, but they were often in dialogue with racial and ethnic others. In "The Kellys," a young immigrant from Cork encounters both the ubiquitous Irish and their diverse neighbors:

> I went to the directory me uncle for to find
> But I found so many Kellys that I nearly lost me mind.
> So I went to ask directions from a friendly German Jew
> But he says please excuse me but me name is Kelly too.
> Dan Kelly runs the railroads, John Kelly runs the seas
> Kate Kelly runs the suffragettes and she looks right good to me.
> Well I went and asked directions from a naturalized Chinese
> But he says please excuse me but me name it is Kell Lee.[46]

Filled with a good deal of self-congratulation and nostalgia for the "old sod," such lyrics were less the products of the immigrants themselves than of a second generation probing its place in American society in relation to other ethnic groups. The fact that stock Irish characters who had frequently been depicted as drunks or buffoons in vaudeville skits were less common in Tin Pan Alley numbers is explained in part by social mobility, often at the expense of recent immigrants and blacks. Some songs, however, reflected increasingly close relations between the Irish and other ethnic groups.

Lyrics often depicted Irish men and women roaming the world and encountering a wide range of others. Intermarriage was a common theme, with Irish men marrying or courting Indian, Hawaiian, or Arab women.[47] The continuing marginality of the Irish was reflected in the sense that audiences laughed at the thought of the Irishman in exotic locations, so central was he to images of the working class and the American city.

By far the most common pairing, however, in such comic romantic songs was the Irish/Jewish match, as in "My Yiddisha Colleen" and "It's Tough When Izzy Rosenstein Loves Genevieve Malone." The humor tended to be more at the expense of the Jews than the Irish, but it displayed a clear affinity between the two groups.[48] Irish Catholics and Jews, two of the nation's most successful ethnic groups, shared a history of oppression in the Old World, conspicuous urban settlement and persistence in the new, and an equal distribution of men and women. In the politics of the early twentieth century, the Irish Tammany Hall political machine was coming to terms with the increasingly large and well-organized Jewish community. And between them, the two groups dominated the entertainment industry.[49] The 1912 William Jerome (Flannery) and Jean Schwartz number "If It Wasn't for the Irish and the Jews" conveyed these affinities:

> Talk about a combination,
> Hear my words and make a note,
> On St. Patrick's Day Rosinsky,
> Pins a shamrock on his coat.
> There's a sympathetic feeling,
> Between the Blooms and McAdoos,
> Why Tammany would surely fall,
> There'd really be no hall at all,
> If it wasn't for the Irish and the Jews.[50]

Interethnic love and marriage was a common theme, first in vaudeville and then in early films, and it became particularly popular with the second generation in the Irish and other immigrant communities. In the early 1920s, the movie, play, and novel *Abie's Irish Rose* captured the imagination of a wide segment of the U.S. public. It sympathetically told the story of the love between a second-generation Jewish immigrant man and a second-generation

Irish American woman. Rose's father, Patrick Murphy, a contractor from County Kerry, represented one possible response to such a match, his priest, another. Patrick is full of ethnic humor and stories about youthful Jewish–Irish fights in the streets of New York. Objecting to the proposed marriage on the basis of stereotypes, Patrick is confronted on his anti-Semitism by Father Whalen, who represents a strain of ethnic and racial tolerance within the Irish American community. The play was wildly successful, running for over 2,300 performances on Broadway, a record that persisted for fourteen years. It also set records in Erie, Pennsylvania, and South Bend, Indiana, home of Notre Dame University. By the summer of 1926, some five million had seen it. It spawned film adaptations, in 1928 and 1946, a weekly radio show during World War II, and was revived twice on Broadway.[51]

With its roots in vaudeville ethnic humor, *Abie's Irish Rose* embodied the second and third immigrant generation's anxieties and aspirations. It signaled a much broader cultural phenomenon that featured Irish–Jewish relationships in scores of ragtime songs, in other stage productions, and in twenty-one other films between 1921 and 1930. Quintessentially nostalgic Irish Tin Pan Alley songs like "Mother Malone" and "Twas Only an Irishman's Dream" were actually the creations of Jewish–Irish teams. Comic and romantic pairings were a staple on the vaudeville stage, and sports fans followed the antics of Jewish and Irish roommates on the New York Giants and the Chicago White Sox.[52] By the twenties, if not earlier, rabbis or other representatives of the Jewish community often spoke at St. Patrick's Day celebrations. Clearly, Irish–Jewish couplings resonated widely and had meaning for their audiences. What was going on here?

One distinct possibility was that the pairing was so unlikely, given cultural differences and frequent conflicts in politics and on the streets, that it was inherently comical. Though they shared city neighborhoods and the vaudeville stage, the Irish and Jews were far more likely to be enemies than friends.[53] Yet the popularity of the songs, plays, and films, and their often subtle treatments of these relationships, indicate some affinity between the two groups— if not in real life, then in the imagination of readers and viewers.

These kinds of films and plays were particularly popular with second-generation ethnic audiences in large cities like New York and Chicago. As they constructed their own new identities, they were drawn to older stock ethnic characters like Abie's and Rose's parents, who helped them to distance themselves from the first generation in their own communities, while they worked out their attitudes toward their counterparts in other communities. Vaudeville's ethnic cross-dressing reappeared with young Jewish and Irish

Catholic characters assuming one another's ethnic backgrounds in unsuccessful efforts to reassure their families. Such performances continued to foreground the available Irish American woman as a vehicle for both comedy and assimilation. "If the melting pot existed," Riv-Ellen Prell concludes, "it was in the cultural imagination of the 1920s."[54]

Another possible explanation is considerable anxiety in various ethnic communities over the issue of intermarriage as the ultimate test case for interethnic relations. Discussions of intermarriage in part gauged the attitudes of these groups toward one another. Would the Irish and new immigrants mix, and if so, on what basis? What identities would the children of such "mixed marriages" carry?[55]

Yet many of the Irish/Jewish plays and films seemed genuinely concerned with using these interethnic love affairs to depict the potential for good relations between the two communities. At their best, these productions conveyed a cultural reaction against the intolerance so widespread in the "Tribal Twenties." In the film version of *Abie's Irish Rose*, a young Abie pledges allegiance to the flag alongside black and Asian youths. Given the strength of ethnic and religious prejudice in these years, it would be a mistake to read too much into these images, but their extreme popularity indicates that many in the second-generation immigrant population longed for the tolerance symbolized in such matches.[56] Underlying all these performances lay a social reality: There were far more Irish American women around than was true for most other ethnic communities.

The unusually large stream of young single Irish women entering American cities and their history of intermarriage meant they were viewed as more eligible than most for such matches, especially with men from immigrant groups that had far fewer women. Memories of marriage between Irish women and African American and Chinese likely enhanced their reputation as eligible partners—and fears of racial amalgamation. Irish–Chinese marriages were still fairly common even after the turn of the century, with the couples often living in Chinatown or Irish Catholic communities.[57]

Irish women were twice as likely as Irish men to marry outside of the ethnic group and more apt to marry with a broad spectrum of races and nationalities than any of the other ethnic groups. Intermarriage, then, even in small numbers, was highly visible. By the 1920s, in the large Irish American third generation, rates of outmarriage were relatively high, anticipating later patterns of intra-Catholic, interethnic marriages uniting Irish Americans with new immigrants.[58] Relations at this most intimate level meant the creation of interethnic families in a generation when such formations were still rare.

The Silver Screen and Urban Realism

Irish American influence can be discerned on the nation's movie screens, in a new generation of urban realist writers, and in other dimensions of the nation's urban culture by the era of the Great Depression. James Cagney, the nation's most popular movie gangster, and other Irish American actors and actresses became models for millions of immigrant youth. Although Irish Americans played vital roles as actors, directors, and producers in early American films, however, their greatest impact on Hollywood came not with their efforts on screen, but rather through campaigns for public purity. Catholic efforts resulted in the first censorship law in Chicago as early as 1907. Pressed by demands for federal decency legislation, and with an eye on the huge audience of first- and second-generation immigrants in American cities, Hollywood moguls developed their own Hollywood Production or Hays Code in 1930. Written by a Jesuit priest, sold to the industry by a Catholic journalist, the code represented less an industry prescription than what a film historian called "a statement of Catholic moral philosophy."[59]

Aimed at providing the Church's seal of approval for Hollywood's product, the original code was voluntary, so sex and violence remained on the screen through the early Depression. The Church intervened directly in 1934, establishing the Legion of Decency, with its own elaborate code and rating system. Every film received a rating published widely every week. Once each year at Mass, Catholics were required to formally pledge to support the system, and many parents used it to monitor their children's cinema viewing. With 11 million Catholics adhering to the Legion at its height, the industry quickly fell into line with a more rigid code and an enforcement system overseen by yet another Irish Catholic. In line with conservative Irish sensibilities, the enforcement body showed far more concern with sex than with violence. By 1938, the new code system was reviewing about 98 percent of all films viewed in U.S. theaters. Studios also submitted films and sometimes even preproduction scripts directly to the Legion of Decency.[60] Beyond indicating the Church's influence on popular culture by the Depression era, Hollywood's choice of personnel clearly signaled the critical position of Irish Catholics as arbiters of decency within the culture.

The Irish mark on popular culture was a product of literacy as much as timing and inclination. Irish Americans represented an unusually literate segment of the immigrant working-class population.[61] Raised in ethnic urban enclaves, having absorbed a modicum of education, they were now perched between their parents' struggles and their own uneasy reach for respectability and recognition. Second- and third-generation Irish American urban authors interpreted much of the transformation of the city—to themselves and their own generation, to the broader middle-class society, and eventually to second-generation immigrants. They offered realism in its various forms, and in the process they told the stories not only of their own people but of many others as well.

James T. Farrell represented the zenith of this new urban realism, beginning in the 1930s. Raised in poverty in an aging tenement, Farrell was sent to live with his middle-class grandparents because his impoverished parents could not provide the upbringing they desired for him. This move out of the old neighborhood and up the social ladder undoubtedly attuned the young writer to the status anxiety of middle-class Irish, who were often only one step from poverty, but the central theme in Farrell's famous urban trilogy, *Studs Lonigan* (1930–1935), was the relations between the Irish and other racial and ethnic groups.

Much of the narrative in *Studs Lonigan* unfolds against the backdrop of the Irish American oscillation between security and terror, their strivings for respectability, and their fear of "invasion" by African Americans and more recent European immigrants in a succession of South Side Chicago neighborhoods. Nowhere do the defensive quality and anxieties of Irish American culture emerge more dramatically. The Lonigan family hopes that Father Gilhooley's construction of a new church and school will anchor their parish and keep theirs a "white man's neighborhood." This defensive parochial conception of urban space later shaped opposition to neighborhood racial integration by Catholics from a variety of ethnic backgrounds.[62]

Eventually, the Lonigan family's only recourse seems to be flight, the occasion for a deep sense of loss reminiscent of the exile from Ireland, but now with racial undertones after a generation in the city. "Bill, I'd rather let the money I made on this building go to hell and not be moving," his father tells Studs. "[T]his neighborhood was kind of like home. We sort of felt about it the same way I feel about Ireland, where I was born." Yet there was no question of remaining with their African American neighbors. "Hell, there is scarcely a white man left in the neighborhood.... Goddamn those niggers!"[63]

As in much of Farrell's fiction, characters and settings are rooted firmly in real locations and in actual experiences. Farrell's Washington Park neighborhood became a great symbol of the racial divide in the interwar years. It provided the venue for frequent clashes—in Farrell's epic *Studs Lonigan* trilogy and in real life—as the area around the park changed from largely Irish to more ethnically mixed and then, increasingly, to African American. The neighborhood's black population grew from 15 percent to 92 percent in the decade between 1920 and 1930.⁶⁴ Father Gilhooley and St. Patrick's stand in for Father Michael Gilmartin of St. Anselm's Parish. Completed in late 1925 in the midst of racial transformation in Farrell's Washington Park neighborhood, the new church became one of the largest African American parishes in Chicago by the late 1920s.⁶⁵ When he'd bought this building, Studs's father Patrick recalls, "Wabash Avenue had been a nice, decent, respectable street for a self-respecting man to live with his family. But now, well, niggers and kikes were getting in."⁶⁶

Irish American creations in song lyrics, prose, and theater performance were interethnic by nature, often with racial difference at their very core. They focused on the relations among the various groups crowded into urban neighborhoods. In the process, a new, multiethnic city culture emerged. To the extent that immigrant youth from various backgrounds embraced the styles, behavior, values, and norms of a new urban culture, they were not those of some distant WASP mainstream, but rather of a newly emerging hybrid ethnic working-class culture. Irish American interpretations of this new culture on the vaudeville stage and in movies embraced ethnic and racial stereotypes, but also displayed a fascination with urban diversity. They provided both a rather strict moral compass for what appeared on the nation's movie screens, and also the model for the urban movie gangster, and for the Hollywood glamour girl who became the idols of immigrant youth. At its best, as in Farrell's unrelenting portrayal of his own community and culture, it could be trenchant, progressive, transcendent. But even at its worst, it shaped much of what it meant to be a young American by the interwar era.

CHAPTER NINE

Making and Unmaking the Working Class

E. P. Thompson, The Making of the English Working Class, and the "New Labor History" in the United States

The Indian historian Rajnarayan Chandavarkar recalls a most unusual salute to a most unusual book. "In the late 1970s, when E. P. Thompson was elected President of the Indian History Congress, and rode into session on the back of an elephant," he writes, "this was a tribute primarily to *The Making*, a book the Canadian historian Bryan Palmer calls "arguably the most influential book in the modern historiography of working-class studies."[1] The data suggests the book's influence well beyond labor history. At the time of Thompson's death, E. J. Hobsbawm noted that he was cited more than any other historian in the twentieth century, and indeed was one of the 250 most cited authors of all time.[2] For more than a generation, *The Making of the English Working Class* has shaped historical writing in Japan, South and Southeast Asia, and Africa, as well as throughout Europe, parts of Latin America, Australia and New Zealand, and, of course, North America.[3]

Despite its celebrated status, however, paradox is central to the book's reception. One example, of course, is the fact that a study so rooted in a particular time and place, one that emphasized the role of English culture and ideas in the creation of a distinctive working-class presence, has had so broad an influence in societies seemingly so different from Thompson's own. Critics have also noted a kind of left-wing nationalism in Thompson's perspective, and yet he was, more than most scholars we could cite, a dedicated internationalist—not just in theory and on the printed page, but in consistent practice.[4] Perhaps the greatest paradox, however, is that although Thompson's work defined the "working class" and the means of studying it for a generation, it also helped to deconstruct the very notion of class, and nowhere was this truer than in the United States.

Socialist Humanism and Radical History in the United States

The Making's great influence in the United States was based on an affinity that was in part political. Despite his extensive family and personal connections and his extremely generous attitude toward younger American historians, Thompson's left-wing version of British values and traditions, particularly English liberalism and humanism, and his opposition to U.S. international policy nurtured what some critics have seen as a kind of anti-Americanism. Yet long after Thompson and other "old guard" New Left colleagues had come to blows with the younger radicals around *New Left Review*, American left intellectuals continued to embrace both *The Making* and its author. Indeed, there was a much greater affinity and a better political fit in the United States than in the U.K.—in part *because of* Thompson's criticism of the United States at the level of policy, government, mainstream politics, and even popular culture. His younger New Left critics in the U.K. might have considered his theory less rigorous and his politics less revolutionary than their own, but his socialist humanist perspective proved particularly attractive for both political and intellectual reasons in the United States.[5] I propose to focus here on the striking affinity between these now-aging radical historians and a book that would seem on the surface a rather awkward fit with the counternarrative of U.S. history they were constructing between the late sixties and the late eighties.

We cannot fully appreciate Thompson's book or even understand how and why it came along at the time that it did without considering the political and intellectual context that shaped it—on the one hand, a highly determinist, structural form of European Marxism (closely associated in the late fifties with Stalinism), and on the other, the highly static and structural character of sociology, particularly American sociology, wherein class became a quantifiable category via modernization theory. This British side of this story is pretty well understood.[6] Likewise, the peculiar trajectory of the postwar

American left helps to explain the warm embrace of *The Making* here by the late sixties. The ideological fit between Thompson's socialist humanism and "looser" conception of class formation and those of a new generation of left intellectuals was perhaps strongest in the United States during the late sixties and the decade of the seventies, just when the "new labor history" was gestating.[7]

One way to gauge the book's effect is to contrast its distance from an earlier generation of American radical historians, Thompson's contemporaries in the late fifties and early sixties, with the enormous influence of its emphasis on working-class self-activity and agency on a younger generation of New Left historians emerging in the late sixties and early seventies. The older group coalesced in Madison, Wisconsin, around the journal *Studies on the Left*. I have no desire to reduce the importance of this early Madison group, but its main contribution to historiography was its evocation of a "corporate liberal" political and intellectual consensus that held sway through much of the twentieth century and fundamentally shaped the character of American liberalism.[8]

This group went through graduate school in the late fifties or early sixties and had connections with the Old Left, but it shared little of the heavy political legacy of Marxists in Europe. On the political side, it was "notable for its heterodoxy," in part at least because of the catastrophic decline of the postwar left and the weak tradition of Marxist scholarship in the United States. In terms of their intellectual pursuits, they were fixed particularly on American business and foreign policy elites, and their hegemony in the nation's political and intellectual history.[9] Most of those in this older New Left group, then, viewed history—and American politics—from the top down rather than the bottom up. Most of them closely analyzed corporate executives and foreign policymakers, but their work also included Eugene Genovese's studies of the southern planter elite.

When they considered workers at all, it was largely in negative terms. Gabriel Kolko, a major figure in this generation, argued that the failure of the nation's immigrant workers to develop a class-conscious labor movement bred disorganization and despair, manifested in widespread social pathologies ranging from insanity to crime and alcoholism. They were, he concluded, "lumpen people in a lumpen society." The group's most important conclusion, historian Jon Weiner notes, "was that virtually all popular and protest movements had been incorporated within the expanding capitalist system, instead of undermining it."[10]

By the late sixties, a very different orientation and group of historians emerged, once again gravitating around Madison, Wisconsin. With the publication of *Radical America* (RA) beginning in 1967, the political and historiographical tables were turned. The journal and the scholar/activists around it championed agency, spontaneity, and wage earners' and slaves' self-activity. "The Marxism *Radical America* adopted was the unorthodox variant developed by E. P. Thompson," Peter Novick writes, "a Marxism that valued working-class culture and consciousness and strove to integrate class analysis with the cultural concerns growing out of Black Nationalism, feminism, and youth culture."[11] Novick misses the decisive influence of the West Indian Marxist scholar C. L. R. James on the group around RA and to some extent on Thompson himself. James brought an emphasis on agency, a popular culture angle, and insistence on the centrality of race, which resonated particularly with younger left scholars in the United States long after the demise of RA. But there is no mistaking the impact of Thompson's work.[12] *Radical America* published socialist feminist writing from factories and community organizations, as well as studies of women's, working-class, and black history. While its focus has changed considerably over the past decade or more, this was also the context for the *Radical History Review*, which was deeply influenced by the new labor history and has carried the banner of new, poststructuralist radical history since the late 1980s.

This younger group of New Left historians tapped into the insights of two older scholars who, not coincidentally, were deeply influenced by and shared some experiences with Thompson. David Montgomery and Herbert Gutman both had backgrounds in the Old Left, though Gutman had left the movement while he was still quite young. After a decade in industrial work, Montgomery left the Communist Party in the mid-fifties, around the same period as E. P. Thompson. While he never produced the sort of sustained critique of Stalinism Thompson marshaled, by the mid-fifties he had come to believe, like Thompson, that the organization was increasingly irrelevant to radical politics. Montgomery's work in particular reflected his industrial experiences, focusing on gritty studies of the workplace and workers' control, on strike activity, and on working-class politics. Gutman's background in the rich left Jewish culture of New York shaped his sensitivity to local working-class cultures. Both scholars sought to connect their research and that of their students with the labor movement.[13]

The "New Labor Historians" and *The Making of the English Working Class*

It is difficult to overstate the hunger for an approach which at once promised common people a place in the historical narrative, allowed one to reconstruct their lives, and provided a language that captured their complexity and contingent quality. In Thompson and the other British Marxists, these historians found not only a theory of class formation more compatible with their own looser understandings of the term, but, more importantly, one that privileged the everyday lives of American workers. "*The Making of the English Working Class* resonated perfectly with the hopes of a generation of radical scholars that common people could make their own history," Alan Dawley argued. "In the United States the book was quickly assimilated to a radical populism which aimed at doing history 'from the bottom up' to show that the poor—seamen, sharecroppers, shoemakers—made history on their own terms and not as part of a consensus with their superiors."[14] "We knew that American history was very different from British history," Sean Wilentz recalls of this group, "but we still wanted to try to do for American working people and their past something of what Thompson had done for the English."[15]

Leaving aside entirely the legacy of the Cold War and the elevation of anticommunism into a sort of civic religion, these labor historians were working against an entrenched Whig tradition that focused on labor institutions, emphasizing the virtue of the business union model while rejecting any notion of "social unionism." They also faced two highly determinist radical traditions—a small group of scholars from the CPUSA, Philip Foner most prominent among them, who were largely writing an institutional narrative of the labor movement from the left; and the *Studies'* more sophisticated top-down interpretation that emphasized the decisive power and influence of American capital—whether in the persons of paternalist slave masters or cosmopolitan "corporate liberals"—and the impotence of popular movements. There was little role in this story for workers, slave or free.

At its best, as in the work of David Montgomery, the new approach provided a sweeping reinterpretation of what Thompson termed the historical "presence" of common people and their everyday lives—at work, in their communities, and even in the more intimate surroundings of family and home. If not in his earlier work, then certainly in its totality, Montgomery demonstrated the impact of workers on the broader history of industrialization, liberalism, and the evolution of the American state and imperialism. Though he is most remembered for his workplace studies, which seem quite distant from *The Making*'s narrative, Montgomery was greatly influenced both by Thompson's notion of the pervasive influence of class and by his insistence on workers' agency. Where Thompson had focused particularly on a literate, articulate, and politicized group of artisan radicals, the key group in Montgomery's "project" of class consciousness was the "militant minority"—a group of socialists, syndicalists, and progressive unionists who sought to bring their workmates together into an aggressive labor movement. More than Thompson had, Montgomery emphasized the diversity of working-class experience. While focusing mainly on male workers, he probed the gendered character of skilled work cultures, considered both race and ethnicity as vital to understanding the evolution of working-class identity, and absorbed the efforts of feminists and others who were attempting to deconstruct the archetypical worker as a white, skilled male. His students have gone much further in documenting the significance of social difference for working-class formation, while emphasizing the pervasiveness of class in the lives of working-class families.[16]

Looking at Montgomery, Gutman, and the younger group who followed in their wake establishes the profound influence of Thompson and *The Making* on a generation of scholars, who in turn transformed our understanding of U.S. social history. In the short run, none of the founders of the new labor history were directly influenced by the book; none of the early foundation texts cited it. At first, the new field was shaped primarily by reactions to older approaches, notably the large body of work associated with the labor economists John R. Commons and Selig Perlman.[17] David Brody's *Steelworkers in America: The Non-Union Era*, which assumed the perspective and evoked the mentality of immigrant steelworkers, was published before *The Making*. David Montgomery's *Beyond Equality: Labor and the Radical Republicans*, which showed that it was essential to understand the politics of the Civil War and Reconstruction through the actions of American workers and their relations with employers and the state, had already appeared by the time the author became aware of Thompson's book. Several of Gutman's pioneering local studies of working-class cultures and protest also came before the appearance of *The Making*.[18] Yet each of these authors, by focusing on workers themselves and the experience of class in and beyond the workplace, demonstrated both the agency and the "presence" of working-class people in the broader narrative of American history.

In each case, *The Making* transformed the author's understanding of the field. Gutman's collaborator Ira Berlin writes that *The Making* had a profound effect on Gutman's thinking. Up to that point he had not conceptualized his local studies in terms of class formation; *The Making* stimulated him to do so. "Thompson's twin nemeses—smug liberalism and vulgar Marxism—were also Gutman's," Berlin wrote. "Thompson's understanding of class... and of class consciousness as the cultural articulation of those experiences, was also Gutman's [and his]... overarching commitment to empirical research [was] also Thompson's. Indeed, it was not so much the emphasis on culture that drew him to Thompson [the connection most observers made] as it was Thompson's explicit avowal, indeed his outright celebration, of human agency." Thompson introduced a theoretical rigor previously absent in Gutman's work.[19] What Gutman did brilliantly was to capture the need of industrialists to transform not only the technology and methods of production, but also the culture and work habits of the people involved. Thompson had shown that this was an uneven, complex, and contentious process in England; Gutman showed that it was far more complex in the United States, for reasons having to do with migration, race, and ethnicity.

Another intellectual basis for the new labor history seems at first to be at odds with Thompson—the influence of social science methods. Thompson was always very skeptical, to some degree hostile, to this approach, but his insistence on scrupulous empirical research paralleled the influence not only of the *Annales* school in France and beyond, but also of quantitative methods. Indeed, it is a combination of Thompson's understanding of class with more systematic research methods that explains the rather dramatic transformation of American historical research between the late 1960s and the early 1980s. Aside from the Cambridge school of demographers, quantitative approaches were much less popular in the U.K., perhaps especially among historians on the left, but in the United States many of the new social history studies inspired by *The Making* saw the harnessing of large amounts of data as vital to reconstructing the lives of common people.[20]

Thompson's deepest and most enduring mark on American working-class historiography concerned the plebian Atlantic world of the eighteenth century. While Marcus Rediker and Peter Linebaugh followed Thompson in their brilliant evocation of the remarkably diverse and insurrectionary early modern maritime world, Al Young did most perhaps to establish the agency of artisans, the crowd, and the working poor in the context of the American Revolution. Rediker and Linebaugh in particular remain unreconstructed "Thompsonists."[21]

Not surprisingly, the earliest Thompsonesque studies focused on a comparable period in the United States, and for a while it seemed that *The Making* provided an admirable model for the social history of early American working-class formation. A generation of young Yankee farm women constituted America's first factory proletariat in New England's textile towns, facing the sort of rigors of industrial work Thompson had described. In cities and smaller industrial communities, they mixed with British, Ulster Irish, and native-born skilled workers, and a population of laboring poor, including free and enslaved blacks, to constitute the American working-class population. By the 1830s, a labor movement and a class culture and politics had emerged resembling the one in Thompson's narrative—trades unions, cooperatives, "Working Men's" institutes, political parties, newspapers, and a small group of organic intellectuals advocating a new perspective on political economy that emphasized a labor theory of value. The activists drew on earlier notions of radical republicanism, not unlike the process Thompson had described in England. By the middle of the nineteenth century, this first generation of American industrial workers had "learned the rules of the game," to use Hobsbawm's famous phrase.[22] As Thompson's artisans had done with the "Rights of the Freeborn Englishman," they reworked the ideology of the new republic and turned it on their social betters in the form of what the new labor historians came to call "labor republicanism," demanding not only better wages, but also shorter hours, universal free education, and other reforms aimed at making the United States a more egalitarian society.[23]

The process was perhaps most advanced in Philadelphia, where the General Trades Union (GTU) drew in more than fifty organizations representing laborers and factory operatives as well as artisans from diverse backgrounds, more than ten thousand workers in all. When the unskilled coal heavers walked off the job over long hours, artisans stopped work too, declaring, "We are all day laborers." In 1835, a huge general strike for shorter hours commenced, involving as many as twenty thousand—far beyond the boundaries of the expansive GTU.[24] The moment of class formation, it seemed, had arrived—and at about the same moment as the Chartist revolt, Thompson's point of class maturation in England. Yet within a few years this promising movement had been destroyed and workers were bitterly divided along ethnic, racial, and religious sectarian lines.

Making and Unmaking: Working-Class Formation and Fragmentation

In his assessment of the paradoxical character of *The Making*, Rajnarayan Chandavarkar notes one irony that towers over others. It seems to have particular relevance for the study of the United States, where the field, so fundamentally shaped by Thompson's book, has been particularly porous to other influences and approaches, and where other forms of constructed identity have tended gradually to displace class as a key analytical category over the past generation. "[I]t is ironical that while Thompson was perhaps best known, and most widely admired, for having demonstrated how the history of a class may be written," Chandavarkar writes, "his method and style of argument may have contributed substantially to the deconstruction and dissolution of the very concept of class."[25] Thompson's emphasis on the diversity of working-class experience, his insistence on the rootedness of class in particular sites and cultures, his general "loosening" of our understanding of class, shifting the stuff of causation from structures and modes of production to experience and agency, has paradoxically led to an emphasis on fragmentation.

The precision of class as a category of analysis loosened as historians' evocation of class experience became more detailed and complex and as Thompson's artisan-based movement appeared more and more unusual over time, particularly in societies like the United States that were characterized increasingly by massive rural and transnational migration of unskilled laborers and by mass production technologies. In other societies as well, but certainly in the United States, gender, race, and other forms of identity appeared vital to explaining the experience of workers and their roles in history. If we have deconstructed and greatly complicated the notions of class and class formation, this process started not with postmodern theory and methods, but rather with *The Making of the English Working Class*.

This process of deconstruction relates in part to chronology. A possibility that Thompson considered later, but not in *The Making*, is the idea that class formation is *never* complete, and that laboring people never permanently constitute a "mature" working class. Rather, the historical experience and "presence" of a working class is best conveyed through a dynamic process of formation and fragmentation over time. Even in the U.K., Hobsbawm, Stedman Jones, and others have emphasized the ongoing process of class formation and argued that if there were a *distinct* era in which the English working class was "made," it was likely long after Thompson's 1830s. Stedman Jones located a distinctive but "defensive" London working-class culture focused more on popular leisure activities than on radical politics as late as the end of the nineteenth century. Likewise, Hobsbawm notes that the material and popular culture, and many of the distinctive institutions of the working class, emerged only in the late nineteenth century. It was only in the wake of this more homogeneous class culture and in the context of massive strikes and political challenges of the early twentieth century that large working-class political parties emerged.²⁶

In the United States, the process of fragmentation was particularly striking. Within a decade of America's first labor movement in the 1830s, its cities were increasingly overwhelmed by a huge tide of immigrants—German, British, and above all, Irish peasants—transforming America's working-class population. Thompson's own discussion of the Irish in the industrial towns of northern England began to suggest divergent class experiences based on ethnicity. Since immigrants represented a much larger proportion of the laboring population in the United States, the significance of ethnicity was far more pronounced here, where organized ethnic and religious intolerance swept the society. By the 1840s nativist movements exploded, and promising local labor movements like the one in Philadelphia splintered along ethnic and religious lines. There Catholic and Protestant handloom weavers who had helped to create the city's vibrant General Trades Union and waged the successful general strike of 1835 now turned on one another in streets and workplaces over which version of the Bible was the proper one for Philadelphia's schoolchildren. In the wake of economic depression, religious sectarianism, and attacks from employers' organizations, the institutional framework for urban working-class society in the United States was largely destroyed. The American narrative looked much more like an "unmaking" than a "making."²⁷

This issue of ethnic, religious, and racial difference loomed far larger from the late nineteenth century through the early twentieth, with massive waves of so-called "new immigrants," who came in much larger numbers and from a much wider range of societies than the "old immigrants" of the mid-nineteenth century. Italians, Poles, Russian and Eastern European Jews, and others each created their own distinct communities and cultures, greatly complicating the task of any organizer who sought to weld them together into an effective working-class movement. Finally, the process became racially fraught, as people of color migrated to American industrial cities from Asia, the American South, and Mexico, raising the prospect of racial conflict. With the "Great Migration" of African Americans to the industrial cities of East and Midwest in the First World War era and the 1920s, giant racial conflagrations erupted, tearing apart even the most promising efforts to organize workers across lines of race and ethnicity. For most of the twentieth century, and in many cases earlier, European immigrant workers and their children toiled alongside blacks and Latinos, fashioning their own identities and institutional and cultural lives in the midst of this ethnic and racial diversity, while retaining some sense of their distinct cultures.²⁸

Herbert Gutman conceptualized this process as one of interaction between these successive waves of migrants and the evolving fabric of an urban industrial society. Each generation of migrants faced anew Thompson's trauma of industrial work discipline and the process of class formation.[29] Each generation of labor activists sought to face the challenge either by excluding the migrants entirely, or by developing strategies to bring their constituents together across these lines.[30] Yet strikes were more frequent, larger, and more violent; socialist movements more common and popular; socialist votes higher; and working-class social and cultural institutions more elaborate in the United States throughout the late nineteenth and early twentieth centuries than in the U.K. during the same period. The problem in the United States was not that the working class never was "made," but rather that it was "remade" continuously over the course of more than a century.

Labor History's "Race Problem"

The key difference between Thompson's narrative for nineteenth-century England and what happened in the United States concerns race. It was not simply a matter of distinct communities organized along racial and ethnic lines. Rather, the process of working-class formation itself was fundamentally racialized. White workers developed a sense of class identity that led them to define, organize, and mobilize "labor" in racial terms, and this process was as intimately linked to slavery as to wage labor, and also to the influx of Asian and even many European migrants who were viewed as less than white. So long as historians saw the wage- and slave-labor systems and the workers engaged in them as separate and distinct, which was the case until the 1990s, this was less of a conceptual problem for them. But, of course, they were separate in neither the labor market nor, more importantly, in the minds of white and black workers.

Though they need not have, working-class historians turned toward Thompson's subjects—wage earners, artisans, and the urban laboring poor—and, in effect, away from slave labor. Indeed, notions of agency and slave community and culture emerged as major themes, particularly in the work of George Rawick, but the study of slaves and their lives tended to be seen as a separate field for a generation.[31] This prevented labor historians from grasping the full complexity of working-class formation in the United States. A self-consciously capacious approach to class still tended to compartmentalize and neglect a large population of the most exploited elements in the working-class population.

David Roediger, whose own approach was deeply influenced by Thompson but even more by W. E. B. Du Bois, looked at precisely the Thompsonian moment in the United States, from the late eighteenth through mid-nineteenth centuries. He not only employed a similar approach and many of the same kinds of sources, he also carried Thompson's argument about working-class agency one step further to explain the racialized character of class formation in the United States in this critical period. As in England, American workers were active agents in their own making as a class, but here the identity was one of a *white* working class. It is yet another testament to *The Making*'s influence that perhaps the most searching critique of the new labor history is framed largely in terms of Thompson's own approach, and particularly his argument regarding workers' agency. In this case, Roediger argued that "whiteness," like class, was a constructed, not a natural identity, that American workers were active agents in the creation of a white working-class identity and movement, and that it was impossible to separate the process of class formation from this process of racial formation.[32]

Following Thompson's (and Raymond Williams's) emphasis on language and culture as the medium through which a notion of class was created and reproduced, Roediger nevertheless largely eschewed the realm of work and exploitation that absorbed much of Thompson's attention and connected his approach with earlier Marxist historiography. Some see Roediger's determination to document the agency of white workers in creating and reproducing racism as largely crowding out the role of the business and political ruling class in this process. It also now seems that the group of working-class abolitionists, which Roediger always acknowledged, was likely larger than he had realized. This group included many German immigrants as well as native-born workers. There were white labor activists who identified with black workers and saw abolition and labor reform as part of the same democratic vision.[33]

Likewise, the idea that even much of the early new labor history failed to engage the problem of race would be to exaggerate a serious under-theorization of the problem. It was a major preoccupation in seminars at Pitt, Rochester, and elsewhere, and a serious element in many of the workplace-community studies begun as dissertations in the late seventies and published in the 1980s. Most labor historians came to acknowledge that it was impossible to understand either class formation or class fragmentation without looking carefully at the whole issue of race; that the gradual and uneven formation of a class identity was interwoven with that of a racial identity; and that white racism was perhaps the most serious obstacle, among many, to the formation of the sort of class consciousness Thompson described for England. Indeed, some of the best work in the field over the past twenty-five years has revolved around precisely these issues.

Even in the British case, however, *The Making* has been criticized for achieving its definition and narrative of class only by ignoring issues of social difference, notably gender, and for failing to weigh the significance of England's imperial status for the process of working-class formation. As in the United States, race was certainly a vital element in various colonial settings and even in the U.K. If it were proper to speak of an American working class, this could not be done in the same way the term was applied in *The Making*.[34]

Thompson as a Teacher

By the 1980s, Thompson's intellectual influence among radical historians in the United States might have receded for at least two reasons. First, with no apologies for doing so, he shifted his time and talents from social history to the transnational movement for peace and disarmament. He campaigned across Europe and elsewhere, in socialist states as well as in the West, for the organizations European Nuclear Disarmament (END) and the Campaign for Nuclear Disarmament (CND) against the deployment of weapons that threatened to destabilize the delicate nuclear balance in the late Cold War period. It was this role more than his social history that won him a spot on the list of those most admired by the English people. (He finished just below the Queen Mother.) Far from slowing down his writing, Thompson was particularly prolific throughout the decade, but his dozens of articles, pamphlets, and books dealt with disarmament issues, and this work left him very little time for writing social history.[35]

A second reason Thompson's influence might have declined had to do with theory: First, while Thompson's approach was mistakenly described as "culturalist" and did target highly structuralist formulations, in fact, the spread of postmodern theory to U.S. circles still challenged the kind of highly empirical, materialist social history Thompson and his supporters celebrated. Also, an increasing emphasis throughout the 1980s on gender, racial and ethnic, and later, sexual identity was capturing the imagination of precisely those historians most apt to embrace the description of "radical." Among labor historians at least, this second challenge proved more significant than the first, as issues of race, ethnicity, and sex and gender came to complicate our understanding of class and how it worked in the U.S. context.

That Thompson's influence persisted through the late twentieth century had to do in part with his teaching. He visited the United States often, and in 1975–1976 Edward and Dorothy Thompson divided the academic year between Rutgers and the University of Pittsburgh, two hotbeds of the new labor history. They left deep marks on the young historians in these programs and on many others who encountered the Thompsons in these and later years.

Teaching, and especially adult education classes, had always been closely linked with Thompson's historical writing. His first two books, a biography of William Morris and *The Making*, came directly out of his teaching experience and, indeed, were aimed much less at academic historians than at well-read and interested workers—the kinds of people Thompson taught in his Workers' Education Association classes and with whom he worked and socialized in the Communist Party. Though it has not been analyzed, this close connection between teaching and writing seemed to persist in the U.S. context. Anyone who saw Thompson lecture would quickly make the connection between his deeply engaging personal style and the compelling quality of his narratives; in many respects, he wrote as he spoke, and vice versa.[36] Although he had retired from English university teaching, I saw him speak a couple of times during the 1972–1973 academic year, which I spent at the Center for the Study of Social History, which Thompson had established at Warwick University in 1968. My recollections of his Pitt lectures on eighteenth- and nineteenth-century England are more vivid, and bring to mind Christopher Hitchens's own recollections of a lecture on enclosure which Thompson gave at Oxford: "All the clichés about bringing history to life had become, for those who listened, vividly and properly true."[37]

In spite of, or perhaps because of all this, the graduate seminar Thompson taught at Pitt in the fall of 1975 came as a bit of a shock. David Montgomery's extremely popular seminars were sometimes developed on the basis of student interests, and they focused on the era since early industrialization. Montgomery's own gritty research at this point was firmly fixed on the period between the late nineteenth century and the 1920s. Besides *The Making*, it was the Thompson *Past and Present* articles on "Time, Work-Discipline and Industrial Capitalism" and "The Moral Economy of the Eighteenth Century English Crowd" that we knew best.[38] The Pitt seminar was loaded with activist-scholars who were undoubtedly ready for a heavy dose of more labor history. Instead, we focused on "England in the Age of the French Revolution," and spent much of our time reading Blake, Wordsworth, Shelley, Wollstonecraft, and other romantic poets and writers. This was certainly not what I had signed up for. For his purposes, Thompson was experimenting with material and questions on romanticism and revolution that had long engaged him and that formed the basis of his last major projects, which were delayed by work in the peace movement and published posthumously—*Witness against the Beast: William Blake and the Moral Law* (New York: New Press, 1993) and *The Romantics: England in a Revolutionary Age* (Suffolk, UK: New Press, 1997).

But the questions raised and the reading we did in the seminar, including all that poetry, served our own purposes as well. The central theme, it turned out, was the relationship between radical intellectuals and popular social movements, one with considerable currency in Pittsburgh and elsewhere in the United States amid a range of rank-and-file movements and strikes in the 1970s. Thompson seemed delighted to be back in the classroom, and we were delighted to have him with us. In between his teaching responsibilities, he attended conferences and delivered lectures at other institutions, coming into contact with many of the labor historians he had not already met through his work at Warwick. By 1980, as Thompson shifted his efforts decisively in the direction of the peace movement, his influence on the "new labor historians" who were transforming the field seemed secure. There was another link for me at least, between this seminar and an interest that flowered only in my later work. These were questions of personality and personal crisis, the significance of experience for political ideals and action, the importance of weighing close personal relationships in assessing the experience of radical activists—all of which came up in the lives of these romantic writers, even if they proved more difficult to fathom and document in the lives of the folks down below.

The Emotional Dimension of Working-Class Experience

Where are we headed today, and what, if anything, does a new trajectory have to do with Thompson and his famous book? Certainly by the standards of his day, and even in comparison to many of today's histories, *The Making* was more concerned to convey what class *felt* like—to endure factory work; to be politically marginalized and excluded from the decision making of society; to have one's children denied a proper education and instead sentenced to a life of hard labor at an early age. Thompson recognized already what many historians seem still not to have learned—that class is not only a material, social, and cultural experience, but is also in a profound sense *emotional*. What we call class consciousness, as a sort of shorthand, involved not only social and political aspirations, but also a world of hurt, resentment, and anger.³⁹ Without such emotions, the element of experience at the heart of Thompson's approach would not mean much. This world of emotions seems remote from the frameworks most social historians employ. Yet if culture was the medium through which working people "handled" class, it was experienced at the personal level and shared socially through emotions. In this sense at least, the personal could indeed be political.⁴⁰

I doubt this is precisely what Thompson meant when he used the phrase "structures of feeling," but there is no doubt that at numerous places in *The Making* the affective side of class is evoked to demonstrate the personal as well as the social costs of industrial work, political exclusion, and class discrimination.⁴¹ Interestingly, when he reached to convey the pervasive but elusive quality of the class experience, Thompson invoked emotions as a metaphor. "The finest-meshed sociological net cannot give us a pure specimen of class," he wrote, "any more than it can give us one of deference or love."⁴²

As late as the 1980s, Thompson still understood himself as a "democratic, libertarian communist."⁴³ Toward the end of his life, however, when he was asked for an "Agenda for Radical History," Thompson found it difficult to prescribe any particular approach, to establish such an agenda, or even to define his own relationship to Marxism. Instead, he spoke of human needs and emotions and the implications of these for how we go about creating a radical history:

> I find a lot in the Marxist tradition ... marked by what is ultimately a capitalist definition of human need. . . . This definition of need, in economic material terms, tends to enforce a hierarchy of causation which affords insufficient priority to other needs: the needs of identity, the needs of gender identity, the need for respect and status among working people themselves.⁴⁴

We continue to read and debate Thompson and his great book, not simply to decide whether or not he got the story straight—clearly the work of feminist historians and other critics has highlighted weaknesses—but rather to recognize how the book can help us understand the power relations that enveloped our historical subjects. We also look to Thompson to judge how to make our own mark not so much upon our profession as upon our society—as individuals, of course, but more importantly as elements in a broader humanity that was always at the center of Thompson's approach to history.

NOTES

INTRODUCTION

1. For various perspectives on social history "from the bottom up" and the "New Labor History," see Peter Novick, *That Noble Dream: The "Objectivity Question" and the American Historical Profession* (Cambridge: Cambridge University Press, 1988); David Brody, "The Old Labor and the New: In Search of an American Working Class," *Labor History* 20:1 (Winter 1979): 11–126; Leon Fink, "John R. Commons, Herbert Gutman, and the Burden of Labor History," *Labor History* 29:3 (1988): 313–322.

2. Leon Fink et al., eds., *Workers across the Americas: The Transnational Turn in Labor History* (New York: Oxford University Press, 2011); Marcel van der Linden, *Workers of the World: Essays toward a Global Labor History* (Boston: Brill, 2008).

3. Robert A. Orsi, *The Madonna of One Hundred and Fifteenth Street: Faith and Community in Italian Harlem, 1880–1950* (New Haven, CT: Yale University Press, 1985). Peter N. Stearns and Jan Lewis, eds., *An Emotional History of the United States* (New York: New York University Press, 1998) contains suggestive essays dealing with the emotional lives of common people. Susan J. Matt and Peter N. Stearns, "Introduction," in Susan J. Matt and Peter N. Stearns, eds., *Doing Emotions History* (Urbana: University of Illinois Press, 2014), 1–13, briefly maps the issues and history of the field. William M. Reddy, *The Navigation of Feeling: A Framework for the History of Emotions* (Cambridge: Cambridge University Press, 2001), though focused primarily on French elites, discusses the theory and implications of such research.

4. The seminal work is David R. Roediger, *The Wages of Whiteness: Race and the Making of the American Working Class* (London: Verso, 1991). The problem of social difference, and especially race relations and racial identity, in working-class experience has been a concern throughout my career and is reflected in most of the essays presented here.

5. This theme is developed more fully in James R. Barrett, *The Irish Way: Becoming American in the Multi-Ethnic City* (New York: Penguin, 2012).

6. Michael K. Rosenow, *Death and Dying in the Working Class, 1865–1920* (Urbana: University of Illinois Press, 2015).

7. George Steinmetz, "Reflections on the Role of Social Narratives in Working-Class Formation: Narrative Theory in the Social Sciences," *Social Science History* 16 (1992): 489–516; Reginia Gagnier, "The Literary Standard, Working-Class Autobiography, and Gender," in Susan Groag Bell and Marilyn Yalom, eds., *Revealing Lives: Autobiography, Biography, and Gender* (Albany: State University of New York Press, 1990); Mary Jo Maynes, *Taking the Hard Road: Life Course in French and German Workers' Autobiographies in the Era of Industrialization* (Chapel Hill: University of North Carolina Press, 1995); Diane Koenker, "Scripting the Revolutionary Worker Autobiography: Archetypes, Models, Inventions, and Markets," *International Review of Social History*, 49 (2004): 371–400.

8. See Susan J. Matt, "Recovering the Invisible: Methods for the Historical Study of the Emotions," in Matt and Stearns, eds., *Doing Emotions History*, 41–53.

9. The impact of emotional language and behavior can show up in unexpected places. Mark Steinberg locates a heavy emotional content in the writings of Russian working-class poets and in the language and action of the Russian Revolution. See Mark D. Steinberg, *Proletarian Imagination: Self, Modernity, and the Sacred in Russia, 1910–1925* (Ithaca, NY: Cornell University Press, 2002); Mark D. Steinberg, "Emotions History in Eastern Europe," in Matt and Stearns, eds., *Doing Emotions History*, 74–95.

10. Richard Sennett and Jonathan Cobb, *The Hidden Injuries of Class* (New York: Random House, 1972).

CHAPTER 1. The Blessed Virgin Made Me a Socialist Historian

An earlier version of this essay appeared in different form in Nick Salvatore, ed., *Faith in History: Catholic Perspectives* (Urbana: University of Illinois Press, 2007). Thanks to Nick Salvatore, Pat Simpson, Jenny Barrett, and members of the University of Illinois History Workshop for helpful comments.

1. Renee Remond in *Essais d'Ego-Histoire* by Maurice Agulhon et al. (Paris, 1987), 294, translated and quoted from the French in Jeremy Popkin, "Historians on the Autobiographical Frontier," *American Historical Review* 104 (June 1999): 726–727.

2. On the "discourse of fear" in American Catholicism through the mid-twentieth century, particularly with regard to sexuality, see Timothy Kelly and Joseph Kelly, "American Catholics and the Discourse of Fear," in Peter Stearns and Jan Lewis, eds., *An Emotional History of the United States* (New York: New York University Press, 1998), 259–277. The Kellys argue that this tendency was in decline by the 1950s, but it certainly sounds familiar to me. See also the early fiction of Mary Gordon and her reminiscence, "The Irish Catholic Church," in Peter Ochiogrosso, ed., *Once a Catholic: Prominent Catholics and Ex-Catholics Reveal the Influence of the Church on Their Lives and Work* (New York: Ballantine Books, 1989), 71–85.

3. Michael Harrington, *The Long Distance Runner: An Autobiography* (New York: Holt, 1988), 4, 240. For an illuminating discussion of the relationship between religious and personal identity, see Robert Wuthnow's essay in "Forum: Sources of Personal Identity: Religion, Ethnicity, and the American Cultural Situation," *Religion and American Culture* 2 (Winter 1992): 1–8. For a distinction between the tight, all-encompassing

identity of the 1950s and the "looser" post–Vatican II Catholic identity, including the nonreligious phenomenon of "cultural Catholics" in the current generation, see Philip Gleason's essay in the same forum, 13–18.

4. Charles Morris, *American Catholics: The Saints and Sinners Who Built America's Most Powerful Church* (New York: Oxford University Press, 1998), 174, 175.

5. Rev. Michael A. McGuire, *Father McGuire's New Baltimore Catechism and Mass* (New York: Benziger, 1953).

6. "Races of Mankind," *Compton's Pictured Encyclopedia*, vol. 7 (Chicago: F. E. Compton, 1928), 2956–2957.

7. Interestingly, historian Elizabeth McKeown, growing up in a small Montana town, isolated from the larger Catholic communities of cities like Chicago, also attributed her early understanding of a world beyond her town—and of the broader Catholic experience—to *Treasure Chest*. See Elizabeth McKeown, "Local Memories," *U.S. Catholic Historian* 21:1 (Spring 2003): 21–22.

8. See *Treasure Chest*, various issues, 1961. On the legacies of Tom Dooley and Michael Harrington, see Maurice Isserman, *The Other American: The Life of Michael Harrington* (New York: Public Affairs, 2000), and James Terence Fisher, *Dr. America: The Lives of Thomas A. Dooley, 1927–1961* (Amherst: University of Massachusetts Press, 1997).

9. See James R. Barrett, "Ethnic and Racial Fragmentation: Toward a Reinterpretation of a Local Labor Movement," in Joe Trotter, Earl Lewis, and Tera Hunter, eds., *African American Urban Experience: Perspectives from the Colonial Period to the Present* (New York: Palgrave Macmillan, 2004), 294–295; Graham Taylor, "An Epidemic of Strikes at Chicago," *The Survey* 42 (August 2, 1919): 645–646.

10. James W. Sanders, *The Education of an Urban Minority: Catholics in Chicago, 1833–1965* (Chicago: University of Chicago Press, 1977), 91, quoted in Eileen McMahon, *What Parish Are You From? A Chicago Irish Community and Race Relations* (Lexington: University of Kentucky Press, 1995), 20; Brother Thomas M. Mulerkins, S.J., *Holy Family Parish, Chicago: Priests and People* (Chicago: Holy Family Parish History Commission, 1923); Ellen Skerrett, "Sacred Space: Parish and Neighborhood in Chicago," in Ellen Skerrett, Edward R. Kantowicz, and Steven M. Avella, *Catholicism, Chicago Style* (Chicago: Loyola University Press, 1993), 143–146, quotes, 143, 145. See also Ellen Skerrett, "The Irish of Chicago's Hull House Neighborhood," in Charles Fanning, ed., *New Perspectives on the Irish Diaspora* (Carbondale: Southern Illinois University Press 2000), 189–222.

11. John T. McGreevy, *Parish Boundaries: The Catholic Encounter with Race in the Twentieth Century Urban North* (Chicago: University of Chicago Press, 1996), 102–103, passim. On the proclivity of Catholic parishes to persist in the process of integration while Jewish and Protestant congregations tended to "flee," see Gerald Gamm, *Urban Exodus: Why the Jews Left Boston and the Catholics Stayed* (Cambridge, MA: Harvard University Press, 1999). On the racial transformation of East and West Garfield Park, including the area around Our Lady of the Angels, see Amanda Irene Seligman, *Block by Block: Neighborhoods and Public Policy on Chicago's West Side* (Chicago: University of Chicago Press, 2005).

12. Evelyn M. Kitagawa and Karl E. Taeuber, eds., *Local Community Fact Book for Chicago, 1950* (Chicago: Chicago Community Inventory, University of Chicago, 1953), 98–101; Evelyn M. Kitagawa and Karl E. Taeuber, eds., *Local Community Fact Book for Chicago, 1960* (Chicago: Chicago Community Inventory, University of Chicago, 1963), 60–61; Chicago Fact Book Consortium, *Local Community Fact Book, Chicago Metropolitan Area, Based on the 1970 and 1980 Censuses* (Chicago: Chicago Review Press, 1984), 59–61; Seligman, "Block by Block," 262.

13. Martin E. Marty, *Modern American Religion*, vol. 3: *Under God Indivisible, 1941–1960* (Chicago: University of Chicago Press, 1996), 417–418; Morris, *American Catholics*, 256.

14. My conception of my world as homogeneous was not unusual. A National Opinion Research Center study in the late sixties found that about 20 percent of Catholics surveyed said they lived in a neighborhood that was "almost all Catholic"—even though this was rarely the case. The study was cited in Andrew M. Greeley, *The American Catholic: A Social Portrait* (New York: Basic Books, 1977), 214.

15. David Cowan and John Kuenster, *To Sleep with the Angels: The Story of a Fire* (Chicago: Ivan R. Dee, 1996), 8.

16. McGreevy, *Parish Boundaries*, 33–35, 109–110; William A. Osborne, *The Segregated Covenant: Race Relations and American Catholics* (New York: Herder and Herder, 1967), 206–208; Cowan and Kuenster, *To Sleep with the Angels*, 8.

17. Cowan and Kuenster, *To Sleep with the Angels*, passim; Suellen Hoy, "Stunned with Sorrow," *Chicago History* 32 (Summer 2004): 4–24; Daniel Greene, "Tragedy in the Parish," *Chicago History* 29 (Spring 2001): 5–19.

18. Julie Billart (1751–1816), a French nun, was the founder and first superior-general of the Sisters of Notre Dame de Namur. Paralyzed in her lower extremities at the age of twenty-one, she was beatified in 1906 and canonized by Pope Paul VI in 1969 on the strength of a series of documented miracles. See Peter Stravinskas, ed., *The Catholic Encyclopedia*, vol. 8 (1907–1912; online edition, Detroit: Thomson Gale, 1999, http://newadvent.org/cathen/).

19. On the general context for this transition from ethnic Catholic to white Catholic, see McGreevy, *Parish Boundaries*, 109–110. Although there was certainly racial discrimination and gang violence against Puerto Ricans, whom we recognized as nonwhite, my neighbors made a distinction between them and African Americans. Perhaps there were many reasons for the distinction, but we were certainly aware that most Puerto Rican families were Catholic and that most African American families were not.

20. On the elaborate network of street gangs in Chicago during the interwar years and entrenched notions of "turf," both still very much alive in the fifties and sixties, see Frederic M. Thrasher, *The Gang: A Study of 1,313 Gangs in Chicago* (Chicago: University of Chicago Press, 1927). On the world of the city's street gangs amid Chicago's changing racial and ethnic demographics, including at the time I was growing up, see Andrew J. Diamond, *Mean Streets: Chicago Youths and the Everyday Struggle for Empowerment in the Multiracial City, 1908–1969* (Berkeley: University of California Press, 2009).

21. See, for example, the racially integrated classrooms and play groups, and the racially diverse Madonnas and saints from countries all over the world, depicted in vari-

ous issues of *Treasure Chest* as early as the mid-fifties: 12 (October 11, 1956); 12 (November 22, 1956); 12 (December 20, 1956); 12 (January 31, 1957); 12 (February 14, 1957); 12 (March 14, 1957); 13 (October 24, 1957); 13 (January 16, 1958).

22. Greeley, *American Catholic*, 112–25.

23. Philip Gleason, "Catholicism and Cultural Change in the 60's," in Ronald Weber, ed., *America in Change: Reflections on the 60's and 70's* (South Bend, IN: Notre Dame University Press, 1972), quote, 91.

24. On the archdiocese's interracial mission, see Osborne, *Segregated Covenant*, 211–220; Steven M. Avella, "Cardinal Meyer and the Era of Confidence," in Skerrett, Kantowicz, and Avella, *Catholicism, Chicago Style*, 120–121; McGreevy, *Parish Boundaries*, 119–120, 136–137, 147. The last quote is from one of our parishioners who objected to the socially oriented message that arrived in the parish in the early 1960s.

25. *Chicago Tribune*, August 13, 1965; Adam Cohen and Elizabeth Taylor, *American Pharaoh: Mayor Richard J. Daley: His Battle for Chicago and the Nation* (Boston: Little, Brown, 2000), 348–349.

26. Osborne, *Segregated Covenant*, 203, 204. On widespread instances of racial violence in and near various ethnic blue-collar neighborhoods in Chicago during the postwar era, see the *Chicago Defender*, May 12, 1964, 3, 17; *Chicago American*, August 3, 1963, 1, clippings in the papers of the Catholic Interracial Council, Box 73, Chicago History Museum; Arnold Hirsch, *Making the Second Ghetto: Race and Housing in Chicago, 1940–1960*, 2nd ed. (Cambridge: Cambridge University Press, 2000); "Massive Resistance in the Urban North: Trumble Park, Chicago, 1953–1966," *Journal of American History* 82 (1995): 551–578. On white violence against African American homeowners on the West Side in particular, see Seligman, "Block by Block," 241–251. John McGreevy ties the events to the culture and perspective of Catholic parishioners in Chicago and elsewhere in *Parish Boundaries*, 93–101, and provides the best treatment of the interracial movement in Chicago and elsewhere.

27. The photograph was reproduced in the September 1963 issue of *Community*, published by Friendship House, a South Side Catholic community dedicated to "the elimination of racial prejudice and discrimination." On the involvement of Chicago religious in civil rights actions in the city and beyond, see McGreevy, *Parish Boundaries*, 171–172. For the growing hostility of some laity to them as a result, see 189–190, and for the chasm that opened between the city's liberal and conservative Catholics in the wake of the summer 1966 open housing demonstrations in Gage Park and Marquette Park, see 184–192 and James R. Ralph, *Northern Protest: Martin Luther King, Jr., Chicago, and the Civil Rights Movement* (Cambridge, MA: Harvard University Press, 1993). For a blue-collar ethnic memoir of growing up in Gage Park's St. Gaul Parish, see Douglas Bukowski, *Pictures of Home: A Memoir of Family and City* (Chicago: Ivan R. Dee, 2004).

28. Maria Romano to Father Mallette, November 30, 1964, Box 3, Folder 8; "Irish Catholic" to Daniel Mallette, [1965], Father Daniel Mallette Papers, Chicago History Museum.

29. On the Catholic Interracial Council in these years, see Karen Joy Johnson, "The Universal Church in the Segregated City: Doing Catholic Interracialism in Chicago, 1915–1963," PhD dissertation, University of Illinois at Chicago, 2013, 390,

and for the racial transformation of a South Side parish in the course of the 1960s and the tensions this produced within the parish among those supporting continued segregation and those supporting peaceful integration, see McMahon, *What Parish Are You From?*

30. James R. Barrett, "Remembering *The Jungle*," *Labor: Studies in Working-Class History of the Americas* 3:4 (Fall 2006): 7–12.

31. On the "new labor history" and the influence of Thompson and Gutman on my own generation of historians, see chapter 9 of this volume.

32. Gareth Stedman Jones, *Outcast London: A Study of the Relations between Social Classes* (Oxford: Oxford University Press, 1970); Carter Goodrich, *The Frontier of Control: A Study of British Workshop Politics* (1921; repr., London: Pluto Press, 1975); David Brody, *Steelworkers in America: The Nonunion Era* (1960; repr., Urbana: University of Illinois Press, 1999); David Montgomery, *Workers' Control in America: Studies in the History of Work, Technology, and Labor Struggles* (New York: Cambridge University Press, 1979). The British influences derived from a year of study at Warwick University in Coventry, England, where E. P. Thompson had established the Center for the Study of Social History. David Brody was the visiting American professor during my year of study there (1972–1973), my first travel outside of the United States.

33. Montgomery was invoking a phrase employed by Robert and Helen Lynd in *Middletown* (New York: Harcourt, Brace and Company, 1929). I thank Kathy Oberdeck for reminding me of the original source of the phrase.

34. John Bodnar, "Immigration, Kinship, and the Rise of Working Class Realism in Industrial America," *Journal of Social History* 14 (1980): 45–65; James R. Barrett, *Work and Community in the Jungle: Chicago's Packinghouse Workers, 1894–1922* (Urbana: University of Illinois Press, 1987), 271–272; James R. Barrett, "*The Transplanted*: Workers, Class, and Labor," *Social Science History* 12 (Fall 1988): 221–31; James R. Barrett, "Women's Work, Family Economy, and Militancy: The Case of Chicago's Immigrant Packinghouse Workers, 1900–1922," in Robert Asher and Charles Stephenson, eds., *Labor Divided: Race and Ethnicity in United States Labor Struggles, 1840–1970* (Albany: State University of New York Press, 1990). Neither Bodnar nor I noted the likely influence of the Church's teachings on the sacredness of family life in relation to these problems. See Leslie Woodcock Tentler, "On the Margins: The State of American Catholic History," *American Quarterly* 45 (March 1993): 104–127.

35. Woodcock Tentler, "On the Margins," 114; Leslie Woodcock Tentler, "Present at the Creation: Working-Class Catholics in the United States," in Rick Halpern and Jonathan Morris, eds., *American Exceptionalism? U.S. Working-Class Formation in an International Context* (New York: St. Martin's Press, 1997), 135, 144; Robert A. Slayton, *Back of the Yards: The Making of a Local Democracy* (Chicago: University of Chicago Press, 1986), 118–123 and passim.

36. Thomas Bell, *Out of This Furnace* (Boston: Little, Brown, 1941). For a fuller argument that traditional religious and other cultural values can provide the basis for radical social movements, see Craig Calhoun, "The Radicalism of Tradition: Community Strength or Venerable Disguise and Borrowed Language?" *American Journal of Sociology* 88 (1983): 886–914. I thank Kathy Oberdeck for the reference.

37. Barrett, *Work and Community in the Jungle*; Upton Sinclair, *The Jungle*, with an introduction and notes by James R. Barrett (Urbana: University of Illinois Press, 1988), xix–xxii; "Remembering *The Jungle*." Alinsky is quoted in Slayton, *Back of the Yards*, 118.

38. Woodcock Tentler, "On the Margins," 111–112, quote on 112. Although I am speaking here of Catholicism, the argument applies to workers' religious lives more generally. When this essay first appeared, I cited the following as indications of a rise in interest in working-class religion among younger labor historians: Kimberly L. Phillips, *AlabamaNorth: African-American Migrants, Community, and Working-Class Activism in Cleveland, 1915–1945* (Urbana: University of Illinois Press, 1999), and Kathryn Oberdeck, *The Evangelist and the Impresario: Religion, Entertainment, and Politics in America, 1884–1914* (Baltimore: Johns Hopkins University Press, 1999). Since then, there has been an unmistakable burgeoning of this interest, particularly on Southern subjects; the work is less developed with regard to working-class Catholics. See, for example, Kenneth Fones-Wolf and Elizabeth Fones-Wolf, *Struggle for the Soul of the Postwar South: White Protestant Evangelicals and Operation Dixie* (Urbana: University of Illinois Press, 2015); Jarod Heath Roll, *The Spirit of Rebellion: Labor and Religion in the New Cotton South* (Urbana: University of Illinois Press, 2010); Christopher D. Cantwell, Heath W. Carter, and Janine Giordano Drake, eds., *The Pew and the Picket Line: Christianity and the American Working Class* (Urbana: University of Illinois Press, 2016); Matthew Pehl, *The Making of Working-Class Religion: Welding Solidarity to the Sacred in the Motor City* (Urbana: University of Illinois Press, 2016); the special issue on Labor and Religion in *Labor: Studies in the Working-Class History of the Americas* 6:1 (2009); and James P. McCartin and Joseph A. McCartin, "Working-Class Catholicism: A Call for New Investigations, Dialogue, and Reappraisal," *Labor: Studies in the Working-Class History of the Americas* 4:2 (2007): 99–110.

39. John T. McGreevy, "Faith and Morals in the United States, 1865 to the Present," *Reviews in American History* 26 (March 1998): 240. Woodcock Tentler, "On the Margins." Woodcock Tentler's article is reprinted with responses from several Catholic historians in *U.S. Catholic Historian* 21 (Spring 2003): 77–126.

40. William H. Sewell, "Toward a Post-Materialist Rhetoric for Labor History," in Lenard Berlanstein, ed., *Rethinking Labor History: Essays on Discourse and Class Analysis* (Urbana: University of Illinois Press, 1993), 17–18. Garry Wills has argued that American intellectuals and social critics generally ignore the pervasive influence of religion in the United States, except when its enormous impact on American politics and culture make this impossible. See Garry Wills, *Under God: Religion and American Politics* (New York: Simon and Schuster, 1990), 15–16.

41. Herbert Gutman, "Protestantism and the American Labor Movement: The Christian Spirit in the Gilded Age," in *Work, Culture, and Society in Industrializing America: Essays in American Working-Class and Social History* (New York: Vintage, 1976), 79–117; Nick Salvatore, "Herbert Gutman's Narrative of the American Working-Class: A Reevaluation," *International Journal of Politics, Culture and Society* 12 (1998): 64–68. Unlike Salvatore, I find Gutman's interest in religion here and elsewhere another sign of his remarkably sensitive approach to working-class life during the earliest stages of the "new labor history." See also "Work, Culture, and Society in Industrializing America,

1815–1919," in Gutman, *Work, Culture, and Industrializing America*, 4–66. We know far more about popular religion among workers in the early and mid-nineteenth than in the twentieth century, though much of this literature emphasizes religion as a source of class fragmentation. For some of the best of this work, see, for example, Bruce Laurie, *The Working People of Philadelphia, 1800–1850* (Philadelphia: Temple University Press, 1980); David Montgomery, "The Shuttle and the Cross: Weavers and Artisans in the Kensington Riots of 1844," *Journal of Social History* 5 (1972): 411–447; and, for a critique, William R. Sutton, "Tied to the Whipping Post: New Labor Historians and Evangelical Artisans in the Early Republic," *Labor History* 36 (Spring 1995): 251–281. As in so much of the new labor history, E. P. Thompson's influence has been enormous. See his classic discussion of Methodism in E. P. Thompson, *The Making of the English Working Class* (New York: Vintage, 1966), 350–400.

42. See chapters 2 and 3 of this volume and James R. Barrett, *William Z. Foster and the Tragedy of American Radicalism* (Urbana: University of Illinois Press, 2000).

43. Compare the treatment of the 1919 riot in Barrett, *Work and Community in the Jungle*, and Dominic Pacyga, "Chicago's 1919 Race Riot: Ethnicity, Class, and Urban Violence," in Raymond A. Mohl, ed., *The Making of Urban America*, 2nd ed. (Wilmington, DE: Scholarly Resources, 1997), with the standard treatment in William M. Tuttle, *Race Riot: Chicago in the Red Summer of 1919* (New York: Atheneum, 1970).

44. David Roediger and James R. Barrett, "Irish Hosts and White Pan-Ethnicity; Or, Who Made the 'New Immigrants' Inbetween?" in Nancy Foner and George Fredrickson, eds., *Not Just Black and White: Immigration and Race, Then and Now* (New York: Russell Sage, 2004); and James R. Barrett and David R. Roediger, "The Irish and the 'Americanization' of the 'New Immigrants' in the Streets and in the Churches of the Urban United States, 1900–1930," *Journal of American Ethnic History* 24 (Summer 2005): 3–33.

45. James R. Barrett, *The Irish Way: Becoming American in the Multi-Ethnic City* (New York: Penguin, 2012).

CHAPTER 2. *Was* the Personal Political?

An earlier version of this essay appeared first in different form in the *International Review of Social History* 53 (December 2008): 395–423. I thank Glenda Gilmore, Marilyn Booth, Kathy Oberdeck, Leslie Reagan, and Diane Koenker for their comments, and Nicole Ranganath, Adam Hodges, and Caroline Merithew for their research assistance.

1. See Harvey Klehr, "The Historiography of American Communism: An Unsettled Field," *Labour History Review* 68 (2003): 61–78; and for a criticism of much of left-wing scholarship for underestimating the influence of Stalinism in the party's history, Bryan Palmer, "Rethinking the History of United States Communism," *American Communist History* 2 (2003): 139–173, with responses by John Earl Haynes, James R. Barrett, Melvyn Dubofsky, and John McIlroy, 175–202. For unusual treatments of sexuality, personal relationships, and the emotional content of communist activism, which have influenced my own approach here, see Kathleen A. Brown and Elizabeth Faue, "Social Bonds, Sexual Politics, and Political Community in the US Left, 1920s to 1940s," *Left History* 7 (Spring 2000): 9–45; Kathleen A. Brown and Elizabeth Faue, "Revolutionary Desire: Redefining

the Politics of Sexuality of American Radicals, 1919–1945," in Kathleen Kennedy and Sharon Ullman, eds., *Sexual Borderlands: Constructing an American Sexual Past* (Columbus: Ohio State University Press, 2003), 273–302.

2. See Alan McIlroy and Alan Campbell, eds., *Party People, Communist Lives: Explorations in Biography* (London: Lawrence and Wishart, 2002), and Kevin Morgan, Gidon Cohen, and Andrew Flinn, eds., *Agents of the Revolution: New Biographical Approaches to the History of International Communism in the Age of Lenin and Stalin* (Oxford: Peter Lang, 2005). For collective biography as a database for the movement's history, see "The CPGB Biographical Project," which describes a large project to collect biographical details on members of the British Communist Party, and Peter Huber, "Working on a New Biographical Dictionary of the Comintern: A Survey," papers presented at the conference, "People of a New Mould?" University of Manchester, April 6–8, 2001. The collection of biographical data on party militants is, of course, an old Soviet tradition. See Diane Koenker, "Scripting the Revolutionary Worker Autobiography: Archetypes, Models, Inventions, and Markets," *International Review of Social History* 49 (2004): 371–400.

3. Edward J. Johanningsmeier, *Forging American Communism: The Life of William Z. Foster* (Princeton, NJ: Princeton University Press, 1994); James G. Ryan, *Earl Browder: The Failure of American Communism* (Tuscaloosa: University of Alabama Press, 1997); James R. Barrett, *William Z. Foster and the Tragedy of American Radicalism* (Urbana: University of Illinois Press, 1999); Bryan D. Palmer, *James P. Cannon and the Origins of the American Revolutionary Left, 1890–1928* (Urbana: University of Illinois Press, 2007).

4. Vivian Gornick, *The Romance of American Communism* (New York: Basic Books, 1977), 18. The forty-seven interviews excerpted in Gornick's book are identified only by pseudonym, and she includes only a very brief description of her anecdotal methods. But hers is by far the most ambitious treatment of the subjective dimensions of Communist Party activism. Many of her respondents are identifiable to someone familiar with the party's history and communist autobiography.

5. My own understanding of autobiography differs somewhat from current postmodern notions of the genre, but my approach has been shaped in various ways by works in the following two notes, as well as by some of the essays in Sidonie Smith and Julia Watson, eds., *Women, Autobiography, Theory: A Reader* (Madison: University of Wisconsin Press, 1998), and especially George Steinmetz, "Reflections on the Role of Social Narratives in Working-Class Formation: Narrative Theory in the Social Sciences," *Social Science History* 16 (1992): 489–516.

6. Reginia Gagnier, "The Literary Standard, Working-Class Autobiography, and Gender," in Susan Groag Bell and Marilyn Yalom, eds., *Revealing Lives: Autobiography, Biography, and Gender* (Albany: State University of New York Press, 1990), 94; Joan Scott, "Experience," in Judith Butler and Joan Scott, eds., *Feminists Theorize the Political* (New York: Routledge, 1992), 22–40; quotation, Phillipe LeJeune, *On Autobiography*, edited and with a foreword by Paul John Eakin, trans. Katherine Leary (Minneapolis: University of Minnesota Press, 1989), ix.

7. Mary Jo Maynes, "Gender and Narrative Form in French and German Working-Class Autobiographies," in Personal Narratives Group, eds., *Interpreting Women's Lives: Feminist*

Theory and Personal Narratives (Bloomington: Indiana University Press, 1989), 104. See also Sidonie Smith and Julia Walton, *Reading Autobiography: A Guide for Interpreting Life Narratives* (Minneapolis: University of Minnesota Press, 2001), 2–4, and James Olney, *Metaphors of Self: The Meaning of Autobiography* (Princeton, NJ: Princeton University Press, 1972).

8. Mary Jo Maynes, *Taking the Hard Road: Life Course in French and German Workers' Autobiographies in the Era of Industrialization* (Chapel Hill: University of North Carolina Press, 1995), 200.

9. Reginia Gagnier, "Social Atoms: Working-Class Autobiography, Subjectivity, and Gender," *Victorian Studies* 30 (1987): 335–362. On working-class autobiography as a distinct genre requiring a different analytical approach, see also Maynes, *Taking the Hard Road*, 33; Gagnier, "The Literary Standard, Working-Class Autobiography, and Gender," 93–114; Koenker, "Scripting the Revolutionary Worker Autobiography," 371–373.

10. Maynes, *Taking the Hard Road*, 200, 154. The emphasis on a conversion that reorients the life narrative around this new central commitment means that communist autobiography bears some resemblance to Christian "conversion narratives," which have received considerable attention from scholars of autobiography. See Smith and Watson, *Reading Autobiography*, 70, 85, 101, 192–193.

11. Kevin Morgan, "Parts of People and Communist Lives," in McIlroy, Morgan, and Campbell, *Party People, Communist Lives*, 10.

12. Interestingly, the central message of the six existential narratives in Richard Crossman's extremely popular collection, *The God that Failed* (New York: Harper, 1950), is that there is no room for the individual in the communist movement.

13. Morgan, "Parts of People and Communist Lives," 10, 11, 12.

14. Theodore Draper: *The Roots of American Communism* (New York: Viking, 1957); and Theodore Draper, *American Communism and Soviet Russia*, 2nd ed. (New York: Vintage, 1986). Draper's interpretation is carried on in the work of Harvey Klehr and John Earl Haynes. See Harvey Klehr and John Earl Haynes, *The American Communist Movement: Storming Heaven Itself* (New York: Twayne, 1992); Harvey Klehr, *Heyday of American Communism: The Depression Decade* (New York: Basic Books, 1984). For Draper's assessments of the New Left scholarship, see Theodore Draper, "American Communism Revisited," *New York Review of Books*, May 9, 1985, 32–37; Theodore Draper, "The Popular Front Revisited," *New York Review of Books*, May 30, 1985, 79–81.

15. Sara Evans, *Personal Politics: The Roots of Women's Liberation and the New Left* (New York: Vintage, 1979).

16. Nell Painter, *The Narrative of Hosea Hudson: His Life as a Negro Communist in the South* (Cambridge, MA: Harvard University Press, 1979), 36–37, 39–40, and Ellen Kay Trimberger, "Women in the Old and New Left: The Evolution of a Politics of Personal Life," *Feminist Studies* 5 (1979): 432–449.

17. Morgan, "Parts of People and Communist Lives," 23.

18. See the voluminous prison correspondence between veteran communist activist Gil Green and his wife and children between 1957 and 1963, and the wartime correspondence between Bill Dunne and his wife Marguerite; Gil Green Papers, Chicago History

Museum, Box 1; William F. Dunne Papers, Tamiment Institute, New York University, Box 1, Folders 10, 11.

19. Hosea Hudson, *Black Worker in the Deep South: A Personal Record* (New York: International Publishers, 1972); William Patterson, *The Man Who Cried Genocide* (New York: International Publishers, 1971); Benjamin Davis, *Communist Councilman from Harlem: Autobiographical Notes Written in a Federal Penitentiary* (New York: International Publishers, 1969); Jack Kling, *Where the Action Is: Memoirs of a US Communist* (New York: International Publishers, 1986); John Williamson, *Dangerous Scot: The Life and Work of an American "Undesirable"* (New York: International Publishers, 1969); Elizabeth Gurley Flynn, *I Speak My Own Piece: Autobiography of the Rebel Girl* (New York: International Publishers, 1955); Elizabeth Gurley Flynn, *The Alderson Story: My Life as a Political Prisoner* (New York: International Publishers, 1963); William Z. Foster, *From Bryan to Stalin* (New York: International Publishers, 1937); William Z. Foster, *Pages from a Worker's Life* (New York: International Publishers,1939); Art Shields, *On the Battle Lines, 1919–1939* (New York: International Publishers, 1986); Charles R. Rubin, *The Log of Rubin the Sailor* (New York: International Publishers, 1973); Ella Reeve Bloor, *We Are Many* (New York: International Publishers, 1940); Gil Green, *Cold War Fugitive* (New York: International Publishers, 1985). Joseph Freeman's *An American Testament* (New York: Farrar and Rinehart, 1936), the work of an accomplished writer published by a large commercial press, differs markedly from most other party biographies. Yet Freeman's central narrative is his gradual maturity as a communist intellectual. I have also read several unpublished autobiographies that seem to fit in this category, despite the fact that their authors were all expelled from the party before they sat down to write: Max Bedacht, Alexander Bittelman, William Dunne, and Samuel Darcy, all in the authors' manuscript collections at the Tamiment Institute, Bobst Library, New York University.

20. Steinmetz, "Reflections on the Role of Social Narratives in Working-Class Formation"; Koenker, "Scripting the Revolutionary Worker Autobiography," 371–400.

21. Foster, *From Bryan to Stalin*; Foster, *Pages from a Worker's Life*; Flynn, *I Speak My Own Piece* and *The Alderson Story*. Both autobiographers focus heavily on their lives before joining the party, yet the narratives are organized around specific movement activities and the lessons drawn from these. Foster, in particular, organizes his stories around problems for which the Communist Party ultimately provided the solution. See chapter 3 of this volume, "Revolution and Personal Crisis." See also the autobiographies cited in n. 11.

22. Denis L. D. Heyck, *Life Stories of the Nicaraguan Revolution*, 122, quoted in Camilla Stivers, "Reflections on the Role of Personal Narrative in Social Science," *Signs: Journal of Women in Society and Culture* 18 (1993): 419.

23. On the peculiarly homosocial masculine character of Foster's narrative, see "Revolution and Personal Crisis"; on the masculine quality of the party's appeal in the 1920s and 1930s, Van Gosse, "To Organize in Every Neighborhood, Every Home: The Gender Politics of American Communists between the Wars." *Radical History Review* 50 (1991): 109–142; and on Flynn's long relationship with Equi, Rosalyn Fraad Baxandall, *Words*

on Fire: The Life and Writings of Elizabeth Gurley Flynn (New Brunswick, NJ: Rutgers University Press, 1987), and Brown and Faue, "Revolutionary Desire," 288.

24. Germaine Bree, "Autobiography," in James Olney, ed., *Studies in Autobiography* (New York: Oxford University Press, 1988), 171–179.

25. Foster, *Pages from a Worker's Life*, 11.

26. Maynes, *Taking the Hard Road*, 154.

27. Painter, *Narrative of Hosea Hudson*, 2.

28. Foster, *From Bryan to Stalin*, 23. For a fuller analysis of Foster's autobiographical writing in the context of his political career, see "Revolution and Personal Crisis." See also Paul F. Douglas, *Six upon the World: Toward an American Culture for an Industrial Change* (Boston: Little, Brown, 1954), 68.

29. Judy Kaplan and Linn Shapiro, eds., *Red Diapers: Growing Up in the Communist Left* (Urbana: University of Illinois Press, 1998); Phil Cohen, ed., *Children of the Revolution* (London: Lawrence and Wishart, 1997).

30. Flynn, *I Speak My Own Piece*; Peggy Dennis, *The Autobiography of an American Communist: A Personal View of a Political Life, 1925–1975* (Westport, CT: Lawrence Hill, 1977); Dorothy Healey and Maurice Isserman, *Dorothy Healey Remembers: A Life in the American Communist Party* (New York: Oxford University Press, 1990); Jessica Mitford, *A Fine Old Conflict* (New York: Knopf, 1977); Mary S. Lovell, *The Mitford Girls: The Biography of an Extraordinary Family* (London: Little, Brown, 2001). For a similar observation regarding the political socialization of French and German women radicals, see Maynes, *Taking the Hard Road*, 159–163.

31. Benjamin Gitlow, *I Confess: The Truth about American Communism* (New York: E. P. Dutton, 1940), and *The Whole of Their Lives: Communism in America—A Personal History and Intimate Portrayal of Its Leaders* (New York: C. Scribner's and Sons, 1948); Louis Francis Budenz, *Men without Faces: The Communist Conspiracy in the United States* (New York: Harper, 1948); Louis Francis Budenz, *This Is My Story* (New York: Whittlesey House, 1947); Whittaker Chambers, *Witness* (New York: Random House, 1952); Elizabeth Bentley, *Out of Bondage: The Story of Elizabeth Bentley* (New York: Devin-Adair, 1951); Bella Dodd, *School of Darkness* (New York: Devin-Adair, 1954). On confessions as an autobiographical genre going back to Rousseau, see Rita Felski, "On Confession," in Sidonie Smith and Julia Watson, eds., *Women, Autobiography, Theory: A Reader* (Madison: University of Wisconsin Press, 1998), 83–95. See also Smith and Watson, *Reading Autobiography*, 85, 146–147, 192. For an early "antimemoir," see Fred Beal, *Proletarian Journey: New England, Gastonia, Moscow* (New York: Hillman-Curl, 1937).

32. Harvey Klehr and John Earl Haynes, *In Denial: Historians, Communism and Espionage* (San Francisco: Encounter Books, 2003), argues for the centrality of espionage to the communist experience and the failure of many New Left historians to engage this dimension of communist history. On the role of espionage, see Harvey Klehr, John Earl Haynes, and Fridrikh Iforevich Firsov, *The Secret World of American Communism* (New Haven, CT: Yale University Press, 1995); Harvey Klehr and Ronald Radosh, *The Amerasia Spy Case: Prelude to McCarthyism* (Chapel Hill: University of North Carolina Press, 1996); Harvey Klehr, John Early Haynes, and Kyrill M. Anderson, *The Soviet World of*

American Communism (New Haven, CT: Yale University Press, 1998); John Earl Haynes and Harvey Klehr, *Venona: Decoding Soviet Espionage in America* (New Haven, CT: Yale University Press, 2002).

33. John Gates, *The Story of an American Communist* (New York: Nelson, 1958); George Charney, *A Long Journey* (Chicago: Quadrangle, 1968); Al Richmond, *A Long View from the Left* (Boston: Houghton-Mifflin, 1973); Vera Buch Weisbord, *A Radical Life* (Bloomington: Indiana University Press, 1977); Dennis, *The Autobiography of an American Communist*; Mitford, *A Fine Old Conflict*; Junius Irving Scales and Richard Nickson, *Cause at Heart: A Former Communist Remembers* (Athens: University of Georgia Press, 1987; repr. 2005).

34. Stivers, "Reflections on the Role of Personal Narrative."

35. *Seeing Red*, directed by Julia Reichert and James Klein (New York: New Day Films, 1984).

36. Harry Haywood, *Black Bolshevik: Autobiography of an Afro-American Communist* (Chicago: Liberator Press, 1978); Painter, *The Narrative of Hosea Hudson*; Kenneth Kann, *Joe Rapoport: The Life of a Jewish Radical* (Philadelphia: Temple University Press, 1981); Steve Nelson, James R. Barrett, and Rob Ruck, *Steve Nelson, American Radical* (Pittsburgh: University of Pittsburgh Press, 1981); Jessie Lloyd O'Connor, Harvey O'Connor, and Susan M. Bowler, *Harvey and Jessie: A Couple of Radicals* (Philadelphia: Temple University Press, 1988); Healey and Isserman, *Dorothy Healey Remembers*; Eugene V. Dennett, *Agitprop, The Life of an American Working-Class Radical: The Autobiography of Eugene V. Dennett* (Albany: State University of New York Press, 1992); Christina Looper Baker, *In a Generous Spirit: A First-Person Biography of Myra Page* (Urbana: University of Illinois Press, 1996). For a perceptive discussion of the methods and context for this genre, see Roy Rosenzweig, "Oral History and the Old Left," *International Labor and Working Class History* 4 (1983): 27–38. For the classic New Left formulation of the "personal is political," see Evans, *Personal Politics*; and for the roots of "second-wave feminism" in the Old Left, see Kate Weigand, *Red Feminism: American Communism and the Making of Women's Liberation* (Baltimore: Johns Hopkins University Press, 2001). On the tension between the Old Left activists' relentlessly political construction of their narratives and a New Left feminist's quest for the relationship between the political and the personal, see Trimberger, "Women in the Old and New Left," 432–449.

37. See Gosse, "To Organize in Every Neighborhood, in Every Home," and on the small number of women on the party's central committee before the Popular Front years, Harvey E. Klehr, *Communist Cadre: The Social Background of the American Communist Party Elite* (Stanford, CA: Hoover Institution Press, 1978), 70–82. For the masculinist subculture in the party, largely derived from the IWW and associated most closely with William Z. Foster, see James R. Barrett, *William Z. Foster and the Tragedy of American Radicalism* (Urbana: University of Illinois Press, 1999), 111–117; Palmer, *James P. Cannon*, 283. Brown and Faue, "Social Bonds, Sexual Politics, and Political Community in the US Left," and Brown and Faue, "Revolutionary Desire: Redefining the Politics of Sexuality of American Radicals, 1919–1945" represent the most substantial discussions of love and sexuality in the movement.

38. O'Connor, O'Connor, and Bowler, *Harvey and Jessie: A Couple of Radicals*, 48, 126.

39. Baker, *In a Generous Spirit*, 120; James G. Ryan, *Earl Browder: The Failure of American Communism* (Tuscaloosa: University of Alabama Press, 1997). On Foster's liaisons, see Klehr, *Communist Cadre*, 72; Oliver Carlson interview with Harvey Klehr, March 20–22, 1978, 68; Harvey Klehr Papers, Special Collections, Robert W. Woodruff Library, Emory University; and Johanningsmeier, *Forging American Communism*, 324; and on Esther Abramovitz's experience, Hutchins Hapgood, *The Spirit of Labor* (New York, 1907; repr. Urbana: University of Illinois Press, 2004), 290–291; Lucy Robins Lang, *Tomorrow Is Beautiful* (New York: Macmillan, 1948), 49, 78; Hutchins Hapgood, *A Victorian in the Modern World* (New York, 1939), 196–207.

40. On "varietism," see Christine Stansell, *American Moderns: Bohemian New York and the Creation of a New Century* (New York: H. Holt, 2001), 225–308. Maynes notes early and frequent sexual contacts in French and German working-class autobiographies. See Maynes, *Taking the Hard Road*, 148–151.

41. Charles Shipman, *It Had to Be Revolution: Memoirs of an American Radical* (Ithaca, NY: Cornell University Press, 1993), 80.

42. Healey and Isserman, *Dorothy Healey Remembers*, 88, 145.

43. Weisbord, *A Radical Life*, 115–116.

44. Shipman, *It Had to Be Revolution*, 126, 127.

45. Rosalyn Baxandall, "The Question Seldom Asked: Women and the CPUSA," in Michael E. Brown, Randy Martin, Frank Rosengarten, and George Snedeker, eds., *New Studies in the Politics and Culture of U.S. Communism* (New York: Monthly Review Press, 1993), 141–162.

46. Carlson interview; Harvey Klehr, *Communist Cadre*, 71–73.

47. Healey and Isserman, *Dorothy Healey Remembers*, 67; Brown and Faue, "Revolutionary Desire," 284–285.

48. Ella Winter, *Red Virtue: Human Relationships in the New Soviet Russia* (New York: Harcourt, Brace and Company, 1933). On the transformation in the personal lives of Russian women in the wake of the revolution, see also Wendy Z. Goldman, *Women, the State, and Revolution: Soviet Family Policy and Social Life, 1917–1936* (Cambridge: Cambridge University Press, 1993).

49. Weisbord, *A Radical Life*, 116.

50. Kann, *Joe Rapoport*, 71. See also Brown and Faue, "Revolutionary Desire," 275–276; Winter, *Red Virtue*.

51. Palmer, *James P. Cannon*, 195–196, 233–234, 313–315.

52. Baker, *In a Generous Spirit*, xviii–xix, 68, 75, 205. See also Brown and Faue, "Revolutionary Desire," 285–286.

53. Erik S. McDuffie, *Sojourning for Freedom: Black Women, American Communism, and the Making of Black Left Feminism* (Durham, NC: Duke University Press, 2011), 98–100, 119–122; Karl Yoneda, *Ganbatte: Sixty Year Struggle of a Kibei Worker* (Los Angeles: University of California, Asian Studies Center, 1983); St. Clare Drake and Horace Cayton, *Black Metropolis: Black Metropolis: A Study of Negro Life in a Northern City*, Introduction by Richard Wright and Harper Torchbook edition Introduction by Everett C. Hughes (New York: Harper & Row, 1962), 136–139; Weigand, *Red Feminism*, 99–100.

54. James Sydney Slotkin, "Jewish Intermarriage in Chicago," PhD dissertation, University of Chicago, 1940, 136, 177–178.

55. Slotkin, "Jewish Intermarriage," 140.

56. Ibid.

57. Ibid., 139–140.

58. Aurelia Johnson to Arnold Johnson, January 22, 1955; March 5, 1955, Box 2, Folder 18, Arnold Johnson Papers, Tamiment Institute, Bobst Library, New York University.

59. Arnold Johnson to Aurelia Johnson, January 1, 1956, Folder 21; January 1, 1957, Folder 23, Box 2, Johnson Papers.

60. Gil Green Papers, Box 1, Chicago History Museum. See also the prison correspondence between Fred Fine and his wife Doris, Fred Fine Papers, Series 1, Chicago History Museum.

61. Brown and Faue, "Revolutionary Desire," 287–293; Brown and Faue, "Social Bonds, Sexual Politics, and Political Community," 32–34; Healey and Isserman, *Dorothy Healey*, 129–130; John D'Emilio, *Sexual Politics, Sexual Communities: The Making of a Homosexual Minority in America* (Chicago: University of Chicago Press, 1984), 58–70; John D'Emilio, "The Founding of the Mattachine Society: An Interview with Henry Hay," *Radical America* 11 (July–August 1977): 29, 32, 34.

62. O'Connor, O'Connor, and Bowler, *Harvey and Jessie*, 48, 206.

63. Baker, *In a Generous Spirit*; Earl Ford and William Z. Foster, *Syndicalism* (Chicago, 1912; repr. Chicago, Charles H. Kerr, 1998), 17.

64. Elizabeth Gurley Flynn, *Rebel Girl: An Autobiography, My First Life (1906–1926)* (New York: International Publishers, 1973), 266. Flynn had not yet joined the CPUSA at the time of the experience.

65. Dennis, *Autobiography of an American Communist*, 77–87, quotations, 86, 87.

66. Leslie J. Reagan, *When Abortion Was a Crime: Women, Medicine, and Law in the United States, 1867–1973* (Berkeley: University of California Press, 1997).

67. Healey and Isserman, *Dorothy Healey Remembers*, 87, quotation, 38. See also Hooper, *In a Generous Spirit*, 136.

68. Weisbord, *A Radical Life*, 167, 168–169.

69. Baker, *In a Generous Spirit*, 187. On the notion of an extended family that appears in many autobiographies, embracing close friends throughout the party and sometimes crossing national boundaries, see Brown and Faue, "Social Bonds, Sexual Politics, and Political Community," 15–16.

70. Healey and Isserman, *Dorothy Healey Remembers*, 88. Whatever the reasons, the party became more "domesticated" in the postwar era. Most of the (overwhelmingly male) members of the party's National Board in the postwar era were married with children.

71. Peggy Dennis, "A Response to Ellen Kay Trimberger's Essay, 'Women in the Old and New Left,'" *Feminist Studies* 5 (1979): 453, quoted in Deborah Gerson, "Is Family Devotion Now Subversive? Familism against McCarthyism," in Joanne Meyerowitz, ed., *Not June Cleaver: Women and Gender in Postwar America, 1945–1960* (Philadelphia: University of Pennsylvania Press, 1994), 170.

72. Healey and Isserman, *Dorothy Healey Remembers*, 89.

73. O'Connor, O'Connor, and Bowler, *Harvey and Jessie*, 207.

74. Gerson, "Is Family Devotion Now Subversive?" 161, 162. On the importance of left-wing summer camps and other children's activities in sustaining party children in the midst of the McCarthy era, see Peggy Dennis's recollections regarding her son Gene in *Autobiography of an American Communist*, 187, and the reminiscences of Peggy Dennis, Sirkka Tuomi Holm, Mary Louise Patterson, and others in Kaplan and Shapiro, *Red Diapers*. See also Paul Mishler, *Raising Reds: The Young Pioneers, Radical Summer Camps, and Communist Political Culture in the United States* (New York: Columbia University Press, 1999).

75. Kaplan and Shapiro, *Red Diapers*, 5–6; and on party youth culture, Mishler, *Raising Reds*; Julia L. Mickenberg, *Learning from the Left: Children's Literature, the Cold War, and Radical Politics in the United States* (New York: Oxford University Press, 2005). For examples of the party's literature for children, see Julia L. Mickenberg and Philip Nel, eds., *Tales for Little Rebels: A Collection of Radical Children's Literature* (New York: New York University Press, 2008).

76. Kaplan and Shapiro, *Red Diapers*, 120; Gornick, *Romance of American Communism*, 3–12.

77. Kaplan and Shapiro, *Red Diapers*, 91–92, 7–11, quotation, 92.

78. Bettina F. Aptheker, *Intimate Politics: How I Grew Up Red, Fought for Free Speech, and Became a Feminist Rebel* (Emeryville, CA: Seal Press, 2006).

79. Dennis, *Autobiography of an American Communist*, 210, 211. Not surprisingly, perhaps, the execution of Julius and Ethel Rosenberg appears as a central trope in the narratives of many red-diaper babies. See, for example, the recollections of Dorothy Zellner (85–87), and Rachel Fast Ben-Avi (131), and for explicit fears that their parents too would be arrested and executed, see the recollections of Stephanie Allan (118), and Bettina Aptheker (284), all in Kaplan and Shapiro, *Red Diapers*.

80. Ethan Bonner, "Witching Hour: Rethinking McCarthyism, If Not McCarthy," *New York Times*, October 18, 1998, section 4, pp. 1, 6, summarizes the scholarship and some of its effects in terms of a rehabilitation of McCarthy-era anticommunism. The most popular account is Ann Coulter's best seller, *Treason: Liberal Treachery from the Cold War to the War on Terrorism* (New York: Crown Forum, 2003). While Coulter relies on the works of John Earl Haynes, Harvey Klehr, and other historians of the CPUSA, and includes references to coverage of this issue in the popular press, these historians do not necessarily agree with her political conclusions. For a major anticommunist reinterpretation of the McCarthy era in light of the Russian archival material, see John E. Haynes, *Red Menace or Red Scare? American Communism and Anticommunism in the Cold War Era* (Chicago: Ivan R. Dee, 1995).

81. Gornick, *Romance of American Communism*, 230, 233. Even many of the autobiographies and interviews of those who left the movement over the years contain similar statements.

82. Ibid., 231.

83. Dennis, *Autobiography of an American Communist*, 215.

84. See, for example, "The Story of Junius Scales, Southerner" (New York, late 1956); "Newsletter from Peggy Wellman," February 22, 1957; and the pamphlet attached to

"Dear Friend" from Families of the Smith Act Victims, June 28, 1956, with photographs of the Henry Winston, Gil Green, Fred Fine, William Norman, and James Jackson families, all materials in Arnold Johnson Papers, Box 2, Folder 24, Tamiment Institute, Bobst Library, New York University. On the strength of domestic ideology in the context of the Cold War, see Elaine Tyler May, *Homeward Bound: American Families in the Cold War Era* (New York: Basic Books, 1988).

85. W. E. B. Du Bois to "Dear Friend," June 20, 1956, Johnson Papers, Box 2, Folder 24.
86. Dennis, *Autobiography of an American Communist*, 215.
87. Gerson, "Is Family Devotion Now Subversive?" 169.
88. Gornick, *Romance of American Communism*, 232.
89. Ibid., 233.
90. Ibid., 239.
91. Ibid., 247–248.
92. Ibid., 13.
93. Ibid., 248. The passion and self-realization achieved through life in the movement and the failure to make a place for the individual within this world is the central theme of Gornick's book.
94. Douglas, *Six upon the World*, 119.

CHAPTER 3. Revolution and Personal Crisis

For research assistance, I thank Adam Hodges and Nicki Ranganath, and for their comments, Randi Storch, David Roediger, David Montgomery, Diane Koenker, Kathy Oberdeck, Marilyn Booth, and members of the University of Illinois History Workshop and the Pittsburgh Seminar in Working Class History, particularly Wendy Goldman. Portions of this article appeared in earlier versions in *Labor History* 43 (Fall 2002): 465–482 and in James R. Barrett, *William Z. Foster and the Tragedy of American Radicalism* (Urbana: University of Illinois Press, 1999).

1. Mary Heaton Vorse, *Men and Steel* (New York: Boni and Liveright, 1920), 60–61.
2. William Z. Foster to Comrade Lozovsky, Sochi, USSR, October 19, 1933, Foster Personnel File, Comintern Papers, f. 495, op. 66, 11, 40–44, Russian State Archive of Social and Political History (RGASPI), Moscow. I thank Dasha Lotoreva for translation of this document from the Russian.
3. Kathleen Brown and Elizabeth Faue, "Social Bonds, Sexual Politics, and Political Community on the U.S. Left, 1920s–1940s," *Left History* 7 (Spring 2000): 9; Sara Evans, *Personal Politics: The Origins of Women's Liberation in the Civil Rights Movement and the New Left* (New York: Knopf, 1979).
4. Foster provides his own accounts of his life in William Z. Foster, *From Bryan to Stalin* (New York: Workers' Library, 1937), and *Pages from a Worker's Life* (New York: International Publishers, 1939). The only other scholarly biography is Edward J. Johanningsmeier, *Forging American Communism: The Life of William Z. Foster* (Princeton, NJ: Princeton University Press, 1993). The Communist Party's conception of Foster and some notion of his standing in the party are conveyed in Arthur Zipser, *Working Class Giant: The Life of William Z. Foster* (New York: International Publishers,

1983); Joseph North, *William Z. Foster, an Appreciation* (New York: International Publishers, 1957); and Elizabeth Gurley Flynn, *Labor's Own—William Z. Foster* (New York: New Century Publishers, 1949). Foster's Comintern personnel file establishes his proletarian bona fides and suggests the high and low points of his career in the party (Foster Personnel File, Comintern Papers). On the significance of Foster's relationship with his parents and his childhood experiences for his later political development, see especially Edward J. Johanningsmeier, "Philadelphia, Skitterneen, and William Z. Foster: The Childhood of an American Communist," *Pennsylvania Magazine of History and Biography* 117 (1993): 287–308.

5. In 1928 the Communist International declared a "Third Period" of capitalist crisis and revolutionary ferment. In this era of "Class against Class," communists were to shun cooperation with reformists and instead assert a strong revolutionary line in all of their political work.

6. Earl C. Ford and William Z. Foster, *Syndicalism* (Chicago: William Z. Foster, 1912; repr. Chicago: Charles H. Kerr, 1990).

7. U.S. House of Representatives, *Investigation of Communist Propaganda: Hearings before a Special Committee to Investigate Communist Activities in the United States*, 71st Congress, 2nd Session, part IV, vol. 1 (Washington, DC: Government Printing Office, 1930), 359.

8. William Z. Foster, *Toward Soviet America* (New York: Coward-McCann, 1932), 213–214.

9. William Z. Foster, *The Twilight of World Capitalism* (New York: International Publishers, 1949), 157. For the continuity in Foster's hyperbolic rhetoric, see Foster, *Toward Soviet America*; William Z. Foster, *The War Crisis: Questions and Answers* (New York: Workers' Library Publishers, [January] 1940); William Z. Foster, "Leninism and Some Practical Problems of the Postwar Period," *Political Affairs* 25 (1946): 99–109.

10. See, for example, Foster, *Twilight of World Capitalism*, 158–159. In considering the relationship between a religious background and future socialist activism among German working-class autobiographers, Mary Jo Maynes found that "religious skepticism appears frequently as an important step on the way." Mary Jo Maynes, *Taking the Hard Road: Life Course in French and German Workers' Autobiographies in the Era of Industrialization* (Chapel Hill: University of North Carolina Press, 1995), 166.

11. See Johanningsmeier, *Forging*, 353.

12. Foster, *From Bryan to Stalin*, 22; quote, Foster, *The Twilight of World Capitalism*, 157.

13. *Syndicalism*; William Z. Foster and J. A. Jones, "The Future Society," *The Toiler* (1914): 7–8; William Z. Foster, "Is Government Necessary to the Operation of Industry?" typescript, William Z. Foster Papers (WZF MSS), RGASPI, f. 615, op. 1, d. 86,11. 26–35; William Z. Foster, *Russian Workers and Workshops* (Chicago: Trade Union Educational League, 1926); Foster, *Toward Soviet America*.

14. Robert Wiebe, *The Search for Order, 1877–1920* (New York: Hill and Wang, 1967); Jerry Israel, ed., *Building the Organizational Society: Essays on Associational Activities* (New York: Free Press, 1972).

15. Henry Steele Commager, ed., *Lester Frank Ward and the Welfare State* (Indianapolis: Bobbs Merrill, 1967); James Quayle Dealey, "Lester Frank Ward," in Dumas Malone, ed., *Dictionary of American Biography*, vol. 19 (New York: Scribner, 1937), 430–431; Clifford Scott, *Lester Frank Ward* (Boston: Twayne Publishers, 1976); and Richard Hofstadter's contrast between Ward and William Graham Sumner in *Social Darwinism in American Thought* (Boston: Beacon Press, 1955). Foster had likely encountered Ward's *Dynamic Sociology* (Philadelphia: University of Pennsylvania Press, 1944).

16. Theodore Draper, *The Roots of American Communism* (New York: Viking Press, 1957), 310.

17. William Z. Foster, "A Statement of the Aims of the Trade Union Educational League," f. 615, op. 1, d. 86,ll. 5–6, WZF MSS; Barrett, *William Z. Foster*, 102–111; Foster, *From Bryan to Stalin*, 138 (quote). For the evolution of Foster's thought from syndicalism through to his embrace of Soviet communism, see *Trade Unionism, the Road to Freedom* (Chicago: International Trade Union Educational League, 1915); *The Great Steel Strike and Its Lessons* (New York: B. W. Huebsch, Inc., 1920); *The Russian Revolution* (Chicago: Trade Union Educational League, 1921); *The Bankruptcy of the American Labor Movement* (Chicago: Trade Union Educational League, 1922).

18. James R. Barrett, "Boring from Within and Without: William Z. Foster, the Trade Union Educational League, and American Communism in the 1920s," in Eric Arnesen, Julie Greene, and Bruce Laurie, eds., *Labor Histories: Class, Politics, and the Working Class Experience* (Urbana: University of Illinois Press, 1998), 319–331. The American affiliate of the Third International changed names several times in the course of the 1920s before emerging as the Communist Party USA in 1929. It was called the Workers' Party of America at the time Foster joined.

19. Harvey Klehr, *The Heyday of American Communism: The Depression Decade* (New York: Basic Books, 1984), 33–34; Roy Rosenzweig, "Organizing the Unemployed: The Early Years of the Great Depression," *Radical America* 10 (1976): 40–41; *New York Times*, March 7, 1930, 1, 2; *Daily Worker*, April 12, 1930, 1. For Foster's description of his prison experiences, see Foster, *Pages from a Worker's Life*, 243–268.

20. William Z. Foster, "The Coal Strike," *Communist* 10 (1931): 595; Theodore Draper, "Communists and Miners—1928–1933," *Dissent* 19 (1972): 377–380; quote, Foster, *Pages from a Worker's Life*, 180; "Minutes of the Central Committee Bureau on the Western Pennsylvania Coal Strike, June 5, 8, 9, 1931," CPUSA Papers, RGASPI, f. 515, op. 1, d. 2355,ll. 1–6, Moscow; "Transcripts of Speeches before the Anglo-American Secretariat of the ECCI," January 3, 1932, Comintern Papers, RGASPI, f. 495, op. 72, d. 164,ll.3–86.

21. Foster, *Pages from a Worker's Life*, 283.

22. Federal Bureau of Investigation files; Solon Bernstein, MD to Earl Browder, New York, September 17, 1932, CPUSA Papers, f. 515, op. 1, d. 2710,l. 75; unnamed physician to U.S. Attorney, Southern District of New York, Attention: Judge Harold Medina, November 4, 1948, document 61-330-485, FOIA File 270, 224; document number 61-330-485; *Daily Worker*, September 15, 22, 1932, 1; Foster quote, "Pre-Plenum Meeting . . . , March 23, 1939," 3.

23. Foster to Lozovsky, October 19, 1933, Foster Personnel File, Comintern Papers, f. 495, op. 66, ll.41–44.

24. Foster to Browder, March 7, 1934, Browder Papers, Microfilm Edition, Reel 1, Section 29; Sam Darcy to James R. Barrett, November 6, 1986, letter in possession of the author.

25. Gil Green, interview by author, New York City, March 10, 1994; Paul Douglas, *Six upon the World* (Boston: Little, Brown 1954), quote, 118–119. On the close relationship between depression and heart disease, see *New York Times*, January 14, 1997, 1, 8. (I thank David Montgomery for calling my attention to the medical research.) On Foster's work routine in the postwar era, see also Arthur Zipser, taped comments in response to questions from James R. Barrett, November 28, 1986, in the author's possession; Johanningsmeier, *Forging American Communism*, 268; and Steve Nelson, James R. Barrett, and Rob Ruck, *Steve Nelson, American Radical* (Pittsburgh: University of Pittsburgh Press, 1981), 291. My thinking on the various aspects of Foster's illness has been stimulated by conversation with Howard Berenbaum, Department of Psychology, University of Illinois at Urbana-Champaign.

26. Steve Nelson, interview by author, November 1986, in the author's possession; John Brophy, interview by William Goldsmith, Washington, DC, notes, Daniel Bell Papers, addendum, Box 1, Folder 20, Tamiment Institute, New York University; Lizabeth Cohen, *Making a New Deal: Industrial Workers in Chicago 1919–1939* (Cambridge: Cambridge University Press, 1990), 314; Foster, *A Manual of Industrial Unionism*, quoted in Cohen, *Making a New Deal*, fn. 39, 502. The pamphlets included *Unionizing Steel* (New York: Workers' Library, 1936); *Organizing Methods in the Steel Industry* (New York: Workers' Library, 1936); *What Means a Strike in Steel* (New York: Workers' Library, 1937); *A Manual of Industrial Unionism Organizational Structure and Policies* (New York: Workers' Library, 1937); and *Railroad Workers, Forward!* (New York: Workers' Library, 1938).

27. Irving Bernstein, *The Turbulent Years: A History of the American Worker, 1933–1941* (Boston: Houghton Mifflin, 1969), 451–455; Max Gordon, "The Communist Party and the Drive to Organize Steel, 1936," *Labor History* 23 (1982): 254, 257–258; Bet Cochran, *Labor and Communism: The Conflict that Shaped American Unions* (Princeton, NJ: Princeton University Press, 1977), 96–97; Klehr, *Heyday of American Communism*, 227–238.

28. Dorothy Healey and Maurice Isserman, *Dorothy Healey Remembers: A Life in the Communist Party* (New York: Oxford University Press, 1990), 74–75. On Foster's influence on organizers in a range of industries, see Herbert March, interview, October 21, 1986, 17–18, 27, United Packing House Workers of America Oral History Project, State Historical Society of Wisconsin, Madison; Vicky Starr, interview, August 4, 1986, 915, 921, ibid.; Alice Lynd and Staughton Lynd, eds., *Rank and File: Personal Histories by Working-Class Organizers* (Princeton, NJ: Princeton University Press, 1981), 74–75; Art Shields, *On the Battle Lines, 1919–1939* (New York: International Publishers, 1986), 217; and Cohen, *Making a New Deal*, 314, 502.

29. Phillipe LeJeune, *On Autobiography*, edited and with a foreword by Paul John Eakin, trans. Katherine Leary (Minneapolis: University of Minnesota Press, 1989), ix; Reginia Gagnier, "The Literary Standard, Working Class Autobiography, and Gender," in Susan Groag Bell and Marilyn Yalom, eds., *Revealing Lives: Autobiography, Biography, and Gender* (Albany: State University of New York Press, 1990), 94.

30. Foster, *Pages from a Worker's Life*, 11.

31. Foster, *Pages from a Worker's Life*, 11; William Z. Foster, "The Human Element in Mass Agitation," *Communist* 18 (1939): 346–352, quotes, 347, 349; Johanningsmeier, *Forging*, 27–71.

32. Elizabeth Gurley Flynn, "The Life of a Great American Working Class Leader," *Communist* 18 (1939): 476–477.

33. Reginia Gagnier, "Social Atoms: Working-Class Autobiography, Subjectivity, and Gender," *Victorian Studies* 30 (1987): 335–364; John Burnett, David Vincent, and David Mayall, eds., *The Autobiography of the Working Class: An Annotated Critical Bibliography*, vol. I (New York: New York University Press, 1984), xvii–xxix. See also Maynes, *Taking the Hard Road*, 33; and Diane P. Koenker, "Scripting the Revolutionary Worker Autobiography: Archetypes, Models, Interventions, and Markets," *International Review of Social History* 49 (2004): 371–400.

34. William Z. Foster, *From Bryan to Stalin*, 59; Lucy Robbins Lang, *Tomorrow Is Beautiful* (New York: Macmillan, 1948), 49; Paul Douglas, *Six upon the World*, 119; Hutchins Hapgood, *The Spirit of Labor* (New York: Duffield and Co., 1907), 290–291.

35. Brown and Faue, "Social Bonds, Sexual Politics, and Political Community," 15–27. On the gendered quality of the party's propaganda and line during the Third Period, when Foster was in his element, see Van Gosse, "To Organize in Every Neighborhood, in Every Home: The Gender Politics of American Communists between the Wars," *Radical History Review* 50 (1991): 109–142. On the "Foster group's" subculture in 1920s party, see Alexander Bittelman, manuscript autobiography, Alexander Bittelman Papers, Tamiment Institute, New York University, 398–399 (quotes), 407–408, 434–435. On women in the party leadership, see Harvey Klehr, *Communist Cadre: The Social Background of the American Communist Party Elite* (Stanford, CA: Hoover Institution Press, 1978), 70–82. On the homosocial world of the migratory worker and hobo, see Frank T. Higbie, *Indispensable Outcasts: Hobo Workers and Community in the American Midwest, 1880–1930* (Urbana: University of Illinois Press, 2003). On Foster's affairs, see Klehr, *Communist Cadre*, 72, and Johanningsmeier, *Forging*, 324.

36. Fraser Ottanellli, *The Communist Party of the United States: From Depression to World War II* (New Brunswick, NJ: Rutgers University Press, 1991), 75–105; Michael Denning, *The Cultural Front: The Laboring of American Culture in the Twentieth Century* (London: Verso, 1996), 3–7, passim.

37. Joseph Starobin, *Communism in Crisis, 1943–1957* (Cambridge, MA: Harvard University Press, 1972), quote, 54; Gil Green, interview by Anders Stephanson, in Michael E. Brown et al., eds., *New Studies in the Politics and History of U.S. Communism* (New York: Monthly Review Press, 1993), 310. On Foster's feelings of inadequacy regarding theory, see Sam Darcy, interview by Theodore Draper, May 11–15, 1957, microfilm series 2.3, roll 8, Theodore Draper Papers, Woodruff Library, Emory University; Benjamin Gitlow, *I Confess* (New York: E. P. Dutton, 1940), 191; "Pre-Plenum Meeting of the National Committee, March 23, 1939," typed stenogram, 3, Philip Jaffe Papers, Box 35, Folder 4, Woodruff Library, Emory University, Atlanta, microfilmed material, reel 1.

38. Quote, James P. Cannon, *The First Ten Years of American Communism* (New York: Pathfinder Press, 1962), 114; Starobin, *American Communism in Crisis*, 224–237; Stalin's

speech before the Anglo-American Secretariat of the Executive Committee of the Communist International, May 6, 1929, quoted at length in Spravka, signed by Comrade Nisov, July 4, 1938, f. 495, op. 66, d. 261,l. 73, Comintern Papers, RGASPI; and "secret memo" by Comrade Belov, January 15, 1938, ll. 69–70 in Comintern Papers, RGASPI. On Foster's final struggles against the "revisionism" of the mid-1950s, see Barrett, *William Z. Foster*, 255–267, and on the general context for the fight, Maurice Isserman, *If I Had a Hammer: The Death of the Old Left and the Birth of the New Left* (New York: Basic Books, 1987), 1–34.

39. William Z. Foster, "Birthday Speech," March 9, 1956, William Z. Foster Papers, f. 615, op. 1, d. 65,l. 7; Bill to Esther, Sylvia, and Joe, Moscow, March 23, 1961, William Z. Foster Papers, f. 615, op. 1, d. 6,l. 85. See also Barrett, *William Z. Foster*, 247–249, 256–257, 269, 270.

40. The personal toll emerges most clearly perhaps in the memoirs of Bolshevik women activists in the midst and in the wake of the Russian Revolution. See, for example, Barbara Clements, *Bolshevik Women* (Cambridge: Cambridge University Press, 1997).

41. Peggy Dennis, The *Autobiography of an American Communist: A Personal View of a Political Life, 1925–1975* (Westport, CT: Lawrence Hill, 1977), 215; Healey and Isserman, *Dorothy Healey*, 30. See also Vivian Gornick, *The Romance of American Communism* (New York: Basic Books, 1977), 57.

42. Ellen Kay Trimberger, "Women in the Old and New Left: The Evolution of a Politics of Personal Life," *Feminist Studies* 5 (1979): 432–449; for similar observations regarding Russian, German, French, and English militants' memoirs, see Koenker, "Scripting the Revolutionary Worker Autobiography"; Maynes, *Taking the Hard Road*; and Gagnier, "Social Atoms." The American communist memoir literature is voluminous. For examples of male memoirs, see, for example, Nelson, Barrett, and Ruck, *Steve Nelson*; Nell Irvin Painter, *The Narrative of Hosea Hudson* (Cambridge, MA: Harvard University Press, 1979); John Williamson, *Dangerous Scot: The Life and Work of an American "Undesirable"* (New York: International Publishers, 1969); Hosea Hudson, *Black Worker in the Deep South* (New York: International Publishers, 1972); Ben Davis, *Communist Councilman from Harlem* (New York: International Publishers, 1969); George Blake Charney, *A Long Journey* (Chicago: Quadrangle, 1968); Harry Haywood, *Black Bolshevik: Autobiography of an Afro-American Communist* (Chicago: Liberator, 1978); Shields, *On the Battle Lines*; Al Richmond, *Long View from the Left* (Boston: Houghton Mifflin, 1973). For examples of the women veterans' narratives, see Dennis, *Autobiography of an American Communist*; Healey and Isserman, *Dorothy Healey*; Jessica Mitford, *A Fine Old Conflict* (New York: Knopf, 1977); Elizabeth Gurley Flynn, *I Speak My Own Piece: Autobiography of the Rebel Girl* (New York: International Publishers, 1955); Vera Buch Weisbord, *A Radical Life* (Bloomington: Indiana University Press, 1977); Christina Looper Baker, *In a Generous Spirit: A First-Person Biography of Myra Page* (Urbana: University of Illinois Press, 1996). For two biographies that try to develop both the personal and the political, see Martin B. Duberman, *Paul Robeson: A Biography* (New York: Knopf, 1988); and Rosalyn Baxandall, *Words on Fire: The Life and Writings of Elizabeth Gurley Flynn* (New Brunswick, NJ: Rutgers University Press, 1987). Vivian Gornick, The

Romance of American Communism, which is based on interviews with veterans of the movement, demonstrates that it is possible to trivialize the political by overemphasizing the personal.

43. Joseph Freeman, *An American Testament* (New York: Farrar and Rinehart, 1936), 294–295. Adulation of Foster's selfless devotion to the cause emerges clearly in the celebration of his sixtieth birthday before a crowd of 18,000 in Madison Square Garden. See *Daily Worker*, March 16, 1941, Section 1, p. 6, Section 2, p. 4; March 18, 1941, 1, 3, 7; Duberman, *Paul Robeson*, 652, fn. 35. The dictionary definition for the term "ascetic"—"anyone who lives with strict self-discipline and abstinence"—seems quite appropriate (*Webster's New Twentieth Century Dictionary of the English Language*, Unabridged 2nd ed. [New York: Fawcett Popular Library, 1983], 108). I do not subscribe to the Freudian use of the term that suggests an ideal personality type who unconsciously derives political principles and behavior as the result of "displaced libido." See Bruce Mazlish, *The Revolutionary Ascetic: Evolution of a Political Type* (New York: Basic Books, 1976). Compare the Freeman quote with Vorse's observation, cited above: "He lives completely outside the circle of self . . . swallowed up by the strike's enormity. What happens to Foster does not matter to him."

44. Wendy Z. Goldman to James Barrett, October 18, 2000.

45. Harold D. Lasswell, *Psychopathology and Politics* (Chicago: University of Chicago Press, 1930), explained such allegiances and behavior in terms of Freud's categories of childhood personality development and Oedipal conflicts. The subject's ambivalent relationship to his father was displaced to the political movement. (Lasswell and his followers tended to assume male subjects.)

46. Morris Ernst and David Loth, *Report on the American Communist* (New York: Henry Holt, 1952), 127. For a summary of postwar approaches to explaining Communist motivation, see Gabriel Almond et al., *The Appeals of Communism* (Princeton, NJ: Princeton University Press, 1954), 183–185. See also Eric Hoffer, *The True Believer: Thoughts on the Nature of Mass Movements* (New York: Harper and Row, 1951); Nathan Leites, *A Study of Bolshevism* (Glencoe, IL: Free Press, 1953).

47. Almond et al., *Appeals of Communism*, 260–261, 279.

48. E. Victor Wolfenstein, *The Revolutionary Personality: Lenin, Trotsky and Gandhi* (Princeton, NJ: Princeton University Press, 1967); Bruce Mazlish, *The Revolutionary Ascetic*.

49. Leo Ribuffo, "The Complexity of American Communism," in *Left, Right, and Center* (New Brunswick, NJ: Rutgers University Press, 1992), 149.

50. For an exception, see Brown and Faue, "Social Bonds, Sexual Politics, and Political Community."

51. William H. Sewell, "Toward a Post Materialist Rhetoric for Labor History," in L. R. Berlanstein, ed., *Rethinking Labor History: Essays on Discourse and Class Analysis* (Urbana: University of Illinois Press, 1993), 15–38; James R. Barrett, "Labor History from the Inside, Out," unpublished essay, October 1994; James R. Barrett, "Working Class Autobiography as a Path Within," unpublished essay in the author's possession, October 1996.

CHAPTER 4. Blue-Collar Cosmopolitans

This essay is dedicated to Thomas E. Barrett Jr. For research, I thank Michael Staudenmaier, and for their reading and helpful suggestions, Toby Higbie, Jenny Barrett, Kathy Oberdeck, the History Workshop at the University of Illinois, and the Labor History Seminar at Newberry Library, especially Sue Levine, Jack Metzgar, Suellen Hoy, Walter Nugent, and Peter Cole. Thanks also to Toby for source suggestions and for allowing me to read and cite his unpublished book manuscript.

1. Pheng Cheah and Bruce Robbins, eds., *Cosmopolitics: Thinking and Feeling Beyond the Nation* (Minneapolis: University of Minnesota Press, 1998).

2. James Clifford, "Traveling Cultures," in *Routes: Travel and Translation in the Late Twentieth Century* (Cambridge, MA: Harvard University Press, 1997), 17–39.

3. Robert K. Merton, "Patterns of Influence: Local and Cosmopolitan Influentials," in *Social Theory and Social Structure* (New York: Free Press, 1957), 441–469, especially 447–448. Merton, in turn, was drawing on the German sociologist Tönnies's familiar distinction between *Gemainschaft* and *Gesellschaft* and the work of other sociologists making similar distinctions. For a discussion of a "new class" of such cosmopolitans operating on a global scale, see Ulf Hannerz, "Cosmopolitans and Locals in World Culture," *Theory, Culture and Society* 7 (1990): 237–252, and the essays by Aihwa Ong and others in Cheah and Robbins, eds., *Cosmopolitics*.

4. Like most scholars, Clifford interprets cosmopolitanism largely in bourgeois terms, but his brief consideration of working-class travelers ("Traveling Cultures," 33–38), together with my reading of twentieth-century sailors' autobiographies and Marcus Rediker's and Peter Linebaugh's work were sources for my own interest in probing the concept of the "cosmopolitan" for understanding certain working-class subcultures. See Marcus Rediker, *Between the Devil and the Deep Blue Sea: Merchant Seamen, Pirates and the Anglo-American Maritime World, 1700–1750* (Cambridge: Cambridge University Press, 1987); Peter Linebaugh and Marcus Rediker, *The Many-Headed Hydra: Sailors, Slaves, Commoners, and the Hidden History of the Revolutionary Atlantic* (Boston: Beacon Press, 2000). I have also been influenced by Toby Higbie's capacious understandings of the diverse spaces and processes involved in working-class self-education. See Frank Tobias Higbie, *Working Knowledge: Learning Power in the Open Shop Era* (Urbana: University of Illinois Press, in press).

5. See, for example, Dominic A. Pacyga, "Villages of Packinghouses and Steel Mills: The Polish Worker on Chicago's South Side, 1880 to 1921," PhD dissertation, University of Illinois at Chicago, 1981. John Bodnar, *The Transplanted: A History of Immigrants in Urban America* (Bloomington: Indiana University Press, 1985) explores immigrants' local experiences within the context of global capitalism.

6. Douglas Wixson, *Worker-Writer in America: Jack Conroy and the Tradition of Midwestern Literary Radicalism, 1898–1990* (Urbana: University of Illinois Press, 1994).

7. Hazel Rowley, *Richard Wright: The Life and Times* (New York: Henry Holt, 2001).

8. Carl F. Kaestle and Janice A. Radway, "A Framework for the History of Publishing and Reading in the United States, 1880–1940," in Carl F. Kaestle and Janice A. Radway, eds., *A History of the Book in America*, vol. 4: *Print in Motion: The Expansion of Publishing*

and Reading in the United States, 1880–1940 (Chapel Hill: University of North Carolina Press, 2009), 7–21.

9. Hilda Satt Polacheck, *I Came a Stranger: The Story of a Hull-House Girl* (Urbana: University of Illinois Press, 1989), is a particularly revealing memoir of a young Jewish immigrant woman whose horizons were enormously expanded by the activities at a Chicago settlement house.

10. Susan Levine, "Workers' Wives: Gender, Class, and Consumerism in the 1920s," *Gender and History* 3, no. 1 (Spring 1991): 45–64.

11. "Organizer, IWW (Doyle)," ms., Don D. Lescohier Papers, Box 1, Folder 1, State Historical Society of Wisconsin. Thanks to Toby Higbie for this source.

12. Toby Higbie, *Working Knowledge* (chapter 2).

13. Hutchins Hapgood, *The Spirit of Labor*, edited and with an introduction and notes by James R. Barrett (1907; repr., Urbana: University of Illinois Press, 2004), 37–38, 75–93. See also William Z. Foster's early reading experiences with Paine and others: William Z. Foster, *From Bryan to Stalin* (New York: International Publishers, 1937), 22.

14. Kathryn J. Oberdeck and Frank Tobias Higbie, "Labour and Popular Print Culture," in Christine Bold, ed., *Oxford History of Popular Print: Volume Six: US Popular Print Culture 1860–1920* (Oxford: Oxford University Press, 2012), 233–252.

15. Higbie, *Working Knowledge* (chapter 2); Douglas Waples and Ralph W. Tyler, *What People Want to Read About: A Study of Group Interests and a Survey of Problems in Adult Reading* (Chicago: University of Chicago Press, 1931).

16. On the "Little Blue Books," see Alan Ruff, *We Called Each Other Comrade: Charles H. Kerr and Company, Radical Publishers* (Urbana: University of Illinois Press, 1997), and "Haldeman-Julius" in Mari Jo Buhle, Paul Buhle, and Dan Georgakis, eds., *Encyclopedia of the American Left*, 2nd ed. (Urbana: University of Illinois Press, 1998).

17. Richard Wright, *Black Boy (American Hunger): A Record of Childhood and Youth* (New York: Harper Perennial, 1993), 151.

18. Erin A. Smith, *Hard-Boiled: Working Class Readers and Pulp Magazines* (Philadelphia: Temple University Press, 2000), especially 79–102.

19. Larry Peterson, "The Intellectual World of the IWW: An American Worker's Library in the First Half of the 20th Century," *History Workshop Journal* 22 (1986): 153–172. Peterson emphasizes the close fit between his grandfather's organizing and political activities in the shop and his reading habits over the years.

20. Frank Tobias Higbie, *Indispensable Outcasts: Hobo Workers and Community in the American Midwest, 1880–1930* (Urbana: University of Illinois Press, 2003), 102; Carl Kaestle and Janice A. Radway, "Epilogue," in *Print in Motion*, 528. See also Harvey J. Graff, *The Legacies of Literacy: Continuities and Contradictions in Western Culture and Society* (Bloomington: Indiana University Press, 1987), 366–368.

21. Higbie, *Indispensable Outcasts*, chapter 1; Hapgood, *Spirit of Labor*, 41–44; James R. Barrett, *William Z. Foster and the Tragedy of American Radicalism* (Urbana: University of Illinois Press, 1999), 23–24; John C. Schneider, "Tramping Workers, 1880–1920: A Subcultural View," in Erik Monkkonen, ed., *Walking to Work: Tramps in American, 1790–1935* (Lincoln: University of Nebraska Press, 1984), 219; Nels Anderson, *The Hobo: The Sociology of the Homeless Man* (Chicago: University of Chicago Press,

1923), 137–149. William Z. Foster offers a stark memoir of the troubles and dangers in "On the Hobo" in *Pages from a Worker's Life* (New York: International Publishers, 1939), 105–133.

22. Higbie, *Working Knowledge* (quote, chapter 2). Melvyn Dubofsky, *We Shall Be All: A History of the IWW* (Chicago: Quadrangle, 1969), remains the definitive study of the IWW.

23. Anderson, *The Hobo*, 171–249; Lynn Weiner, "Sisters of the Road: Women Transients and Tramps," in Monkkonen, ed., *Walking to Work*, 171–188.

24. James Green, *Death in the Haymarket: A Story of Chicago, the First Labor Movement, and the Bombing that Divided Gilded Age America* (New York: Pantheon, 2006), 59–66, 94, 138–139, quote, 139; Hartmut Keil and John B. Jentz, eds., *German Workers in Chicago: A Documentary History of Working Class Culture from 1850 to World War One* (Urbana: University of Illinois Press, 1998); Bruce C. Nelson, *Beyond the Martyrs: A Social History of Chicago's Anarchists* (New Brunswick, NJ: Rutgers University Press, 1988); Hartmut Keil and Heinz Ickstadt, "Elements of German Working-Class Culture in Chicago, 1880–1890," in Hartmut Keil and John Jentz, eds., *German Workers' Culture in the United States, 1850–1920* (Washington, DC: Smithsonian Institution Press, 1988); Dorothee Schneider, *Trade Unions and Community: The German Working Class in New York City, 1870–1900* (Urbana: University of Illinois Press, 1994).

25. "Peripatetic Philosophers" *New York Times*, May 29, 1910, reprinted in Tony Michels, ed., *Radical Jews: A Documentary History* (New York: New York University Press, 2014), 174–78; Irving Howe, with the assistance of Kenneth Lebo, *World of Our Fathers: The Journey of the East European Jews to America and the Life They Made* (New York: Harcourt, Brace, Jovanovich, 1976); Hutchins Hapgood, *The Spirit of the Ghetto*, edited by Moses Rischin (Cambridge: Harvard University Press, 1967); Tony Michels, *A Fire in Their Hearts: Jewish Socialists in New York* (Cambridge, MA: Harvard University Press, 2005).

26. Susan A. Glenn, *Daughters of the Shtetl: Life and Labor in the Immigrant Generation* (Ithaca, NY: Cornell University Press, 1990); Sydney Stahl Weinberg, *The World of Our Mothers: The Lives of Jewish Immigrant Women* (Chapel Hill: University of North Carolina Press, 1988); Nan Enstad, *Ladies of Labor, Girls of Adventure: Working Women, Popular Culture, and Labor Politics at the Turn of the Twentieth Century* (New York: Columbia University Press, 1999).

27. "Peripatetic Philosophers," quote, 178.

28. Daniel Katz, *All Together Different: Yiddish Socialists, Garment Workers, and the Labor Roots of Multiculturalism* (New York: New York University Press, 2011), 63–83, 127–139.

29. Jennifer Guglielmo, *Living the Revolution: Italian Women's Resistance and Radicalism in New York City, 1880–1945* (Chapel Hill: University of North Carolina Press, 2010), especially 139–175; Kenyon Zimmer, *Immigrants against the State: Yiddish and Italian Anarchism in America* (Urbana: University of Illinois Press, 2015); Donna R. Gabaccia and Fraser M. Ottanelli, eds., *Italian Workers of the World: Labor Migration and the Formation of Multiethnic States* (Urbana: University of Illinois Press, 2001); Gary Mormino and George Pozzetta, *The Immigrant World of Ybor City: Italians and Their Latin Neighbors*

in Tampa (Urbana: University of Illinois Press, 1987); Caroline Waldron Merithew, "Anarchist Motherhood: Toward the Making of a Revolutionary Proletariat in Illinois Coal Towns," in Donna R. Gabaccia and Franca Iacovetta, eds., *Women, Gender, and Transnational Lives* (Toronto: University of Toronto Press, 2002), 217–246.

30. See chapter 7 of this volume.

31. Marcus Rediker, *Outlaws of the Atlantic: Sailors, Pirates, and Motley Crews in the Age of Sail* (Boston: Beacon Press, 2014); Foster, *Pages from a Worker's Life*, 17; Charles Rubin, *The Log of Rubin the Sailor* (New York: International Publishers, 1973), 99–100.

32. Bill Bailey, *The Kid from Hoboken: An Autobiography* (San Francisco: Lithographic Prepress, 1993), 216–218, quote, 216.

33. Ulf Hannerz, "Cosmopolitans and Locals in World Culture," *Theory, Culture and Society* 7 (1990): 239.

34. Linebaugh and Rediker, *Many-Headed Hydra*.

35. Quoted in W. E. Home, *Merchant Seamen: Their Diseases and Their Welfare Needs* (New York: Dutton, 1922), 39.

36. Foster, *Pages from a Worker's Life*, 75–77, quotes, 80, 82.

37. Quotations from Leon Fink, *Sweatshops of the Sea: Merchant Seamen in the World's First Globalized Industry, from 1812 to the Present* (Chapel Hill: University of North Carolina Press, 2011), 132.

38. Rubin, *Rubin the Sailor*, 34, 58, 60, 64, 97, 99–100.

39. Christine Stansell, *American Moderns: Bohemian New York and the Creation of a New Century* (New York: Henry Holt, 2001), 273–286; Hapgood, *Spirit of Labor*, 262–292; George Chauncey, *Gay New York: Gender, Urban Culture, and the Making of the Gay Male World, 1890–1940* (New York: Basic Books, 1994), 72–86; Hutchins Hapgood, *An Anarchist Woman* (New York: Duffield and Co., 1909). See the pioneering work of the late Allan Berube on the Marine Cooks and Stewards Union, an interracial, leftwing, and gay-friendly union organized in the Great Depression, in Allan Berube, John DEmilio, and Estelle B. Freedman, eds., *My Desire for History* (Chapel Hill: University of North Carolina Press, 2011), especially 259–320. The ethnic, racial, and sexual diversity of the sailors' experiences as well as their travels is particularly striking.

40. Sterling D. Spero and Abram L. Harris, *The Black Worker* (New York: Columbia University Press, 1931), 430.

41. Murray Kempton, "George," in *Part of Our Time: Some Ruins and Monuments of the Thirties* (New York: Modern Library, 1998 [1955]), quotes, 307–308, 306.

42. William H. Harris, *Keeping the Faith: A. Philip Randolph, Milton P. Webster, and the Brotherhood of Sleeping Car Porters, 1925–1937* (Urbana: University of Illinois Press, 1991 [1977]), quote, 15. Archibald Motley Sr. and his family represented the sophistication and status of the porters. He married outside of the community and lived in a largely white, more middle-class neighborhood. He raised a son, Archibald Jr., who became a prominent painter, and mentored a nephew, Willard, who wrote best selling novels and screenplays.

43. William H. Harris, *The Harder They Run: Black Workers since the Civil War* (New York: Oxford University Press, 1982), 78.

44. Beth Tompkins Bates, *Pullman Porters and the Rise of Protest Politics in Black America, 1925–1945* (Chapel Hill: University of North Carolina Press, 2001), 18–19.

45. Nixon interview, Studs Terkel, *Hard Times: An Oral History of the Great Depression* (New York: Pantheon Books, 1970), 117.

46. Alex Haley and Malcolm X, *The Autobiography of Malcolm X: As Told to Alex Haley* (New York: Ballantine Books, 1987), 73–78.

47. W. C. Handy, *Father of the Blues: An Autobiography* (New York: Da Capo Press, 1991 [1941]), 201.

48. Perry Bradford, *Born with the Blues: Perry Bradford's Own Story* (New York: Oak Publications, 1965), 48.

49. Quoted in Jervis Anderson, *A. Philip Randolph: A Biographical Portrait* (Berkeley: University of California Press, 1986 [1972]), 160. James R. Grossman draws a direct connection between the distribution of the *Chicago Defender*, largely through the agency of Chicago Pullman porters and the concentration of migration to the city from the Mississippi Delta. See James R. Grossman, *Promised Land: Chicago, Black Southerners, and the Great Migration* (Chicago: University of Chicago Press, 1991), 74–78.

50. Jack Santino, *Miles of Smiles, Years of Struggle: Stories of Black Pullman Porters* (Urbana: University of Illinois Press, 1989), 81, 86, quote, 9.

51. Ibid., quote, 69.

52. On the Brotherhood of Sleeping Car Porters, see William Hamilton Harris, *Keeping the Faith: A. Philip Randolph, Milton P. Webster, and the Brotherhood of Sleeping Car Porters, 1925–1937* (Urbana: University of Illinois Press, 1977); and on the role of the porters in the emerging civil rights movement, Beth Tompkins Bates, "Mobilizing Black Chicago: The Brotherhood of Porters and Community Organizing, 1925–1935," in Eric Arnesen, ed., *The Black Worker: A Reader* (Urbana: University of Illinois Press, 2007), 195–221; Beth Tompkins Bates, "A New Crowd Challenges of the Old Guard in the NAACP, 1933–1941," *American Historical Review* 102 (April 1997): 340–377.

53. Sidney G. Tarrow, *The New Transnational Activism* (New York: Cambridge University Press, 2005), especially 3–14.

54. On ethnically segmented working-class cultures in the United States and the fitful development of a broader American working-class identity, see chapter 7 of this volume; and on the diverse identities of immigrant workers in the context of strike activity, David Montgomery, "Immigrants, Industrial Unions, and Social Reconstruction in the United States, 1916–1923," *Labour/Le Travail* 13 (Spring 1984): 101–114; David Montgomery, "Racism, Immigrants, and Political Reform," *Journal of American History* 87:4 (March 2001): 1253–1274. See also Caroline Waldron (Merithew), "The Great Spirit of Solidarity: The Illinois Valley Mining Communities and the Formation of Interethnic Consciousness, 1889–1917," unpublished PhD dissertation, University of Illinois at Urbana-Champaign, 2000; Thomas Mackaman, "The Foreign Element: New Immigrants and American Industry, 1914–1924," unpublished PhD dissertation, University of Illinois at Urbana-Champaign, 2009.

55. Steve Nelson, James R. Barrett, and Rob Ruck, *Steve Nelson, American Radical* (Pittsburgh: University of Pittsburgh Press, 1981), 16–17.

56. John Wiite, "My Early Years in the United States," John Wiite Papers, State Historical Society of Wisconsin, Box 1, Folder 12, quote, 3. My thanks to Toby Higbie for drawing my attention to this document.

57. Vivian Gornick, *The Romance of American Communism* (New York: Basic Books, 1977), quotes, 3, 4, 6. See also the evocation of Jewish socialist and communist debate in the streets of Depression-era Brooklyn in Alfred Kazin, *A Walker in the City* (New York: Harcourt, Brace, and World, 1951), 141–146, and his cosmopolitan world of reading and discussion in his neighborhood of Brownsville, passim.

58. Gornick, *Romance*, quote, 6–7.

59. Ibid.

60. Ibid., quote, 8.

61. Richard Wright, excerpt from *American Hunger*, in Richard Crossman, ed., *The God that Failed* (New York, 1959), 139–140.

62. Paul C. Mishler, *Raising Reds: The Young Pioneers, Radical Summer Camps, and Communist Political Culture in the United States* (New York: Columbia University Press, 1999); Julia L. Mickenberg, *Learning from the Left: Children's Literature, the Cold War, and Radical Politics in the United States* (New York: Oxford University Press, 2005); Julia L. Mickenberg and Philip Nel, eds., *Tales for Little Rebels: A Collection of Radical Children's Literature*, with Foreword by Jack Zipes (New York: New York University Press, 2008). See also chapter 2 of this volume.

63. Robin D. G. Kelley, *Hammer and Hoe: Alabama Communists during the Great Depression* (Chapel Hill: University of North Carolina Press, 1990); Robin D. G. Kelley, " 'Comrades, Praise God for Lenin and Them!': Culture and Ideology among Black Communists in Alabama, 1930–1935," *Science and Society* 52 (Spring 1988): 59–82.

64. Barbara Ransby, *Ella Baker and the Black Freedom Movement: A Radical Democratic Vision* (Chapel Hill: University of North Carolina Press, 2003); Baker quoted in Ellen Cantarow and Susan Gushee O'Malley, "Ella Baker: Organizing for Civil Rights," in Ellen Cantarow, Susan Gushee O'Malley, and Susan Hartman Strom, eds., *Moving the Mountain: Women Working for Social Change* (New York: Feminist Press, 1980), 64.

65. Oberdeck and Higbie, "Labour and Popular Print Culture"; Jon Bekken, " 'No Weapon So Powerful': Working-Class Newspapers in the United States," *Journal of Communication Inquiry* 12 (1988): 104–119; Jon Bekken, "Working-Class Newspapers, Community and Consciousness in Chicago, 1880–1930," PhD dissertation, University of Illinois, Urbana-Champaign, 1992; Sally M. Miller, ed., *The Ethnic Press in the United States: A Historical Analysis and Handbook* (Westport, CT: Greenwood Press, 1987); Dirk Hoeder and Cristiana Harzig, eds., *The Immigrant Labor Press in North America: An Annotated Bibliography*, 3 vols. (Westport, CT: Greenwood Press, 1987).

66. Kimberley L. Phillips, *AlabamaNorth: African-American Migrants, Community, and Working-Class Activism in Cleveland, 1915–45* (Urbana: University of Illinois Press, 1999). See also Steven Hahn, *A Nation under Our Feet: Black Political Struggles in the Rural South from Slavery to the Great Migration* (Cambridge, MA: Harvard University Press), 461, as cited in Oberdeck and Higbie, "Labor and Popular Print Culture."

CHAPTER 5. The Bohemian Writer and the Radical Woodworker

An earlier version of this essay appeared in different form as the introduction to Hutchins Hapgood, *The Spirit of Labor* (Urbana: University of Illinois Press, 2004; original publication, 2007). The essay is dedicated to the memory of Steve Sapolsky.

The epigraph is from Hutchins Hapgood, *The Spirit of Labor*, edited and with an introduction and notes by James R. Barrett (Urbana: University of Illinois Press, 2004), 221–222.

1. Hutchins Hapgood, *A Victorian in the Modern World* (New York: Harcourt, Brace and Company, 1939), quotes, 186, 186–187.

2. Hapgood, *Victorian*, passim.

3. Michael D. Marcaccio, *The Hapgoods: Three Earnest Brothers* (Charlottesville: University of Virginia Press, 1977).

4. Robert Bussell, *From Harvard to the Ranks of Labor: Powers Hapgood and the American Working Class* (University Park: Pennsylvania State University Press, 1999).

5. On Hapgood's radical literary culture and circle of friends, see Christine Stansell, *American Moderns: Bohemian New York and the Creation of a New Century* (New York: H. Holt, 2001).

6. Hapgood, *Spirit of Labor*, 37–39, 85–88.

7. Ibid., 54.

8. Ibid., 85.

9. Ibid., 138–139.

10. Stansell, *American Moderns*, 16.

11. Moses Rischin, "Introduction to Hutchins Hapgood," *The Spirit of the Ghetto* (Cambridge, MA: Harvard University Press, 1967), viii. For the influence of the *Advertiser* and the writers around it on Hutchins Hapgood, see also Hapgood, *Victorian*, 137–172.

12. Stansell, *American Moderns*, 18–25, quote, 24–25. On the phenomenon of Progressive Era reform-oriented journalists "dressing up" to cross class lines in search the authentic working-class experience, see Frank Tobias Higbie, "Crossing Class Boundaries: Tramp Ethnographers and Narratives of Class in Progressive Era America," *Social Science History* 21 (Winter 1999): 559–592; Kathryn Oberdeck, "Popular Narratives and Working-Class Identity: Alexander Irvine's Early Twentieth Century Literary Adventures," in Eric Arnesen, Julie Greene, and Bruce Laurie, eds., *Labor Histories: Class, Politics, and Working-Class Experience* (Urbana: University of Illinois Press, 1998), 201–229; Mark Pittenger, "A World of Difference: Constructing the 'Underclass' in Progressive Era American," *American Quarterly* 49 (March 1997): 26–65.

13. Stansell, *American Moderns*, 24–25; Hapgood, *Victorian*, 141–143; Rischin, "Introduction."

14. On the production of *The Autobiography of a Thief*, see Hapgood, *Victorian*, 166–172. The evidence that Hapgood shared his royalties is suggested in a series of correspondence with lower-class collaborators. See, for example, Anton Johannsen to Hutchins Hapgood, Corte Madera, California, April 13, 1914, Hapgood Family Papers, Beinecke Library, Yale University, Box 4, Folder 117; Hutchins Hapgood to Terry Carlin, New York, March 31, 1914, Ibid., Box 2, Folder 40.

15. Reginia Gagnier, "Social Atoms: Working-Class Autobiography, Subjectivity, and Gender," *Victorian Studies* 30 (Spring 1987), 335–364. This phenomenon is remarkably similar across autobiographies from numerous societies, whatever their other differences. On British workers' autobiographies, see John Burnett, David Vincent, and David Mayall, eds., *The Autobiography of the Working Class: An Annotated Ciritcal Bibliography*, vol. 1 (New York, 1984), xvii–xxix; on French and German, Mary Jo Maynes, *Taking the Hard Road: Life Course in French and German Workers' Autobiographies in the Era of Industrialization* (Chapel Hill: University of North Carolina Press, 1995), 33; and on Russian, Diane Koenker, "Scripting the Revolutionary Worker Autobiography: Archetypes, Models, Inventions, and Markets," *International Review of Social History* 49 (2004): 371–400. On the problem of personality or lack of it in the autobiographies of working-class radicals in the United States, see chapters 2 and 3 of this volume..

16. Hapgood, *Victorian*, 189.

17. Hutchins Hapgood to Neith Boyce Hapgood, Chicago, October 9, 1905 (quote); Hutchins Hapgood to Neith Boyce Hapgood, Chicago, October 7, 1905, Hapgood Family Papers, Box 12, Folder 363, Yale Collection of American Literature, Beinecke Rare Book and Manuscript Library, Yale University.

18. Hutchins Hapgood, *An Anarchist Woman* (New York: Duffield and Co., 1909).

19. On the tensions between women labor activists and middle-class women reformers in New York, Chicago, and Boston, see Nancy Schrom Dye, *As Equals and as Sisters: Feminism, the Labor Movement, and the Women's Trade Union League of New York* (Columbia: University of Missouri Press, 1980), 45–47, 52–56, 120; Elizabeth Anne Payne, *Reform, Labor, and Feminism: Margaret Dreier Robbins and the Women's Trade Union League* (Urbana: University of Illinois Press, 1988), 48, 60–64; Sarah Deutsch, *Women and the City: Gender, Space, and Power in Boston, 1870–1940* (New York: Oxford University Press, 2000), 248.

20. *Federation News*, July 2, 1938, 8; November 16, 1935, 12. My thanks to Suellen Hoy for these references.

21. Marcaccio, *The Hapgoods*, 146.

22. Hapgood, *Victorian*, 186.

23. *Chicago Record Herald*, March 26, 1903, 2; December 27, 1903, 6; *The Economist*, September 5, 1903, 299, clippings in Bessie Louise Pierce Papers, Box 86A, Chicago Historical Society; Dorothy Richardson, "Trade Unions in Petticoats," *Lelsie's Monthly Magazine*, 1904, 489–500; Steven Sapolsky, "Class Conscious Belligerents: The Teamsters and the Class Struggle in Chicago, 1901–1905," unpublished seminar paper, University of Pittsburgh, 1974, 1–2; David Montgomery, *Workers' Control in America: Studies in Work, Technology, and Labor Struggles* (New York: Cambridge University Press, 1979), 57–58; *Arbeiterzeitung*, April 3, 1903, quoted in Georg Leidenberger, "'The Public Is the Labor Union': Working Class Progressivism in Turn of the Century Chicago," *Labor History* 36 (Spring 1995): 194.

24. Philip S. Foner, *History of the Labor Movement in the United States*, vol. 3: *The Policies and Practices of the American Federation of Labor, 1900–1909* (New York: International Publishers, 1973), 27.

25. John R. Commons, "The Teamsters of Chicago," in John R. Commons, ed., *Trade Unionism and Labor Problems* (Boston: Ginn and Company, 1905) 36–64; Sapolsky, "Class Conscious Belligerents"; Leidenberger, "'The Public Is the Labor Union,'" 198–199; David Witwer, *Corruption and Reform in the Teamsters Union* (Urbana: University of Illinois Press, 2003), 22–28. See also Ernest Poole, "How a Labor Machine Held Up Chicago, and How the Teamsters' Union Smashed the Machine," *The World's Work* (July 1904): 896–905.

26. Poole, "How a Labor Machine Held Up Chicago," 896.

27. William English Walling, "Can Labor Unions Be Destroyed?" *The World's Work* (December 1905): 6955.

28. *Chicago Tribune* July 31, 1904, clipping in Pierce Papers, Box 86A. On the national trends, see Foner, *Policies and Practices of the American Federation of Labor*, 32–60, especially 59–60. On the Chicago Employers' Association and its offensive against the unions, see Isaac Marcosson, "Labor Met by Its Own Methods," *The World's Work* 7 (January 1904): 4313; and Isaac Marcosson, "The Fight for the Open Shop," *The World's Work* (December 1905): 6955.

29. Graham Taylor, *Chicago Commons through Forty Years* (Chicago: Chicago Commons Association, 1936), 118.

30. Jane Addams, *Twenty Years at Hull House, with Autobiographical Notes*, with an introduction and notes by James Hurt (Urbana: University of Illinois Press, 1990), 109, quote, 131.

31. Hapgood, *Spirit of Labor*, 109.

32. Addams, *Twenty Years at Hull House*, 131.

33. Hapgood, *Spirit of Labor*, 115–118, quotes, 117, 118.

34. Hutchins Hapgood to Neith Boyce Hapgood, Chicago, October 9, 1905, Hapgood Family Papers, Beinecke Library, Yale University, Box 5, Folder 363.

35. Hapgood, *Spirit of Labor*, 213.

36. Hutchins Hapgood, "Seen from the Outside: An Aspect of Hull House," *Chicago Evening Post*, March 17, 1905, clipping, Hapgood Family Papers, Beinecke Library, Yale University, Box 27, Folder 792.

37. Stansell, *American Moderns*, 85–86; Roger A. Bruns, *The Damnedest Radical: The Life and World of Ben Reitman, Chicago's Celebrated Social Reformer, Hobo King, and Whorehouse Physician* (Urbana: University of Illinois Press, 1987); Dill Pickle Papers, Newberry Library, Chicago; Franklin Rosemont, ed. and intro., *The Rise and Fall of the Dill Pickle: Jazz-Age Chicago's Wildest and Most Outrageously Creative Hobohemian Nightspot* (Chicago: Charles H. Kerr, 2004); and Slim Brundage, *From Bughouse Square to the Beat Generation: Selected Ravings*, edited and introduced by Franklin Rosemont (Chicago: Charles H. Kerr, 1997) evoke the fit between working-class radicalism and Chicago bohemia from the early twentieth century through the post–World War II era. See also Alison Jesse Smith, *Chicago's Left Bank* (Chicago: H. Regnery Company, 1953); Albert Parry, *Garrets and Pretenders: A History of Bohemianism in America* (New York: Covici, Friede, 1933), 175–211; and Dale Kramer, *Chicago Renaissance: The Literary Life in the Midwest, 1900–1930* (New York: Appleton-Century, 1966), which all emphasize the bohemian literary angle.

38. Hutchins Hapgood to Neith Boyce, Chicago, May 27, 1905, Hapgood Family Papers, Box 12, Folder 361; September, 1905, Ibid., Folder 364; n.d., 1905, Ibid., Folder 365; Hutchins Hapgood to Robert Herrick, May 22, 1905, Ibid., Box 4, Folder 104.

39. David J. Hogan, *Class and Reform: School and Society in Chicago, 1880–1930* (Philadelphia: University of Pennsylvania Press, 1985), 3; John Allswang, *A House for All Peoples* (Lexington: University of Kentucky Press, 1971), 17–22; Allen Spear, *Black Chicago: The Making of a Negro Ghetto, 1890–1920* (Chicago: University of Chicago Press, 1967), 129–166; William M. Tuttle, *Race Riot: Chicago in the Red Summer of 1919* (New York: Atheneum, 1970), 74–107; James R. Grossman, *Land of Hope: Chicago, Black Southerners, and the Great Migration* (Chicago: University of Chicago Press, 1989). For the increasing proportion of African Americans in laboring and manufacturing jobs in Chicago between 1900 and 1920, compare the tables in Spear, *Black Chicago*, 30–33, 152–154.

40. W. E. B. DuBois, *Souls of Black Folk* (Chicago: A. C. McClurg and Company, 1903).

41. Hutchins Hapgood to Neith Boyce Hapgood, Chicago, December 6, 1905, Ibid., Box 12, Folder 365.

42. Neith Boyce Hapgood to Robert Morss Lovett, New York City, January 18, 1906, Ibid., Box 5, Folder 144.

43. Marcaccio, *The Hapgoods*.

44. Hapgood quotes in Hapgood, *Victorian*, 207, 581.

45. Marcaccio, *The Hapgoods*, 160–164. There is even some question as to whether the play *Enemies* was written entirely by Neith Boyce. See Mary Kay Trimberger, ed., *Intimate Warriors: Portraits of a Modern Marriage, 1899–1944* (New York: Feminist Press, 1991), 5, 6, 180.

46. Hapgood, *Victorian*, 432–447, quote, 434; Marcaccio, *The Hapgoods*, 194–204.

47. Philip S. Foner, *History of the Labor Movement in the United States*, vol. 5: *The AFL in the Progressive Era* (New York: International Publishers, 1980), 7–31; Michael Kazin, *Barons of Labor: The San Francisco Building Trades and Union Power in the Progressive Era* (Urbana: University of Illinois Press, 1987), 205–208; Clarence Darrow, *The Story of My Life* (New York: Scribner, 1932), 172–184; Anton Johannsen [AJ] to Hutchins Hapgood [HH], October 24, 1911, St. Louis, Hapgood Family Papers, Box 4, Folder 117; AJ to HH, Dec. 25, [1912?], Corte Madera, CA, Hapgood Family Papers, Box 4, Folder 117.

48. Hapgood, *Victorian*, 289.

49. Solon De Leon, ed., *The American Labor Who's Who* (New York: International Publishers, 1925), 116; Kazin, *Barons of Labor*, 299; AJ to HH, Chicago, September 28, 1935, Hapgood Family Papers, Box 4, Folder 117.

50. *Chicago Tribune*, June 3, 1946.

51. William J. Adelman, *Haymarket Revisited: A Tour Guide of Labor Sites and Ethnic Neighborhoods Connected with the Haymarket Affair* (Chicago: Illinois Labor History Society, 1976).

CHAPTER 6. Americanization from the Bottom Up

I wish to thank Jenny Barrett, Carol Leff, Vernon Burton, David Brody, Dirk Hoerder, Marianne Debouzy, Catherine Collomp, Bruno Ramirez, James Grossman, Robert Wiebe, David Thelen, and Fred Hoxie for their comments. I am particularly grateful to the late Mark Leff for his suggestions and encouragement. I also wish to acknowledge the Newberry Library for its support in the form of a Lloyd Lewis Fellowship and to thank Youn-jin Kim and Toby Higbie for their research assistance. This essay originally appeared in the *Journal of American History* 79 (December 1992): 996–1020.

1. Clinton C. Dewitt, "Industrial Teachers," in U. S. Bureau of Education, *Proceedings, Americanization Conference, 1919* (Washington, DC: U.S. Government Printing Office, 1919), 119. See also Howard Hill, "The Americanization Movement," *American Journal of Sociology* 24 (May 1919): 633–634; Stephen Meyer, "Adapting the Immigrant to the Line: Americanization in the Ford Factory, 1914–1921," *Journal of Social History* 14 (1980): 67–82. On the symbol of the melting pot, see Werner Sollors, *Beyond Ethnicity: Consent and Descent in American Culture* (New York: Oxford University Press, 1986), 76–101.

2. John Higham, *Strangers in the Land: Patterns of American Nativism, 1859–1925* (New York: Atheneum, 1971), 234–263; John F. McClymer, "The Americanization Movement and the Education of the Foreign-Born Adult, 1914–1925," in Bernard J. Weiss, ed., *American Education and the European Immigrant, 1840–1940* (Urbana: University of Illinois Press, 1982), 96–116; John F. McClymer, *War and Welfare: Social Engineering in America, 1890–1925* (Westport, CT: Greenwood Press, 1980), 105–152; Rivka Shpak Lissak, *Pluralism and Progressives: Hull House and the New Immigrants, 1890–1919* (Chicago: University of Chicago Press, 1989), 3–4, 74–81; Ruth Hutchinson Crocker, *Social Work and Social Order: The Settlement Movement in Two Industrial Cities, 1889–1930* (Urbana: University of Illinois Press, 1992), 213–214; Edward G. Hartmann, *The Movement to Americanize the Immigrant* (New York: Columbia University Press, 1948).

3. Kathy Peiss, *Cheap Amusements: Working Women and Leisure in Turn-of-the-Century New York* (Philadelphia: Temple University Press, 1986), 11–33; Susan Glenn, *Daughters of the Shtetl: Life and Labor in the Immigrant Generation* (Ithaca, NY: Cornell University Press, 1990), 159–160; David Nasaw, *Children of the City: At Work and Play* (Garden City, NJ: Anchor Doubleday, 1985), 68–73; Roy Rosenzweig, *Eight Hours for What We Will: Workers and Leisure in an Industrial City, 1870–1920* (Cambridge: Cambridge University Press, 1983), 148–150.

4. Karl Mannheim, "The Problem of Generations," in *Essays on the Sociology of Knowledge*, (New York: Oxford University Press, 1952), 276–322; Alan Spitzer, "The Historical Problem of Generations," *American Historical Review* 78 (December 1973): 1353–1385; David Montgomery, *Workers' Control in America: Studies in Work, Technology, and Labor Struggles* (New York: Cambridge University Press, 1979), 9–10; John Bodnar, *The Transplanted: A History of Immigrants in Urban America* (Bloomington: Indiana University Press, 1985), 85–93.

5. E. J. Hobsbawm, *Labouring Men: Studies in the History of Labour* (London: Weidenfeld and Nicolson, 1968), 344–345.

6. Ewa Morawska, *For Bread with Butter: The Lifeworlds of East Central Europeans in Johnstown, Pennsylvania, 1890–1940* (New York: Cambridge University Press, 1985), 22–62; Caroline Golab, *Immigrant Destinations* (Philadelphia: Temple University Press, 1977), 75–100; Victor Greene, *The Slavic Community on Strike: Immigrant Labor in Pennsylvania Anthracite* (South Bend, IN: Notre Dame University Press, 1968), 13–32; Glenn, *Daughters of the Shtetl*, 1–7; Peter Gottlieb, *Making Their Own Way: Southern Blacks' Migration to Pittsburgh, 1916–1930* (Urbana: University of Illinois Press, 1987), 1–62; John Bodnar, Roger Simon, and Michael P. Weber, *Lives of Their Own: Blacks, Italians, and Poles in Pittsburgh, 1900–1960* (Urbana: University of Illinois Press, 1982), 29–54; James R. Grossman, *Land of Hope: Chicago, Black Southerners, and Migration, 1916–1930* (Chicago: University of Chicago Press, 1989). Bodnar, *The Transplanted*, emphasizes the transformation of immigrant culture and everyday life over cultural continuity.

7. Linda Schneider, "The Citizen Striker: Workers' Ideology in the Homestead Strike of 1892," *Labor History* 23 (Winter 1982): 47–66; Linda Schneider, "Republicanism Reinterpreted: American Ironworkers, 1860–1892," in Marianne Debouzy, ed., *A l'ombre de la Statue de la Liberté: Immigrants et Ouvriers dans la Republique Americaine, 1880–1920* (Saint-Denis: Presses Universitaires de Vincennes, 1988), 211; Rosenzweig, *Eight Hours for What We Will*, 65–90; Richard J. Oestreicher, *Solidarity and Fragmentation: Working People and Class Consciousness in Detroit, 1875–1900* (Urbana: University of Illinois Press, 1986), 30–67, 172–214; David Emmons, *The Butte Irish: Class and Ethnicity in an American Mining Town, 1875–1925* (Urbana: University of Illinois Press, 1989); James R. Barrett, *Work and Community in the Jungle: Chicago's Packinghouse Workers, 1894–1922* (Urbana: University of Illinois Press, 1987), 38–44, 119–131.

8. Leon Fink, *Workingmen's Democracy: The Knights of Labor and American Politics* (Urbana: University of Illinois Press, 1983); Eric Foner, "Class, Ethnicity, and Radicalism in the Gilded Age: The Land League and Irish-America," *Marxist Perspectives* 1 (Summer 1978): 6–55; Richard Schneirov, "Political Cultures and the Role of the State in Labor's Republic: The View from Chicago, 1848–1877," *Labor History* 32 (Summer 1991): 376–400; David Brundage, "Irish Land and American Workers: Class and Ethnicity in Denver, Colorado," in Dirk Hoerder, ed., *"Struggle a Hard Battle": Essays on Working-Class Immigrants* (DeKalb: Northern Illinois University Press, 1986), 46–67; David Montgomery, "Labor and the Republic in Industrial America: 1860–1920," *Le Mouvement Sociale* 110 (1980): 211–215.

9. Nick Salvatore, "Some Thoughts on Class and Citizenship," in Debouzy, ed., *A l'ombre de la Statue de la Liberté*, 215–230; Catherine Collomp, "Les organizations ouvrieres et la restriction de l'immigration aux Etats-Unis a la fin du dix-neuvieme siecle," in Debouzy, ed., *A l'ombre de la Statue de la Liberté*, 231–246; Catherine Collomp, "Unions, Civics, and National Identity: Organized Reaction to Immigration, 1881–1897," *Labor History* 29 (Fall 1988): 471–474; A. T. Lane, "American Unions, Mass Immigration, and the Literacy Test: 1900–1917," *Labor History* 25 (Winter 1984): 5–25.

10. David Roediger, *The Wages of Whiteness: Race and the Making of the American Working Class* (London: Verso, 1991), 71–112, 179–180; Gwendolyn Mink, *Old Labor and New Immigrants in American Political Development: Union, Party, and State, 1875–1920* (Ithaca, NY: Cornell University Press, 1986), 228–235; Collomp, "Unions, Civics, and

National Identity," 463–464; Alexander Saxton, *The Indispensable Enemy: Labor and the Anti-Chinese Movement in California* (Berkeley: University of California Press, 1971); Lawrence Glickman, "Inventing the 'American Standard of Living': Gender, Race and Working-Class Identity, 1880–1925," *Labor History* 34 (1993): 221–235.

11. Roediger, *Wages of Whiteness*, 133–163; Kerby A. Miller, "Green over Black: The Origins of Irish-American Racism," paper, 1969 (in author's possession). My thanks to Professor Miller for allowing me to cite this fine work.

12. Montgomery, *Workers' Control in America*; Robert Asher, "Union Nativism and the Immigrant Response," *Labor History* 23 (1982): 325–348.

13. Herbert Gutman, *Work, Culture, and Society in Industrializing America: Essays in Working-Class and Social History* (New York: Vintage, 1976), 7–9, 22–25; Hartmann, *Movement to Americanize the Immigrant*, 165–173.

14. W. M. Roberts, "Promotion of Education in Industry," in U.S. Bureau of Education, *Proceedings, Americanization Conference*, 145; Meyer, "Adapting the Immigrant to the Line," 67–82; and Stephen Meyer, *The Five Dollar Day: Social Control in the Ford Motor Company, 1908–1921* (Albany: State University of New York Press, 1981), 123–164, especially 151, 156. For other company programs, see David Brody, *Steelworkers in America: The Nonunion Era* (New York: Harper Torchbooks, 1969), 190–197; Gerd Korman, "Americanization at the Factory Gate," *Labor and Industrial Relations Review* 18 (1965): 396–419; Lizebeth Cohen, *Making a New Deal: Industrial Workers in Chicago, 1919–1939* (New York: Cambridge University Press, 1990), 163, 165; for a more general discussion, Stuart Brandes, *American Welfare Capitalism, 1880–1940* (Chicago: University of Chicago Press, 1976), 58–60, 78–79, 116–117; Daniel Nelson, *Managers and Workers: Origins of the New Factory System in the United States, 1880–1920* (Madison: University of Wisconsin Press, 1975), 144–145.

15. Meyer, *Five Dollar Day*, 56; Nelson, *Managers and Workers*, 81; "Family Records" [1919], 23, Box 120, Mary Heaton Vorse Papers (Archives of Labor History and Urban Affairs, Wayne State University, Detroit); Andrea Grazziosi, "Common Laborers, Unskilled Workers, 1890–1915," *Labor History* 22 (Fall 1981): 512–544; Richard Edwards, *Contested Terrain: The Transformation of the Workplace in the Twentieth Century* (New York: Basic Books, 1979), 30–34, 63–65; David Montgomery, *The Fall of the House of Labor: The Workplace, the State, and American Labor Activism* (Cambridge: Cambridge University Press, 1987), 92–93; Cohen, *Making a New Deal*, 167–168; Brody, *Steelworkers in America*, 28; Gerd Korman, *Industrialization, Immigrants, and Americanizers: The View from Milwaukee, 1866–1921* (Madison: University of Wisconsin Press, 1967), 62–63.

16. Montgomery, *Workers' Control in America*, 43; Montgomery, *Fall of the House of Labor*, 89–91; Glenn, *Daughters of the Shtetl*, 154–160.

17. Gutman, *Work, Culture, and Society*, 3–76; Donna Gabaccia, *Militants and Migrants: Rural Sicilians Become American Workers* (New Brunswick, NJ: Rutgers University Press, 1988); Bruno Cartosio, "Sicilians in Two Worlds," in Debouzy, ed., *A l'ombre de la Statue de la Liberté*, 127–138; Gary Mormino and George Pozzetta, *The Immigrant World of Ybor City: Italians and Their Latin Neighbors in Tampa* (Urbana: University of Illinois Press, 1987); Irving Howe, *World of Our Fathers: The Journey of the East European Jews to America and the Life They Made* (New York: Harcourt, Brace, and Jovanovich,

1976), 287–304; Moses Rischin, *The Promised City: New York's Jews, 1870–1914* (New York: Harper, 1970), 162–168; Michael G. Karni, "Finnish Immigrant Leftists in America: The Golden Years, 1900–1918," in Hoerder, ed., *"Struggle a Hard Battle,"* 199–266; "Interview with Leo Laukki, Chicago, July 10, 1919," Folder 15, Box 21, David J. Saposs Papers (State Historical Society of Wisconsin, Madison); Mary Cygan, "Political and Cultural Leadership in an Immigrant Community: Polish-American Socialism, 1880–1950," PhD dissertation, Northwestern University, 1989; Joseph Stipanovich, "Immigrant Workers and Immigrant Intellectuals in Progressive America: A History of the Yugoslavian Socialist Federation, 1900–1918," PhD dissertation, University of Minnesota, 1977.

18. "Interview with John S. Wasko, Homestead," Folder 8, Box 26, Saposs Papers.

19. Steve Nelson, James R. Barrett, and Rob Ruck, *Steve Nelson, American Radical* (Pittsburgh: University of Pittsburgh Press, 1981), 16.

20. Rudolph J. Vecoli, "'Free Country': The American Republic Viewed by the Italian Left, 1880–1920," in Debouzy, ed., *A l'ombre de la Statue de la Liberté*, 75–76; Miller, "Green over Black"; Roediger, *Wages of Whiteness*, 133–163; Barrett, *Work and Community in the Jungle*, 202–224; Dominic Pacyga, *Polish Immigrants and Industrial Chicago: Workers on the South Side, 1880–1922* (Columbus: Ohio State University Press, 1991), 212–227; Arnold Hirsch, "Race and Housing: Violence and Communal Protest in Chicago, 1940–1960," in Peter D'A. Jones and Melvin Holli, eds., *The Ethnic Frontier: Essays in the History of Group Survival in Chicago and the Midwest* (Grand Rapids, MI: Eerdmans, 1977), 350–355.

21. Julianna Puskas, "Hungarian Immigration and Socialism," in Debouzy, ed., *A l'ombre de la Statue de la Liberté*, 145–150; Mary Cygan, "Political and Cultural Leadership"; Robert Park, *The Immigrant Press and Its Control* (New York: Harper and Brothers, 1922), 107–109; Timothy L. Smith, "Introduction," in Ivan Molek, *Slovene Immigrant History, 1900–1950: Autobiographical Sketches* (New York: Dover, 1979), xix–xx; and David Shannon, *The Socialist Party* (Chicago: Quadrangle, 1967), 43–48.

22. On the "Americanization" of the Communist Party in the mid-1920s, see Theodore Draper, *American Communism and Soviet Russia: The Formative Period* (New York: Vanguard, 1960), 272–275; Irving Howe and Lewis Coser, *The American Communist Party: A Critical History, 1919-1957* (Boston: Beacon Press, 1957). On the Americanism of the Popular Front, see Fraser Ottanelli, *The Communist Party of the United States: From the Depression to World War II* (New Brunswick, NJ: Rutgers University Press, 1991), 83–105; Harvey Klehr, *The Heyday of American Communism: The Depression Decade* (New York: Basic Books, 1984), 167–206; Maurice Isserman, "The 1956 Generation: An Alternative Approach to the History of American Communism," *Radical America* 14 (March–April 1980): 43–51; George Watt, interview by Maurice Isserman, January 7, 1978, in Isserman's possession, quoted in Maurice Isserman, *Which Side Were You On? The American Communist Party during the Second World War* (Middletown, CT: Wesleyan University Press, 1982), 9–14.

23. John Hutchinson to Editor, *United Mine Workers Journal*, June 15, 1921, 21; David Allan Corbin, *Life, Work, and Rebellion in the Coal Fields: The Southern West Virginia*

Miners, 1880–1922 (Urbana: University of Illinois Press, 1981), 242; "Interview with Mike Connolly, Pittsburgh" [1919], Folder 9, Box 26, Saposs Papers.

24. Glickman, "Inventing the 'American Standard of Living'"; Peter Shergold, *Working-Class Life: The American Standard in Comparative Perspective, 1899–1913* (Pittsburgh: University of Pittsburgh Press, 1982); Barrett, *Work and Community in the Jungle*, 142–146; Mary McDowell, "The Struggle for an American Standard of Living," in Caroline Hill, ed., *Mary McDowell and Municipal Housekeeping* (Chicago: Millar Publishing, 1938), 62–66, especially 66.

25. Howard Wilson, *Mary McDowell, Neighbor* (Chicago: University of Chicago Press, 1928), 100; Alice Henry, *The Trade Union Woman* (New York: D. Appleton, 1915), 56; Alan Dawley, *Struggles for Justice: Social Responsibility and the Liberal State* (Cambridge, MA: Harvard University Press, 1991), 257–260.

26. For Ethelbert Stewart's 1905 statement, see Barrett, *Work and Community in the Jungle*, 139; Winthrop Talbot, ed., *Americanization* (New York: H. W. Wilson, 1917), 307, 305, 177–178; Peter Roberts, *The New Immigration: A Study of the Industrial and Social Life of Southeastern Europeans in America* (New York: Macmillan, 1912), 195.

27. Wilson, *Mary McDowell*, 99; William M. Leiserson, *Adjusting Immigrant and Industry* (New York: Harper, 1924), 234–245; Neil Betten, "Polish-American Steelworkers: Americanization through Industry and Labor," *Polish American Studies* 33 (Autumn 1976): 31–42; David J. Saposs, "The Problem of Making Permanent Trade Unionists out of the Recently Organized Immigrant Workers," 1919, Folder 5, Box 21, Saposs Papers.

28. Greene, *Slavic Community on Strike*, 157–158; Barrett, *Work and Community in the Jungle*, 195–196; Brody, *Steelworkers in America*, 214–262. The contention that immigrants were easier to organize and more loyal in strikes recurred often in David Saposs's interviews with union officials in the period immediately after World War I. See "Digest of Interviews with Trade Union Officials" [1919], 3–4, Folder 15, Box 21, Saposs Papers; "Interview with Dennis Lane, president, Amalgamated Meat Cutters and Butcher Workmen of North America," Folder 2, Box 26, Saposs Papers; and other interviews in Boxes 21 and 22, Saposs Papers.

29. Higham, *Strangers in the Land*, 239–242; John McClymer, "Gender and 'the American Way of Life': Women in the Americanization Movement," *Journal of American Ethnic History* 10 (Spring 1991): 5–6; U.S. Labor Department, Naturalization Bureau, *Suggestions for Americanization Work among Foreign-Born Women* (Washington, DC: U.S. Government Printing Office, 1921); Harriet P. Dow, "Home Classes for Foreign-Born Women," in U.S. Education Department, *Proceedings, Americanization Conference*, 128–135; George J. Sanchez, "'Go after the Women': Americanization and the Mexican Immigrant Woman, 1915–1929," in Ellen Carol DuBois and Vicki L. Ruiz, eds., *Unequal Sisters: A Multi-Cultural Reader in U.S. Women's History* (New York: Routledge, 1990), 257.

30. Colette Hyman, "Labor Organizing and Female Institution Building: The Chicago Women's Trade Union League," in Ruth Milkman, ed., *Women's Work and Protest: A Century of US Women's Labor History* (New York: Routledge, Kegan Paul, 1985), 35–36; Agnes Aitkin, "Teaching English to Our Foreign Friends, Part II: Among the Italians," *Life and Labor* 1 (October 1911): 309; Violet Pike, "New World Lessons

for Old World Peoples, Lesson VI: Joining the Union," *Life and Labor* 2 (March 1912): 90; Nancy Schrom-Dye, *As Equals and as Sisters: Feminism, the Labor Movement, and the Women's Trade Union League of New York* (Columbia: University of Missouri Press, 1980); Elizabeth A. Payne, *Reform, Labor, and Feminism: Margaret Dreier Robbins and the Women 's Trade Union League* (Urbana: University of Illinois Press, 1988), 85–86; Leiserson, *Adjusting Immigrant and Industry*, 297–331; James R. Barrett, "Women's Work, Family Economy, and Labor Militancy: The Case of Chicago's Packinghouse Workers, 1900–1922," in Robert Asher and Charles Stephenson, eds., *Labor Divided—Race and Ethnicity in United States Labor Struggles, 1835–1960* (Albany: State University of New York Press, 1990), 260–262.

31. See David Montgomery, "Nationalism, American Patriotism, and Class Consciousness among Immigrant Workers in the United States in the Epoch of World War I," in Hoerder, ed., *"Struggle a Hard Battle,"* 327–351.

32. David Brody, *Labor in Crisis: The Steel Strike of 1919* (Philadelphia: Lippincott, 1965), 73; Brody, *Steelworkers in America*, 221, 223; Betten, "Polish-American Steelworkers," 36–38; Montgomery, *Fall of the House of Labor*, 384–385.

33. Fernando Fasce, "Freedom in the Workplace? Immigrants at the Scovill Manufacturing Company, 1915–1921," in Debouzy, ed., *A l'ombre de la Statue de la Liberté*, 107–121, especially 116.

34. Brody, *Steelworkers in America*, 214–230; Frank Serene, "Immigrant Steelworkers in the Monongahela Valley: Their Communities and the Development of a Labor Consciousness," PhD dissertation, University of Pittsburgh, 1979; Emmons, *Butte Irish*, 255–291, 340–397; Barrett, *Work and Community in the Jungle*, 188–239; David J. Goldberg, *A Tale of Three Cities: Labor Organization and Protest in Patterson, Passaic, and Lawrence, 1916–1921* (New Brunswick, NJ: Rutgers University Press, 1989); Montgomery, *Workers' Control in America*, 93–101; David Montgomery, "Immigrants, Industrial Unions, and Social Reconstruction in the United States, 1916–1923," *Labour/Le Travail* 13 (Spring 1984): 104–109.

35. *Report of Proceedings of the Thirty-Ninth Annual Convention of the American Federation of Labor*, Atlantic City, New Jersey, June 9–23, 1919 (Washington, DC: U.S. Government Printing Office, 1919), 135–144; Glenn, *Daughters of the Shtetl*, 4–5, 218–222; J. M. Budish to David J. Saposs, November 16, 1918, Folder 7, Box 1, Saposs Papers; Sam Levin interview by David J. Saposs, December 26, 1918, Folder 15, Box 21, Saposs Papers.

36. James R. Barrett, "Comment: Polish Immigrants and the Mentality of the Unskilled Immigrant Worker, 1900–1922," *Polish American Studies* 46 (Spring 1989): 100–107; Adam Walaszek, "Was the Polish Worker Asleep? Immigrants, Unions, and Workers' Control in America, 1900–1922," *Polish American Studies* 46 (Spring 1989): 74–79; Adam Walaszek, " 'For in America Poles Are Like Cattle': Polish Peasant Immigrants and Work in America, 1890–91," in Debouzy, ed., *A l'ombre de la Statue de la Liberté*, 95–105; Montgomery, "Nationalism, Patriotism, and Class Consciousness."

37. James R. Barrett, "Ethnic and Racial Fragmentation: Toward an Interpretation of a Local Labor Movement," in Joe Trotter, Earl Lewis, and Tera Hunter, eds., *African American Urban Studies: Historical, Contemporary and Comparative Perspectives* (New York: Palgrave, 2004), 287–309; Dawley, *Struggles for Justice*, 235–236.

38. Higham, *Strangers in the Land*, 234–263; Gary Gerstle, *Working-Class Americanism: The Politics of Labor in a Textile City, 1914–1960* (Cambridge: Cambridge University Press, 1989), 43–46; Dawley, *Struggles for Justice*, 257–260; Brody, *Steelworkers in America*, 190–198; *National Provisioner*, September 25, 1920, 18–20, 25–26, 42–43; Barrett, *Work and Community in the Jungle*, 243–263; Meyer, *Five Dollar Day*, 169–189; Goldberg, *Tale of Three Cities*, 148–162; Korman, *Industrialization, Immigrants, and Americanizers*, 148–166; Ronald Edsforth, *Class Conflict and Cultural Consensus: The Making of a Consumer Society in Flint, Michigan* (New Brunswick, NJ: Rutgers University Press, 1987); Montgomery, "Nationalism, Patriotism, and Class Consciousness," 334–335; Montgomery, *Fall of the House of Labor*, 438–439, 454–457.

39. William Preston, Jr., *Aliens and Dissenters: Federal Suppression of Radicals, 1903–1933* (New York: Harper and Row, 1966), 88–117, 208–237; Robert K. Murray, *Red Scare: A Study in National Hysteria* (New York: McGraw-Hill, 1964); Dawley, *Struggles for Justice*, 243–251.

40. *American Labor Year Book, 1923–24* (New York: Labor Research Association, 1924), 143. For comparable rhetoric, see "Labor's Fourteen Points," *Survey*, November 30, 1918, 265; *New Majority*, January 18, 1919, 8–9; Illinois Federation of Labor, *Proceedings of the Convention, 1918* (Springfield, IL, 1919), 134–159.

41. Gerstle, *Working-Class Americanism*; Thomas Gobel, "Becoming American: Ethnic Workers and the Rise of the CIO," *Labor History* 29 (Spring 1988): 173–198. See also the story of Dobie Dobrejcak in Thomas Bell's novel *Out of This Furnace* (Pittsburgh: University of Pittsburgh Press, 1976 [1941]), 259–413.

CHAPTER 7. Inbetween Peoples

This essay originally appeared in the *Journal of American Ethnic History* 16 (1997): 3–44. I thank my coauthor David Roediger, who provided much of the thinking behind the essay. Thanks also go to David Montgomery, Steven Rosswurm, Susan Porter Benson, Randy McBee, Neil Gotanda, Peter Rachleff, Noel Ignatiev, the late Peter Tamony, Louise Edwards, Susan Hirsch, Isaiah McCaffery, Rudolph Vecoli, Hyman Berman, Sal Salerno, Louise O'Brien, Liz Pleck, Mark Leff, Toby Higbie, Micaela di Leonardo, Dana Frank, and the Social History Group at the University of Illinois.

1. The epigraph is from John A. Fitch, *The Steel Workers* (New York: Russell Sage Foundation, 1910), 147. Joe Sauris, interview with Joseph Loguidice, July 25, 1980, Italians in Chicago Project, copy of transcript, Box 6, Immigration History Research Center, University of Minnesota, St. Paul.

2. See, for example, Gerald Rosenblum, *Immigrant Workers: Their Impact on American Labor Radicalism* (New York: Basic Books, 1973); C. T. Husbands, "Editor's Introductory Essay," in Werner Sombart, *Why Is There No Socialism in the United States?* (White Plains, NY: M. E. Sharpe, 1976 [1906]), xxix.

3. Robert Orsi, "The Religious Boundaries of an Inbetween People: Street *Feste* and the Problem of the Dark-Skinned 'Other' in Italian Harlem, 1920–1990," *American Quarterly* 44 (September 1992): 335. Michael Omi and Howard Winant, *Racial Formation in the United States: From the 1960s to the 1980s* (New York: Verso, 1986), 64–65; Gary

Gerstle, "Working Class Racism: Broaden the Focus," *International Labor and Working Class History* 44 (1993): 38–39.

4. Sombart, *No Socialism*, 27–28; Stanford M. Lyman, "Race Relations as Social Process: Sociology's Resistance to a Civil Rights Orientation," in Herbert Hill and James E. Jones, Jr., eds., *Race in America: The Struggle for Equality* (Madison: University of Wisconsin Press, 1993), 374–383; cf. Omi and Winant, *Racial Formation*, 15–17, for useful complications on this score; Thomas F. Gossett, *Race: The History of an Idea in America* (Dallas: Southern Methodist University Press, 1963); Barbara Solomon, *Ancestors and Immigrants* (Cambridge, MA: Harvard University Press, 1956); Gloria A. Marshall, "Racial Classification: Popular and Scientific," in Sandra Harding, ed., *The "Racial" Economy of Science* (Bloomington: Indiana University Press, 1993), 123–124. On Park regarding race and ethnicity, see also Omi and Winant, *Racial Formation*, 15–17; Stow Persons, *Ethnic Studies at Chicago, 1905–1945* (Urbana: University of Illinois Press, 1987), 602.

5. For historical invocations of "ethnicity" to explain situations experienced at the time as racial, in otherwise brilliant works, see Mary C. Waters, *Ethnic Options: Choosing Identities in America* (Berkeley: University of California Press, 1990), 79; Werner Sollors, *Beyond Ethnicity: Consent and Descent in American Culture* (New York: Oxford University Press, 1986), 38–39. See also Michael Banton, *Racial Theories* (Cambridge: Cambridge University Press, 1988); David Theo Goldberg, "The Semantics of Race," *Ethnic and Racial Studies* 15 (October 1992): especially 554–55. The most devastating critique of the "cult of ethnicity" remains Alexander Saxton's review essay on Nathan Glazer's *Affirmative Discrimination* in *Amerasia Journal* 4 (1977): 141–150. See also Gwendolyn Mink, *Old Labor and New Immigrants in American Political Development* (Ithaca, NY: Cornell University Press, 1986), especially 46, n. 1.

6. Peggy Pascoe, "Miscegenation Law, Court Cases, and Ideologies of 'Race' in Twentieth Century America," *Journal of American History* 83 (June 1996): 44–69; Peggy Pascoe, "Race, Gender, and Intercultural Relations: The Case of Interracial Marriage," *Frontiers: A Journal of Women's Studies* 12 (1991): 5–17; Paul Spickard, *Mixed Blood: Intermarriage and Ethnic Identity in Twentieth-Century America* (Madison: University of Wisconsin Press, 1989), appendix A, 374–375. See Paul Siu, *The Chinese Laundryman: A Study of Social Isolation* (New York: New York University Press, 1987), 143, 250–271.

7. We borrow "inbetween" from Orsi, "Religious Boundaries of an Inbetween People," passim, and also from John Higham, *Strangers in the Land: Patterns of American Nativism, 1860–1925* (New York: Atheneum, 1963 [1955]), 169. Herbert Gutman and Ira Berlin, "Class Composition and the Development of the American Working Class, 1840–1890," in Gutman, *Power and Culture: Essays on the American Working Class*, edited by Ira Berlin (New York: Pantheon, 1987), 380–394, initiates vital debate on immigration and the "remaking" of the U.S. working class over time. We occasionally use the phrase "new immigrants," the same one contemporaries sometimes employed to distinguish more recent and "less desirable" from earlier immigrant peoples, but we do so critically. To use the term indiscriminately tends not only to render Asian, Latin, and other non-European immigrants invisible, but also to normalize a racialized language we are trying to explicate.

8. Lawrence Glickman, "Inventing the 'American Standard of Living': Gender, Race and Working-class Identity, 1880–1925," *Labor History* 34 (Spring–Summer, 1993): 221–235; David Montgomery, *Beyond Equality: Labor and the Radical Republicans, 1862–1872* (Urbana: University of Illinois Press, 1981), 254; Richard Williams, *Hierarchical Structures and Social Value: The Creation of Black and Irish Identities in the United States* (New York: Cambridge University Press, 1990); E. P. Thompson, *Customs in Common: Studies in Traditional Popular Culture* (New York: New Press, 1993), 320.

9. On *guinea*'s history, see David Roediger, "*Guineas, Wiggers* and the Dramas of Racialized Culture," *American Literary History* 7 (Winter 1995): 654–668. On post-1890 usages, see William Harlen Gilbert, Jr., "Memorandum Concerning the Characteristics of the Larger Mixed-Blood Islands of the United States," *Social Forces* 24 (March 1946): 442; *Oxford English Dictionary*, 2nd ed. (Oxford: Oxford University Press, 1989), vol. 6, 937–938; Frederic G. Cassidy and Joan Houston Hall, eds., *Dictionary of American Regional English* (Cambridge: Oxford University Press, 1991), 838; Harold Wentworth and Stuart Berg Flexner, *Dictionary of American Slang* (New York: Crowell, 1975), 234; Peter J. Tamony, research notes on *guinea*, Tamony Collection, Western Historical Manuscripts Collection, University of Missouri, Columbia.

10. Tamony's notes on *hunky* (or *hunkie*) speculate on links to *honkie* (or *honky*) and refer to the former as an "old labor term." By no means did *Hun* refer unambiguously to Germans before World War I. See, e.g., Henry White, "Immigration Restriction as a Necessity," *American Federationist* 4 (June 1897): 67; Paul Krause, *The Battle for Homestead, 1880–1892: Politics, Culture and Steel* (Pittsburgh: University of Pittsburgh Press, 1992), 216–217; Stan Kemp, *Boss Tom: The Annals of an Anthracite Mining Village* (Akron, OH: Saalfield, 1904), 258; Thames Williamson, *Hunky* (New York: Coward McCann Inc., 1929), slipcover; Thomas Bell's *Out of This Furnace* (Pittsburgh: University of Pittsburgh Press, 1976 [1941]), 124–125; David Brody, *Steelworkers in America* (New York: Harper Torchbooks, 1969), 120–121; Josef Barton, *Peasants and Strangers* (Cambridge, MA: Harvard University Press, 1975), 20. Theodore Radzialowski, "The Competition for Jobs and Racial Stereotypes: Poles and Blacks in Chicago," *Polish American Studies* 22 (Autumn 1976): n. 7; Upton Sinclair, *Singing Jailbirds: A Drama in Four Acts* (Pasadena, CA: n.p., 1924). Remarks regarding *mill hunky* in the 1970s are based on Barrett's anecdotal observations in and around Pittsburgh at the time. See also the *Mill Hunk Herald*, published in Pittsburgh throughout the late 1970s.

11. John Dollard, *Caste and Class in a Southern Town* (Garden City, NY: Doubleday, 1949), 93; Barry Goldberg, "Historical Reflections on Transnationalism, Race, and the American Immigrant Saga," unpublished paper delivered at the Rethinking Migration, Race, Ethnicity, and Nationalism in Historical Perspective Conferences, New York Academy of the Sciences, May, 1990. Confusion regarding citations has in the past led David Roediger to attribute "not yet white ethnic" to immigration historian John Bukowczyk rather than Goldberg.

12. Albert S. Broussard, "George Albert Flippin and Race Relations in a Western Rural Community," *Midwest Review* 12 (1990): 15, n. 42; J. Alexander Karlin, "The Italo-American Incident of 1891 and the Road to Reunion," *Journal of Southern History* 8 (1942); Gunther Peck, "Padrones and Protest: 'Old' Radicals and 'New' Immigrants in

Bingham, Utah, 1905–1912," *Western Historical Quarterly* (May 1993): 177; Dan Georgakas, *Greek America at Work* (New York: n.p., 1992), 12, 16–47; Andrea Yvette Huginnie, *"Strikitos": Race, Class, and Work in the Arizona Copper Industry, 1870–1920* (New Haven, CT: Yale University Press, 1991); Ruth Shonle Cavan and Katherine Howland Ranck, *The Family and the Depression: A Study of One Hundred Chicago Families* (Chicago: University of Chicago Press, 1938), 38–39; Isaiah McCaffery, "An Esteemed Minority? Greek Americans and Interethnic Relations in the Plains Region," unpublished paper, University of Kansas, 1993; see also Donna Misner Collins, *Ethnic Identification: The Greek Americans of Houston, Texas* (New York: AMS Press, 1991), 201–211. For the African American slang, Clarence Major, ed., *From Juba to Jive: A Dictionary of African-American Slang* (New York: Viking, 1994), 213.

13. Donna Gabaccia, "The 'Yellow Peril' and the 'Chinese of Europe': Global Perspectives on Race and Labor, 1815–1930," in Jan Lucassen and Leo Lucassen, eds., *Migrations, Migration History, History: Old Paradigms and New Perspectives* (Berlin: Peter Lang, 1997).

14. George E. Cunningham, "The Italian: A Hindrance to White Solidarity in Louisiana, 1890–1898," *Journal of Negro History* 50 (January 1965): 34, includes the quotes.

15. Higham, *Strangers in the Land*, 66; Gary R. Mormino and George E. Pozzetta, *The Immigrant World of Ybor City: Italians and Their Latin Neighbors in Tampa, 1885–1985* (Urbana: University of Illinois Press, 1987), 241; Micaela DiLeonardo, *The Varieties of Ethnic Experience* (Ithaca, NY: Cornell University Press, 1984), 24, n. 16; Georgakas, *Greek America at Work*, 16. See also Karen Brodkin Sacks's superb "How Did Jews Become White Folks?" in Steven Gregory and Roger Sanjek, eds., *Race* (New Brunswick, NJ: Rutgers University Press, 1994).

16. Quoted in Brody, *Steelworkers*, 120; W. Lloyd Warner and J. O. Low, *The Social System of the Modern Factory—The Strike: A Social Analysis* (New Haven, CT: Yale University Press, 1947), 140; Gershon Legman, *The Horn Book* (Hyde Park, NY: University Books, 1964 [1953]), 486–487; *Anecdota Americana: Five Hundred Stories for the Amusement of Five Hundred Nations That Comprise America* (New York: Nesor Publishing Co., 1934), 98; Nathan Hurvitz, "Blacks and Jews in American Folklore," *Western Folklore* 33 (October 1974): 304–307; Emory S. Borgardus, "Comparing Racial Distance in Ethiopia, South Africa, and the United States," *Sociology and Social Research* 52 (January 1968): 149–156; F. James Davis, *Who Is Black? One Nation's Definition* (University Park: Pennsylvania State University Press, 1991), 161.

17. Thomas G. Dyer, *Theodore Roosevelt and the Idea of Race* (Baton Rouge: Louisiana State University Press, 1980), 131, 143–144; Miriam King and Steven Ruggles, "American Immigration, Fertility and Race Suicide at the Turn of the Century," *Journal of Interdisciplinary History* 20 (Winter 1990): 347–369. On *stock*, see M. G. Smith's "Ethnicity and Ethnic Groups in America: The View from Harvard," *Ethnic and Racial Studies* 5 (January 1982): 17–18.

18. On race and naturalization law, see D. O. McGovney, "Race Discrimination in Naturalization, Parts I–III," *Iowa Law Bulletin* 8 (March 1923), and "Race Discrimination in Naturalization, Part IV," *Iowa Law Bulletin* 8 (May 1923): 211–244; Charles

Gordon, "The Race Barrier to American Citizenship," *University of Pennsylvania Law Review* 93 (March 1945): 237–258; Stanford Lyman, "The Race Question and Liberalism," *International Journal of Politics, Culture, and Society* 5 (Winter 1991): 203–225. On the racial status of Finns, A. William Hoglund, *Finnish Immigrants in America, 1908–1920* (Madison: University of Wisconsin Press, 1960), 112–114; Peter Kivisto, *Immigrant Socialists in the United States: The Case of Finns and the Left* (Rutherford, NJ: Farleigh Dickinson University Press, 1984). The whiteness of Armenians was also sometimes at issue, even if they lived on "the west side of the Bosphorus." See *In Re Halladjian et al*, C.C.D., Mass., 174 Fed. 834 (1909), and *U.S. v. Cartozian*, 6 Fed. (2nd) (1925), 919.

19. *U.S. v. Bhagat Singh Thind*, 261 U.S. 204; Joan M. Jensen, *Passage from India: Asian Indian Immigrants in North America* (New Haven, CT: Yale University Press, 1988), 246–269. On the nonwhite status of Asians, see Jensen, *Passage from India*; *In Re Ah Yup*, 1 Fed. Cas. 223 (1878); *In Re Saito*, C.C.D. Mass., 62 Fed. 126 (1894); *Ozawa v. U.S.*, 260 U. S. 178 (1922). Williams, *Hierarchical Structures*; David Montejano, *Anglos and Mexicans in the Making of Texas, 1836–1986* (Austin: University of Texas Press 1987); Sharon M. Lee, "Racial Classifications in the U.S. Census, 1890–1990," *Ethnic and Racial Studies* 16 (January 1993): 79; Tomas Almaguer, *Racial Faultlines: The Historical Origins of White Supremacy in California* (Berkeley: University of California Press, 1994), 55–57; George Sanchez, *Becoming Mexican American: Ethnicity, Culture and Identity in Chicano Los Angeles, 1900–1945* (New York: Oxford University Press, 1993), 29–30.

20. Oscar Handlin, *Race and Nationality in American Life* (Boston: Beacon Press, 1957), 205; Cunningham, "Hindrance to White Solidarity," 33–35; and especially Jean Scarpaci, "A Tale of Selective Accommodation: Sicilians and Native Whites in Louisiana," *Journal of Ethnic Studies* 3 (1977): 44–45, noting the use of "dago clause" to describe the provision. For the Irish, see David R. Roediger, *The Wages of Whiteness: Race and the Making of the American Working Class* (London: Verso, 1991), 140–143; Steven P. Erie, *Rainbow's End: Irish-Americans and the Dilemmas of Urban Machine Politics, 1840–1985* (Berkeley: University of California, 1988) 25–66 and 96, table 10.

21. Reginald Horsman, *Race and Manifest Destiny: The Origins of American Racial Anglo-Saxonism* (Cambridge, MA: Harvard University Press, 1981), 250–253; Dyer, *Idea of Race*, 131; Mink, *Old Labor and New Immigrants*, 224–227.

22. Dyer, *Idea of Race*, 29–30 and 10–44, passim. Stephen Thernstrom, Ann Orlov, and Oscar Handlin, eds., *Harvard Encyclopedia of Ethnic Groups* (Cambridge, MA: Harvard University Press, 1980), 379; quotes, Dyer, *Idea of Race*, 55, 66, 132.

23. Dyer, *Idea of Race*, 132, and for Roosevelt's revealing exchanges with Madison Grant, 17.

24. Higham, *Strangers in the Land*, 238–262.

25. Quoted in Mink, *Old Labor Immigrants*, 71–112, 109–110; Grant quote, Higham, *Strangers In the Land*, 156–157. In his *The Old World and the New* (New York: Century, 1914), the reformer and sociologist E. A. Ross maintained that "ethical endowment" was innate, and that Southern Europeans lacked it.

26. Jane Addams, *Twenty Years at Hull House* (New York: Macmillan, 1910); Mink, *Old Labor and New Immigrants*, 223 and 226 for the quotes.

27. James Weinstein, *The Corporate Ideal in the Liberal State, 1900–1918* (Boston: Beacon Press, 1968).

28. Stephen Meyer III, *The Five Dollar Day: Labor Management and Social Control in the Ford Motor Company, 1908–1921* (Albany: State University of New York Press, 1981), 176–185; Higham, *Strangers in the Land*, 138, 261–262, 316–317.

29. Cf. Dyer, *Idea of Race*, 42–44, 63, 130–131; Higham, *Strangers in the Land*, 317; John F. McClymer, "The Americanization Movement and the Education of the Foreign-Born Adult, 1914–1925," in Bernard J. Weiss, ed., *American Education and the European Immigrant, 1840–1940* (Urbana: University of Illinois Press, 1982), 96–116; Herbert Gutman, *Work, Culture and Society in Industrializing America: Essays in Working-Class and Social History* (New York: Vintage, 1976), 7–8, 22–25. On the curricula in factory-based Americanization programs, see Gerd Korman, "Americanization at the Factory Gate," *Labor and Industrial Relations Review*, 18 (1965): 396–419.

30. Higham, *Strangers in the Land*, 263.

31. Quotes from Higham, *Strangers in the Land*, 273, 321. See also 300–330 passim. On the triumph of terror and exclusion and the consequent turn by leading liberal intellectuals to a defeatism regarding "race and ethnicity," see Gary Gerstle, "The Protean Character of American Liberalism," *American Historical Review* 99 (October 1994): 1055–1067.

32. Richard Slotkin, *Gunfighter Nation: The Myth of the Frontier in Twentieth-Century America* (New York: Atheneum, 1992); Michael Rogin, " 'The Sword Became a Flashing Vision': D. W. Griffith's 'The Birth of a Nation,' " in *Ronald Reagan, the Movie: And Other Essays in Political Demonology* (Berkeley: University of California Press, 1987), 190–235. "Incontestably mulatto" comes from Albert Murray, *The Omni-Americans: New Perspectives on Black Experience and American Culture* (New York: Outerbridge and Dienstfrey, 1983), 22; Zena Pearlstone, ed., *Seeds of Prejudice: Racial and Ethnic Stereotypes in American Popular Lithography, 1830–1918*, forthcoming. See especially Michael Rogin, "Blackface, White Noise: The Jewish Jazz Singer Finds His Voice," *Critical Inquiry* 18 (Spring 1992): 417–453; Michael Rogin, "Making America Home: Racial Masquerade and Ethnic Assimilation in the Transition to Talking Pictures," *Journal of American History* 79 (December 1992): 1050–1977.

33. Gads Hill Center, "May Report" (1915) and "Minstrel Concert" flyer, Gads Hill Settlement Papers, Chicago Historical Museum. Thanks to Steven Rosswurm for identifying this source. See also Elisabeth Lasch-Quinn, *Black Neighbors: Race and the Limits of Reform in the American Settlement House Movement, 1890–1945* (Chapel Hill: University of North Carolina Press, 1993), especially 14–30, quote 22; Lyman, "Assimilation-Pluralism Debate," 191; Krause, *Battle for Homestead*, p. 218.

34. Kathleen Neils Conzen, David A. Gerber, Ewa Morawska, George E. Pozzetta, and Rudolph J. Vecoli, "The Invention of Ethnicity: A Perspective from the U.S.A.," *Journal of American Ethnic History* 12 (Fall 1992): 27.

35. Stanley Lieberson, *A Piece of the Pie: Black and White Immigrants since 1880* (Berkeley: University of California Press, 1980), 301–359; John Bodnar, Roger Simon, and Michael Weber, *Lives of Their Own: Blacks, Italians and Poles in Pittsburgh, 1900–1960* (Urbana: University of Illinois Press, 1982), 141–149; Suzanne Model, "The Effects of

Ethnicity in the Workplace on Blacks, Italians, and Jews in 1910 New York," *Journal of Urban History* 16 (November 1989): 33–39.

36. Model, "The Effects of Ethnicity in the Workplace"; See also Sterling D. Spero and Abram L. Harris, *The Black Worker* (New York: Atheneum, 1969 [1931]), 149–181, 221; David Ward, *Poverty, Ethnicity and the American City, 1840–1925* (Cambridge: Cambridge University Press, 1989), 211.

37. Harold M. Baron, *The Demand for Black Labor: Historical Notes on the Political Economy of Racism* (Cambridge, MA: Radical America, 1971), 21–23; Spero and Harris, *Black Worker*, 174–177; Edward Greer, "Racism and U.S. Steel," *Radical America* 10 (September–October 1976): 45–68; Paul F. McGouldrick and Michael Tannen, "Did American Manufacturers Discriminate against Immigrants before 1914?" *Journal of Economic History* 37 (September 1977): 723–746; Allan Kent Powell, *The Next Time We Strike: Labor in Utah's Coal Fields, 1900–1933* (Logan: Utah State University Press, 1985), 92; John R. Commons, "Introduction to Volumes III and IV," in John R. Commons et al., *History of Labour in the United States*, 4 vols. (New York: Kelley, 1966 [1935]), vol. 3, xxv. Bodnar, Simon, and Weber, *Lives of Their Own*, 5; quote, Montgomery, *Fall*, 243. For the cartoon, see Ernest Riebe, *Mr. Block* (Chicago: Charles H. Kerr, 1984 [1913]), unpaginated. See also David M. Gordon, Richard Edwards, and Michael Reich, *Segmented Work, Divided Workers: The Historical Transformations of Labor in the United States* (Cambridge: Cambridge University Press, 1982), 141–143.

38. Ross, as quoted in Lieberson, *A Piece of the Pie*, 25; Brody, *Steelworkers in America*, 120; Peter Speek, "Report on Psychological Aspect of the Problem of Floating Laborers," U.S. Commission on Industrial Relations Papers (June 25, 1915), 31. Thanks to Toby Higbie for the citation. Huginnie, *"Strikitos"*; Georgakas, *Greek America at Work*, 17; John Bukowczyk, "The Transformation of Working-Class Ethnicity: Corporate Control, Americanization, and the Polish Immigrant Middle Class in Bayonne, New Jersey, 1915–1925," in Robert Asher and Charles Stephenson, eds., *Labor Divided: Race and Ethnicity in United States Labor Struggles, 1835–1960* (Albany: State University of New York Press, 1990), 291; Higham, *Strangers in the Land*, 173. See also Alexander Saxton, *The Indispensable Enemy: Labor and the Anti-Chinese Movement in California* (Berkeley: University of California Press, 1971), 281; Richard W. Steele, "No Racials: Discrimination against Ethnics in American Defense Industry, 1940–42," *Labor History* 32 (Winter 1991): 66–90.

39. Jean Scarpaci, "Immigrants in the New South: Italians in Louisiana's Sugar Parishes, 1880–1910," *Labor History* 16 (Spring 1975): 165–183; Lieberson, *Piece of the Pie*, 346–350. The judgment changed briefly in African Americans' favor in the early 1920s. See Peter Gottlieb, *Making Their Own Way: Southern Blacks' Migration to Pittsburgh, 1916–30* (Urbana: University of Illinois Press, 1987), 126, 162; Baron, *Demand for Black Labor*, 22; quotes from Lieberson, *Piece of the Pie*, 348; Thaddeus Radzialowski, "The Competition for Jobs and Racial Stereotypes: Poles and Blacks in Chicago," *Polish American Studies* 33 (Autumn 1976): 16.

40. Lieberson, *Piece of the Pie*, 299–327; John Bodnar, Roger Simon, Michael Weber, "Blacks and Poles in Pittsburgh, 1900–1930," *Journal of American History* 66:3 (1979): 554.

41. Bodnar, Simon, and Weber, *Lives of Their Own*, 141, table 16.

42. Steve Nelson, James R. Barrett, and Rob Ruck, *Steve Nelson, American Radical* (Pittsburgh: University of Pittsburgh Press, 1981), 16.

43. Model, "Effects of Ethnicity," 41–42. Cf. Bodnar, Simon, and Weber, *Lives of Their Own*, 141.

44. Bell, *Out of This Furnace*, 124; Attaway, *Blood on the Forge* (New York: Monthly Review Press, 1941, repr. 1987), 122–123.

45. Roger Horowitz, "'Without a Union, We're All Lost': Ethnicity, Race and Unionism among Kansas City Packinghouse Workers, 1930–1941," unpublished paper given at the Reworking American Labor History conference, State Historical Society of Wisconsin, April 1992, 4. On marriage between Catholics but across "ethnic" lines, see Paul Spickard, *Mixed Blood*, 8, 450, n. 70.

46. Mark Wyman, *Round Trip to America: The Immigrants Return to Europe, 1880–1930* (Ithaca, NY: Cornell University Press, 1993) 10–12; see also Michael J. Piore, *Birds of Passage: Migrant Labor and Industrial Societies* (Ann Arbor: University of Michigan Press, 1978), passim.

47. See Arnold Shankman, "This Menacing Influx: Afro-Americans on Italian Immigration to the South," *Mississippi Quarterly* 31 (Winter 1977–1978), 82, 79–87 passim; Scarpaci, "Immigrants in the New South," 175; Robert Asher, "Union Nativism and Immigrant Response," *Labor History* 23 (Summer 1982): 328; Gabaccia, "'Chinese of Europe'"; Scarpaci, "Sicilians and Native Whites," 14.

48. Scarpaci, "Sicilians and Native Whites." For the quotation, Harold David Brackman, "The Ebb and Flow of Race Relations: A History of Black-Jewish Relations through 1900," PhD dissertation, University of California, Los Angeles, 1977, 450. See Loewen, *Mississippi Chinese*, 58–72; Youn-Jin Kim, "From Immigrants to Ethnics: The Life Worlds of Korean Immigrants in Chicago," PhD dissertation, University of Illinois at Urbana Champaign, 1991.

49. Adam Walaszek, "'For in America Poles Work Like Cattle': Polish Peasant Immigrants and Work in America, 1880–1921," in Marianne Debouzy, ed., *In the Shadow of the Statue of Liberty: Immigrants, Workers and Citizens in the American Republic, 1880–1920* (Urbana: University of Illinois Press, 1992), 86–88, 90–91; Bodnar, Simon, and Weber, *Lives of Their Own*, 5, 60.

50. David R. Roediger, *Towards the Abolition of Whiteness: Essays on Race, Politics, and Working-Class History* (London: Verso, 1994), 163; Tamony Papers, on "hunkie," excerpting "American Tramp and Underworld Slang"; Scarpaci, "Immigrants in the New South," 174; Andrew Neather, "Popular Republicanism, Americanism and the Roots of Anti-Communism, 1890–1925," PhD dissertation, Duke University, 1993, 242; Model, "Effects of Ethnicity," 33; Bodnar, Simon, and Weber, *Lives of Their Own*, 60.

51. Bodnar, Simon, and Weber, *Lives Of of Their Own*, 60; Neather, "Roots of Anti-Communism," 138–223; James Barrett, "Americanization from the Bottom Up: Immigration and the Remaking of the Working Class in the United States, 1880–1930," *Journal of American History* 79 (December 1992): 1009

52. Barrett, "From the Bottom Up," 1002. The classic recognition of this reality is found in Du Bois, *The Philadelphia Negro*, 332–333. See also Higham, *Strangers in the Land*, 305, 321–322.

53. Neather, "Roots of Anti-Communism," 235–240; Mink, *Old Labor and New Immigrants*, 71–112; Messer-Kruse, " 'Chinese Exclusion and the Eight-Hour Day': Ira Steward's 'Political Economy of Cheap Labor,' " unpublished paper, University of Wisconsin, Madison, 1994, 13 and passim. The classic expression of both the biological and cultural racism and much else is Samuel Gompers and Herman Guttstadt, "Meat vs. Rice: American Manhood against Asiatic Coolieism: Which Shall Service?" (San Francisco: American Federation of Labor, 1902). On the distinction between opposition to coolies and to the Chinese "race," see Andrew Gyory, "Rolling in the Dirt: The Origins of the Chinese Exclusion Act and the Politics of Racism, 1870–1882," PhD dissertation, University of Massachusetts at Amherst, 1991, especially chapters 4–6.

54. Gyory, "Rolling"; Glickman, "American Standard," 221–235.

55. Krause, *Battle for Homestead*, 216.

56. Catherine Collomp, "Unions, Civics, and National Identity: Organized Labor's Reaction to Immigration, 1881–1897," in Debouzy, ed., *Shadow of the Statue of Liberty*, 240, 242, 246.

57. Asher, "Union Nativism," quotes, 328; Neather, "Roots of Anti-Communism," 242; White, "Immigration Restriction as a Necessity," 67–69; A. A. Graham, "The Un-Americanization of America," *American Federationist* 17 (April 1910): 302, 303, 304.

58. Gompers, as quoted in Arthur Mann, "Gompers and the Irony of Racism," *Antioch Review* 13 (1953): 212; Mink, *Old Labor and New Immigrants*, 97; and David Brody, *In Labor's Cause: Main Themes on the History of the American Worker* (New York: Oxford University Press, 1993), 117. Cf. Prescott F. Hall, "Immigration and the Education Test," *North American Review* 165 (1897): 395; cf. Lydia Kingsmill Commander, "Evil Effects of Immigration," *American Federationist* 12 (October 1905). See also Neather, "Roots of Anti-Communism," 242, 267.

59. McGovern, quoted in David Montgomery, *The Fall of the House of Labor: The Workplace, the State and American Labor Activism, 1865–1925* (New York: Cambridge University Press, 1987), 25; Asher, "Union Nativism," 339, 338–42. "Internal protectionism" is Mink's term, from *Old Labor and New Immigrants*, 203; Lieberson, *Piece of the Pie*, 341–344. Cf. the explicit Anglo-Saxonism of *Railroad Trainmen's Journal*, discussed in Neather, "Roots of Anti-Communism," 267–268.

60. Lieberson, *Piece of the Pie*, 342–43; Gabaccia, "Chinese of Europe"; Mink, *Old Labor and New Immigrants*, 108. See also A. T. Lane, *Solidarity or Survival: American Labor and European Immigrants, 1830–1924* (Westport, CT: Greenwood Press, 1987). Graham, "The Un-Americanizing of America," 302–304, ran in the same 1910 issue of the *American Federationist* as "Where Yanks Meet Orientals" and "The International Fraternity of Labor." J. A. Edgerton's "Brotherhood of Man," *American Federationist* 12 (April 1905): 213, ran an issue before Augusta H. Pio's "Exclude Japanese Labor." On "race suicide," see Lizzie M. Holmes's review of *The American Idea* in *American Federationist* 14 (December 1907): 998.

61. Asher, "Union Nativism," passim; Mink, *Old Labor and New Immigrants*, 198–203.

62. Philip S. Foner, *History of the Labor Movement in the United States*, 3 vols. (New York: International Publishers, 1964), vol. 3, 256–281; Asher, "Union Nativism," 345, for the quote.

63. Barrett, "From the Bottom Up," 1010 and passim; cf. Brody, *In Labor's Cause*, 128.

64. Asher, "Union Nativism," 330; Covington Hall, "Labor Struggles in the Deep South," unpublished ms., Labadie Collection, University of Michigan, 1951, 122, 138, 147–148, 183; *Voice of the People*, March 5, 1914; Roediger, *Towards the Abolition of Whiteness*, 149, 150, 175, n. 75. See also Peck, "Padrones and Protest," 172.

65. Speek, "Floating Laborers," 31, 34, 36; plasterer quoted in Asher, "Nativism," 330.

66. *New Majority*, November 22, 1919, 11. See John Howard Keiser, "John Fitzpatrick and Progressive Unionism, 1915–1925," PhD dissertation, Northwestern University, 1965, 38–41; William D. Haywood, *Big Bill Haywood's Book* (New York: International Publishers, 1929) 241–242; James R. Barrett, *Work and Community in the Jungle: Chicago's Packinghouse Workers, 1894–1922* (Urbana: University of Illinois Press, 1987), 138–142.

67. Du Bois, as quoted in Thomas Holt, "The Political Uses of Alienation: W. E. B. DuBois on Politics, Race and Culture," *American Quarterly* 42 (June 1990): 313; Peck, "Padrones and Protest," 173.

68. Dominic A. Pacyga, *Polish Immigrants and Industrial Chicago: Workers on the South Side, 1880–1930* (Columbus: Ohio State University Press, 1991), 172; Barrett, *Work and Community in the Jungle*, 172–174. If newly organized Poles read John Roach's "Packingtown Conditions," *American Federationist* 13 (August 1906): 534, they would have seen strikebreaking described as an activity in which "the illiterate southern negro has held high carnival" and have wrongly learned that the stockyards strike was broken simply by black strikebreakers, "ignorant and vicious, whose predominating trait was animalism."

69. Gompers, "Talks on Labor," *American Federationist* 12 (September 1905): 636–637.

70. Quoted in Robert L. Allen and Pamela P. Allen, *Reluctant Reformers: Racism and Social Reform Movements in the United States* (Washington, DC: Howard University Press, 1974), 213; Mark Pittenger, *American Socialists and Evolutionary Thought, 1870–1920* (Madison: University of Wisconsin Press, 1993); Higham, *Strangers in the Land*, 172. London's animus was characteristically directed against both "racial" and "semi-racial" groups, against "Dagoes and Japs." See his *The Valley of the Moon* (New York: Macmillan, 1913), 21–22.

71. Roediger, *Towards the Abolition of Whiteness*, 158–169; Powell, *Next Time We Strike*, 436, n. 11; Barry Goldberg, " 'Wage Slaves' and 'White Niggers,' " *New Politics* (Summer 1991): 64–83.

72. Warren C. Whatley, "African American Strikebreaking from the Civil War to the New Deal," *Social Science History* 17 (1993): 525–558; Allen and Allen, *Reluctant Reformers*, 183; Roach, "Packingtown Conditions," 534; Radzialowski, "Competition for Jobs," 8, n. 7, and passim; Leslie Fishel, "The North and the Negro, 1865–1900: A Study in Race Discrimination," PhD dissertation, Harvard University, 1953, 454–471; Ray Ginger, "Were Negroes Strikebreakers?" *Negro History Bulletin* (January 1952): 73–74; on the "niggerscab" image, see Roediger, *Towards the Abolition of Whiteness*, 150–153.

73. Higham, *Strangers in the Land*, 172, 321–322; Mink, *Old Labor and New Immigrants*, 234; James R. Barrett, "Ethnic and Racial Fragmentation. Toward an Interpretation of a Local Labor Movement," in Joe Trotter, Earl Lewis, and Tera Hunter, eds., *African American Urban Studies: Historical, Contemporary and Comparative Perspectives* (New York: Palgrave Macmillan, 2004), 287–309; Quinn, "Americanism and Immigration,"

American Federationist 31 (April 1924): 295. Gompers linked support for the 1924 restrictions to "maintenance of racial purity and strength." See Brody, *In Labor's Cause*, 117.

74. Scarpaci, "Immigrants in the New South," 177; Radzialowski, "Competition for Jobs," 17.

75. The first quote is from David Montgomery to Jim Barrett, May 30, 1995. On Old World prejudices, see Orsi, "Religious Boundaries of an Inbetween People," 315; Gary Mormino, *Immigrants on the Hill: Italian-Americans in St. Louis* (Urbana: University of Illinois Press, 1986). For popular anti-Semitism in Poland in the era of massive Polish and Eastern European Jewish immigration to the United States, see Celia S. Heller, *On the Edge of Destruction: Jews of Poland between the Two World Wars* (New York: Schocken, 1977), 38–76.

76. Ronald L. Lewis, *Black Coal Miners in America: Race, Class, and Community Conflict, 1780–1900* (Lexington: University of Kentucky Press, 1987), 110; Allen and Allen, *Reluctant Reformers*, 180. For a recent expression of the common oppression argument, see Paul Berman, "The Other and the Almost the Same," in Paul Berman, ed., *Blacks and Jews: Alliances and Arguments* (New York: Delacorte Press, 1994), 11–30.

77. Peck, "Padrones and Protest," 172–73; "The Greatness of the Greek Spirit," [Chicago] *Saloniki*, January 15, 1919; Georgakas, *Greek America at Work*, 17; Kivisto, *Immigrant Socialists*, 127–28; Thomas Lee Philpott, *The Slum and the Ghetto: Neighborhood Deterioration and Middle Class Reform, Chicago, 1880–1930* (New York: Oxford University Press, 1978), 195.

78. Brackman, "Ebb and Flow of Conflict," 461–464; Marilyn Halter, *Between Race and Ethnicity: Cape Verdean American Immigrants, 1860–1965* (Urbana: University of Illinois Press, 1993), 146–149; Gary Mormino and George Pozzetta, *The Immigrant World of Ybor City: Italians and Their Latin Neighbors in Tampa* (Urbana: University of Illinois Press, 1987), 241.

79. Radzialowski, "Competition for Jobs," 14, n. 20.

80. Rogin, "Making America Home," 1053; Robert W. Snyder, *The Voice of the City: Vaudeville and Popular Culture in New York* (New York: Oxford University Press, 1989), 120; Lewis Erenberg, *Steppin' Out: New York Nightlife and the Transformations of American Culture, 1890–1930* (Chicago: University of Chicago Press, 1981), 195; Rogin, "Blackface, White Noise," 420, 437–448; Brackman, "Ebb and Flow of Conflict," 486.

81. Collins, *Ethnic Identification*, 210–211; Georgakas, *Greek America at Work*, 9–12; Hodding Carter, *Southern Legacy* (Baton Rouge: Louisiana State University Press, 1966), 106; John B. Kennedy, "The Knights of Columbus History Movement," *Current History* 15 (December 1921): 441–443; Herbert Aptheker, "Introduction," in W. E. B. DuBois, *The Gift of Black Folk* (Millwood, NY: Kraus-Thomson, 1975 [1924]), 7–8; Rudolph J. Vecoli, "'Free Country': The American Republic Viewed by the Italian Left, 1880–1920," in Debouzy, ed., *Shadow of the Statue of Liberty*, 38, 33, 34, for the quotes from the Italian-American press; and [Chicago] *Daily Jewish Courier*, August 1912.

82. See Noel Ignatiev, *How the Irish Became White* (New York: Routledge, 1996).

83. Barrett, *Work and Community in the Jungle*, 219–223; cf, William M. Tuttle, Jr., *Race Riot: Chicago in the Red Summer of 1919* (New York: Atheneum, 1974); cf. Roberta Senechal, *The Sociogenesis of a Race Riot* (Urbana: University of Illinois Press, 1990). On the highpoint for Polish and Lithuanian American nationalism in the World War

I era, see Victor Greene, *For God and Country: The Rise of Polish and Lithuanian Ethnic Consciousness in America, 1860–1910* (Madison: University of Wisconsin Press, 1975), chapters 7–9.

84. Radzialowski, "Competition for Jobs," 16; *Glos Polek*, July 31, 1919; cf. *Daily Jewish Courier*, April 22, 1914; *Narod Polski*, August 6, 1919, Chicago Foreign Language Press Survey.

85. Luigi Villari, "Relazione dell dott. Luigi Villari gugli Italiani nel Distretto Consolare di New Orleans," *Bolletino Dell Emigrazione* (Italian Ministry of Foreign Affairs, Royal Commission on Emigration, 1907), 2439, 2499, 2532. Thanks to Louise Edwards for the source and the translations.

86. Barrett, "From the Bottom Up," especially 1012–1013; John McClymer, "Gender and the 'American Way of Life': Women in the Americanization Movement," *Journal of American Ethnic History* 11 (Spring 1991): 5–6.

87. Niles Carpenter and Daniel Katz, "The Cultural Adjustment of the Polish Group in the City of Buffalo: An Experiment in the Technique of Social Investigation," *Social Forces* 6 (September 1927): 80–82. For further evidence of such "indifference," see Scarpaci, "Immigrants in the New South," 175; Edward R. Kantowicz, *Polish American Politics in Chicago, 1888–1940* (Chicago: University of Chicago Press, 1975), 149.

88. Gary Gerstle, *Working Class Americanism: The Politics of Labor in a Textile City, 1914–1960* (New York: Cambridge University Press, 1989); Roger Horowitz, *Negro and White, Unite and Fight! A Social History of Industrial Unionism in Meatpacking, 1930–90* (Urbana: University of Illinois Press, 1997); Rick Halpern, *"Down on the Killing Floor": Black and White Workers in Chicago's Packinghouses, 1904–1954* (Urbana: University of Illinois Press, 1997); Michael Goldfield, "Race and the CIO: The Possibilities for Racial Egalitarianism in the 1930s and 1940s," *International Labor and Working Class History* 44 (1993): 1–32.

89. Dominic Capeci, *Race Relations in Wartime Detroit* (Philadelphia: Temple University Press, 1984); Gerstle, *Working-Class Americanism*, 290; Arnold R. Hirsch, *Making the Second Ghetto: Race and Housing in Chicago, 1940–1960* (Chicago: University of Chicago Press, 1998). See also Thomas Sugrue, "The Structures of Poverty: The Reorganization of Space and Work in Three Periods of American History," in Michael B. Katz, ed., *The Underclass Debate: The View from History* (Princeton, NJ: Princeton University Press, 1993), 85–117; Russell A. Kazal, "Revisiting Assimilation: The Rise, Fall, and Reappraisal of a Concept in American Ethnic History," *American Historical Review* 100 (1995): 468–470. The little information we have on late strikes suggests that they more likely involved recent southern white migrants than "ethnics." See Nelson Lichtenstein, *Labor's War at Home: The CIO in World War II* (New York: Cambridge University Press, 1982), 125–126; Joshua Freeman, "Delivering the Goods: Industrial Unionism in World War II," in Daniel J. Leab, ed., *The Labor History Reader* (Urbana: University of Illinois Press, 1985), 398–400.

90. David R. Colburn and George E. Pozzetta, "Race, Ethnicity, and the Evolution of Political Legitimacy," in David Farber, ed., *The Sixties: From Memory to History* (Chapel Hill: University of North Carolina Press, 1994), 130–138.

CHAPTER 8. Irish Americanization on Stage

My thanks to Kathy Oberdeck, Jenny Barrett, and Kotaro Nakano for their comments. An earlier version of this essay first appeared in different form in *History for the Public* (Osaka, Japan), 10 (2013): 1–19. It also draws on material in *The Irish Way: Becoming American in the Multi-Ethnic City* (New York: Penguin, 2012).

1. "Hissed Off the Stage by Angry Irishmen," *New York Times*, January 25, 1907, 3; "Egg Russell Brothers in a Brooklyn Theatre," *New York Times*, February 1, 1907, 1; M. Alison Kibler, "The Stage Irishwoman," *Journal of American Ethnic History* 24 (Spring 2005): 5–7; Geraldine Maschio, "Ethnic Humor and the Decline of the Russell Brothers," *Journal of Popular Culture* 26 (Summer 1992): 81–92; Kathryn J. Oberdeck, *The Evangelist and the Impresario: Religion, Entertainment, and Cultural Politics in America, 1884–1914* (Baltimore: Johns Hopkins University Press, 1999), 201.

2. Mick Moloney, "Irish-American Popular Music," in J. J. Lee and Marion R. Casey, eds., *Making the Irish American* (New York: New York University Press, 2005), 382, quote, 383; David R. Roediger, *The Wages of Whiteness: Race and the Making of the American Working Class* (London: Verso, 1991), 118–119.

3. On the British tradition, see G. C. Duggan, *The Stage Irishman: A History of the Irish Play and Stage Characters from the Earliest Times* (London: Longman's Green, 1937); Declan Kiberd, "The Fall of the Stage Irishman," *Genre: A Quarterly Devoted to Generic Criticism* 12 (Winter 1979): 451–454; Kathleen Donovan, "Good Old Pat: An Irish American Stereotype in Decline," *Eire-Ireland* 15:3 (1980): 6–14. On derogatory comic caricature in nineteenth-century British print culture, see L. Perry Curtis, *Apes and Angels: The Irishman in Victorian Caricature*, rev. ed. (Washington, DC: Smithsonian Press, 1997).

4. Roediger, *Wages of Whiteness*, 133–163; Eric Lott, *Love and Theft: Blackface Minstrelsy and the American Working Class* (New York: Oxford University Press, 1993); Michael Rogin, *Blackface, White Noise: Jewish Immigrants in the Hollywood Melting Pot* (Berkeley: University of California Press, 1996), 56–58, Moloney, "Irish-American Popular Music," 383.

5. Dale T. Knobel, "A Vocabulary of Ethnic Perception: Content Analysis of the American Stage Irishman, 1820–1860," *Journal of American Studies* 15 (1981): 45–71; Patricia L. Ireland, "Blarney Streets: The Staging of Ireland and Irish-America by the Chicago Manuscript Company," PhD dissertation, Southern Illinois University, 1998, 201 and passim.

6. Harrigan, quoted in "Mr. Harrigan as Actor and Maker of 'Documents,'" *New York Times*, September 3, 1893, 16; Harley Erdman, *Staging the Jew: The Performance of an American Ethnicity, 1860–1920* (New Brunswick, NJ: Rutgers University Press, 1997), 89.

7. Moloney, "Irish-American Popular Music," 389; "American Playwrights on the American Drama," *Harper's Weekly*, February 2, 1889, 98; W. D. Howells, *Selected Literary Criticism*, Vol. 2: *1886–1897*, edited by David J. Nordloh (Bloomington: Indiana University Press, 1993), 25, both quoted in Jon W. Finson, "Realism in the Late Nineteenth Century American Musical Theatre: The Songs of Edward Harrigan and David Braham," in Jon W. Finson, ed., *Collected Songs: Edward Harrigan and David Braham*, vols.

27–28 of *Music of the United States of America* (Madison: University of Wisconsin Press, 1977), xxvii; Finerty, quoted in Charles Fanning, *Finley Peter Dunne and Mr. Dooley: The Chicago Years* (Lexington: University Press of Kentucky, 1978), 158. For a sketch of Five Points in the era of Harrigan's greatest popularity, see "Not for Open Saloons," *New York Times*, January 25, 1895, 9.

8. Krystyn R. Moon, *Yellowface: Creating the Chinese in American Popular Music and Performance, 1850s–1920s* (New Brunswick, NJ: Rutgers University Press, 2005), 53. See also James H. Dormon, "Ethnic Cultures of the Mind: The Harrigan-Hart Mosaic," *American Studies* 33 (Summer 1992): passim.

9. Quoted in E. J. Kahn Jr., *The Merry Partners: The Age and Stage of Harrigan and Hart* (New York: Random House, 1955), 69.

10. Mixed-race Irish–Chinese marriages remained popular in early twentieth-century plays like *Patsy O'Wang: An Irish Farce with a Chinese Mix-Up* (1895). See Robert G. Lee, *Orientals: Asian Americans in Popular Culture* (Philadelphia: Temple University Press, 1999), 78–81.

11. Harrigan's play and the street tune are both quoted in Moon, *Yellowface*, 50. On the rise of the Chinese hand laundry, see Mary Tin Yi Lui, *The Chinatown Trunk Mystery: Murder, Miscegenation, and Other Dangerous Encounters in Turn-of-the-Century New York City* (Princeton, NJ: Princeton University Press, 2005), 55–58; and on the laundryman's perceived femininity, Ronald Takaki, *Strangers from a Different Shore: A History of Asian Americans* (New York: Penguin, 1989), 92–93.

12. *Irish World and Industrial Liberator*, July 12, 1879, 5; Alexander Saxton, *Indispensable Enemy: Labor and the Anti-Chinese Movement in California* (Berkeley: University of California Press, 1971). See also, Moon, *Yellowface*, 49–51.

13. On *The Mulligan Guards' Ball*, see Dennis McNulty, "Blackface as Irish Mask? Liminality and Resistance in Irish Blackface Performance," 2005, unpublished seminar paper in the author's possession; Lauren Onkey, *Blackness and Transatlantic Irish Identity: Celtic Soul Brothers* (New York: Rutledge, 2010), 71–76; Catherine Eagan, "'I Did Imagine . . . We Had Ceased to Be White-Washed Negroes': The Racial Formation of Irish Identity in Ireland and America," PhD dissertation, Boston College, 2000; on the musical renderings of Chinese-Irish intermarriage, see Moon, *Yellow Face*, 51–52; and on the affinity between Irish and African Americans in Harrigan's plays, Robert Toll, *Blacking Up: The Minstrel Show in Nineteenth Century America* (New York: Oxford University Press, 1974), 247, 249.

14. Joyce Flynn, "Melting Plots: Patterns of Racial and Ethnic Amalgamation in American Drama before Eugene O'Neill," *American Quarterly* 38 (1986): 430.

15. Robert W. Snyder, "The Irish and Vaudeville," in Lee and Casey, eds., *Making the Irish American*, 406.

16. Alexander Saxton, "Blackface Minstrelsy and Jacksonian Ideology," *American Quarterly* 27 (1975): 14–15; Roediger, *Wages of Whiteness*, 119; Lott, *Love and Theft*, 190–191.

17. Robert W. Snyder, "Big Time, Small Time, All around the Town: New York Vaudeville in the Early Twentieth Century," in Richard Butsch, ed., *For Fun and Profit: The Transformation of Leisure into Consumption* (Philadelphia: Temple University Press,

1990), 119; Michael Davis, *The Exploitation of Pleasure* (New York: Russell Sage Foundation, 1910).

18. Davis, *Exploitation of Pleasure*, table 8, 30. See also David Nasaw, *Going Out: The Rise and Fall of Public Amusements* (New York: Basic Books, 1993), 23–32.

19. Richard Butsch, *The Making of American Audiences: From Stage to Television* (New York: Cambridge University Press, 2000), 141–146; Davis, *Exploitation of Pleasure*, 30; Nasaw, *Going Out*, 168–171, 186–204.

20. Snyder, "Big Time, Small Time," 120.

21. Gavin Roger Jones, *Strange Talk: The Politics of Dialect Literature in Gilded Age America* (Berkeley: University of California Press, 1999), 173–177; Moloney, "Irish American Popular Music," 387.

22. Moloney, "Irish American Popular Music"; Flynn, "Melting Plots," 426, quote, 429; "Dramatic and Musical," *New York Times*, November 13, 1900, 6; Paul Antoine Distler, "Ethnic Comedy in Vaudeville and Burlesque," in Myron Matlaw, ed., *American Popular Entertainment* (Westport, CT: Greenwood Press, 1979), 38; Rogin, *Blackface, White Noise*, 53.

23. Moon, *Yellowface* 114.

24. Ibid., 140–142; Lee, *Orientals*, 34–35, 61–5; Lott, *Love and Theft*, 48.

25. Gunther Barth, *City People: The Rise of Modern City Culture in Nineteenth Century America* (New York: Oxford University Press, 1980), 193. See also Thomas J. Schlereth, *Victorian America: Transformations in Everyday Life, 1876–1915* (New York: Harper Perennial, 1991), 232–233.

26. Hartley Davis, "In Vaudeville," *Everyone's Magazine* 24 (August 1905): 238, quoted, James H. Dormon, "European Immigrant/Ethnic Theatre in Gilded Age in New York: Reflections and Projections of Mentalities," in William Pencak, Selma Berrol, and Randall M. Miller, eds., *Immigration to New York* (Philadelphia: Balch Institute Press, 1991), 165.

27. Snyder, "The Irish and Vaudeville," 407; Paul Antoine Distler, "Ethnic Comedy in Vaudeville and Burlesque," in Matlaw, ed., *American Popular Entertainment*, 36; Sabine Haenni, *The Immigrant Scene: Ethnic Amusements in New York, 1880–1920* (Minneapolis: University of Minnesota Press, 2008), 14–16.

28. Stephen Whitfield, *In Search of American Jewish Culture* (Waltham, MA: Brandeis University Press, 1999), quote, 51. On the increasing diversity of vaudeville audiences, see Snyder, "Big Time, Small Time," 125; M. Alison Kibler, *Rank Ladies: Gender and Hierarchy in American Vaudeville* (Chapel Hill: University of North Carolina Press, 1999), 25, 34–36; Mary Carbine, "The Finest outside the Loop: Motion Picture Exhibition in Chicago's Black Metropolis, 1905–1925," *Camera Obscura* 23 (1990): 9–41. On the balance of slapstick, nostalgia, and urban realism, see Oberdeck, *Evangelist and the Impresario*, 91–108, 97–98.

29. Nasaw, *Going Out*, 52–53.

30. Armond Fields and L. Marc Fields, *From the Bowery to Broadway: Lew Fields and the Roots of American Popular Theatre* (New York: Oxford University Press, 1993), 32–33, 85, first quote, 32; George Peter Murdock, ed., *Studies in the Science of Society* (Freeport, NY: Books for Libraries Press, 1969), second quote, 21. See also Moon, *Yellowface*, 148–150.

31. Rogin, *Blackface, White Noise*, 56–58, quote, 56.

32. Donovan, "Good Old Pat," 6–14; Oberdeck, *Evangelist and the Impresario*, 198–204; Kibler, *Rank Ladies*, 60–69.

33. Snyder, "Irish and Vaudeville," 406–409, quote 407; Kibler, *Rank Ladies*, 55–57, 63–64, 71–74; Charles Fanning, *The Irish Voice in America: 250 Years of Irish American Fiction* (Lexington: University of Kentucky Press, 2000), 179–182; Carl Wittke, "The Immigrant Theme on the American Stage," *Mississippi Valley Historical Review* 39 (September 1952): 222–223. The comic pretensions of the upwardly mobile Irish were a constant refrain in Finley Peter Dunne's popular "Mister Dooley" columns and books.

34. Ireland, "Blarney Streets," 197–198; *New York Tribune*, March 28, 1903, 1; *Managers' Report Book*, p. 252, Boston, April 27, 1903, Keith/Albee Collection, Special Collections, University of Iowa Library. Thanks to M. Alison Kibler for directing me to this source.

35. "Irish Comedian Must Go," *Chicago Tribune*, May 1902, 1; M. Alison Kibler, "Pigs, Green Whiskers, and Drunken Widows: Irish Nationalists and the 'Practical Censorship' of McFadden's Row of Flats in 1902 and 1903," *Journal of American Studies* 42 (December 2008): 489–514; Donovan, "Good Old Pat," 13. The United Irish Societies quote is in Oberdeck, *Evangelist and the Impresario*, 201; Nasaw, *Going Out*, 167.

36. Oberdeck, *Evangelist and the Impresario*, 343–349; *Managers' Report Book*, 8, 124, Keith/Albee Collection, quoted, Kibler, *Rank Ladies*, 56.

37. Fanning, *Irish Voice in America*, 219.

38. On Irish defensiveness and obsession with respectability, see Kerby A. Miller, *Emigrants and Exiles: Ireland and the Irish Exodus to North America* (New York: Oxford University Press, 1988), 497–499, quote, 498; Thomas Rowland, "Irish Americans and the Quest for Respectability in the Coming of the Great War, 1900–1917," *Journal of American Ethnic History* 15 (Winter 1996): 3–31. On the changing composition of the audience for musical theater at the end of the nineteenth century, see Dormon, "Ethnic Cultures of the Mind," 37.

39. Fanning, *Irish Voice in America*, 153–176; Chris McNickle, "When New York Was Irish, and After," in Ronald H. Bayor and Timothy J. Meagher, eds., *The New York Irish* (Baltimore: Johns Hopkins University Press, 1996), 345–346.

40. Kibler, "The Stage Irishwoman," 5–30; Kibler, "Pigs, Green Whiskers, and Drunken Widows," 11–14. The characterization of "belligerent masculinity" is from Meagher, *Making of Irish America*, 243. On the working-class character of the A.O.H., see Miller, *Emigrants and Exiles*, 534–35. See also "Riot in Theatre over an Irish Play," *New York Times*, November 28, 1911, 1, 3; "Egg Riot at Theatre; Irishmen in a Rage," *New York Tribune*, March 28, 1903, 1.

41. Timothy Meagher, "Introduction," in Timothy Meagher, ed., *From Paddy to Studs: Irish American Communities in the Turn of the Century Era, 1880–1920* (Westport, CT: Greenwood Press, 1986), 2.

42. *Managers' Report Book*, p. 297, Boston, April 27, 1903, Keith/Albee Collection. Thanks to M. Alison Kibler for this reference.

43. Kibler, *Rank Ladies*, 34–36; Nasaw, *Going Out*, 53–56, 167–168.

44. "All Races to War on Play Ridicule," *Chicago Tribune*, April 25, 1913, 5; quote, "Anti-Defamation Move Becomes Nationwide," November 14, 1913, 14; "To Boycott the

Stage Jew," *New York Times*, April 25, 1913, 3. On protests against ethnic caricatures on the part of several different ethnic groups, see M. Alison Kibler, *Censoring Racial Ridicule: Irish, Jewish, and African American Struggles over Race and Representation, 1890–1930* (Chapel Hill, NC: University of North Carolina Press, 2015).

45. Oberdeck, *Evangelist and the Impresario*, 341–349; "Stage Folk Dispute Virtues of Make-Up," *New York Times*, July 15, 1923, E6.

46. Lyrics in Mick Moloney, *Far from the Shamrock Shore: The Story of Irish-American Immigration through Song* (New York: Crown, 2002), 34.

47. Williams, *'Twas Only an Irishman's Dream: The Image of Ireland and the Irish in American Popular Song Lyrics, 1800–1920* (Urbana: University of Illinois Press), 192–194.

48. Ibid., quote, 190.

49. Rogin, *Blackface, White Noise*, 57–58.

50. This and the previous paragraph draw on Williams, *'Twas Only an Irishman's Dream*, 194–199, song lyrics quoted, 196. See also Moloney, "Irish-American Popular Music," 393–396; Moloney, *Far from the Shamrock Shore*, 36–37.

51. "Comedies for All," *New York Times*, August 29, 1926, X1; Ann Nichols, *Abie's Irish Rose: A Novel* (New York: Grosset and Dunlap, 1927), 75–79, 95–98, 101–106; Riv-Ellen Prell, *Fighting to Become Americans: Jews, Gender, and the Anxiety of Assimilation* (Boston: Beacon Press, 1999), 72–77; Rudolf Glanz, *Jew and Irish: Historic Group Relations and Immigration* (New York: Walden Press, 1966), 105–106; Joseph M. Curran, *Hibernian Green on the Silver Screen: The Irish and American Movies* (New York: Greenwood Press, 1989), 36; Ted Merwin, "The Performance of Jewish Identity in Anne Nichols's 'Abie's Irish Rose,'" *Journal of American Ethnic History* 20 (Winter 2001): 3–37; Rogin, *Blackface, White Noise*, 104; Lester D. Friedman, *Unspeakable Images: Ethnicity and the American Cinema* (Urbana: University of Illinois Press, 1991), 58–60; Mari Kathleen Fielder, "Fatal Attraction: Irish-Jewish Romance in Early Film and Drama," *Journal of American Ethnic History* 20:4 (Fall 1985): 6–18; Eric Goldstein, *The Price of Whiteness: Jews, Race and American Identity* (Princeton, NJ: Princeton Univeristy Press, 2006), 134, 135.

52. Edward T. O'Donnell, "Abie's Irish Rose," *Irish Echo*, May 19, 2004; *Irish Echo*, November 4–10, 2009, 18; "Moe and Jawn Practice Their Abie's Irish Rose Jokes," *Chicago Tribune*, April 15, 1928, A3; Erdman, *Staging the Jew*, 120; "Abie Sings an Irish Song," [1913] Words and Music by Irving Berlin in Charles Hamm, ed., *Irving Berlin: Early Songs* (Madison, WI: Published for the American Musicological Society by A-R Editions, 1994); Mick Maloney, *If It Wasn't for the Irish and the Jews*, CD, Compass Records, 2009. Thanks to Ed O'Donnell, Jo Kibbee, and Jeff Magee for their suggestions on this theme. On Berlin's early career, see Michael Freeland, *Irving Berlin* (New York: Stein and Day, 1974). See also Rogin, *Blackface, White Noise*, 58; Whitfield, *In Search of American Jewish Culture*; Williams, *'Twas Only an Irishman's Dream*, 198–199.

53. Timothy J. Meagher, "Abie's Irish Enemy: Irish and Jews, Social and Political Realities and Media Representations," in Ruth Barton, ed., *Screening Irish America: Representing Irish American in Film and Television* (Dublin: Irish Academic Press, 2009), 45–58.

54. Prell, *Fighting to Become Americans*, quote, 77. On intermarriage in the third generation and beyond, see Will Herberg, *Protestant, Catholic, Jew: An Essay on American*

Religious Sociology (Chicago: University of California Press, 1955); Harold Abramson, *Ethnic Diversity in Catholic America* (New York: Wiley, 1973), 51–99; Joel Perlmann, "The Romance of Assimilation? Studying the Demographic Outcomes of Ethnic Intermarriage in American History," Working Paper No. 230 (Jerome Levy Economics Institute, Bard College, 1988), especially table 9; Perlmann, "Demographic Outcomes of Ethnic Intermarriage in American History: Italian Americans through Four Generations," Working Paper No. 372 (Jerome Levy Economics Institute, 2000), especially table 13; Julius Drachsler, "Intermarriage in New York City: A Statistical Survey of the Amalgamation of European Peoples," PhD dissertation, Columbia University, 1921, 56; Stephen Steinberg, *The Ethnic Myth: Race, Ethnicity and Class in America* (Boston: Beacon Press, 1989), 68.

55. For the experiences of an Irish Catholic woman who married her Jewish employer and the struggles of their son in a Catholic school, see "The Experiences of a Jew's Wife," *American Magazine* 78 (December 1914), 49–53, 83–86. My thanks to Edward T. O'Donnell for directing me to this source.

56. Bruce M. Stave and John F. Sutherland, with Aldo Salerno, eds., *From the Old Country: An Oral History of European Migration to America* (New York: Twayne, 1994), 185–187, 190; Fielder, "Fatal Attraction," 12, 13; Richard Alba, *Ethnic Identity: The Transformation of White America* (New Haven, CT: Yale University Press, 1990), 59–61; cf. Michael Hout and Joshua R. Goldstein, "How 4.5 Million Irish Immigrants Became 40 Million Irish Americans: Demographic and Subject Aspects of the Ethnic Composition of White Americans," *American Sociological Review* 59 (February, 1994), 64–82. Thanks to Gillian Stevens for this citation.

57. Tyler Anbinder, *Five Points: The New York City Neighborhood that Invented Tap Dance* (New York: Free Press, 2001), 389–390, 314, 320, 263; Graham Hodges, "'Desirable Companions and Lovers': Irish and African Americans in the Sixth Ward, 1830–1870," in Bayor and Meagher, eds., *The New York Irish*, 107–124; Sarah Deutsch, *Women and the City: Gender, Space, and Power in Boston, 1870–1940* (New York: Oxford University Press, 2000), 86–89; John Kuo Wei Tchen, "Quimbo Appo's Fear of Fenians: Chinese-Irish-Anglo Relations in New York City," in Meagher and Bayor, eds., *The New York Irish*, 128–130; Lui, *Chinatown Trunk Mystery*, 154–160.

58. Drachsler, "Intermarriage in New York City," passim, especially 56; Bronwen Walter, *Outsiders Inside: Whiteness, Place, and Irish Women* (New York: Routledge, 2000), 34–35; Thomas J. Archdeacon, *Becoming American: An Ethnic History* (New York: Free Press, 1983), 139–140; Hasia R. Diner, *Erin's Daughters: Irish Immigrant Women in the Nineteenth Century* (Baltimore: Johns Hopkins University Press, 1983), xiv, 8–9, 30–34, 51; William Z. Ripley, "Races in the United States," *Atlantic Monthly* 102 (December 1908): 745–759; Herberg, *Protestant, Catholic, Jew*; Harold Abramson, *Ethnic Diversity in Catholic America* (New York: Wiley, 1973), 51–99; Perlmann, "The Romance of Assimilation," especially table 9; Perlmann, "Demographic Outcomes of Ethnic Intermarriage," especially table 13. See also R. J. R. Kennedy, "Single or Triple Melting Pot? Intermarriage Trends in New Haven, 1870–1940," *American Journal of Sociology* 49:4 (January 1944): 331–339; R. J. R. Kennedy, "Single or Triple Melting Pot? Intermarriage in New Haven, 1870–1950," *American Journal of Sociology* 58:1 (July 1952): 56–59.

59. Frank Walsh, *Sin and Censorship: The Catholic Church and the Motion Picture Industry* (New Haven, CT: Yale University Press, 1996); Curran, *Hibernian Green*, quote, 49.

60. Charles Morris, *American Catholics: The Saints and Sinners Who Built America's Most Powerful Church* (New York: Vintage Books, 1998), 196–209; Curran, *Hibernian Green*, 48–52; Thomas Doherty, *Hollywood's Censor: Joseph I. Breen and the Production Code Administration* (New York: Columbia University Press, 2009), 56–60.

61. Lawrence J. McCaffrey, "Diaspora Comparisons and Irish-American Uniqueness," in Charles Fanning, ed., *New Perspectives on the Irish Diaspora* (Carbondale: Southern Illinois University Press, 2000), 22.

62. James T. Farrell, *Studs Lonigan: A Trilogy Comprising Young Lonigan, The Young Manhood of Studs Lonigan, and Judgement Day* (Urbana: University of Illinois Press, 1993), 375–376, 455–458, 560; Lauren Onkey, "James Farrell's *Studs Lonigan* Trilogy and the Anxieties of Race," *Eire-Ireland* 40 (Fall/Winter 2005): 105; John McGreevy, *Parish Boundaries: The Catholic Encounter with Race in the Twentieth Century North* (Chicago: University of Chicago Press, 1996), passim. Anxieties about the encroachment of "new immigrants" were also characteristic of the work of earlier writers like the popular novelist and journalist Maurice Egan, who deplored the fact that the immigrant Irish were "fading away before the swarm of newcomers . . . the outcasts of old nations." See Fanning, *Irish Voice in America*, 205.

63. Farrell, *Studs Lonigan*, 454, 455.

64. Charles Fanning and Ellen Skerrett, "James T. Farrell and Washington Park," *Chicago History* 7 (1979): 87. On the black migration, see James G. Grossman, *Land of Hope: Chicago, Black Southerners, and the Great Migration* (Chicago: University of Chicago Press, 1989); Chicago Commission on Race Relations, *The Negro in Chicago: A Study of Race Relations and a Race Riot* (Chicago: University of Chicago Press, 1922). Washington Park itself became a Mecca for white and especially for African American radicals in the era of the Great Depression. See Richard Wright, *Black Boy* (New York: Harper and Row, 1946) and St. Clair Drake and Horace Cayton, *Black Metropolis: A Study of Negro Life in a Northern City* (New York: Harcourt, Brace, 1945).

65. Edgar M. Branch, *Studs Lonigan's Neighborhood and the Making of James T. Farrell* (Newton, MA: Arts End Books, 1996), 15–16; Ellen Skerrett, "The Catholic Dimension," in Lawrence McCaffrey, Ellen Skerrett, Michael Funchion, and Charles Fanning, eds., *The Irish in Chicago* (Urbana: University of Illinois Press, 1987), 52; Charles Fanning, "The Literary Dimension," in McCaffrey, Skerrett, Funchion, and Fanning, eds., *The Irish in Chicago*, 128–129.

66. Farrell, *Studs Lonigan*, 18. See also Chicago Commission on Race Relations, *The Negro in Chicago*.

CHAPTER 9. Making and Unmaking the Working Class

An earlier, shorter version of this essay (in a different form) appeared in *Historical Reflections/Reflections Historique* 41 (Spring 2015): 7–18. For facilitating the essay, I have to thank Antoinette Burton and Stephanie Seawell, and for helpful comments, Jenny Barrett, Bryan Palmer, David Roediger, Leon Fink, and Bruce Levine.

1. Rajnarayan Chandavarkar, "The Making of the Working Class: E. P. Thompson and Indian History," *History Workshop Journal* 43 (Spring 1997): 179.

2. "E. P. Thompson Obituary," *The Independent*, August 30, 1993, cited in Bryan D. Palmer, "Homage to Edward Thompson, Part II," *Labour/LeTravail* 33 (Spring 1994): 14, fn. 2. See also E. J. Hobsbawm, *Interesting Times: A Twentieth Century Life* (New York: Pantheon Books, 2002), 214.

3. Frederick Cooper, "Work, Class and Empire: An African Historian's Retrospective on E. P. Thompson," *Social History* 20:2 (May 1995): 235–241; Chandavarkar, "The Making of the Working Class," 177–196.

4. Chandavarkar, "The Making of the Working Class"; Bryan D. Palmer, "Paradox and the Thompson 'School of Awkwardness,'" in *E. P. Thompson: Objections and Oppositions* (London: Verso, 1994), 205–227. Chandavarkar is concerned primarily with what he sees as the contradictions in *The Making*, while Palmer notes Thompson's attraction to and investigation of the paradoxes of industrialization.

5. Kate Soper, "Socialist Humanism," in Harvey Kaye and Keith McClelland, eds., *E. P. Thompson: Critical Perspectives* (Philadelphia: Temple University Press, 1990), 204–221; Kate Soper, "Thompson and Socialist Humanism," in Roger Fieldhouse and Richard Taylor, eds., *E. P. Thompson and English Radicalism* (Manchester: Manchester University Press, 2013), 121–142; Palmer, *E. P. Thompson*, 69–86.

6. Scott Hamilton, *The Crisis of Theory: E. P. Thompson, the New Left and Postwar British Politics* (Manchester: Manchester University Press, 2011), 49–226; Perry Anderson, *Arguments within English Marxism* (London: New Left Books, 1980); Palmer, *E. P. Thompson*, 69–86; Michael D. Bess, "The Historian as Activist," *American Historical Review* 98 (February 1993): 18–38; Michael Newman, "Thompson and the Early New Left," in Fieldhouse and Taylor, eds., *E. P. Thompson*, 158–180.

7. William Sewell, "How Classes Are Made: Critical Reflections on E. P. Thompson's Theory of Working-Class Formation," in Kaye and McClelland, eds., *E. P. Thompson*, 54–56; cf. Peter Way, "'The Something that Has Called Itself Marxism,'" in "Thompson's *The Making of the English Working Class* at Fifty," *Labour/Le Travail* 71 (Spring 2013): 161–167, especially 163; Nina Power, "Thompson's Concept of Class: The Flesh and Blood of Self-Emancipation," in Fieldhouse and Richard Taylor, eds., *E. P. Thompson*, 143–157.

8. Gabriel Kolko, *The Triumph of Conservatism: A Reinterpretation of American History* (New York: Free Press, 1963); James Weinstein, *The Corporate Ideal in the Liberal State* (Boston: Beacon Press, 1968); James Weinstein and David Eakins, eds., *For a New America: Essays in History and Politics from Studies on the Left* (New York: Vintage, 1970).

9. Peter Novick, *That Noble Dream: The "Objectivity Question" and the American Historical Profession* (Cambridge: Cambridge University Press, 1988), quote, 424; Paul Buhle, "Madison: An Introduction"; James Weinstein, "Studies on the Left"; and James Gilbert, "The Intellectuals and the First New Left," all in Paul Buhle, ed., *History and the New Left: Madison, Wisconsin, 1950–1970* (Philadelphia: Temple University Press, 1990), 24–31, 113–117, 118–126.

10. Gabriel Kolko, *Main Currents in Modern American History* (New York: Harper & Row, 1977), quote, 99; Jonathan M. Weiner, "Radical Historians and the Crisis in American History, 1959–1980," *Journal of American History* 76:2 (September 1989): 408.

11. Novick, *That Noble Dream*, quote, 424; Paul Buhle, *Radical America* and Me," in *History and the New Left*, 216–232.

12. Paul Buhle, *C. L. R. James: The Artist as Revolutionary* (London: Verso, 1988); for a particularly creative piece that brings Thompson and James together, Peter Linebaugh, "What if C. L. R. James Had Met E. P. Thompson in 1792?" *Urgent Tasks* 12 (Summer 1981): 108–110. Thompson shows an uncharacteristic deference to James in the remarkable 1983 documentary film *Talking History: C. L. R. James and E. P. Thompson*, Penumbra Productions, London, 1983, directed by H. O. Nazareth. The film is still available online through Concordia Media, U.K., at www.concordmedia.uk. On the film and its context, see Utathya Chattopadhyaya, "Talking History: E. P. Thompson, C. L. R. James, and the Afterlives of Internationalism," *Historical Reflections/Reflexions Historique* 41 (Spring 2015): 111–128.

13. James R. Barrett, "Class Act: An Interview with David Montgomery," *Labor: Studies in Working-Class History of the Americas* 1:1 (2004): 25–57; Weiner, "Radical Historians," 410–412; "Interview with Herbert Gutman," in Herbert G. Gutman, *Power and Culture: Essays on the American Working Class*, edited by Ira Berlin (New York: Pantheon, 1987), 329–356.

14. Alan Dawley, "E. P. Thompson and the Peculiarities of the Americans," *Radical History Review* 19 (Winter 1978–1979): quote, 39.

15. Sean Wilentz, *Chants Democratic: New York City and the Rise of the American Working Class, 1780–1850*, 2nd ed. (New York: Oxford University Press, 2004), quote, xii–xiii.

16. James R. Barrett, "Remembering David Montgomery (1926–2011), His Scholarship, and His Mentorship," *Labor/Le Travail* 70 (Fall 2012): 203–223; David Montgomery, *The Fall of the House of Labor: The Workplace, the State, and American Labor Activism, 1865–1925* (Cambridge: Cambridge University Press, 1987), quote, 3. Montgomery has been faulted for focusing primarily on skilled male workers. Contrast my assessment here with Elizabeth Faue, "Retooling the Class Factory: United States Labor History after Marx, Montgomery, and Postmodernism," *Labour History* 82 (May 2002): 109–119. Feminist criticisms of Thompson have been even sharper; see, for example, Joan Scott, "Women in *The Making of the English Working Class*," in *Gender and the Politics of History* (New York: Columbia University Press, 1988), 68–91; Roger Fieldhouse, Theodore Koditschek, and Richard Taylor, "E. P. Thompson: An Introduction," in Fieldhouse and Taylor, eds., *E. P. Thompson*, 9–10.

17. John R. Commons et al., *History of Labor in the United States*, 4 vols. (New York: Macmillan, 1918–1935); John R. Commons et al., eds., *A Documentary History of American Industrial Society*, 10 vols. (New York: Russell and Russell, 1958); Selig Perlman, *A History of Trade Unionism in the United States* (New York: Macmillan, 1922); Selig Perlman, *A Theory of the Labor Movement* (New York: Macmillan, 1928). On the Commons tradition in the field and the departure by the new labor historians, see David Brody, "The Old Labor and the New: In Search of an American Working Class," *Labor History* 20:1 (Winter 1979): 111–126; Shelton Stromquist, "Perspectives on the New Labor History: The Wisconsin School and Beyond," *International Labor and Working Class History* 39:3 (Spring 1991): 81–88; Leon Fink, "John R. Commons, Herbert Gutman, and the Burden of Labor History," *Labor History* 29:3 (1988): 313–322.

18. David Brody, "David Montgomery, Field Builder," *Labor: Studies in Working-Class History of the Americas* 10:1 (Spring 2013): 53–56; Barrett, "Class Act"; "Interview with Herbert Gutman."

19. Ira Berlin, "Introduction," in Gutman, *Power and Culture*, quotes, 18, 19.

20. Many of the studies inspired by *The Making* also employed such methods. See Roy Rosenzweig, *Eight Hours for What We Will: Workers and Leisure in an Industrial City, 1870–1920* (Cambridge: Cambridge University Press, 1983); Shelton Stromquist, *A Generation of Boomers: The Pattern of Railroad Labor Conflict in Nineteenth-Century America* (Urbana: University of Illinois Press, 1987); Peter Rachleff, *Black Labor in the South: Richmond, Virginia, 1865–1890* (Philadelphia: Temple University Press, 1984); James R. Barrett, *Work and Community in the Jungle: Chicago's Packinghouse Workers, 1894–1922* (Urbana: University of Illinois Press, 1987); Susan Hirsch, *Roots of the American Working Class: The Industrialization of Crafts in Newark, 1800–1860* (Philadelphia: Temple University Press, 1978). My emphasis here is on historical writing on the American working class, but a similar observation might be made of many young American historians of the 1970s and early 1980s who were working on other societies. See, for example, the work of Diane Koenker on Russia, James Cronin on England, and William Sewell on France.

21. Marcus Rediker, *Between the Devil and the Deep Blue Sea: Merchant Seamen, Pirates, and the Anglo-American Maritime World, 1700–1750* (Cambridge: Cambridge University Press, 1987); Peter Linebaugh and Marcus Rediker, *The Many-Headed Hydra: Sailors, Slaves, Commoners, and the Hidden History of the Revolutionary Atlantic* (Boston: Beacon Press, 2000); Alfred F. Young, *The Shoemaker and the Tea Party: Memory and the American Revolution* (Boston: Beacon Press, 1999).

22. Alan Dawley, *Class and Community: The Industrial Revolution in Lynn* (Cambridge, MA: Harvard University Press, 1976); Bruce Laurie, *The Working People of Philadelphia, 1800–1850* (Philadelphia: Temple University Press, 1980); Sean Wilentz, *Chants Democratic: New York City and the Rise of the American Working Class, 1780–1850* (New York: Oxford University Press, 1984); Hirsch, *Roots of the American Working Class*; David Montgomery, "The Working Classes of the Preindustrial City, 1780–1830," *Labor History* 9:1 (1983): 3–22. Much of this work is synthesized in Bruce Laurie, *Artisans into Workers: Labor in Nineteenth Century America* (Urbana: University of Illinois Press, 1997). On the first generation of industrial workers learning "the rules of the game," see E. J. Hobsbawm, "Custom, Wages, and Workload in the Nineteenth Century," in *Laboring Men: Studies in the History of Labor* (New York: Basic Books, 1964). In a rare, explicitly comparative piece, Leon Fink finds that the optimistic reading of working-class culture in these studies of early industrialization turned far gloomier in studies of the twentieth. See Leon Fink, "Looking Backward: Reflections on Workers' Culture and Certain Conceptual Dilemmas in Labor History," in *In Search of the Working Class: Essays in American Labor History and Political Culture* (Urbana: University of Illinois Press, 1994), 175–200.

23. David Montgomery, *Beyond Equality: Labor and the Radical Republicans, 1862–1872* (New York: Alfred A. Knopf, 1967); Wilentz, *Chants Democratic*; Leon Fink, "The New Labor History of the Powers of Historical Pessimism: Consensus, Hegemony, and the Case of the Knights of Labor," *Journal of American History* 75:1 (June 1988): 116.

24. Laurie, *The Working People of Philadelphia*, quote, 91.

25. Chandavarkar, "The Making of the Working Class," quote, 177.

26. E. J. Hobsbawm, "The Making of the Working Class," in *Workers: Worlds of Labor* (New York: Pantheon, 1984); Gareth Stedman Jones, "Working-Class Culture and Working-Class Politics in London, 1870–1900: Notes on the Remaking of a Working Class," *Journal of Social History* 7:4 (Summer 1974): 460–508, especially 498–500. See also Anderson, *Arguments within English Marxism*, 43–49.

27. Laurie, *The Working People of Philadelphia*; David Montgomery, "The Shuttle and the Cross: Weavers and Artisans in the Kensington Riots of 1844," *Journal of Social History* 5:4 (Summer 1972): 411–466.

28. James R. Barrett, "The World of the Worker," in Ronald H. Bayor, ed., *Oxford Handbook of American Immigration and Ethnicity* (New York: Oxford University Press, 2016); James R. Barrett, "Unity and Fragmentation: Class, Race, and Ethnicity on Chicago's South Side, 1900–1922," *Journal of Social History* 18:1 (1984): 37–56; Bryan D. Palmer, "Social Formation and Class Formation in Nineteenth-Century North America," in David Levine, ed., *Proletarianization and Family History* (New York: Academic Press, 1984), 229–308; Herbert Gutman and Ira Berlin, "Class Composition and the Development of the American Working Class, 1840–1890," in Gutman, *Power and Culture*, 380–394.

29. Herbert Gutman, "Work, Culture, and Society in Industrializing America, 1815–1919," in *Work, Culture, and Society in Industrializing America: Essays in American Working-Class and Social History* (New York: Vintage, 1977), 11, fn. 8; David Montgomery, "Gutman's Nineteenth Century America," *Labor History* 19 (Summer 1978): 419.

30. Robert Asher, "Union Nativism and the Immigrant Response," *Labor History* 23 (Summer 1982): 325–348; Catherine Collomp, "Unions, Civics, and National Identity: Organized Reaction to Immigration, 1881–1897," *Labor History* 29 (Fall 1988): 450–474; Alexander Saxton, *The Indispensable Enemy: Labor and the Anti-Chinese Movement in California* (Berkeley: University of California Press, 1971); Gwendolyn Mink, *Old Labor and New Immigrants in American Political Development: Union, Party, and State, 1875–1920* (Ithaca, NY: Cornell University Press, 1986).

31. Herbert Hill, "The Problem of Race in American Labor History," *Reviews in American History* 24:2 (June 1996): 180–208; David Roediger, "Labor in White Skin: Race and Working Class History," in Mike Davis and Michael Sprinker, eds., *The Year Left 3: Reshaping the US Left* (London: Verso, 1988); George P. Rawick, *From Sundown to Sunup: The Making of the Black Community* (Westport, CT: Greenwood, 1972); Eugene D. Genovese, *Roll, Jordan, Roll: The World the Slaves Made* (New York: Pantheon Books, 1974).

32. David R. Roediger, *The Wages of Whiteness: Race and the Making of the American Working Class* (London: Verso, 1991).

33. Bruce Laurie, *Beyond Garrison: Antislavery and Social Reform* (Cambridge: Cambridge University Press, 2005). See also Edward Magdol, *The Anti-Slavery Rank and File: A Social Profile of the Abolitionists' Constituency* (Westport, CT: Greenwood Press, 1986).

34. Joan Scott, "Women in *The Making of the English Working Class*," in *Gender and the Politics of History*, 68–91; Anna Clark, *The Struggle for the Breeches: Gender and the Making of the British Working Class* (Berkeley: University of California Press, 1995);

Robert Gregg, "Class, Culture, and Empire: E. P. Thompson and the Making of Social History", *Journal of Historical Sociology* 11:4 (December 1998): 419–460.

35. For two very different takes on Thompson's embrace of the peace movement and its relationship to his theoretical and scholarly position, see Bess, "The Historian as Activist"; Richard Taylor, "Thompson and the Peace Movement: From CND in the 1950s and 1960s to END in the 1980s," in Fieldhouse and Taylor, eds., *E. P. Thompson*, 181–201.

36. On Thompson's writing and teaching and its relationship to the earlier tradition of workers' education in England, see Peter Searby and the Editors, "Edward Thompson as a Teacher: Yorkshire and Warwick," in John Rule and Robert Malcolmson, eds., *Protest and Survival: Essays for E. P. Thompson* (London: Merlin Press, 1993), 1–23; and Margaret Jacob, "Working-Class Auto-Didacts: The Making of E. P. Thompson," in "Thompson's *The Making of the English Working Class* at Fifty," *Labour/Le Travail* 71 (Spring 2013): 156–160. See also Roger Fieldhouse, "Thompson, the Adult Educator," in Fieldhouse and Taylor, eds., *E. P. Thompson*, 25–47.

37. Hitchens, "Minority Report," *The Nation*, September 27, 1993, 306, quoted in Palmer, *E. P. Thompson*, 103.

38. E. P. Thompson, "Time, Work-Discipline and Industrial Capitalism," *Past and Present* 38 (1967): 59–97; E. P. Thompson, "The Moral Economy of the English Crowd in the Eighteenth Century," *Past and Present* 50 (1971): 76–136.

39. Richard Sennett and Jonathan Cobb, *The Hidden Injuries of Class* (New York: Random House, 1972).

40. "[It is] through the missing term, 'experience', [that] structure is transmuted into process and the subject re-enters into history.... And at 'experience' we were led on to reexamine all those dense, ... complex and elaborated systems by which familial and social life is structured and social consciousness finds realization and expression ... kinship, custom, the visible and invisible rules of social regulation, hegemony and deference, symbolic forms of domination and resistance, religious faith and millennial impulses, manners, laws, institutions and ideologies ... all them joined, at a certain point, in common human experience, which itself (as distinctive *class* experience) exerts its pressure on the sum." E. P. Thompson, *The Poverty of Theory and Other Essays* (New York: Monthly Review Press, 1978), quote, 170–171. Joan Scott has been particularly critical of the concept of experience as a determining factor, identifying it as unexamined and essentialist, but, as Sewell notes, the concept resides at the very heart of Thompson's theory of class formation, and it remains a vital element in writing history from below. It was this dedication to capturing the *experience* of class, presumably, that led Thompson to acquire and learn how to operate a handloom while writing *The Making*. See Joan W. Scott, "Experience," in Judith Butler and Joan W. Scott, eds., *Feminists Theorize the Political* (New York: Routledge, 1992); William Sewell, "How Classes Are Made," 55–56, 59–65; on Thompson's handloom, E. J. Hobsbawm, "Edward Palmer Thompson, 1924–1993," *Proceedings of the British Academy* 90 (1996): 524, as cited in Bryan D. Palmer, "Paradox and Polemic; Argument and Awkwardness: Reflections on E. P. Thompson," Keynote Address, "Fifty Years of E. P. Thompson's *The Making of the English Working Class*," University of London, June 25, 2013, 5. I am grateful to Bryan Palmer for allowing me to read and cite the unpublished paper.

41. Raymond Williams, *Problems in Materialism and Culture: Selected Essays* (London: New Left Books, 1980), 31–49. Thompson identified "structures of feeling" as a constituent of class consciousness in E. P. Thompson, *The Making of the English Working Class* (London: Gollancz, 1963), 9.

42. Thompson, *The Making*, 9.

43. Thompson, *Poverty of Theory*, 189, quoted in Harvey Kaye, *The British Marxist Historians: An Introductory Analysis* (Cambridge: Polity, 1984), 170.

44. E. P. Thompson, "Agenda for a Radical History," *Radical History Review* 36 (1986), reprinted in E. P. Thompson, *Making History: Writings on History and Culture* (New York: New Press, 1994), quote, 362.

SELECTED BIBLIOGRAPHY

Addams, Jane. *Twenty Years at Hull House*. New York: Macmillan, 1910.
Anderson, Nels. *The Hobo: The Sociology of the Homeless Man*. Chicago: University of Chicago Press, 1923.
Barrett, James R. "Class Act: An Interview with David Montgomery." *Labor: Studies in Working-Class History of the Americas* 1:1 (2004): 25–57.
Barrett, James R. *The Irish Way: Becoming American in the Multi-Ethnic City*. New York: Penguin, 2012.
Barrett, James R. "Remembering David Montgomery (1926–2011), His Scholarship, and His Mentorship." *Labor/Le Travail* 70 (Fall 2012): 203–223.
Barrett, James R. *William Z. Foster and the Tragedy of American Radicalism*. Urbana: University of Illinois Press, 1999.
Barrett, James R. *Work and Community in the Jungle: Chicago's Packinghouse Workers, 1894–1922*. Urbana: University of Illinois Press, 1987.
Bell, Thomas. *Out of This Furnace*. Boston: Little, Brown, 1941.
Brody, David. "The Old Labor and the New: In Search of an American Working Class." *Labor History* 20:1 (Winter 1979): 11–126.
Brody, David. *Steelworkers in America: The Nonunion Era*. New York: Harper Torchbooks, 1969.
Brown, Kathleen, and Elizabeth Faue. "Social Bonds, Sexual Politics, and Political Community on the U.S. Left, 1920s–1940s." *Left History* 7 (Spring 2000): 9–45.
Buhle, Paul, ed. *History and the New Left: Madison, Wisconsin, 1950–1970*. Philadelphia: Temple University Press, 1990.
Clifford, James. *Routes: Travel and Translation in the Late Twentieth Century*. Cambridge, MA: Harvard University Press, 1997.
Fieldhouse, Roger, and Richard Taylor, eds. *E. P. Thompson and English Radicalism*. Manchester: Manchester University Press, 2013.
Fink, Leon. "The New Labor History of the Powers of Historical Pessimism: Consensus, Hegemony, and the Case of the Knights of Labor." *Journal of American History* 75:1 (June 1988): 115–136.

Fink, Leon. *Sweatshops of the Sea: Merchant Seamen in the World's First Globalized Industry, from 1812 to the Present*. Chapel Hill: University of North Carolina Press, 2011.

Gagnier, Reginia. "The Literary Standard, Working-Class Autobiography, and Gender." In Susan Groag Bell and Marilyn Yalom, eds., *Revealing Lives: Autobiography, Biography, and Gender*. Albany: State University of New York Press, 1990.

Gagnier, Reginia. "Social Atoms: Working-Class Autobiography, Subjectivity, and Gender." *Victorian Studies* 30 (1987): 335–362.

Gornick, Vivian. *The Romance of American Communism*. New York: Basic Books, 1977.

Gutman, Herbert. *Work, Culture, and Society in Industrializing America: Essays in American Working-Class and Social History*. New York: Vintage, 1976.

Gutman, Herbert G. *Power and Culture: Essays on the American Working Class*. Edited by Ira Berlin. New York: Pantheon, 1987.

Hamilton, Scott. *The Crisis of Theory: E. P. Thompson, the New Left and Postwar British Politics*. Manchester: Manchester University Press, 2011.

Hannerz, Ulf. "Cosmopolitans and Locals in World Culture." *Theory, Culture and Society* 7 (1990): 237–251.

Hapgood, Hutchins. *The Spirit of Labor*. Edited with an introduction and notes by James R. Barrett. Urbana: University of Illinois Press, 2004 (originally published 1907).

Higbie, Frank Tobias. *Indispensable Outcasts: Hobo Workers and Community in the American Midwest, 1880–1930*. Urbana: University of Illinois Press, 2003.

Higbie, Frank Tobias. *Working Knowledge: Learning Power in the Open Shop Era*. Urbana: University of Illinois Press, in press.

Higham, John. *Strangers in the Land: Patterns of American Nativism, 1860–1925*. New York: Atheneum, 1963.

Hirsch, Arnold. *Making the Second Ghetto: Race and Housing in Chicago, 1940–1960*. Chicago: University of Chicago Press, 2000.

Johanningsmeier, Edward J. *Forging American Communism: The Life of William Z. Foster*. Princeton, NJ: Princeton University Press, 1994.

Kaestle, Carl F., and Janice A. Radway. "A Framework for the History of Publishing and Reading in the United States, 1880–1940." In Carl F. Kaestle and Janice A. Radway, eds., *A History of the Book in America*, vol. 4: *Print Motion: The Expansion of Publishing and Reading in the United States, 1880–1940* (pp. 7–21). Chapel Hill: University of North Carolina Press, 2009.

Kaplan, Judy, and Linn Shapiro, eds. *Red Diapers: Growing Up in the Communist Left*. Urbana: University of Illinois Press, 1998.

Kaye, Harvey, and Keith McClelland, eds. *E. P. Thompson: Critical Perspectives*. Philadelphia: Temple University Press, 1990.

Linebaugh, Peter, and Marcus Rediker. *The Many-Headed Hydra: Sailors, Slaves, Commoners, and the Hidden History of the Revolutionary Atlantic*. Boston: Beacon Press, 2000.

Mannheim, Karl. "The Problem of Generations." In *Essays on the Sociology of Knowledge* (pp. 376–322). New York: Oxford University Press, 1952.

Matt, Susan J., and Peter N. Stearns, eds. *Doing Emotions History*. Urbana: University of Illinois Press, 2014.

McCartin. James P., and Joseph A. McCartin. "Working-Class Catholicism: A Call for New Investigations, Dialogue, and Reappraisal." *Labor: Studies in the Working-Class History of the Americas* 4:2 (2007): 99–110.

McGreevy, John T. *Parish Boundaries: The Catholic Encounter with Race in the Twentieth Century Urban North.* Chicago: University of Chicago Press, 1996.

Mink, Gwendolyn. *Old Labor and New Immigrants in American Political Development: Union, Party, and State, 1875–1920.* Ithaca, NY: Cornell University Press, 1986.

Montgomery, David. *The Fall of the House of Labor: The Workplace, the State, and American Labor Activism.* Cambridge: Cambridge University Press, 1987.

Nelson, Steve, James R. Barrett, and Rob Ruck. *Steve Nelson, American Radical.* Pittsburgh: University of Pittsburgh Press, 1981.

Novick, Peter. *That Noble Dream: The "Objectivity Question" and the American Historical Profession.* Cambridge: Cambridge University Press, 1988.

Oberdeck, Kathryn J., and Frank Tobias Higbie. "Labour and Popular Print Culture." in Christine Bold, ed., *Oxford History of Popular Print*, vol. 6: *US Popular Print Culture 1860–1920*. Oxford: Oxford University Press, 2012.

Omi, Michael, and Howard Winant. *Racial Formation in the United States: From the 1960s to the 1980s.* New York: Verso, 1986.

Orsi, Robert. "The Religious Boundaries of an Inbetween People: Street *Feste* and the Problem of the Dark-Skinned 'Other' in Italian Harlem, 1920–1990." *American Quarterly* 44 (September 1992): 313–347.

Palmer, Bryan D. *E. P. Thompson: Objections and Oppositions.* London: Verso, 1994.

Rediker, Marcus. *Between the Devil and the Deep Blue Sea: Merchant Seamen, Pirates, and the Anglo-American Maritime World, 1700–1750.* Cambridge: Cambridge University Press, 1987.

Roediger, David R. *The Wages of Whiteness: Race and the Making of the American Working Class.* London: Verso, 1991.

Sennett, Richard, and Jonathan Cobb. *The Hidden Injuries of Class.* New York: Random House, 1972.

Sinclair, Upton. *The Jungle.* With an introduction and notes by James R. Barrett. Urbana: University of Illinois Press, 1988.

Spero, Sterling P., and Abram L. Harris. *The Black Worker.* New York: Atheneum, 1969 (originally published 1931).

Stansell, Christine. *American Moderns: Bohemian New York and the Creation of a New Century.* New York: H. Holt, 2001.

Steinberg, Mark D. *Proletarian Imagination: Self, Modernity, and the Sacred in Russia, 1910–1925.* Ithaca, NY: Cornell University Press, 2002.

Thompson, E. P. *The Making of the English Working Class.* New York: Vintage, 1966.

Tuttle, William M., Jr. *Race Riot: Chicago in the Red Summer of 1919.* New York: Atheneum, 1970.

INDEX

Abie's Irish Rose, 186–188
Abraham Lincoln Battalion, 132
Addams, Jane, 109, 113–114
affirmative action, white ethnic opposition to, 174
AFL. *See* American Federation of Labor
African Americans, 13, 15–16, 19–20, 23, 25, 125, 132, 135, 146, 148–149, 151, 156–162, 164–173, 177, 199; in Chicago neighborhoods, 212n19; class fragmentation and, 201; in Harrigan plays, 178–179; intermarriage with Irish, 188; liberation, 174; in the minds of white workers, 202; negative stereotypes, 184; as stockyards workers, 61; in urban realist novels, 190–191; in vaudeville, 181–182
Africans, 150, 152
Alinsky, Saul, 28
Allen, Stephanie, 51
Amalgamated Clothing Workers of America, 103, 140
American Federation of Labor (AFL), 111, 127–128; employment discrimination and, 162; immigration restriction and, 168
American Legion, 168
American Plan, 142
American standard of living, 134–135, 137, 162
Americanism, 136
Americanization, 112–144, 154–156, 165–166, 173; and the Communist Party, 245n22;
from the bottom up, 2, 3, 31, 112–144; vaudeville and, 180–182
anarchism, 110–111
Ancient Order of Hibernians, 181, 184, 263n40
Anglo-Saxonism, 164, 166, 170–171
Annales school, 1–2, 198
anti-Catholicism, 183
anti-Chinese sentiment, 127, 135, 162–163, 167–168, 256n53; in Harrigan plays, 178–179
anti-lynching sentiment among immigrants, 171
anti-Mexican sentiment, 167
anti-Semitism, 161, 169, 187; in Poland, 258n75
Aptheker, Bettina, 51
Aptheker, Herbert, 51
Asians, 25, 152, 169, 201
atheism, 226n10
autobiography, 2, 217n5; defined, 35–36; bourgeois, 35, 67; Catholic, 7–32; Communist, 34, 36–37, 55–57, 72, 223n69; confessional antimemoirs, 40; conversion narratives, 39, 218n10; oral biographies, 40; personal crises in, 53; personal in the political, 52, 55–56, 59; Soviet model, 38; women militants', 39–40, 56; working class 3, 4, 35–36, 65–68, 218n9, 239n15; women's, 72

Back of the Yards, 26–27
Back of the Yards Council, 28
Barrett, James: antiwar movement, 21, 24; class awareness, 22–23; civil rights, 20–21; father, 11, 16, 21; grandfather, 11; *Irish Way, The*, 31; Marxism, 23–25; mother, 17–18; and "new labor history," 25–29; perceptions of race, 16–20; unions, attitudes toward, 22
Barrett, Jenny, 24
Bell, Thomas, 28
Billart, Blessed Julie, 15, 212n18
biographies, 34
blackface minstrelsy, 156, 167, 170, 181; audiences, 180; Chinese in, 181; Irish and, 176–177; in vaudeville, 180
Bodnar, John, 27, 214n34
Boyce, Neith, 117–119
Braham, David, 177
British, 125–127, 164, 199
British Marxist historians, 1–2, 196
Broadway, 187
Brody, David, 26–27, 197, 214n32
Browder, Earl, 63, 66, 70–71; personal relationships, 42, 45
Buffalo, New York, 173

Cagney, James, 189
Canadians, 125
Cannon, James P., 45, 70
Cape Verdeans, 170
Castro, Fidel, 11
Catholicism, 13–14, 61, 160; civil rights and, 213n27; movie industry and, 189; Legion of Decency, 189
Catholic Church, Chicago, 13–14; Catholic Interracial Council (CIC), 20, 22; Catholic Worker, 20; Office of Urban Affairs, 20; Vatican II, 18–19; Young Christian Students (YCS), 20
Catholics marrying Jews, 46–47
Chandavarkar, Rajnaryan, 192, 199, 200, 267n4
Chartists, 199
Chicago, 46; Communist Party in, 62–63, 69; ethnic groups, 116; gangs, 212n20; labor movement, 102, 109–114; neighborhoods, 213n27; stockyards, 135–136, 142; Washington Park, 190–191; Teamsters, 111–112; teachers' union, 137. *See also* Back of the Yards
Chicago Area Draft Resistance (CADRE), 24
Chicago Federation of Labor, 111, 119–120, 166
Chicago neighborhoods: Back of the Yards, 26–27; Garfield Park, 12, 13; Humboldt Park, 12, 13; North Lawndale, 12; West Side, 10
Chicago parishes: Holy Family, 12; Our Lady of the Angels (OLA), 12–15, 31; Our Lady of Sorrows Basilica, 19; Saints Cyril and Methodius, 14–15; Visitation, 20
Chinese, 16, 148, 162–164, 169; conflicts with Irish, 178–179; in Harrigan plays, 178–179; intermarriage with Irish, 178, 188; in vaudeville, 181–183
CIO. *See* Congress of Industrial Organizations
citizenship, 151–156; classes, 129
civil liberties, 134, 143
civil rights: movement, 20; backlash against, 174
Civil Rights Congress, 40
Clifford, James, 232n4
Cohan, George M., 179
Cold War, 40–41, 196; Communist historiography and the, 60, 74; domestic ideology and the, 225n84
Comintern. *See* Communist International
Commons, John R., 197
Communist International (Comintern), 43, 46, 49, 59, 63, 69; Popular Front, 69; Third Period, 60
Communist Party, USA, 2, 33, 59–60, 132, 142, 195; Americanization and, 245n22; child-bearing, attitudes in, 49–50; children and, 48–52, 224n74; Czechoslovakia, invasion of, 41; espionage and, 40, 56, 220n32; family metaphor for, 223n69; Freudian interpretations, 231n43; historians, 196; historiography, 73–76; intermar-

riage, Jews and gentiles, 46; interracial marriages, 45; Khrushchev's revelations, 40, 54; name changes, 227n18; New Left histories of, 221n36; personal life, 73–74; personal relationships, 41–48; Popular Front, 71, 133; prison correspondence, 47; psychohistory and, 73–75; revisionist literature, in, 56, 224n80; Third Period, 54, 226n5; women in, 72; youth activities, 50–51. *See also* homosexuality

Communist Party of Great Britain, 34, 40, 205

Congress of Industrial Organizations (CIO), 51, 66, 103, 143

Constitution of the United States, 134

cosmopolitanism, 2; working class, 44, 77–101

Croatians, 131, 149, 158–159

cross-dressing: racial, 156, 167, 170; ethnic, 181, 187–188; class, 238n12

Czechs, 156

DeFelice, Maxine, 51

Dennis, Eugene, 49, 53

Dennis, Peggy, 40, 49–51, 53–54

depression, 59; emotional illness, 64; heart disease and, 228n25

domesticity, cult of, 53

Du Bois, W. E. B., 53, 116, 167, 203

Egan, Father John, 20

emotions, 31–32, 34, 51, 206–207; autobiographies in, 38; class consciousness, basis for, 4, 23; political activism, role in, 4–5

Families Committee of Smith Act Victims, 53

Farmer-Labor Party, 143

Farrell, James T., 190–191

Father McGuire's New Baltimore Catechism No. 2, 9, 18

Filipinos, 151

films, 156, 188–189; white supremacy and, 170

Finns, 130, 152

Fink, Leon, 269n22

Fitzpatrick, John, 119, 166

Five Points neighborhood, 177

Flynn, Elizabeth Gurley, 38, 40, 49, 53, 67, 69; Irish Catholic, 60–61

Foner, Philip, 196

Ford Motor Company, 122, 142; Five Dollar Day, 122, 129; Sociological Department, 129

foremen, 129–130, 160

Foster, Esther Abramovitz, 42, 68

Foster, William Z., 38–39, 55, 219n21; asceticism, 73; Catholicism and, 60–61; children and, 48; depression, 62; early influences on, 60; in election of 1932, 63–64; "Fosterism," 70; illness, 63, 65, 71; marriage, 42; Marxism, 69–72; personal crisis, 58–76; personality, 73, 76; in Soviet Union, 71; syndicalism, 60, 68, 70; women and, 69

free love, 108

Freeman, Joseph, 72–73, 219n19

French, 164

Frontier of Control, The, 26

gay rights movement, 48

gender, 56–67, 68–69, 81, 86–87, 197, 200, 204, 229n35, 268n16

Germans, 111, 125–127, 164; as abolitionists, 203; in Harrigan plays, 179; in vaudeville, 181–182

Gerson, Deborah, 51, 53–54

Goldman, Emma, 108

Goldman, Wendy, 73

Gompers, Samuel, 162, 163, 165, 167

Goodrich, Carter, 26

Gordon, Mary, 210n2

Gornick, Vivian, 34, 55, 217n4

Grant, Madison, 154

Great Migration, 157, 201

Great Steel Strike, 58

Greeks, 23, 129, 149–150, 160–161, 167, 169–170

Green, Deborah, 54

Green, Gil, 47

Guineas (*Ginnies*), 145, 149, 154, 166–167
Gutman, Herbert, 26, 30, 159, 195, 197–198, 215n41, 201

Hapgood, Hutchins, 102–121
Hapgood, Norman, 103, 105
Hapgood, Powers, 103
Hapgood, William Powers, 103
Harrigan, Edward, 177–179
Harrington, Michael, 7–8, 10
Hart, Tony, 177–178
Hay, Harry. *See* gay rights movement
Haymarket Tragedy, 110
Healey, Dorothy, 40, 42, 44, 50
Herenvolk democracy, 173
Higbie, Toby, 232n4
Higham, John, 158, 162
Hitler-Stalin Pact, 54
hobos, 104
Hobsbawm, E. J., 125, 192, 199–200
homosexuality, 235n39; communists and, 47–48
House Un-American Activities Committee (HUAC), 54
Howells, William Dean, 178
Hudson, Hosea, 39
Hull House, 12, 109, 114
Hungarians, 46, 136, 154, 160, 163
Hunkies, 145, 149–150, 154, 157–158, 160–162, 167, 250n10

immigrants, 61, 122–124, 145–174; Asian, 146; "new," 157, 249n7; and racial consciousness, 168–174; racist names for, 145, 149–150, 154, 157–158, 160–162, 166–167, 250n10
immigration: decline, 157; restriction, 173
Industrial Workers of the World (IWW), 38, 41–42, 48–49, 62, 69, 110, 142, 165
Ingersoll, Robert, 104
intellectual history, plebian, 29
intermarriage, 154, 186; interracial, 54, 147–148; Inter-Racial Council, 155; Irish and Jews, 186–187, 265n55; Jews and gentiles, 46; Soviet Union sanctioned, 46

Irish, 13, 16, 38, 111, 112, 125–126, 152, 160, 164, 166; blackface minstrelsy and, 176, 181; on British stage, 176; Chicago race riot, 31–32; Clan na Gael, 184; communists, 60–61; Gaelic League, 184; in film industry, 188–189; in Harrigan plays, 177–179; and intermarriage with Asian and African Americans, 178–179, 188; neighborhood change, 266n62; race riots and, 172; and search for respectability, 184; stage Irishman and, 176, 177, 183–185; and theater protests, 175, 184; vaudeville and, 179–185
Irish Way, The, 31
Italians, 13, 23, 31, 145–146, 149–150, 152–154, 157–161, 164, 166–168; ambivalent racial status, 172; attitudes of radicals toward African Americans, 171; in vaudeville, 181
IWW. *See* Industrial Workers of the World

James, C. L. R., 195
Japanese, 151, 162, 166–167, 169
Jews, 12, 16, 46–47, 130, 149, 160–161, 170; attitudes toward African Americans, 171; Anti-Defamation League, 184–185; Irish and, 185–187; on race riots, 169; Russian and East European, 120; in vaudeville, 181–185
Jim Crow, 155–156
Johannsen, Anton, 104–121
Johannsen, Maggie, 109
Johnson, Aurelia, 47
Johnson-Reed Immigration Act of 1924, 156, 173
Jones, Gareth Stedman, 26
Jungle, The, 25–26

Karsner, Rose, 45
Kennedy, John, 13
Knights of Columbus, 160
Knights of Labor, 125, 127, 171
Koreans, 161
Ku Klux Klan, 155, 170

Latina/os, 23, 25
Lenin, Vladimir, 71

Linebaugh, Peter, 198
literacy, 157
Lodge, Henry Cabot, 163
Loguidice, Joseph, 145–146, 156
London, Jack, 167–168, 257n70
Louisiana, 152–153, 168
Lovestone, Jay, 70
Lower East Side, 106, 118, 120; in Harrigan plays, 177; in vaudeville, 182
Lozovsky, Solomon, 59
Luhan, Mabel Dodge, 103, 104, 114

Madison, Wisconsin, 194–195
Making of the English Working Class, The, 192–207
Mallette, Father Daniel, 21
Marxism, 61–62, 70, 193–195, 198, 203, 207
mass consumption, 156
mass culture, 143, 156, 180
Mattachine Society. *See* gay rights movement
Maynes, Mary Jo, 35, 39
McCarthy era, 48, 52, 54, 56–57
McGreevy, John, 14, 21–22, 30
McNamara brothers, 119
Mexicans, 23, 125, 150, 158, 166, 170
"militant minority," 62, 197
modernism, working-class, 114
Montgomery, David, 26–27, 195–197, 205; *Workers' Control in America*, 27
Morgan, Kevin, 34, 36–37
Morris, Charles, 9
Motley, Archibald, Sr., 235n42

National Committee for Organizing Iron and Steel Workers, 136, 139
National Industrial Conference Board, 155
Native Americans, 152
naturalization, 152–153
Nelson, Steve (Stjepan Mesarosh), 131–132, 158–159
new labor history, 26, 192–207; religion and, 215n38
New Left, 59, 193–195; historians, 36, 40–41
New Left Review, 193

New York, 103–106, 114, 120; Communist Party in, 63; unemployed demonstrations in, 63. *See also* Five Points neighborhood; Lower East Side
North Carolina, 51

O'Connor, Harvey, 48, 50
O'Connor, Jessie Lloyd, 48, 50
Orsi, Robert, 2
Osborne, William, 20
Outcast London, 26
Out of This Furnace (1941), 28, 149

packinghouse workers, 25, 31, 160, 172
Page, Myra (Dorothy Markey), 42, 45, 48–50
Paine, Tom, 82–84, 104
Painter, Nell, 39
Palmer, Bryan, 192, 267n4
Parish Boundaries, 22
Park, Robert, 147
Parsons, Lucy, 110–111
Passing of the Great Race (1916), 154–155
Perlman, Selig, 197
Philadelphia, 39, 60, 199; General Trade Union, 199, 201; nativist violence, 201
Pittsburgh, 27, 29, 58, 158, 206
Poles, 13–14, 46–47, 135, 136, 146, 148–149, 151, 154, 159–161, 170; on race riots, 168–169, 172
Portuguese, 149, 170
Progressive reformers, 155
Protestants, 12, 13
Puerto Ricans, 13, 15, 149–150; in Chicago neighborhoods, 212n19
Pullman, 170; strike, 110

Queen Mother, 204

race, 145–174, 200; class fragmentation and, 202–205; identity and, 31; labor markets and, 156–162, strikebreaking and, 167
race riots, 116, 141, 150, 173–174; in Chicago, 31, 171–172, 213n26; "new immigrants" and, 171; as "pogroms," 169, 172

Index · 281

racism, 2, 3, 127, 132; as acculturation, 31; folklore, 151; unions and, 162–168
Radical America, 194–195
Radical History Review, 195
Rapoport, Joe and Sheba, 44–45
Rawick, George, 202
"red-diaper babies," 40, 51
Rediker, Marcus, 198
Red International of Labor Unions (RILU), 62
Red Scare, 123, 142–143
religion: attitudes of labor historians toward, 29–30; basis for class identity, 25–32, 30
Remond, Renee, 7–8
Riis, Jacob, 109
Roediger, David, 203
Roosevelt, Theodore, 151, 153
Rosenberg, Ethel and Julius, 51, 224n79
Russian Revolution, 62
Russians, 129
Rutgers University, 205

St. Frances Cabrini Hospital, 24
Saint Patrick's Day, 187
San Francisco, 40
Scandinavians, 125, 164
Scots, 46
Scott, Joan, 35, 271n40
Serbs, 131
settlement houses, 233n9
sexuality, 42–44, 92, 107–108, 216n1
Shipman, Charles, 42–44
Sicilians, 149, 157
Sinclair, Upton, 25–26
slavery, 202
Slavic immigrants, 31, 149, 158–159, 162, 168
Slayton, Robert, 27
Slovaks, 13–14, 19, 136, 161
Slovenians, 149
Smith Act trials, 53
socialist humanism, 193–195
Socialist Labor Party, 132
Socialist Party, 62, 127, 133, 142, 168
Sombart, Werner, 147
Soviet Union, 46, 49, 59, 62

Spanish Civil War, 46, 132
Spirit of Labor, The, 102–118
Spirit of the Ghetto, The, 106, 117
Stalin, Joseph, 46, 70
Stalinism, 192, 195
Stedman Jones, Gareth, 200
Steelworkers in America, 26–27
Steffens, Lincoln, 105
strikebreaking, 168, 257n68
strikes, 111–113, 134, 137, 139–140, 155, 201; bituminous coal, 63; Chicago 1919, 11–12; Gastonia, 49; 1934 wave, 64; oil refinery, 158; Philadelphia general strike, 199; racist hate, 173–174, 259n89; steel, 70, 149; after World War I, 168; writings, 65–66
Studies on the Left, 194, 196
Studs Lonigan (1930–1935), 190–191
subjective, history of the: class and emotions, 4–5, 206–207, 210n8; communist, 34–35, 37, 41, 55; defined, 2; personal crisis in, 52, 55; reasons to study; 4, 59–60; working-class, 1–5, 32–76
syndicalism, 62, 68, 70

Taylor, Graham, 112, 113
Tentler, Leslie Woodcock, 27–28
theater riots, 175, 183–184
Thompson, Dorothy, 206
Thompson, E. P., 2, 26, 148, 214n32, 192–207; C. L. R. James and, 268n12; class consciousness and, 272n41; on class and experience, 271n40; feminist criticisms of, 268n16; on Marxism, 207; in peace movement, 204, 271n35; on romantic poets, 205–206; as a teacher, 204–206; Workers Education Association, 205
Tin Pan Alley, 176, 185–186
Trade Union Educational League (TUEL), 62, 69
Treasure Chest, 10–11
Trotskyist movement, 45
Tucker, Sophie, and the racial line, 170

unions, educational programs, 140
United Farm Workers (UFWA), 24

United Hebrew Trades, 165
United Irish Societies, 175, 183–184
United Kingdom, 176, 192–193, 196–198, 200–201, 202, 204–206
United Mine Workers of America, 103, 130, 136
United Packinghouse Workers–CIO, 28
University of Illinois, Chicago campus, 23, 25; Newman House, 24
University of Pittsburgh, 203, 205
University of Rochester, 203
urban culture, 3; Irish role in creation of interethnic, 31, 175–191
urban realism, 189–191

Valentino, Rudolph, and the racial line, 170
vaudeville, 170, 179–183; Americanization and, 182; blackface in, 180; Irish and, 175–176, 180–183; nickelodeons in, 180; xenophobia in, 181
Vorse, Mary Heaton, 58

Ward, Lester Frank, 61
Warwick University, 205–206, 214n32
Washington, Booker T., 168
Weisbord, Albert, 43–44, 50
Weisbord, Vera Buch, 43–44, 49–50
Western Federation of Miners (WFM), 150, 167, 169

whiteness, 3, 145–147, 148, 150–151, 157, 202–204; Americanization and, 173–174; in immigrant consciousness, 168–174; unions and, 167
Why Is There No Socialism in the United States? (1906), 147
Williams, Raymond, 203
Wills, Garry, 215n40
Wilson, Woodrow, 153
women's suffrage, 137
Women's Trade Union League (WTUL), 137–138
working class: family values and, 27; religion, role in, 26–30
working-class formation, 142–144; ethnocultural, 125, 130; ethnically segmented, 3, 126
working-class fragmentation, 141–142, 199–202
working-class history, 1, 192–207
World War I, 123, 125, 129, 132, 136–140, 155, 157, 168, 170
World War II, 50, 144, 158, 173–174

Yiddish, 182–183; culture, 118, 195
Young, Alfred F., 198
Young Communist League, 46
Young Pioneers, 51

www.ingramcontent.com/pod-product-compliance
Lightning Source LLC
Chambersburg PA
CBHW070754230426
43665CB00017B/2357